Nostalgic Empires

Nostalgic Empires

The Crisis of the European Union Related to Its Original Sins

Hèctor López Bofill

LEXINGTON BOOKS
Lanham • Boulder • New York • London

Published by Lexington Books
An imprint of The Rowman & Littlefield Publishing Group, Inc.
4501 Forbes Boulevard, Suite 200, Lanham, Maryland 20706
www.rowman.com

86-90 Paul Street, London EC2A 4NE

British Library Cataloguing in Publication Information Available

Library of Congress Cataloging-in-Publication Data

Names: López Bofill, Hèctor, author.
Title: Nostalgic empires : the crisis of the European Union related to its original sins / Hèctor López Bofill.
Description: Lanham, Maryland : Lexington Books, 2023. | Includes bibliographical references and index.
Identifiers: LCCN 2023034693 (print) | LCCN 2023034694 (ebook) | ISBN 9781666920963 (cloth) | ISBN 9781666920970 (ebook)
Subjects: LCSH: European Union--History. | European cooperation--History. | Europe--Economic integration.
Classification: LCC JN30 .L674 2023 (print) | LCC JN30 (ebook) | DDC 940--dc23/eng/20230905
LC record available at https://lccn.loc.gov/2023034693
LC ebook record available at https://lccn.loc.gov/202303469

This book is for my beloved grandmother Maria Martí López who passed away in 2023 at the age of 100 and was an exceptional witness of some events explained in these pages.

Contents

Acknowledgments

Nostalgic Empires offers my view on the European Union according to my general theory on the foundation of power. As a constitutional law scholar, I have spent some time of my academic career exploring the sources of constitutional creation. But the European integration process, and particularly its decay over the last decade, prompted me to ask myself about the origins of that peculiar form of power sharing. As mentioned further in the text, one key that triggered my investigation was a comment provided by Timothy Snyder in his book *The Road to Unfreedom* (London: The Bodley Head, 2018, p. 67) in which it was suggested that Europeans had restrained their imperial impulses in order to forge what today is the European Union.

Such an appreciation revealed one factor that had usually been omitted in the historical and legal studies on European integration, namely, the relationship between the loss of the Empires and the move toward sovereignty sharing. So, my first aim in writing this book was to unveil such an interaction between imperial implosion and European agreement.

Delving into the formation of the European Communities, however, it soon became evident that, on the one hand, the postwar western European governments had not voluntarily relinquished their empires but rather had been forced to abandon the colonies that they occupied and joined the process of integration to ensure their continuity at least as *nation-states*.

On the other hand, studying the evolution of those nation-states within the framework of that supranational organization showed that the European rulers hoped to develop imperial policies under a different dress covered and fostered by the European constitutive structure. My idea was that the association between the nation-states' imperial ambitions and the integration process went well, while it provided political and economic results that entrenched the member states as nations. When these interests diverged, and the needs of stabilization and expansion of one member could not be satisfied without harming the others and the organization as a whole, there emerged the disruptions that introduced ongoing existential threats to the project. I had the perception, and the reader will judge if I am right, that the present crisis surrounding the European Union represents a revival of the European nationalistic pretensions that erupted in the imperial age and that had been silenced through European integration since then. That is why I have subtitled the book *The Crises of the European Union Related to Its Original Sins*.

I'm in debt to some scholars that have read some parts of this book and have kindly spent some of their time discussing the ideas that are here expressed. Though most of them are legal scholars, others come from different fields, and, in that case, they had provided me a crucial bibliography, particularly on contemporary history and economics, to which I could not have had otherwise access if I had confined myself to the legal literature. Thousands of thanks to Richard Albert, Pau Bossacoma, Marc Carrillo, Víctor Ferreres, Fernando Guirao, Jaime Lluch, Alejandro Sáiz-Arnaiz, Carles Sirera, Aïda Torres, Joseph Weiler, and Michael Wilkinson. I cannot leave out a big thanks to my English reviewer, Mathew Barton, without whom I could not have delivered my thoughts to the English-speaking world. It was a privilege as well to work with my publishers at Lexington Books, who always believed in this project.

Eternal thanks and love to my wife, Hye Young Yu, and my son, Marcel López Yu, for their patience and their sympathy toward my academic and political obsessions.

Introduction

The Defeated Empires in the Origins of European Integration

I

In a political world characterized by the struggle of peoples to dominate and exploit others, spaces grounded in concepts of liberty, equality, and pluralism are exceedingly rare, and they can only emerge within a context of weakness that affects all parties involved. The European Union has represented one such exceptional political construct, where different nations have coexisted by transferring sovereignty rights to a common entity and creating a body of law that binds both the citizens of member states and their institutions.[1]

The collaboration among nations that were once engaged in deadly conflicts was only made possible due to the fragility caused by the preceding sequence of devastations. It took a state of complete devastation in western Europe to alter the competitive and nihilistic dynamics that had driven the various powers until 1945. Even in such an extreme conjuncture, the impulse to collaborate only arose when the European powers, which had previously dominated large territories in America, Asia, Africa, and Oceania, realized that their empires were inevitably heading toward extinction.

These actors also recognized that an alternative model to capitalist liberal democracy, which had established itself in eastern Europe and exerted significant influence through Communist and Social Democratic parties in countries like Italy and France, posed a threat to the postwar power structures. Political alliances and mutual recognition emerged when it became clear that domination was no longer feasible or when the prospect of subjugation to another power, namely the complete defeat of a national project, loomed large.

The central idea of this book is that the current state of the European Union is the result of the weakness experienced by its founding members and subsequent joiners. Only this weakness can explain the willingness of powerful nations to relinquish their imperial aspirations in favor of a discourse centered on transnational liberties and welfare.

However, it will be demonstrated that the delicate balance of weakness that has provided political stability and integration within the European framework is now in jeopardy and may ultimately collapse due to two main factors: firstly, the excessive and disproportionate strength of one partner, and secondly, the excessive fragility of other partners, to the extent that a crack-down on any one of them could trigger a chain reaction capable of ruining the entire continental project.

The collapse of one or more of these partners may be induced by both external and internal factors, with external pressure exerted by non-European global powers or even by supposed European partners themselves. This book will explore the various tensions that have besieged the European project from its inception to the present.

In a way, the triumph of democratic free-market economies in western Europe, with decisive support from the United States, over their opposing models in 1989, masked the profound deficiencies underlying European integration for nearly two decades. The global economic crises that erupted in 2008 brought these deficiencies back to the surface, and in subsequent years, they took on various political forms.

However, the argument put forth in this contribution maintains that the manifestations of the European crisis that emerged after 2008 had deeper roots, and the causes of these shortcomings affecting the formation of a multinational European Union must be traced back to the very origins of the integration project.

II

Western European States entrenched themselves as nation-states after losing their empires.

The tacit agreement underlying the supposed liberal and pluralistic European experiment might sound as following: the abandonment of the overseas territories had to be compensated with a staunch defense of the mainland's national cohesion in places like France, Belgium, the Netherlands, Italy, the United Kingdom, Portugal, or Spain. The stability that the nation-state sought within the European framework in order to survive required the complicity of that supranational structure in silencing national and social domestic dissidence.

When it was no longer possible for European powers to dominate large territories, how could the remnants and fragments maintain themselves as states? The answer, from the 1950s until the 2000s seemed evident: the creation, deepening, and enlargement of the European Communities in the first instance, and of the European Union from 1992.[2] But such an agreement grounded on an existential need, which at the end of the day offered the promise of welfare and democracy, had another side that was not so positive nor brilliant but also dependent on nationalist and imperialist impulses.

Indeed, the survival of the European nation-states might be recognized as the main achievement of the European process, particularly if we take into account that the integration was conceived in times in which such survival was uncertain. But that led to a scenario, the one in which we are still living, defined by the evaporation of any European common project.

Rather than a matter of a continental union, Europe was, is, and probably will be just a matter *of the continuity of the nation-states* that compound it with their corresponding struggles to dominate and to plunder other social and national groups.

III

We will explore the evolution of imperialism as a defining background of the nation-states in Western Europe and examine to what extent the persistence of this imperial dynamic threatens the core of the European Union project. My contention is that although imperialism is fundamentally incompatible with a supranational organization seeking political integration based on democracy and human rights, it has been consistently promoted within the framework of the European Union.

European nation-states have retained their nationalistic and imperialistic impulses, even after losing most of their former empires. As we will see, conflicts arose precisely when the creation and consolidation of supranational power made it clear that member states' imperialist aspirations needed to be curtailed. Member states' authorities resorted to breaching the rules, disobedience, and even secessionism from the European Union, as Brexit demonstrated.

Nationalistic imperialism or plurinational integration? It is challenging to reconcile imperialism with plurinational integration. However, in certain circumstances, the former becomes unavoidable to ensure the survival of the collective entity. The sustainability of the European experiment depends on striking a balance between nationalistic imperialism and inclusive values rooted in pluralism. As outlined in the following pages, such a balance appears more elusive than ever, looking at present events.

This becomes particularly evident in contexts where sovereign nation-states face existential threats. Similar to the foundation of the European Communities during the expansion of Communism in Eastern Europe at the onset of the Cold War, the need to defend and protect a political framework based on freedom, equality, and economic prosperity required more than mere aspirations. It necessitated maintaining a certain level of nationalistic reaffirmation.

National self-sufficiency, nevertheless, would lead to the possibility of doing without the collective project or even to display a political strategy *against* the partners. Those attitudes have been envisaged during the evolution of the European organization but, maybe with the exception of Brexit, they had not been shown in a radical fashion. The single market, economic growth and the welfare of the citizenry restrained such radicalisms until the time in which successive waves of shocks unchained them. By the beginning of the 2020s, the political center had evaporated in most of the European member states. Centrist parties faced a process of minoritization in places like Italy, had to associate to far-left or far-right allies in order to support the government (as in Spain) or had to tackle with permanent contestation in a more or less convulsive manner as happened in France during Macron's presidency.

The social fabric that had supported the political center and, thus, the political stability in the European Union area came unstuck. The time of the industrial societies that had provided lifelong employment, pensions, and social peace (idealized as such a scenario might be) were gone, as were gone the sources of exploitation under the European influence that had entrenched such an industrial and economic development able to produce reserves of stability.

The narrative exposed herein holds that European integration played a crucial role in smoothing the consequences of losing empires, to maintain social and political cohesion while the European economic predation toward other regions of the globe was diminishing. But even the European architecture became insufficient to pay off the complete emancipation of the territories that had formed the European Empires, territories in other parts of the world that would not only gain access to full control of their resources and their technological potentials but that would be in conditions to challenge the European powers that once dominated them.

IV

The decolonization triggered after World War II finished for the western European nations, at best, with a little more of a European piece of land.

But a piece of land in Europe was still something. It could have been worse; it could have happened that some of such European states in which nationalisms flourished within their borders would have to face up to secessionist movements able to make them split. The Union ensured, thus, the mutation from being a colonial power to being a European nation-state, prevented the decline of those European nations and not only did the ghost of their extinction vanish, but there was bestowed to them, on some occasions, a sense of regained grandeur. Alan S. Milward once wrote that European integration came to the rescue of the European nation-states,[3] nation-states that would otherwise have had serious problems going forward. According to Milward's and other neo-realist authors' interpretations, European integration,[4] beginning with postwar western European integration, was not a glide-path toward any real and substantial political union, but on the contrary, a means to effectively reinvigorate national power. The pooling of sovereignty was mainly conceived to allow certain nation-states to render their postwar reconstruction models economically, politically, and socially viable.[5]

The European enterprise, theoretically committed to the ideals of democracy, rule of law, and fundamental rights, contributed to whitewash the atrocities perpetrated by some of those western European colonial powers while withdrawing from their former possessions. The recognition of fundamental rights, for instance, first within the framework of the Council of Europe and afterward also within the framework of the European Union, was managed to bound the authorities of such states without involving them in what had happened in their colonies. On the one hand, such rights contributed to confer legitimacy to the supranational project but, on the other hand, they fostered the oblivion of the overseas European domination that had nourished the allocation of wealth and power defining the European states' positions in relation to the other members of the club. Just as European integration allowed the Germans or the Italians to forget the horrors that their regimes carried out during World War II, including the invasion of European territories organized under colonial parameters, it also allowed the French, the Dutch, the Portuguese, or the Belgians to forget their colonial wars of the 1950s, 1960s, and 1970s.

The pretended European postwar new beginning, grounded on the principles of liberal democracy, nevertheless collided with various impediments until the present, most of them basically related to the decision of ensuring the national continuity of the units that played the main role in the integration and, consequently, by treating the existential threats against such national sovereignties with the same contempt in terms of rights or democracy that had been displayed in the times of the empires against the colonized peoples.

We shall see some examples about such disguise in tackling with social challenges able to undermine the national essence of the member states, but I may advance some of the topics that will deserve my preferential attention in this essay and that can be grouped in three main lines of discussion:

1. the sub-state national minorities able to bring into question the territorial integrity of a given European state;

2. the sway of extra-European migrations in some cases directly related to the colonial past (and the populist and authoritarian backlash that such non-European population transfers have triggered within the local political debate); and
3. the consequences of what I called the "capitalist occupation" that have opened several chasms among societies of different European Members, particularly from the 2008 economic crash, and that have blurred the trust in a common project not founded upon the domination of a given national agent upon others.

Minorities, migrations, occupations, and "internal colonization" in a space wrapped up with the promises of welfare, stability, and inclusion that have concealed the structures of abuse and coercion once exercised in distant places and now defined in day-to-day European governance.

The sub-state national minorities within larger polities, for instance, somehow demonstrated that plurinationalism may subsist within an imperialist context in the same fashion that different nation-states might coexist within a European supranational structure endowed with expansionist aims. However, the collaboration of such national minorities within former colonial empires was possible given their participation in the benefits of the domination exercised overseas.

It is not casual that once the size of the colonial empire began to decrease, that the national minorities within the European metropolis also displayed a strategy to strengthen the self-rule and ultimately to claim for political independence. The history of Scottish and Catalan nationalist movements regarding the United Kingdom and Spain respectively is in some way linked to the decline of the empires to which they belonged.

The resurrection of Scottish nationalism overlapped with the fragmentation of the British Empire during the second half of the twentieth century while the Catalan political vindications erupted precisely once Spain lost the remnants of its possessions in America and in the Pacific at the hands of the incipient expansionism of the United States of America by the end of the nineteenth century.

The European Communities and later the European Union provided the coverage for the European parts of those former empires to be preserved disregarding the loss of their overseas possessions but also offered a supposed framework to solve disputes pacifically and respecting human rights and the rule of law from which the sub-state national minorities might satisfy some of their interests in terms of allocation of power and wealth.

As we will examine later, Catalonia attempted to perpetrate a secession hoping that the European Union would refrain Spanish central authorities from reacting violently in order to stifle their struggle for political emancipation. In Scotland, a referendum on self-determination was permitted (and was lost) within a context in which the United Kingdom belonged to the European Union, a circumstance that later changed.

On the one hand, thus, European integration contributed to tie together sub-state nations within European polities that had experienced a conversion from their condition of global empires to reduced European nation-states. After all, Europe provided a single market (once the previous market defined by the empire was vanishing) from which the agents of such national minorities also obtained profit. The integration focused to strengthen bargaining capabilities vis-à-vis third states, without the European Union, related to exterior common trade policy or investment policy also contributed to pacify the domestic confrontation between national majorities and minorities within member states. Somehow, common European Union policies in economic fields in their relationship to territories that once constituted the colonies of some Western European powers worked as the placebo of an empire that did not exist anymore. On the other hand, the creation of a common European space of liberties and democracy debilitated the possibilities of cajoling dissidence within the member states through the traditional coercive and authoritarian means that endangered such systems that had historically built political unity through the logic of force.

V

The Yugoslavia that we had after the fall of Communism at the beginning of the nineties may well have taken place in Great Britain or in France in the collapse of their colonialist projects. The United Kingdom, in fact, experienced such a kind of instability through the Northern Irish troubles that were tamed once the British government was engaged with the European horizon (only to make it unconfident again, with another range of confusion both in Northern Ireland and Scotland, when the United Kingdom's withdrawal from the Union was executed).

The case of France and the struggle for the preservation of the European territorial integrity was still more complicated since anti-colonialist revolts coincided with the end of the fighting in the *metropole* to expel the occupant. National minorities might have played another more relevant role in the immediate French postwar period, able to threaten French centralism, but the Germans had renounced to play seriously the minorities' card after the 1940s invasion while the Vichy government, though maintaining most of its jurisdiction upon southern France and, consequently, upon non-French minorities, represented a French nationalistic project always suspicious of any opposition coming from those nationalisms.

The combination of the crises of empire with the ethnonational tensions within European territory might have been lethal for postwar France, and to some degree it might be considered, as we shall see, that both disruptions lay behind the Fourth Republic's collapse by the middle of the 1950s. To some extent, we might explain under which manifestations both fractures are still crossing today's political and social context in France.

Also in Belgium, they had to undertake a new domestic organization within their linguistic communities once the colonial adventure in Congo was concluded. Renouncing the external forms of domination forces a political community to rethink itself, and European states found that such a moment of mourning after the colonial humiliation was more easily suffered with the help of a technocratic apparatus from above.

Though every European former colonial power (the British one, the French one, the Belgium one) followed a particular path in their decline, in all of them there was a risk that the emancipation of overseas territories could have overlapped with the disintegration of the "core nation" leading to a definitive existential default. All of them, to some extent or another, turned to Europe to guard against such a risk to their respective national essences.

VI

Not only could a European territorial crisis have challenged the member states but also social convulsions might have shocked national unity, as nearly occurred in Italy by the second half of the 1940s, a danger that overshadowed Italian politics several times during the postwar decades.

After all, one of the most marked features of postwar western European societies in the aftermath of World War II was their poverty.[6] The obliterated France, Italy, West Germany, or even Britain (which had been exhausted after years of military struggle and in fact had to relinquish some of its possessions) had less to offer to their populations from the material point of view. This differed from the socioeconomic model that was being developed in the east of Europe.

The principal risk faced by the "European Rump States" was the possibility that the Soviet Union might obliterate all of them. The overwhelming military (and soon nuclearized) power led by Moscow may have fallen upon the fragile western European units. Stalin displayed a kind of remarkable soft power through the western European Communist parties, notoriously in Italy and France, that could well have attracted those areas to the periphery of the Soviet empire.

A solution to prevent such dissolutive inertias of the European nation-states was to reach an agreement with the other European peers or, more precisely, to reach an agreement among *the elites* of these decadent empires. There was a need to find some channels of solidarity in order to contain the *débâcle*, some common *fora* conceived to exchange the concerns of their members, the main of which was to preserve the system of power of their respective national artifacts.

Such an exchange between elites was, of course, sheltered by the economic, political, and military capacities of the United States of America. In its condition of former colony, the United States authorities of the postwar were reluctant to support the fading European empires in their struggles to stifle the decolonization movements in different parts of the globe. In addition to that, the American approach to the aim of the political and military domination of the world was rarely grounded on the old European strategy of direct ruling upon a population taking profit of an exploitation of the commodities produced in those territories. Instead, initiatives coming from Washington administrations preferred to ensure enclaves to provide a rapid mobilization of the United States military resources while exercising mediated control on governments in America, Africa, or Asia via the creation of a legal and political framework full of complicities with the local elites in order to recognize privileges for the American corporations present in those places. The United States authorities' performances on the path to building their hegemony within the context of the Cold War represented a model for those elites of the European nations that were losing their possessions. The decolonization of vast west and central African territories from France, for instance, somehow followed the American pattern in allowing formal independences while maintaining cultural and economic influences through co-opting the local elites in order to create a legal and political framework favorable to French private agents (not to mention the agreements on French military presence in the Sahel and in other parts of the continent, as the 2013–2014 French operation in Mali revealed). Great Britain maintained similar ties with its former colonies in Africa and Asia disregarding, as in the French case, the retention of overseas territories still directly administrated by the metropole. At any rate, from the 2010s even such a structure of indirect domination exercised by the old European Empires upon formally independent states entered into crisis basically due to the progressive penetration of non-European superpowers such as the People's Republic of China both by controlling local governmental apparatuses and by investing in extracting all sources of raw materials and commodities. The European Communities were founded while the European nation-states were losing the direct rule exercised by the western European partners upon entire populations in Africa, Asia, and America and, once constituted the European Union, their institutions and their member states faced existential crises while losing even the indirect rule upon Africa in favor of other non-European powers.

They had lost their empires, they had been reduced to a "provincialized" condition in political, military, and economic terms;[7] but at least there was a chance through a common understanding to save European fragments under homogeneous social, cultural, and economic conditions provided through the improvement of material and technological conditions, the consolidation of the welfare state, and the expansion of shared narratives through the extraordinary development of the media system able to confirm the sense of belonging to a national community, the sense of "us."

Immediately after the war, the various nation-states, big and small, retreated into their own shells through what has been defined as a "national corporatism" presuming a strong governmental involvement in economic life in order to supersede the precarious material conditions.[8] The Keynesian post-1945 consensus involved, thus, a specific compromise between business and labor and a prescribed role for the state in mediating this compromise aimed at both the maximization of growth in national wealth and the stabilization of the capitalist system.

Later, the years of European integration from the signature of the Treaty of the European Coal and Steel Community in 1951 to the Great Depression of 2008 coincided with the burgeoning career of the European nation-state as a device of power in its process of industrialization, urbanization, and democratization.[9] The state's administrative presence stretched itself through the most remote parts within its borders; education and health were services provided to all citizens, income per capita skyrocketed encouraging massive consumption, and national broadcasts created the emotional resorts in order to homogenize the citizenry identities. As Susan Cotts Watkins[10] demonstrated in analyzing collected data on European families between 1870 and 1960, whereas in 1870 differences on rates of fertility and marriage (and illegitimacy) were much greater within countries than between them, by 1960 in France, in the United Kingdom or in the German Federal Republic the family was "nationalized" by creating similar patterns of social practices and demographic integration.

European nation-states were also the field in which the so-called modernization theory was applied. Conceived as an academic artifact to confer legitimacy to United States foreign policy during the Cold War in its fight against Communism, this theory assumed the absolute priority of economic growth as the first step toward the consolidation of stable representative democracies even accepting that, to achieve such a goal, the system of government in which the modernization would take place need not necessarily be democratic.[11] European states nation-building during the postwar derived from such intellectual struggle encompassing both constitutional democracies but also places, such as Spain or Portugal, that still had not transited through the path toward democracy.[12] In addition, the modernization doctrine provided a staggering coverage for shaping a supranational structure beyond the states' democratic checks (the European Communities) in which free-handed technocrats might develop their ideas in order to foster the economic growth and social welfare that the states needed to cement their national uniformity. As Giandomenico Majone once wrote,[13] the European integration project has been from the beginning a zone in which the reliance upon qualities such as expertise, credibility, fairness, or independence has always been considered more important than reliance upon direct political accountability grounded on a majoritarian model of democracy.

The Golden Age of the European supranational experiment, under which we may qualify the history of the European Communities and the European Union during the second half of the twentieth century, was also the Golden Age of their nation-states. The nation-states have been therefore during the process of the European Union construction (and still now) the main provision for welfare, stability, and defense, as well as regulation.[14] They remain a multi-purpose creation retaining all the powers not transferred to the supranational level including that of withdrawing from the Union.

VII

It is startling to see to what extent European imperialism and its decline has been neglected while analyzing both the origins of European integration and the present crises of the European Union.[15] To summarize one of the theses that I hold in this book, I argue that by the third decade of the twenty-first century we are witnessing the final dissolution of Western European nation-states as colonial empires. Yet, there might have come the time that some of the former colonized territories by the Europeans have become powers able to colonize Europe. That had been already characterized the dynamics between western Europe and the United States of America during a substantial part of the twentieth century and the current century might reflect other non-European powers growth of influence on European territories and peoples. Even the Old Continent might be transformed in the frontline of a clash between global powers, replicating at a major scale what was already anticipated by the Cold War (which maybe we can name the *First* Cold War considering that we are nowadays living the *second* one).

My idea is that the European Communities–European Union represented the last bet to maintain the global influence of the western European states in spite of their respective empires' dismantling. But what happened at the turn of the millennium was that the former territories subjugated by European powers, though they had acceded to formal independence almost half a century before, became fully socially, politically, militarily, and, above all, economically emancipated from their former masters. Territories in the Far East or in the Middle East, such as China, India, Singapore, Israel, Qatar, or the Arab Emirates, only to mention a few examples, experienced the transition from being objects of European domination to be themselves subjects of domination and even, as notoriously happened in the case of China, global superpowers. If in the past some of such territories had been scrambled by the Europeans, there now may be envisaged a situation in which the European nation-states might be scrambled by non-European powers. Indeed, though that happened by a power that was half European (the Soviet Union), that was the outcome of World War II, and the evolution of European integration from that time was an attempt, maybe failed, to overcome such a situation.

VIII

Under my point of view, the 2008 crash, and the economic and political consequences that derived from it displayed during the decade of the 2010s and the first part of the 2020s, represented the visible signs of that process of power replacement that necessarily impacted in the European integration struggle.

The causes of the present European decadence are, of course, rooted in what had happened *before* the foundation of any regional supranational organization: the self-destruction of the European powers during the cycle that was triggered from 1914.

In that regard, the continental supranational building might be recognized as a sort of palliative in order to overcome the attempt at European collective suicide developed in World Wars I and II (accompanied by local warfare in several points of the European geography) a palliative that, as corresponds with that sort of remedies, can slow down the agony but, in judging the present circumstances, would probably not impede the death of the whole body.

The most intelligent of the Nazis, the legal theorist Carl Schmitt,[16] had already realized shortly after Germany's defeat in 1945 to what degree the former European stability had relied on the imperialist expansion of those European powers according to the allocation of areas of influence agreed among them.[17] Schmitt deplored as well the process of total war in European soil that had caused the ruin of that balance while making the world enter into a new global phase marked by nihilism and the threat of nuclear destruction masqueraded by the expansion of humanitarian internationalism.[18]

As was described by the mentioned author, the territorial state as a delimitation of the authority circumscribed in a particular space emerged once the idea of the medieval *Res publica christiana,* in which both ecclesiastic and secular authorities claimed for universal jurisdiction, was abandoned in favor of limited spaces unified under a single authority.[19] The great discoveries that, by the beginning of the Modern Age, opened up non-European territories as a field of unlimited European land-taking, also allowed such European territorial entities to foster a kind of universal vision inherited from the Middle Age through the association between nation and religion.[20] European expansionism to non-European territories, given the European's superior technology combined with such religious and imperial missions, laid the ground for genocidal and tyrannical practices overseas but, as Schmitt observed, *limited* inter-European warfare by conceiving it as a public law status between formally equal sovereigns.

Global European expansion beyond Europe made it possible to maintain the European system stable. The European Communities and, subsequently, the European Union was an attempt to regain such an inter-European equilibrium though the *Großraum* respectively held by the different European nation-states had been eroded. In other words: the Union emerges as the heir of European imperialism once the direct rule upon the vastness of transoceanic extensions disappeared.

Momentary, political domination was replaced by European predominance in the economic realm, and with that aim, as we shall consider, was in great measure displayed the European Union common trade policy (and the European common agricultural policy) that somehow represented an exception to the liberal mandates of globalization by maintaining a privileged position for Europe. The immediate post-colonial phase was accompanied by the European powers still exercising economic extortion against the former colonies through the collapse of commodity prices, loans at high interest, a multilateral aid system that emphasized potential return on investment, and the trade and maritime transport enjoyed by the wealthiest nations. Even trade unions of the industrialized world performed as another instrument of neocolonialism by imposing constant price increases for Western manufactures while insisting on the protection of industrialized nations' domestic markets.[21]

But the question that the European system is currently facing, according to my vision, is how such inter-European stability may be sustained once the global projection of each European power has been severely undermined to the point that some of the former European empires have even to deal with the danger of secessionism within their own European territorial borders or to the "capitalist occupation" in terms of investment and debt held by agents from the former colonies. Effective globalization has allowed us to envisage a change in the roles: those that were once subjugated began to transform themselves into those able to subjugate.

IX

The analysis offered in the following pages shall, furthermore, underline a basic contradiction that to my view crosses the European construction from the beginning. Such contradiction has, at some point, some relationship with the idea of extending the imperialist contexts that characterized the colonialist period to other subtler forms of domination. One thing that was founded on violence and extortion is developed under the same principles, though exhibited in a softer way.

Economic liberalism (together with political liberalism) has theoretically constituted the core of the European project, even surrounded by a sort of messianic aura.[22] Indeed, the development of the free market, the freedom of trade, movement, and employment for nationals became the emblematic structure of the European integration to which would be added the progress in individual freedom as well as prosperity, hand in hand with democratic institutions.[23]

But the dark side of such a liberal (and to some extent idyllic) picture is marked by the circumstance that the plan leading to the European construction was decisively implemented through *the continuity of traditions that were anti-liberal*. Among such traditions my narrative will remark on the following:

1. The survival of elements coming from authoritarian regimes. Some of those cadres that had been engaged with the totalitarian regimes before 1945 not only remained occupying prominent positions in national politics and administration but they exercised an important clout in shaping and consolidating the European level of governance. The pattern was even more visible in the field of the relations that the European economic elites had displayed during the prewar and the war times that decisively hatched the pan-European oligarchy that was behind the creation of the European Communities (a group that would even include Jean Monnet).
2. The aforementioned decolonization disasters that affected the old western European empires. In some cases, as in France, the wars of decolonization had been mostly organized through the personnel that had collaborated with the Germans during the occupation and the Vichy regime so, somehow, the two anti-liberal strands were linked in their influence toward the idea of Europe that was outlined in the origins of the integration and that reaches our present.
3. The resurrection of hard-line nationalistic, xenophobic and populist movements not only with growing electoral success but with

> progressive ability of infiltration in the resorts of the state apparatus from the military to the judiciary, a cycle that in some places was related to a fascist background that was not so distant and that persisted given a supposed smooth transition from an authoritarian regime to a democracy (as in Spain) while in others reemerged in spite of the totalitarian past that was pretended to be surmounted (as, for instance, the presence of far-right elements in the German Federal army testifies).

If we have in the last decade witnessed such a revival of the anti-liberal Europe that has happened in my view because it did not disappear with the European developments that departed from the Schuman Declaration but it rather found within the supranational framework a place to be channeled and even to thrive.[24] Although the official discourses on the building of the European integration historical narrative have tried to conceal such a dark past, the wounds that the abuses left are likely to fester again in the European present.

In 2017, for instance, on initiative of the European Parliament, the House of European History opened to the public with the supposed purpose to provide a room of debate on the European past and to examine the discursive practices of Europeanization.[25] However, the spirit of the different exhibitions presented in the mentioned House stressed an optimistic and ascendant narrative in which concepts such as "democracy," "progress," "liberty," "peace," or "humanism" played a prominent role while allusions to "colonialism," "genocide," "slavery," or "state terror" were at best only suggested and were characterized as the shadows that the success of the integration had happily set aside. The present contribution, notwithstanding, is precisely focused on the terms "colonialism," "genocide," "slavery," and "state terror" and devoted to analyze to what extent they are still influencing the hopes and lacks of European politics, European identity and the European *telos*.

The need to replace the mechanisms of looting upon the former colonies practiced by the old European Empires through a kind of liberal prosperity within Europe was not an abstract ideal but a tangible aspiration, and urgency after the devastation of World War II.

Both, Britain and France, for instance, were from the mid nineteenth century able to sustain their trade deficits through colonial appropriations. As Thomas Piketty observed in his work *Capital in the Twenty-First Century*[26] in Britain by the turn of the twentieth century accumulated assets as the consequence of the colonial empire provided an income about 10 percent higher than its domestic "metropolitan" product, which allowed a fairly significant group to live off this boon. In the case of France, the second most important colonial empire, the dividends, interests, royalties, rents, and other revenue on assets that French citizens owned in the country's overseas possessions and other foreign countries surpassed during the first decade of the twentieth century France's domestic "metropolitan" product by some 6 percent. That was equal to the total industrial output of the northern and eastern *départements*.

Between 1880 and 1914, both Britain and France received significantly more goods and services as a result of their colonialist domination means than they exported themselves (their trade deficits averaged 1–2 percent of national income throughout this period) but since their income from overseas assets totaled more than 5 percent of the national income their balance of payments was positive, which enabled them to increase their holdings outside the *metropole* year after year (both within the dominions and within other formally independent territories) in a way that the world worked to increase consumption by the colonial powers and, at the same time, became more and more indebted to those same powers.

That situation changed dramatically with World Wars I and II, the Great Depression, and, finally, the decolonization through which these vast stocks outside the *metropole* would eventually evaporate. Since colonialism could not provide the trade surpluses that ensured the standards of living of the British and French population within the European territories, prosperity and the maintenance of economic growth had to be found within another frame: by exchanging goods, services, and capitals within the other former European powers that were seeking to recover from the disasters of war and the division of the continent.

One of my principal claims here is that the European integration project is the product of both the European imperialist usurpations that strengthened the path of European industrial and technological supremacy before the wars of the twentieth century and the dramatic aspiration to retain the privileges of that supremacy in terms of welfare for their populations once those European powers had to renounce the instruments of coercion (basically because they were not able to sustain them) that had enforced the imperial structures.

X

Supporting free trade, movement of goods, and capitals beyond borders, the internationalization of the economy and, in short, what we later would call "globalism" had been a matter of European losers.

Quinn Slobodian[27] convincingly argued that the direct precedent of the liberalization trend that inspired the creation of the European Common Market had been provided by the Austrian School of economists as a reaction to the collapse of the Austro-Hungarian Empire at the end of World War I. The small Austrian republic that resulted from the scattering of ethnicities, languages, and cultures that for centuries had integrated a single political unity could not survive without trading, firstly, with the former subjects of the deposed emperor that now were citizens of independent states.

Economy, and the prosperity that the free exchange of goods would promote, was conceived as an alternative to regain the welfare that political disruption had diminished. What von Mises, Haberler, Hayek, and others were planning in the offices of Vienna's Chamber of Commerce was the consolidation of an ideological and legal framework able to boost economic growth disregarding the vicissitudes experienced by the different sovereign nations given the advent of mass democracy. Economic liberalism as a remedy against political fragmentation: that was the deep philosophy of the intellectuals gathered in Vienna by the establishment of the Republic of Austria in 1919. Unsurprisingly, shortly after the burial of the Austro-Hungarian Empire, Czechs and the new Austria deployed solid relations grounded in extensive mutual trade[28] not to mention the prospect of closing the ties between Austria and the Weimar Republic in which the old ideal of building a Great Germany was embodied (and that finally the Nazis would achieve through the *Anschluss,* albeit from an authoritarian perspective and at the cost of Austria's political disappearance).

Austrian liberalists' concerns would be similar to those that dominated the founders of European integration more than thirty years later when they found their countries in a parallel position as the one that Austria had held after the military defeat: devastated and with an empire in the process of being dismantled. Still, the interwar experience had shown the Western European elites from 1945 were thinking about the future of the continent to which path mass democracy and populism may lead, in the absence of supranational constraints: to the mortal fight between the totalitarianism of the right and the totalitarianism of the left (with the latter controlling half of Europe once Hitler fell into his particular Walhalla).

However, and in spite of the internationalism that embedded the liberal economic vision, both the postwar liberalism and its interwar Austrian precedent saw in the rules that had to secure property rights, safe trade, access to goods, and capitals circulation, a range of mechanisms designed *for the nation's sake*. The ideal relied on ensuring the execution of an ordo-liberal mercantilist program within a heterogeneous union of states in a form according to which economic growth (or, at least, the economic growth of their respective oligarchies) served for the robustness of their national cohesion. When von Mises, for instance, imagined the thriving society that the application of his liberal rooted theories would bring thought, precisely, on the Austria that floated from the disaster of World War I (and the latter may help to understand Mises's sympathy for Austrian fascism in the thirties just like his willingness to collaborate as economic advisor of the Dollfuss government).

The late Weimar Germany also succumbed to the temptation of focusing on economic rationality with the intention to regain international standing and influence. Nevertheless, the German interwar project to impose a capitalist market system by curtailing political participation and fostering social inequality would indeed, by the beginning of the thirties, seriously weaken liberal democracy's ability to respond to threats of political extremism when they later emerged fully fledged.[29] Such a move would to some extent resemble the correlation between the German response to the 2010s crises of the euro by imposing austerity measures and the rise of nationalistic and populist movements across Europe during the following years. The attempt to take economic matters out of the public domain of democratic power and accountability links the policies displayed within the European Union in recent times both with the principles that inspired the first movements toward European integration after World War II and with the intellectual atmosphere between both world wars that sought to find a margin protected from far-left and far-right extremes.[30]

A not-so-distant path than that described regarding Austria and Germany before the 1930s was certainly taken by the France that Monnet conceived while contributing to the founding of the European Communities: the aim was not the dissolution of the nation within an ethereal international magma but the erection of a strong France without turning to wars of conquest and annexation. The European Communities and later the European Union grounded their appeal by promising a *nationally* prosperous horizon without having to fight a war to obtain it.

The nationalistic project, however, forced, by the beginning of the communities, to moderate the liberal strands of economic integration. As we shall see in more detail, particularly by developing the French evolution within the European integration, the liberal vision grounded on removing all the barriers to the free movement of factors of production, had initially to coexist with the attempt to orchestrate a set of uniform practices into being by state intervention.[31]

The complete destruction that the war had left and the need to ensure a minimum welfare for the citizenry in times of reconstruction, in order to confer legitimacy to the project, paved the way to conceive some sort of social structures within the nation-states compatible with the western European attempt to unify economic life through the workings of the market. Corporatism, in short, with its inheritance of both fascist and socialist practices, was going to be essential during the building of the postwar western European states and would represent an exception to the liberal economic global system that was being defined through the structures designed at Bretton Woods. The boundaries to liberal capitalism settled in order to reconstruct European economies and to ensure a minimal material welfare would still be present in most members of the European Communities in its essentials at least until the aftermath of the 1970s oil crisis.

It was precisely such a succession of economic crises that jolted Europe and the world from the 1970s (together with the disintegration of the Soviet bloc in the 1990s and, consequently, the disappearance of the liberal counter model) that fostered the freeing of markets from Statist interference and led to cuts in social expenditures as well as to the weakening of trade unions and other mechanisms to contain the expansion of capital, the concentration of wealth and the growth of inequality.

The 2008 Great Slump, under the imperatives of monetary stability, and the powerful impact that it had in Europe, represented the climax of the triumph of liberal economic aspirations, even at the expense of deteriorating the political atmosphere with an authoritarian regression in some contexts and the threat to the core of the supposed European values as established from 1945. We are going to analyze such cycles from the European Communities' foundations to the present: the moderated initial liberalism constrained by the remnants of corporatism and exceptionalism regarding to global trade, the expansion of the ordo-liberal strand from the 1980s, and the austerity apotheosis from the 2010s.

XI

European integration was not conceived to water down the nation-states in a post-national continental entity but was a framework created by such states to make them stronger in their identities. Europe was used to make France, Germany, Italy, or Spain greater in spite of the circumstances or, at least, to allow their survival as national bodies within a sea of dangers. That explains why all the attempts to conceive Europe as a "single public space" in which transnational deliberations are developed by transnational agents within a common cultural frame have always failed.[32] Nobody was really interested in that cultural development able to transcend the nation, except maybe a group of intellectuals and academics who benefited from the material conditions that the same national system from which they wrote provided.

Nation-states prevailed, they were on the top of the scale of political loyalty within the population and, indeed, their authorities used the European institutions to maximize their respective national interests. Every European institutional amendment was rather a matter on how to preserve and even expand the influence of a given nation-state within the supranational structure, it had always been a matter on what Europe could do for the nation-state rather than what a nation-state could do for Europe (and what the European nationalisms would at any rate *never* do would be to dissolve themselves in favoring the consolidation of a "European *demos*" able to form a "European identity" competing with the local identities).

Even the possibilities generated by the establishment of a free movement of people and workers had been insufficient to generate a sense of supranational belonging since, at the end of the day, only the elites, being European civil servants, entrepreneurs, or university students of the Erasmus program, or those that had nothing to lose, benefited from the creation of a free transit space (and those advantages did not tell anything about personal identities and loyalties of the mentioned groups). The majority of the French or the Germans remained respectively in France or Germany and, consequently, gave continuity to their French and German identities.[33]

Paradoxically, the creation of a supranational organization had been the answer offered by the nation-states' governments to achieve, in the times that followed decolonization, the old dream of the pre-liberal (and absolutist) state devoted to building a strong and centralized administrative machinery in order to eliminate internal national diversity. As we shall see, the meager recognition of both the right of the people's self-determination and the minority nations within Europe, and particularly within western Europe, reflected that. The supranational artifact that was likely to mute the voracity of the state nationalism deeply contributed to consolidate it and, with such a movement, the failure of the emergence of a European *demos* was ensured (at the same time that the seed of the comprehensive fragmentation of the project was planted). The European Union contained the disruptions on identity that had marked European history until 1945. The veil of the continental organization, and the economic prosperity that it brought, provided simultaneously the confidence in the nationalistic projects built around the member states.

It has been such national confidence, embodied in the original agreement on exchanging the overseas empire for the mainland's national cohesion, the one that nonetheless blew up with the multiple crises experienced in the recent past: the economic crisis (the one that exploded from 2008, the one derived from the COVID-19 pandemic, and that following the war in Ukraine) the immigration crisis, the Brexit issue, the subnational secessionist movements or the challenges to the European Union's borders. And, in the background, there is a more profound and pressing crisis that encompasses the others and that explains the European Union's decline, namely, *the nostalgia for the empire* that has been aroused within the European nation-states in which both some of their politicians and relevant parts of their societies think to find the way to disentangle all the conflicts that besiege them.

One obvious extreme of the imperial "nostalgia" might be represented by Brexit, the divorce with a possible European empire in order to regain the British former global influence and, particularly, to strengthen ties with those territories that once were under the British Crown jurisdiction (or in which the British Monarch is still the head of state as in Canada, Australia, or New Zealand). Why belong to a club in which linguistic and cultural differences are profound when you may still enjoy the cultural profits of your previous expansion?[34] As we shall see, the cost of such an odyssey is the discontent of national minorities within the British borders, which may push to create their own states in order to reattach themselves to the European order or, at least, to facilitate a particular legal regime that may expand the European acquis in some parts of the United Kingdom, as happened in Northern Ireland with the so called Irish Protocol to the agreement on British withdrawal from the European Union.

But the nostalgic imperial dreams might be revealed by other manifestations, such as the more direct coercive measures adopted to erode national minorities existing within the European borders of a particular member state or the capitalist occupation exercised by a group of central and northern European states to entrench their dominant position toward the southern and eastern peripheries of Europe. The question would be, thus, if such wishes to revive the respective *national* empires are compatible with the survival of the European Union. For the moment, Brexit provided a radiant "no" as an answer.

XII

The story here unfolded concerns mainly western European states and, particularly, the founders of the European Union (France, Germany, Italy, Belgium, the Netherlands, and Luxembourg) with two important ramifications in Great Britain and in the Iberian Peninsula (Spain and Portugal) which acceded later to the integration process.

In the eastern European scenario, even though some attempts of using the European Union project with the aim of revisiting imperial dreams (as notoriously has been the case of Orbán's Hungary) most of those countries, especially the ones created after the collapse of the Communist area, were satisfied enough if the Union contributed to ensure their political independence.

For the Baltic states, for instance, the linkage to the European project provided the coverage to protect themselves against the resurrection of Russian expansionism, which began to appear as a tangible danger by the Russo-Georgian short war in 2008 and was perceived as an imminent threat as long as the conflict between Russia and Ukraine recrudesced from 2014. The fast Baltic alignment with Brussels proved in this fashion to be more successful than the experiences of those states that remained aside or that sought to join the European Union when Russia had strengthened itself and frustrated any attempt of detachment from its sphere of influence, as in the mentioned Ukrainian case.[35] Regarding the former Soviet Union satellites (or even regarding the former Soviet Union republics) the European Union appeared from 1989, in sum, as a safeguard against a predictable return of Russian imperialism.

Eastern Europe, consequently, and given their condition of imperialist victims rather than that of imperialist perpetrators, remained outside of the equation relating European integration as a solution to surmount the loss of a colonial empire. The imperial nostalgia and irredentism that might define the project of some eastern European country (or maybe I should call it the wish for an empire that never was) would not be in that way relevant enough to describe the integration of that member within the European Union as a means to regain what was left in the dismantling of an empire. That is why the developments within the eastern European members of the Union, amid some exceptions related to Poland, Hungary, or the effects of Russian aggression against Ukraine upon such territories, will not be analyzed in the following pages. Instead, my interest shall be rather centered in examining European integration as the scenario in which western European powers abandoned their structures of domination upon global Empires to transfer them to the nation-state.

XIII

Before World War II, most of the states founded with the fall of the Central Empires were certainly a melting pot of nationalities with several levels of recognition both in the domestic constitutional order and in international law. The Peace Treaties that followed the Great War lumped together many peoples in single states, called some of them "State People" and entrusted them with the government, silently assumed that others (such as the Slovaks in Czechoslovakia, and the Croats and Slovenes in Yugoslavia) were equal partners in the government, while they were not.[36]

Such treaties had also created within the central and eastern European states a third group of nationalities called "minorities," thereby adding to the many burdens of the new entities the trouble of observing special regulations for that part of the population. No wonder that Mussolini, for instance, when writing after the 1938 crisis in the Sudeten believed that Czechoslovakia's delicate situation of that time was precisely because such a state was not only a union between Czechs and Slovaks but a "Czech-Germano-Polono-Magyaro-Rutheno-Rumano-Slovakia" federation.[37]

The failure of the system of the protection of ethnic "minorities" designed within the framework of the League of Nations after World War I was replaced, once World War II approached its end and during its aftermath, by the necessity to accommodate the waves of refugees that the collapse of the Nazi order had caused.[38] The solution, particularly in central and eastern Europe, relied on agreeing to the consolidation of ethnically purified nation-states strong enough to grant protection to the newcomers, which instead of coexisting would be dispersed among other peoples, and thereby integrated in *the same national structure*.

The first assumption on the road of the creation of a supranational entity such as the European Union required, thus, *the galvanization of national peoples within the same political and cultural framework*, a goal that, deprived of the imperialist impulse, coincided to some extent with a model of ethnicity that the Nazis had done more than anyone to push through.[39]

The continuity of the "mainland" nation states in spite of the cruel confrontations of the twentieth century was still more evident in western Europe which, with the exception of the Republic of Ireland, Iceland, Norway, the regaining of Alsace and Lorraine by France, and the territories assigned to Italy by the end of World War I, presented *the same* territorial borders as those inherited from the nineteenth century, and maybe, as we shall see, that explains why claims of statehood have resurrected among small nations within larger states in the western Europe of the twenty-first century, that is, in the area in which ethnic cleansings and transfers of population had been less relevant during the time that Hobsbawm called the "Age of the Extremes."[40]

XIV

European postwar arrangements may be characterized as an updating of an agreement between agents that have been, and would be, redefined after a conflict in a similar mode as the movement experienced by the Peace of Westphalia around three centuries before. But, whereas in Westphalia what was being outlined was the state itself as a machinery of centralized power, in the "Neo Pax Westphalica" that postwar European integration represented, the European state was transformed in terms of national homogenization and modernization.

The movement that has been characterized as "renouncing sovereignty" to allow income growth[41] (and, thus, to ensure social stability) through integration might probably be reshaped in a more specific sense by remarking that the western European powers have relinquished *territorial expansion* to fulfill their national ambitions. But that does not mean that national communities' representatives do not think of their national interest in the first instance, nor that all the material and political gains obtained through the strategy of integration are not to be applied to reassert the respective nation among the others. In other words: the change in the means of domination has not jeopardized *the intention of continuing to exercise such a domination*.

The European construct had in this vein the double effect, on the one hand, of consolidating internal national identities through economic growth, technological development, and the use of governmental machinery and, on the other hand, to reorganize the external role of such state-grounded identities under common guidelines regarding to which there was leeway for the members to follow or to dodge in function of their correspondent *raison d'état*.

To put it in classical terms, rather than debilitating their sovereign attributions, the European Union certainly contributed to reinforce both internal and external sovereignty. Through the apparent conduction of a common agreement, the final outcome was rather the ensuring of a *space of independence* that otherwise, that is, without such a Union, would have been unsteady or collapsing.

With the compact that the constitutive treaties designed, everyone had something to win while they had the opportunity to surmount losses that would be at any rate suffered given the global scenario. Even after the adoption of decision-making mechanisms such as the replacement, regarding some powers, of unanimity by qualified majority rule, there was defined a structure in which, after all, no member was obliged to do what their supreme authorities did not want to. It was precisely when those terms changed, when national parliaments and governments began to be constrained by the dictum coming from Brussels (or, better said, from the debt pay-back imperatives coming from the European Central Bank, the Commission, and the International Monetary Fund) that all the European legal framework began to crack.

The integration struggle led by the founders of the European space was marked, thus, by the *need* to regain power through national cohesion within a wasted world. Such need united those ones that were losing their global influence (such as France, Belgium, or the Netherlands) with those ones that *had already lost all* their imperial pretensions in the havoc of war (such as Germany and Italy). The European Union, in the same way that has happened with all the great things that humanity has invented in the science of governing itself with peace and prosperity, didn't come from strength but *from weakness*. It was, thus, a matter of time, that some of the agent's gaining of power or that the persistence of the decadence of other agents would lead European shared aspirations into a cul-de-sac.

The win-win situation for all the participants, in the sense that all the nation-states would become stronger within the European cover, has become by the beginning of the 2020s an act of wishful thinking. History never stops and never allows long periods of tranquility, particularly if someone has the opportunity to impose themselves upon others.

XV

The comment developed above leads me to brief methodological considerations on the spirit of these lines; this book is not an academic contribution sustained by exhaustive empirical data in a path usually transited by studies on European integration. It is, rather, a cultural diagnosis, the kind of interpretation of what has been traditionally included by the studies of humanities under the term "essay," that is, an attempt to add some knowledge pending further discussions and explorations.

All in all, *Nostalgic Empires* is an interpretation grounded on a basic epistemological premise concerning history and social sciences: the basic political motivation of a human group *is to gain more power* or, at least, not to lose the power that it has been exercising. Somehow, we would still follow the path envisaged by Nietzsche in defining his idea on the will of power: "[W]hat man wants," wrote Nietzsche, "what the smallest part of any living organism wants is an increase in power,"[42] only that in our case in the place of "the man" or in the place of "the smallest part of any living organism" may be referred to the main agent of our concerns: the European nation-state.

To put it in the terms of the so-called realist schools of thought on international relations (or its derivatives), the European nation-states within the framework of European integration still consider themselves (and they did so from the beginning) *to be ultimate ends*.[43] That has been a traditional adagio observed by realists concerning the performance of sovereign states within the framework of global relations, but I still would apply it to the political and economic exchanges between the member states in every stage of the evolution of the European project.

According to my view, nation-states constituted in European member states only look after their national interests but, differently to what happened in the Europe existing before the creation of the European Steel and Coal Community, they progressively renounced to display the traditional strategies that they have used to safeguard such interests before 1945 and that had characterized the interactions among them (and between them and other extra-European actors) before that time: balance of power, imperialism, colonialism, or universal dominion.

Instead, as a result of the profound weakness that surrounded the European powers by the second half of the 1940s, the aim to look after their respective national interests and to maximize influence in both the continent and the world as national realities required them to set aside the responses primarily relying on bare imperialism and domination and to tame them through the logic of political negotiation.

In such circumstances I have carved up my theoretical framework by insisting on the impossibility of eliminating the conflictive nature of relations displayed through nation-states in spite of the fact that such conflicts have been more or less displaced to more capillary forms of domination than those expressed in the past when they were the cause of "European civil wars." I tend therefore to disagree on such theories on European integration, which seek to find different motivations to that of the aim of gaining power within a context of geopolitical interests, in order to explain the European states' attitudes in the building of a "closer union."

For Andrew Moravcsik for instance[44] the broad lines of European integration are marked by economic interests provided by commercial advantages, by the consolidation of European governments' bargaining power and by the enhancement of the credibility of interstate commitments.[45] Moravcsik thinks that once put in motion, a supranational framework creates its own dynamics, some of which would not be under the control of the states. But under my vision, the states have always retained the decision on the essentials, which were policies related to the states' desire to maximize their status *as nations*.

When for example Moravcsik argues that De Gaulle's policies toward Europe (including his veto of United Kingdom membership in the 1960s) was driven primarily by economic interests (particularly, by the search for export markets for French farm surpluses) and not by a conception of French grandeur,[46] he forgets that supporting the French farm interests was for the general a crucial way to protect French *national* interests as well. Farming was also a kind of grandeur. Geopolitical ideology is not only developed through armies and nuclear weapons (which were also a relevant issue both in the French postwar policies and in the French position toward European integration) but also by promoting the growth of the primary sector and the welfare of the people whose livelihoods depend on it (as certainly has happened regarding any human civilization since the beginning of time). More precisely: if the European Common Agricultural Policy effectively contradicted and defied the very foundations of the common market grounded on economically liberal principles, it was because it was called to satisfy nationalistic interests that went beyond the liberal economic logic. They were rather attached to the will of domination than to liberalism: they were specifically conceived to protect the European market from more competitive farming producers of other areas of the world.[47] The model supported by France in agricultural matters, to sum it up, was consequent with the general French expectation on the European project under De Gaulle's presidency, that is, to shape a power able to balance the global imperialism of the United States by reinforcing sovereignty of the Western European nation-states under French leadership.[48]

As we have already suggested, from the 2008 global crises onward, once the states perceived that the Union was not the place to maximize their gain of power, the integration project fell under an existential threat. The economic crash began to extend the awareness among the European governments according to which it would be more beneficial to them to develop unilateral policies than to reach consensus with the other European members such as the ones derived from the negotiations on amending the treaties requiring the unanimity of all the actors. Indeed, while the reform of the treaties from the 1986 European Single Act had been frequent and in the direction of enhancing integration[49] from the entering into force of the Lisbon Treaty in 2009, in the midst of the economic downfall, there have been almost no further amendments if we except again those related to Brexit,[50] which were rather dismemberments than proper amendments.[51] If in some moment there had been an aspiration to progress toward a federalist Europe, states quickly introduced checks on those struggles through treaty amendments, and the interpretation thereof by the respective constitutional courts.

In my analysis, all the benefits obtained through integration, including most notoriously the economic ones, may be appreciated as *externalities* from the struggle of underpinning the nation-states' position among their peers. Economic integration would not be, thus, an end in itself but (following authors like Gowa[52] or Grieco[53]) means to manipulate "high politics" related to the defense of national identity.

Another of the topics that has marked the studies on the recent evolution of the European Union relies on observing the degeneration of the both the organization and its member states in terms of democratic space. The euro crisis that reached its first peak by 2012 has been appreciated as the turning point that paved the way to the democratic demolition and the spread of authoritarianism through monetary policy, economic stability criteria, and bailouts subjected to conditionality and the application of austerity measures.[54] But under my interpretation, as also was denounced by several authors,[55] the undermining of democratic values and the siege to fundamental liberties beyond individual economic freedom was *inherent to the European integration project from the outset*, basically because the economic order that the European Communities sought to consolidate had been built under the rapacity and the capital accumulation that the agonic empires had absorbed from the colonies.

XVI

Regarding the founders of European integration, let's take the case of France. France was struggling in rebuilding pacific relations with its former enemy, an amputated Germany, while it was suffering outrageous defeats overseas.[56]

The war was not still concluded when the Brazzaville Declaration was issued on the future of the French empire, in which it was insisted that the overseas populations did not want any kind of independence different to "the independence of France," but the bloody clampdowns that spread across some of the French colonies from 1945 suggested that that was not true.[57]

Only three years after the end of Nazi occupation, the French sought to suppress a nationalistic rebellion that erupted in Madagascar. The troops assigned to that region did not behave themselves very differently from how the Nazis did in France during World War II. They did many hideous things: French platoons annihilated entire towns, committed massive rapes and tortures, and murdered around thirty thousand people.[58]

The end of the war also brought a vicious repression in Syria at the hands of the French authorities. While Prime Minister Faris al-Khoury attended at the founding conference of the United Nations presenting Syria's claim for independence from the Mandate, French planes were bombing Damascus and the colonial authorities tried to arrest the democratically elected Syrian leaders.

Between the signature of the European Coal and Steel Community Treaty in Paris in 1951 and the conclusion of the European Economic Community Treaty in Rome in 1957, the French army had in 1954 been crushed at Dien Bien Phu and shortly afterward had to experience the humiliating withdrawal from Indochina in the agreements of Geneva (on July 21, 1954). French colonialism experienced in Indochina a terrible wave of devastation of social structures that outlined the path that wars of national liberation were going to adopt: Ho Chi Minh's guerrilla began to recruit civil population for its cause in order to infiltrate themselves among the French colonial staff, from the domestic service of officials to farmers who produced food for the French army, the insurgents were in the position to interrupt the normal functioning of public authority in those territories. The revolutionaries in Vietnam and Laos perpetrated all sorts of acts of terror to prepare the French troops for even more savage acts of counterterrorism against the native population, which led to a spiral of hatred and annihilation undermining the economic and political stability also within the *metropole*.

In November 1954, insurrection burst out in a territory that even being in northern Africa was considered a French metropolitan administrative structure: Algeria. Such a territory had also been the scenario in which French people and other Europeans had established themselves permanently in large numbers. While the negotiations both on Tunisian and Moroccan independence went forward, the approximately one million French settlers, determined to maintain their political and economic domination over Algeria's nine million Muslims, would not make things easy.

Certainly, the Algerian question derived in a bloodshed that, at the same time, would lead the French Fourth Republic to collapse. A brand-new constitutional regime around the figure of De Gaulle would be erected revealing, thus, and even more sharply than in the case of Indochina, to what extent a crisis within the periphery of an empire might threaten the core of the national empire itself and the need to find a solution along with the other European partners surrounded by similar circumstances.

XVII

The Netherlands too had faced a traumatic process with Indonesian's independence in the second half of the 1940s.[59] Supposedly, western European nations emerging from the brutal totalitarian occupation in their own country would be willing to strengthen the values of liberalism and democracy. But one of the first things that the Dutch did after liberating themselves from the Nazis was raise an army and send it halfway across the world to stifle Indonesian aspirations of becoming sovereign.[60]

The Japanese conquest had revealed the weakness of the Western colonial powers in east Asia and fostered the growth of nationalist movements once the occupation ceased. In the first instance, following the Japanese capitulation, the British exercised colonial administration both in the Dutch Indies and in French Indochina.[61] Such a movement organized through the South-East Asia Command under Lord Louis Mountbatten, backed by a massive presence of troops, allowed both France and the Netherlands to return to the overseas territories that they had lost during the war.[62] It showed, as well, the British proneness to work shoulder to shoulder with the rest of the Western European powers in order to restore the colonial orderk; they feared that anti-colonial nationalism might start a chain reaction affecting British territories as certainly happened, eventually, in India or in Malaya.[63] The immediate postwar period saw the revival of colonization as a common European project that had dominated global relations for the last centuries.[64]

In Indonesia, the nationalist guerrilla had after the war sustained an anti-colonial struggle for four years and, in spite of the fact that the Dutch tried to reestablish their colony, the nationalist insurgents succeeded in attaining independence except in two eastern provinces, called Netherlands New Guinea, which remained under Dutch dominion until 1962.

The Indonesian uprising severely damaged the Dutch economy. The East Indies accounted for 14 percent of the GDP of the Netherlands after the war, and represented a vital source of oil, rubber, and other raw materials to be processed at home.[65] Indonesian independence caused a demographic convulsion with the repatriation of the European inhabitants from the colony. The Dutch experience in Indonesia shows to what extent, only with reluctance and after a ferocious fight, the European nations would renounce their former imperial dominions. No wonder that, once defeat was inevitable, the former empires would focus themselves on ensuring at least the full control of the territory and the population that they still retained in Europe. With the loss of the East Indies colonies, and given the recent experience of World War II as well, the Netherlands appeared as a small and vulnerable piece of land that vitally urged an economic cooperation within the European space.

As Mathieu Segers explained, the postwar Netherlands was perhaps more than ever at the mercy of international politics.[66] The forces of the Cold War were much too powerful for the small country on the North Sea. In fact, the final Dutch capitulation in Indonesia in 1949 was substantially motivated by the American threats of exclusion from NATO and the Marshall Plan.[67] The Netherlands was forced to cast its lot in with the Old Continent, where it had to deal with troubled and headstrong western European powers over which it had no control, but with which it had to establish relations in a way it had never had to do before. It had been precisely such a sense of vulnerability that had made the Netherlands prepare itself for European integration even before the end of World War II, by founding Benelux with Belgium and Luxembourg.

XVIII

Belgium would have to manage too at the end of the 1950s, shortly after the approval of the Treaty of Rome, with the claims of independence in the former possession of the Belgian kings: Congo.

Even though the Belgian government and the young king Baudouin were embarked on a program of democratization of that territory, the pressure for emancipation, accompanied by great disruptions and violence, made the Belgium dominion upon Congo unsustainable, and the transfer of sovereignty was accelerated in 1960 during a chaotic abandonment of the region.[68]

For Belgian leaders, including the socialist leader Paul Henry Spaak, the Congo was the jewel in the Belgian crown that had to be retained at all costs. Precisely by 1960–1961 when the socialists began a period of electoral dominance, Belgium underwent some of the most violent social upheavals related to the disastrous management of the decolonization question. The final withdrawal from the Congo in 1964 freed Belgium from the contradictions of its colonial policy but only to transfer the disarrangements related to national and linguistic pluralism to the European scenario.[69]

From the four members of the recently created European Economic Community that had been "liberated" from the yoke of the fascism by the Allies in the ending of World War II: France, the Netherlands, Belgium, and

Luxembourg; only the latter, the tiny Luxembourg, had not been directly handling the dismantling of an empire.

Even Italy, a defeated military power that had been forced to renounce control over Libya and Eritrea, managed to return to one of its former colonial possessions in the Horn of Africa. In 1950, Rome obtained a trusteeship over Somalia that allowed it to guide that country's transition to independent government, which Somalia eventually achieved in 1960.[70]

Afterward, new western members of the European club such as Great Britain, Spain, or Portugal had acceded to the European project following an astonishing history of territorial losses (enormous in the case of Great Britain, beginning with Indian and Pakistani independence in 1947; not so relevant in the case of Spain with the loss of some African possessions in the 1970s, but still hurtful given the decadence that the Spanish empire had been suffering since the nineteenth century).

In short, by the beginning of the European integration process, a trend that would be stretched over time as long as other old imperial powers would join the European Communities, the European nation-states were making efforts to establish a democratic and liberal order within the borders of the European continent while defending their colonial ambitions by force in an atmosphere of grisly human rights violations.

Already by the creation of the United Nations, in which both France and Great Britain, the largest imperial powers, were founding members and would become permanent members of the security council, contributed to shape an international order grounded on human rights but both were reluctant to extend the recognition of human rights to their colonies (and worked together to secure their colonial ambitions even with other European powers).[71]

Such a paradox in the recognition of human rights at the supranational level able to fortify the European liberal and democratic order but *denying* the same liberties to the subjects of the colonies would also later be translated into the European transnational mechanisms of protection of rights, being the Council of Europe or the devices that would be progressively developed within the framework of the European Communities and the European Union.

In fact, both Great Britain and France created a legal groundwork for *suspending* the basic rights that they had previously voted to support in the European Convention of Human Rights. Great Britain was, nevertheless, brought before the European Commission of Human Rights by the Greek government both in 1956 and 1957 for violating the European Convention in the repression of the anti-colonial resistance in Cyprus while France, even being one of the founding members of the European Convention in 1950, did not ratify the document until 1974 once the decolonization wars, including those in northern Africa, were over.

As we shall see, the remnants of such a dialectic (human rights for the Europeans in Europe but not for the colonies) still appears in conflicts involving the repression of national movements within European nation-states, even affecting supposed European citizens.

The indifference toward human rights in the former colonies from the beginning of the European project has been translated to the indifference toward migrants or even toward those Europeans who are able to threaten the national identity of member states by forming part of other national identities within said states who seek to build those nations in defiance of said states.

XIX

I emphasize the connection between the decolonization processes and the building of the European Union because the issue of self-determination is one of the main axes of this contribution to explain the current crises of the continent, in general, and that of the supranational organization, in particular.

According to my vision, the tacit agreement of such European rump states that have seen their colonial possessions disappear was to get into European collective transformation under the condition of not touching their European borders. A united Europe, under such premises, was seen by the nation-state's elites as a safeguard against any further fragmentation of their European metropolitan area.

The closest that a European state was to suffer the abridgment of the implicit agreement had been the aforementioned example of France regarding Algeria. As explained, Algeria was considered French mainland. But, first, Algeria is, in spite of the French efforts to formally annex it to the metropolitan area, *not* Europe; and second, Algerian independence happened at the beginning of the formation of the European system, when the nuances of the terms of agreement had no time to be ripe enough.

My thesis on self-determination explains, thus, focusing on the following steps of the European political developments, why Algeria had a chance to become independent and, for instance, Corsica hadn't. Formally, as we shall see, that difference between Algeria and Corsica was because the measure adopted by the states incorporated in the European project was to foster a *very limited interpretation of the right of people's self-determination* that the rest of the deteriorated members of the club were eager to accept.

European powers, and particularly former western European empires, reluctantly accepted the "external" decolonization of their overseas dominions (in most cases with wars in between). But seeing the decomposition of their empires was a bitter pill only able to be swallowed as long as the "*internal colonization*" in the form of the subjection of national minorities existing within the borders of the European mainland areas of such powers was guaranteed.

In other words, the loss of empire was tolerable only if the core of the European national community concerned was secured. Algeria or Indochina may separate from France, but France would not be dissolved at the expenses of all the national minorities (the Bretons, the Basques, the Catalans, the peoples from Occitania, the Corsicans, and so on) that the French have subjugated for centuries within European soil. I intentionally use here the expression "internal colonialism," though it might be deemed inaccurate for the mainstream of political science. In spite of its European origins through the Marxist-Leninist tradition, the idea of "internal colonialism" has been usually applied in the Latin American and the United States literature in relation to the plight of racial and indigenous minorities.[72] But throughout this work I think of "internal colonialism" as *developed within industrialized and economically advanced European realities*.[73] I employ such a term in the relationship between the majority and minority nations within the European nation-states even when they are presented in a single political unity (the French, the Spanish, the Belgians, etc.). The entrenchment of the structures of domination exercised by the "core nation" toward the peripheries within the borders of some western European states belonged to the same imperial impulse that once pushed those western European nations to subjugate countless peoples in America, Africa, Asia, or Oceania.[74] Somehow, the liberal and democratic ideals fostered from the European instances have contributed to whitewash such a dynamic of national oppression developed among the "core nation" and peripheral nationalisms within the European borders of an EU member state.

Yet one of the main arguments examined in the following pages is that such a "colonial" situation between majority and minority nations (concealed by the erection of supposed constitutional democracies within the European area) has been backed up by the parallel development of the European integration process. In my account, thus, one of the main aims of the creation of a European supranational organization relies on *the preservation of the national status quo* (that is, the allocation of power between dominant nations constituted in states and sub-state minorities) within the existing European Union member states.

Only to mention another example provided by European authorities on their lukewarm reception of any claim coming from sub-state minorities able to destabilize a member state, we may refer to the Conference on the Future of Europe developed as a citizen-led series of debates and discussions from April 2021 to May 2022. Though the proposal for a clarity mechanism on exercising the right to self-determination (mainly promoted by some sub-state national communities within Spain such as the Catalans and the Basques) was the *second* most voted issue by the citizenry within the bloc related to the future of Europe, the selection of the members that compounded the conference plenary was conveniently co-opted by the nation-states representatives and the European authorities in order to marginalize such a proposal and to avoid its inclusion in the recommendations for the European Union action. Even within the supposed liberal democratic space that the Union represents, the reinforcement and the discussion around the right to self-determination is more than both the national and the supranational instances may withstand.

XX

As we shall see, if we may identify the "internal colonization" with its classic meaning alluding to a direct territorial occupation such a concept might well also refer to what I call the "capitalist occupation," which marks the economic supremacy that one nation exercises upon other groups.

The former western European empires exercised direct rule, "territorial occupation," upon their former colonies before the success of the respective national emancipation movements in Africa or Asia, but the *metropoles* still maintained some sort of "capitalist occupation," in some cases by controlling the access to raw materials in those places and the trade between the new sovereign state and Europe (from an advantaged position for the latter) during the decades that followed the break up. As has been noticed by several authors, the decolonization process was accompanied through the continuity of Western imperialism by other means, mainly by trade situations of dependence covered through the performance of global economic institutions promoting the persistence of inequality and economic exploitation.[75]

My caveat here is that the same structures of both "territorial occupation" and "capitalist occupation" have been developed, once the European influence upon the former colonial world vanished, *toward European actors within the European borders*. In some cases, "territorial occupation" and "capitalist occupation" have been successively displayed, in others, simultaneously.

The "capitalist occupation" was particularly notorious during the euro crisis and its consequences during the second decade of the twenty-first century. Sovereignty and equality among the member states had not deprived some members (Germany and other Northern and Central European member states) from cajoling, using economic dependence, other member states, with the coverage of the European Union institutions and global economic organizations such as the International Monetary Fund.

The "capitalist occupation" may be, thus, exercised through the authorities of a member state in association with its private sector upon both the authorities of another member state and its social agents, even to the extent of causing a disruption in the chain of political representation and participation, as the Greek situation demonstrated at the peak of the euro crisis. But "capitalist occupations" may also overlap "territorial occupations" when one member state trusts in facing the debt repayment obligations to which its central authorities have been committed through the economic spoliation of a minority nation displayed through the devices of political domination.

As I shall argue, the fear that internal national disputes within a debtor state may put at risk the fulfillment of such state's economic commitments helps to explain why both European Union institutions and powerful member states such as the German Federal Republic have turned a blind eye toward experiences of "territorial occupation," which have been reasserted through violations of the principles of democracy and respect for human rights.

XXI

The narrow interpretation of the right to people's self-determination concerning the nations within the European Union member states national borders, which has provided the legal and the legitimacy basis to maintain "internal colonization," shall be the focus of the first chapter of our analysis.

Portugal and, particularly, Spain, will appear (in their political developments from their respective transitions to democracy in the 1970s and their incorporation into the European Economic Community in the 1980s to the present) as examples on how the principle of renouncing dominion over overseas colonies to ensure metropolitan territorial unity under the coverage of the European institutions has been put in motion.

At the first stage, something similar may have been said on the evolution of the United Kingdom since its accession to the same European organization in 1973 after the disintegration of the old empire and the struggles to retain some pieces of its metropolitan territory as happened in Northern Ireland. But the British example (which in the 2010s appeared to be more open to the secession of mainland territories, as the 2014 Scottish independence referendum demonstrated) expressed in fact a radicalization of the imperial aspirations within the English space, even at the cost of losing Scotland and Northern Ireland, with the decision to withdraw from the European Union, as was decided in the 2016 Brexit referendum.

The British, and particularly the English, were somehow the first to break with the agreement on entrenching the national state within the European Union in exchange for relinquishing empire. That possibly happened because the English believed that the resurrection of their Empire *was possible precisely by leaving the European Union*. The story of Brexit, presented in the second chapter of this contribution leads one to investigate another phenomenon that embeds all the analyzed cases of western European countries: to what extent the hubris of the political actors within the *center* of such national states, what may be characterized as a new wave of state nationalism, is the main factor that in reality allows the fragmentation of political unity.[76]

Since hubris always brings in its heart the seed of self-destruction, the unchained desire to gain more power for the nation turns to a new experience of collapse. The latter was expressed in a sublime manner by the Spanish philosopher José Ortega y Gasset, in describing the crises that Spain had to face, with losing Cuba and Puerto Rico and managing the first challenges coming from Catalan and Basque separatism (which, especially the Catalan one, have recently reappeared with strength). Ortega y Gasset wrote that the Spanish problem lay precisely in the center of Spain, within the elites coming from the old kingdom of Castile whose eagerness for power and inability to offer a common project to the Spanish peripheral nations brought Spain to ruin. Consequently, Ortega y Gasset stated that "Castile made Spain and Castile unmade Spain."[77] *Mutatis mutandis* the same assertion by Ortega y Gasset may be applied nowadays not only to the present Spain but also to the United Kingdom and the threat of English isolation that Brexit, through the eventual loss of Scotland and Northern Ireland, might cause: "England made the United Kingdom and England (through Brexit) unmade it" might well be said.

XXII

The third chapter of this contribution would also be dedicated to the role of European integration, and particularly the influence of the European Communities in their first decades of history to provide cohesion to a country that had been on the verge of political and territorial disintegration by the end of World War II: Italy.

We shall connect all the cleavages that had crossed this state from the postwar, which had resurrected in several instances up to and including the present, and we shall see to which extent the seizing of the European Communities first and the European Union after, had come to the rescue of Italy in order to ensure its national unity. I will take the rise of Italian far-right movements around the figures of Salvini (*Lega)* and Meloni (*Fratelli d'Italia)* to explore some considerations on the link between rights and national sovereignty that pose an additional high voltage signal in the relationship between the European instances and the member states that participate in them.

The fourth chapter is devoted to the analysis of the foundational motivations in creating the European communities to strengthen France as a nation-state. From being defeated and occupied by Germany in World War II to appearing as a major power by the end of the conflict, the European framework of economic integration provided France an opportunity to modernize its economy and to grow.

We shall see that most of the problems that currently besiege France are related firstly with the unsustainability of the social and labor standards that had been possible because some European economic policies had served French interests by shielding the European market from global liberalization, and secondly, with the consequences of colonialism and the disruption that the immigration from the former dominions to the mainland has caused in French society through the problems of poverty, marginalization, religious radicalization, and terrorism. Terrorism, which has severely struck France during recent decades, might be considered as the revenge of the colonized against the decadent former powers. The failure of the European project is in this regard also attached to the inability to build a common continental structure to deal with the population fluxes given the obsession within such states to preserve their respective national identities.

The exchange between national (metropolitan) entrenchment and European integration experienced through immigration and its impact in the national and political imaginary of the European societies represents one of its more profound breaches, particularly in countries such as the aforementioned France and Italy, but also in some eastern European countries such as the members of the Visegrád Group, that struggled to stop the flux of refugees coming mainly from Syria through Greece and the Balkans at one of the peaks of the Syrian crisis in 2015. Something similar, though in a smaller scale, might be said about the onslaughts against African migration caused at the borders of the Spanish enclaves of Ceuta and Melilla mostly committed by Moroccan authorities but blessed by the European ones, including those ascribed to the supposed political left. The popular reaction against immigration, particularly from Africa and the Middle East, the indifference toward the deaths of migrants in the Mediterranean and the rise of far-right extremism has something to do with the described nostalgia of the empire.

Finally, the fifth chapter will be centered on the example of a nation-state that had embraced the European project due to its total collapse but that, disregarding the dramatic origins of its pro-European appeals, has become the main power in Europe: Germany. The future developments of the German Federal Republic will clarify if the bulk of the continent will continue on the track of eluding imperial temptations or, on the contrary, will follow the path of gaining the power that such a community would deserve in accordance with its economic, demographic and political weight. As we shall see, another possibility emerges on the horizon that, somehow related to German complacence in maintaining the status quo and slipping through the path of technological, military, and economic backwardness, would drag the continent to the dependence of another global superpower and, consequently, would transform Europe in a kind of new colonial dominion similar to the situation displayed by the end of World War II regarding the western European dependence toward the United States and the eastern European one toward the Soviet Union, respectively. The hot war in Ukraine caused by the Russian invasion in February 2022 and the strong dependence on Russian energetic resources that this situation revealed (together with Germany's economic vulnerability worsened by the conflict with inflation and lack of growth) probably suggests that by the time of concluding this work (summer 2023) we are closer to the second hypothesis than to the first. Putting it differently: it has precisely been the lack of Germany's imperial reassertion, even having the opportunity to achieve it after the euro zone crisis, the context that led to its dependence on other global empires.

If there is, thus, some European member state in which the already mentioned difficult balance between nationalistic imperialism and plurinational integration has been achieved, it is that one in which nationalistic imperialism has been completely abolished from the public sphere from the conclusion of World War II.

Relinquishing imperialism, even in the midst of the possibility to regain political power through the condition of economic hegemony, has supposed for the Federal Republic of Germany to place itself in a critical position once warfare again affected the core of European dynamics. The lack of imperial ambitions, which might be associated to the lack of territorial expansionism, represented the reliance on power resources and raw materials that were in hands of powers that were confronting Germany and the Union, notoriously from Russia and China. The revival of Germany as a hard power might be envisaged as a way out for the West to restrain Russia's ambitions, but such a change of dynamic might on the other hand endanger the stability within the union that has been precisely grounded on the German authorities' reluctances to display an explicit nationalistic policy. The balance within the European Union has been partially grounded on the German authorities' political self-restraint, but that contention, that from the times of German reunification pushed forward the consolidation of a closer union was insufficient to tackle with the emergence of a military challenge.

XXIII

The history of the German Federal Republic is important for my narrative since it reveals, as generally happens in eastern Europe, the main reason for the national weakness that fostered European integration: the presence of the

Soviet Union and the threat of a completely different social and economic system. The pro-European feelings in the recently created West Germany in the 1950s, the 1960s, and the 1970s, meant that the Federal Republic had to commit to having both a welfare state and to a space of human rights. The Germany protective of human rights and democracy was activated as a counter model to the Communist regimes.

It would be interesting to see how long the German Federation as a constitutional democracy remains stable in the wake of economic and military confrontations among global superpowers. The end of the Cold War brought German national reunification through the absorption of the former German Democratic Republic and the opening of a backyard of influence in the eastern European countries that once were satellites of the Soviet Union (or a part of it). But until the beginning of the 2010s, social and economic costs still represented a limitation on German resurrection. It was not until its relevant role showed during the crises of the euro and the sovereign debt from 2010 that a future of German hegemony could be envisaged and, still, further economic crises erupted as both the consequence of the COVID-19 pandemic and the Ukrainian war, undermining German prospects of confirming its power within Europe and the world.

German evolution, indeed, will probably depend on the course of events involving Russia, considering that if there is a place in Europe dominated by the dreams of imperial revival, that is Putin's kingdom. A threatening Russia could maintain German self-restriction and the opportunity to stretch its influence over eastern Europe buffer states only through economic and cultural means (which would include its role as a safeguard of liberties and democracy in a similar way as West Germany operated while facing the Communist threat). But a straightforwardly imperial Russia, as finally has become palpable, may call both to strengthen German military responses and to curtail Germany's horizon as a pluralistic democracy. The question will be, in other words, if it is viable for Germany to carry on in exercising soft power upon eastern Europe or if it will be induced to develop harder and more explicit ways of domination as it used to do in the past, at least to refrain Russian's expansive ambitions in the continent and to overcome the burden for its economy represented by the lack of raw materials and trade coming from that area.

Other considerations shall be developed concerning the relationship of Germany as the leading agent of the European Union, with the People's Republic of China. A German-European reassertion might increase the tension between both sides of Eurasia but it is more likely, when these lines are written, that what Germany spearheads would be a European neutrality in an eventual conflict between the military, technological, and rising economic power that is China and the Anglo-Saxon world led by the United States.

As we shall see, the European economic and technological dependence on China, consented and even fostered by German authorities and expressed both through several investment agreements and trade exchanges, would have enormous consequences in the European domestic power arrangements, including the consideration of Europe as a democratic and human-rights friendly space, and might reduce European influence in the world even further.

XXIV

In sum, the story told in this book is the story of colonies and their relationship to the European integration project, being the former colonies belonging to the western European powers, the colonies in which some European states were on the verge of being transformed by the aftermath of World War II under the influence of both the United States and the Soviet Union and the colony that Europe as a whole might become under the ascendance of another global power such as China.

We shall begin, nevertheless, with the smallest part of the puzzle, which would be the European "internal colonies," since we believe that fundamental developments on the future concerning the union are at stake in the response given at the European level to demands of national self-determination within Europe, developments in which the status of democracy or human rights are involved and consequently is also involved the position of European Union authorities in their relation to other regions of the world.

On occasion of the trials during the last throes of the Spanish Francoist regime against some Basque activists, the so-called Burgos Trial, the French philosopher Jean-Paul Sartre, who had developed a few years previously a leading intellectual role criticizing the French involvement in repressing Algeria's independence, admitted in 1971 that "large nations contain colonies within their borders" and pointed out the case of the Basque Country within Spain as an example of such internal colonization developed by a European state. In the same contribution, Sartre remarked that repression against Basques was fully visible under Franco's dictatorship, but it would be "more ambiguous" in the case that, as happened, the Spanish regime would itself be transformed into a liberal democracy.[78]

A harsher criticism on the "internal colonialism" than the one expressed by Jean-Paul Sartre came from the Occitan thinker Robert Lafont. Such an author adopted one of the perspectives also shared in the following pages according to which a relevant strategy of the western European nation-states to maintain the territorial integrity of their European mainland relied on distinguishing between the land included within their European borders and the colonies that had been progressively separating from the metropole from the conclusion of World War II and were acquiring the status of sovereign states. As we shall see, such a distinction through the performance of western European political and diplomatic actors characterized the developments of international law which were assumed by the European Law system from the beginning of the formation of the European Communities to the present. According to Lafont, thus,

> The most corrupting falsification is found in the separation maintained between the analysis of the metropolitan facts (the realization of national unity) and that of the colonial facts (the conquest and then loss of the empire) This artificial distinction has been imposed even on the "regionalists," who until very recently did not think to compare the conquest of Occitania with the war in Algeria and, over the centuries, the successful integration of the populations became provincial with the failed integration of Muslims from North Africa.[79]

The European Union appeared as an active agent devoted to legitimize, in the name of democracy and the rule of law, the repression that had been in the previous centuries exercised by the apparatuses of the modern states toward the non-state nations existing within their borders. As such, while the European Union was perceived by small nation-states as a safeguard that big European states would not invade them, as had happened until World War II, it was also the device that tolerated the perpetuation of the national domination of the nation-states upon their sub-state entities.

The European Union allows treatments and behaviors against non-state minority nations that would not be permitted between the nation-states belonging to its club. The level of violence displayed, for instance, by Spain to crush the pacific and democratic pro-independence movement of Catalonia would not be admitted if it were, let's say, a Germany of the XXI century devoted to the annexation of Luxembourg or Austria to its dominions. The Catalan case, given the pacific demand, has revealed sharply such a contradiction in proclaiming the values of democracy and human rights on a continental scale while European instances do nothing to prevent the crippling of such principles exercised by one of its members ensuring its territorial integrity.

It has been stated that the European integration process has provided an almost miraculous way of performing according to which the negotiations between the members, such as the ones concerning the amendment of treaties, take place within a non-coercive system of unanimous voting.[80] However, what such a picture overlooks is that a peaceful understanding between nation-states is sustainable as long as the nation-states are able to threaten with violence the claims coming from the internal bodies that they don't like. In other words, peaceful negotiations between sovereign actors within

Europe have been possible because they are sovereign and the exercise of the monopoly of force by the states' central authorities toward secessionist regions or other dissidents is not contested.

Repression and human rights violations happened in Catalonia from 2017 but it has also been experienced in other European territories such as the Basque Country, Corsica, or when the United Kingdom belonged to the organization, Northern Ireland. European integration had stopped conflicts between nation-states, and even has helped to minimize the tension between western Europe and the eastern European bloc during the Cold War, but, in an opposite direction, has not avoided national conflicts exploding within nation-states and, at worse, has contributed to maintaining a certain silence in relation to these struggles.

Under the formula of "the internal affair" regarding the conflicts between sub-state nations and nation-state central authorities, the European Union has dodged any implication to entrench a common space of democracy and fundamental rights for all its citizens disregarding their national (and sub-national or sub-state) allegiance. The involvement of the European authorities *against* the member states in order to protect the minorities existing within such states (not only national minorities but also political minorities) would lead to the reassertion of a supranational European power that at this moment, and leaving aside the fact that the union lacks coercive power, no European nation-state is likely willing to tolerate.

NOTES

1. So famously stated by the European Court of Justice Judgement Case C-6/64 *Flaminio Costa v E.N.E.L.* of July 15, 1964.

2. See Timothy Snyder, *The Road to Unfreedom: Russia, Europe, America* (London: The Bodley Head, 2018), 67.

3. Alan S. Milward, *The European Rescue of the Nation-State* (London and New York: Routledge, 2000, first edition 1992).

4. See Perry Anderson, *The New Old World* (London and New York: Verso, 2009), 14.

5. See Fernando Guirao, *The European Rescue of the Franco Regime, 1950–1975* (Oxford: Oxford University Press, 2021), 2.

6. Chris Bickerton, *European Integration from Nation-States to Member States* (Oxford: Oxford University Press, 2012), 76.

7. The idea of a "provincializing Europe" was popularized by Chakrabarty (see Dipesh Chakrabarty, *Provincializing Europe: Postcolonial Thought and Historical Difference* [Princeton, NJ: Princeton University Press, 2007], 3–6), but he borrowed the phrase from H.-G.Gadamer, most likely from "Karl-Jaspers-Preis Laudatio für Jeanne Hersch," *Heidelberger Jahrbücher* 37 (1993), 151–58, who located this

impression in the early years of his childhood already in the aftermath of World War I. For a description of this process of Europe's provincialization by the end of the Great War (that would be still more acute in the aftermath of World War II and the lose of the overseas' Empires by the Western Powers); see Adam Tooze, *The Deluge: The Great War, America, and the Remaking of the Global Order, 1916–1931* (New York: Penguin Books, 2014), 6 (note 8). The vicissitudes of the term's "provincializing Europe" coining might be also found in the same source.

8. Walter Laqueur, *Europe in Our Time: A History 1945–1992* (London: Penguin, 1992), 54–55.

9. Stanley Hoffmann, "Obstinate or Obsolete? The Fate of the Nation-State and the Case of Western Europe," *Daedalus* 95, no. 3 (Summer 1966): 889.

10. Susan Cotts Watkins, *From Provinces into Nations: Demographic Integration in Western Europe 1870–1960* (Princeton, NJ: Princeton University Press, 1991).

11. See Nils Gilman, *Mandarins of the Future: Modernization Theory in Cold War America* (Baltimore, MD: Johns Hopkins University Press, 2007); Nils Gilman, "Modernization Theory Never Dies," *History of Political Economy* 50, no. 1 (December 2018): 133–51.

12. Carles Sirera Miralles, "Neglecting the 19th century: Democracy, the Consensus Trap and Modernization Theory in Spain," *History of the Human Sciences* 28, no. 3 (April 2015): 51–67.

13. Giandomenico Majone, "The Politics of Regulation and European Regulatory Institutions," in *Governing Europe*, eds. Jack Hayward and Anand Menon (Oxford: Oxford University Press, 2003), 311.

14. Anderson, *The New Old World*, 108.

15. There are, nevertheless, remarkable exceptions but instead of offering a general theory on the impact of the decolonization processes on the political and legal configuration of the European Union, as I am devoted to do, approaches are rather focused on the creation of the European Common Market in order to redefine the international trade once the independence of former colonies was entrenched. See, for instance, Giuliano Garavini, *After Empires: European Integration, Decolonization, and the Challenge from Global South, 1957–1986* (New York: Oxford University Press, 2012); and Peo Hansen and Stefan Jonsson, "Building Eurafrica: Reviving Colonialism through European Integration, 1920–1960," in *Echoes of Empire: Memory, Identity, and Colonial Legacies*, eds. Kalypso Nicolaidis, Berny Sèbe, and Gabrielle Maas (New York: IB Tauris, 2015).

16. So described by Snyder; see Timothy Snyder, *On Tyranny: Twenty Lessons from the Twentieth Century* (London: The Bodley Head, 2017), 68.

17. See Carl Schmitt, *Nomos der Erde: Im Volkerrecht Des Jus Publicum Europaeum* (Berlin: Duncker & Humblot, 2012), particularly 54–69. Schmitt concluded such an essay on International Law in 1945 but he did not publish it until 1950, ironically the same year of the Schuman Declaration.

18. On the use of absolute destructive weapons against an absolute enemy see Carl Schmitt, *Theorie des Partisanen: Zwischenbemerkung zum Begriff des Politischen* (Berlin: Duncker & Humblot, 2002), 94–95.

19. Schmitt, *Nomos der Erde*, 26–32.

20. See on Schmitt's work Martti Koskenniemi, "International Law as Political Theology: How to Read *Nomos der Erde*?" *Constellations* 11, no. 4 (December 2004): 492–511.

21. Garavini, *After Empires*, 32.

22. See Joseph Weiler, "The Political and Legal Culture of European Integration: An Exploratory Essay," *International Journal of Constitutional Law* 9, no. 3 (2011): 678–94, 683.

23. Dieter Gosewinkel, "Introduction. Anti-liberal Europe—A Neglected Source of Europeanism," in *Anti-liberal Europe: A Neglected Story of Europeanization*, ed. Dieter Gosewinkel (New York and Oxford: Berghahn, 2015), 5.

24. See Christian Joerges, "Europe a *Grossraum*? Shifting Legal Conceptualizations of the Integration Project," in *Darker Legacies of Law in Europe: The Shadow of National Socialism and Fascism over Europe and Its Legal Traditions*, eds. Christian Joerges and Navraj Singh Ghaleigh (Oxford and Portland, OR: Hart Publishing, 2003).

25. Astrid Van Wegenberg, "Europe on Display: A Postcolonial Reading of the House of European History," *Politique Européenne* 66, no. 4 (October 2019): 44–71.

26. Thomas Piketty, *Capital in the Twenty-First Century* (Cambridge, MA: The Belknap Press of Harvard University Press, 2014), 120–22.

27. See Quinn Slobodian, *Globalists. The End of the Empire and the Birth of Neoliberalism* (Cambridge, MA: Harvard University Press, 2018) particularly chapter 1.

28. See Mark Mazower, *Hitler's Empire: Nazi Rule in Occupied Europe* (London and New York: Penguin, 2008), 35.

29. See Michael Wilkinson, "Authoritarian Liberalism in the European Constitutional Imagination: Second Time as a Farce?" *European Law Journal* 21, no. 3 (May 2015) 313–39.

30. See Michael Wilkinson, *Authoritarian Liberalism and the Transformation of Modern Europe* (Oxford: Oxford University Press, 2021), 3.

31. John Gillingham, *European Integration 1950–2003: Superstate or New Market Economy?* (Cambridge: Cambridge University Press, 2003).

32. *See* Peter Häberle, *Gibt es eine europäische Öffentlichkeit? Vortrag gehalten vor der Juristischen Gesellschaft zu Berlin am 15 Dezember 1999* (Berlin and New York: Walter de Gruyter, 2000).

33. See Luuk van Middelaar, *The Passage to Europe. How a Continent Became a Union* (New Haven, CT, and London: Yale University Press, 2014), 212–25.

34. See, for instance, Niall Ferguson, *Empire. How Britain Made the Modern World* (London: Penguin Books, 2004), xxiv.

35. Snyder, *The Road to Unfreedom*, 111–57.

36. Hannah Arendt, *The Origins of Totalitarianism* (San Diego, New York, and London: Harvest/HBJ Book, 1973, first edition 1951), 270.

37. Quoted by Ripka in Hubert Ripka, *Munich: Before and After: A Fully Documental Czechoslovak Account of the Crises of September 1938 and March 1939* (London: Victor Gollancz, 1939), 117.

38. *See* Keith Lowe, *Savage Continent: Europe in the Aftermath of World War II* (London: Penguin Books, 2013), 230–48.

39. See, among many others, Ian Kershaw, "War and Political Violence in Twentieth-Century Europe," *Contemporary European History* 14, no. 1 (February 2005) 114; Mazower, *Hitler's Empire*, 603.

40. Eric Hobsbawm, *The Age of Extremes. A History of the World, 1914–1991* (New York: Vintage Books, 1994).

41. See Branko Milanovic, "What If Putin's True Goals Are Different? The Trade-Off between Sovereignty and Income," *Global Equality and More*, June 2, 2022. Available at https://branko2f7.substack.com/p/what-if-putin-true-goals-are-different?r=16uxt&s=w&utm_campaign=post&utm_medium=web.

42. Friedrich Nietzsche, *The Will to Power: An Attempted Revaluation of All Values* (New York: Barnes & Noble, 2013, translation by Anthony M. Ludovici) § 702.

43. Georg Schwarzenberger, *Power Politics* (London: London Institute of World Affairs/Stevens & Sons, 1951), 13.

44. Andrew Moravcsik, *The Choice for Europe: Social Purpose and State Power from Messina to Maastricht* (London: UCL Press, 1998), 3.

45. Notice that, in contrast with my position, Moravcsik is likely to understand the increase of state bargaining power of important governments not as way of direct domination but a form of cooperation between the European States, on the one hand, and between European states and extra-European actors on the other. For a critic of Moravcsik's approach, see Robert H. Lieshout; Mathieu L. L. Segers, and Johanna Maria van der Vleuten, "De Gaulle, Moravcsik and the Choice for Europe: Soft Sources, Weak Evidence," *Journal of Cold War Studies* 6, no. 4 (November 2004) 89–139; and Wolfram Kaiser, Brigitte Leucht, and Morten Rasmussen, "Origins of a European Polity: A New Research Agenda for the European Union History," in *The History of the European Union: Origins of a Trans- and Supranational Polity 1950–72*, eds. Wolfram Kaiser, Brigitte Leucht, and Morten Rasmussen (London and New York: Routledge, 2009), 6–9.

46. Moravcsik, *The Choice for Europe*, 83–84.

47. See, for instance, Rosemary Fennell, *The Common Agricultural Policy: Continuity and Change* (Oxford: Oxford University Press, 1997).

48. See Michael Sutton, *France and the Construction of Europe, 1944–2007. The Geopolitical Imperative* (New York and Oxford: Berghahn Books, 2007), 1–14.

49. After establishing the Treaty on European Union (1992), the constituent treaties were amended by the European Union accessions of Austria, Finland, and Sweden (1995), the Treaties of Amsterdam (1997) and Nice (2001), the accession of a further twelve states (Cyprus, Czech Republic, Estonia, Hungary, Latvia, Lithuania, Malta, Poland, Slovakia, Slovenia [Treaty of Accession 2003 entering into force on May 1, 2004] plus Bulgaria and Romania [Treaty of Accession 2005 entering into force on January 1, 2007]); and following the failure of the Treaty Establishing a Constitution for Europe (2005) was passed the reform provided by the Treaty of Lisbon (concluded in 2007 and in force since 2009).

50. Apart from the amendments to the constitutive treaties resulting from the United Kingdom withdrawal from 2009 might be only mentioned (1) the reform to Article 136 of the Treaty on the Functioning of the European Union in order to allow the establishment of a permanent mechanism to safeguard the financial stability of the

Euro area as a whole, the European Stability Mechanism (which entered into force on January 1, 2013) and (2) the European Union accession of Croatia (Treaty of Accession 2011 entering into force on July 1, 2013).

51. On the difference between constitutional amendments and constitutional dismemberments, in our context applied to the European Constitutive Treaties though the "constitutional" character of such rules are very arguable; see Richard Albert, "Constitutional Amendment and Dismemberment," *The Yale Journal of International Law* 43, no. 1 (Winter 2018): 1–84.

52. Joanne Gowa, *Allies, Adversaries and International Trade* (Princeton, NJ: Princeton University Press, 1994).

53. Joseph M. Grieco, *Cooperation among Nations: Europe, America and Non-Tariff Barriers to Trade* (Ithaca, NY: Cornell University Press, 1990).

54. See Michael Wilkinson, "Authoritarian Liberalism as Authoritarian Constitutionalism," in *Authoritarian Constitutionalism*, eds. Helena Alviar García and Günter Frankenberg (Cheltenham: Edward Elgar Publishing, 2019), 317–18.

55. See, for instance, Etienne Balibar, "The Rise and Fall of the European Union: Temporalities and Teleologies," *Constellations* 21, no. 2 (August 2014): 202–12; and Michael Wilkinson, "The Reconstruction of Postwar Europe: Lineages of Authoritarian Liberalism," *LSE Law, Society and Economy Working Papers* 5 (2016). Available at www.lse.ac.uk/collections/law/wps/wps.htm.

56. See, among many others, Tony Judt, *Postwar. A History of Europe Since 1945* (London: Penguin Books, 2005), 278–309.

57. Mark Mazower, *Governing the World. The History of an Idea* (London: Allen Lane, 2012), 251–52.

58. Anthony Clayton, *The Wars of French Decolonization* (Abingdon and New York: Routledge, 2013), 79–87.

59. Elizabeth Buettner, *Europe after Empire: Decolonization, Society, and Culture* (Cambridge: Cambridge University Press, 2016), 78–105.

60.See Yuval Noah Harari, *21 Lessons for the 21st Century* (London: Jonathan Cape), 10.

61. John Springhall, *Decolonization since 1945: The Collapse of European Overseas Empire* (Basingstoke/New York: Palgrave, 2001), 31.

62. *See*, for instance, Christopher Bayly and Tim Harper, *Forgotten Wars: Freedom and Revolution in Southeast Asia* (Cambridge, MA: Belknap Press, 2006), 137–89; and Nicholas J. White, "Reconstructing Europe through Rejuvenating Empire: The British, French, and Dutch Experiences Compared," in *Post-War Reconstruction in Europe: International Perspectives, 1945–1949*, eds. Mark Mazower, Jessica Reinisch, and David Feldman (Oxford: Oxford University Press, 2011).

63. Fabian Klose, "Europe as a Colonial Project: A Critique of Its Anti-Liberalism," in *Anti-liberal Europe: A Neglected Story of Europeanization*, ed. Dieter Gosewinkel (New York and Oxford: Berghahn, 2015), 52.

64. See Mariano Delgado, "Kolonialismusbegründung und Kolonialismuskritik: Der Januskopf Europas gegenüber der außereuropäischen Welt," in *Herausforderung Europa: Wege zu einer europäischen Identität*, eds. Mariano Delgado and Matthias Lutz-Bachmann (Munich: Beck, 1995).

65. Garavini, *After Empires*, 48.

66. Mathieu Segers, *The Netherlands and European Integration, 1950 to Present* (Amsterdam: Amsterdam University Press, 2020), 9.

67. Marc Michel, *Décolonisation et émergence du Tiers monde* (Paris: Hachette, 1993), 139.

68. Ian Kershaw, *Roller-Coaster. Europe 1950–2017* (London: Allen Lane/Penguin Books, 2018), 67–68.

69. So Garavini, *After Empires*, 50.

70. Antonio Maria Morone, *L'ultima colonia: Come l'Italia è tornata in Africa 1950–1960* (Bari: Laterza, 2011).

71. For example, in the secret section of a circular to the British colonies dated March 28, 1949, the British colonial secretary Arthur Creech-Jones referred to the Universal Declaration of Human Rights as a potential "source of embarrassment" (quoted by Klose, "Europe as a Colonial Project," 52).

72. See Beatriz Chaloult and Yves Chaloult, "The Internal Colonialism Concept: Methodological Considerations," *Social and Economic Studies* 28, no. 4 (December 1979): 85–99. See also Barbara Arneil, *Domestic Colonies: The Turn Inward to Colony* (Oxford: Oxford University Press, 2018).

73. The closest use of the term *internal colonialism*, to the one that I allude to in these pages, is provided by Michael Hechter's work *Internal Colonialism: The Celtic Fringe in British National Development* (New Brunswick, NJ; and London: Transaction Publishers,1999).

74. On the concept of "core nation" *see* Krishan Kumar, "Nation States as Empires, Empires as Nation States: Two Principles, One Practice?," *Theory and Society,* 39, no. 2 (March 2010): 119–43. See also, Antoni Simon Tarrés, *La unitat d'Espanya com a valor polític: Una arqueologia intel·lectual* (Catarroja, Palma and Barcelona: Editorial Afers, 2022), 50–52. According to Hannah Arendt, "[N]ation-States are in effect empires in miniature," see Arendt, *The Origins of Totalitarianism*, 153. On the idea of empire as a political center subjugating peripheries, see Michael W.Doyle, *Empires* (Ithaca, NY: Cornell University Press, 1986), 12.

75. See, among many others, Antony Anghie, *Imperialism, Sovereignty and the Making of International Law* (Cambridge: Cambridge University Press, 2004); David Harvey, *The New Imperialism* (Oxford: Oxford University Press, 2003); or James Tully, "Modern Constitutional Democracy and Imperialism," *Osgoode Hall Law Journal*, 46, no. 3 (Fall 2008): 461–93.

76. I developed the idea of political hubris affecting the Spanish central authorities while confronting the Catalan secessionist challenge in Hèctor López Bofill, "Hubris, Constitutionalism, and 'the Indissoluble Unity of the Spanish Nation': The Repression of Catalan Secessionist Referenda in Spanish Constitutional Law," *International Journal of Constitutional Law*, 17, no. 3 (July 2019): 943–69.

77. José Ortega y Gasset, *España Invertebrada: Bosquejo de algunos Pensamientos Históricos* (Madrid: Alianza, 1988), 33. First edition 1922.

78. Jean Paul Sartre, *Life/Situations: Essays Written and Spoken* (New York: Pantheon Books, 1977), 136–61.

79. Robert Lafont, *Per una teoria de la nació: El cas de França* (Catalan translation by Miquel Martí i Pol; Barcelona: Edicions 62, 1969), 12 (first edition under the title *Sur la France*, 1968).

80. See Moravcsik, *The Choice for Europe*, 60.

Chapter 1

Boundaries and Self-Determination

I

In the beginning the history of the right of peoples to self-determination was a matter of the European Peoples. Such a right was conceived by those powers that were likely to win the Great War in order to debilitate still more those that were going to lose.

Notwithstanding the latter statement, one of the first demands for self-determination in the modern fashion would be invoked by a power that was going to be defeated in World War I: imperial Germany. During the armistice with the new Bolshevik regime in Russia in December 1917, and the following negotiations that would lead to the conclusion of the Brest-Litovsk Treaty, the German side invoked the people's self-determination right to redraw the borders in eastern Europe.

The logic managed by the German negotiation team at Brest would nonetheless be adjusted to the same pattern of seeking the adversary's territorial dynamiting that would mark the subsequent position of the western powers about the territorial question at issue in the European war. In occasion with the armistice with Russia, the German government saw in the recognition of self-determination an opportunity to dismember the former Tsarist empire and to attract the non-Russian states founded from that area (from the Baltic states to Ukraine and Georgia) to German influence.[1]

The Bolsheviks, beginning with Lenin (who had already argued in favor of self-determination in his debate with Rosa Luxemburg on Poland's national cause and had analyzed the 1905 Norwegian referendum on dissolving the Union with Sweden), accepted the proposal to organize international relations through the mentioned principle in spite of the fact that such a movement would represent the removal from Russia of a considerable part of its former territory.[2] If the Soviet regime came to terms with Germany through such onerous concessions, it was probably because of its extreme fragility and the certain risk that a refusal of the conditions offered at Brest would trigger a German invasion.

At any rate, the Brest-Litovsk negotiations between Germany and the Bolsheviks forced the Western powers to offer an alternative vision of the liberal and democratic peace requirements that would design the global order emergent from the Great War. Such was the context that inspired the most famous wartime declaration by U.S. President Wilson, the so-called Wilson's Fourteen Points, supposedly heralding American backing for self-determination, democracy, and a League of Nations, though neither democracy nor self-determination appeared explicitly in the text or in the speech with which Wilson delivered the Fourteen Points to Congress on January 8, 1918.[3]

The allusions to the idea of the right to self-determination were rather inferred from several manifestations entailed in Wilson's declaration. In this way, the U.S. president called for Belgium to be evacuated and restored (Point 7), "without any attempt to limit the sovereignty which she enjoys in common with all other free nations." Alsace-Lorraine was to be returned and any occupied French territory was to be "freed" from German domination (Point 8). Italy's boundaries were to be determined "along clearly recognizable lines of nationality" (Point 9); and with regard to the peoples of the Habsburg and Ottoman empires (Point 12), the Balkans (Point 11) and Poland (Point 13), it was foreseen that they would be vested with "international guarantees" in the aim of ensuring to them "an absolutely unmolested opportunity of autonomous development," which in some cases, as in the Polish one, would even embrace the respect for their full independence. As a conclusion of his program, Wilson would emphasize the need to form "a general association of nations" to guarantee "political independence and territorial integrity to great and small states alike" (Point 14).[4]

The Fourteen Points declaration, in short, outlined what would be interpreted as the doctrine of the People's self-determination both as a logical corollary of popular sovereignty and as synonymous with the principle that governments must be based on the "consent of the governed,"[5] but such ideas, despite a mention to the colonies in Point 5, were primarily conceived to be applied in a very specific circumstance: the redrawing of the states of central and eastern Europe.

Wilson's declaration was devoted particularly (1) to face up to the disintegration of the Russian empire (which, as we have seen, had been already precipitated by the time of the declaration); (2) to organize Germany's predictable territorial loses both in western and in eastern Europe; and (3) to arrange the fragmentation of the Ottoman and the Austro-Hungarian Empires. The new and small states that would be forged in central and eastern Europe under the coverage of the aforementioned principles, in the mind of the western liberal state's rulers, had to serve as buffer states in order to contain, on the one hand, an eventual expansion of the Bolshevik revolution and, on the other hand, to prevent any resurrection of German imperialism. The principle of the self-determination of peoples, associated with the right of a nation to shape its own full sovereign state, was thus designed to implement the plan that the U.S. administration had for postwar Europe and, generally, was subordinated to the geostrategic interests of the Allies. The proclaimed principle of self-determination of peoples was in its origins a European issue and, specifically, aside from Belgium, Alsace-Lorraine and some disputed territories between Austria and Italy, a central and eastern European issue.

Wilson's proposal, of course, was not intended to be applied to the ones that would win the war. The latter might explain why, differently as to what has happened in the aftermath of World War II, self-determination was not primarily thought to be invoked within the framework of the colonial claims; by 1918, the idea to let the people decide on their own political status had to be reconciled with the interests of Britain or France, which were colonial powers[6] and that would, indeed, entrench their overseas dominions to an unprecedented level in terms of the world's land surface. In fact, the territories colonized by those defeated powers in World War I, as in the case of Germany and its dominions spread across Africa, Asia, or Oceania were going to be transferred to the administration of some of the war's triumphant powers.

With regard to the colonial question, what concerned Wilson were not the rights of the oppressed peoples so much as the violence of inter-imperialist competition as would be reflected in Point 5 of the Fourteen Points when it called for the claims of the rival powers to be settled not by war, but by "a free, open-minded, and absolutely impartial adjustment."[7] Concerning the local population inhabiting those territories administered by a colonial power, the declaration only provided that "the interests of the populations concerned must have equal weight with the equitable claims of the government whose title is to be determined" a consideration, significantly focused on "the interests" of the subordinate populations rather than on their "voice" democratically expressed, that would be entirely compatible with a deeply paternalistic view of colonial government.

But a wide understanding of the right to self-determination would not only have had consequences for the European colonial powers that had maintained (or even widened) their overseas possessions after World War I, but it would have also endangered the core of the United States' political interests, though the American appetite for colonies was meager. Being aware of that, Wilson himself made clear that his concept on self-determination would not be applied to the American scene. According to the U.S. president, thus, "America does not consist of groups. A man who thinks of himself as belonging to a particular national group in America has not yet become an American."[8] An eventual translation of the right to self-determination to the question of the indigenous peoples (not to mention to the African Americans) would have been potentially explosive for American political stability. After all, Wilson was heading the first cabinet of Southern Democrats to govern the United States since Secession, and his presidency was perceived as a vindication of the reconciliation of White America half a century after the end of the Civil War.

Self-determination was only applied to others, and particularly, to those that had been defeated in a conflict. The aftermath of World War I represented the recognition of the right to self-determination of ethnic majorities that once belonged to central and eastern European empires understood as the right to constitute a new sovereign state, but also, at least in the beginning of the establishment of the system of the League of Nations, self-determination obliged the new states to respect the minorities existing within their borders through a system of treaties.[9] From the very beginning, self-determination, thus, was not only understood in its external dimension (that is, the people's right to create an independent state) but also in its internal dimension (the people's right to access to the frame of government that they freely decide within an existing state).[10] Again, nonetheless, the imposition to sign treaties on minorities (which, in another sense, were hardly enforced in the 1930s, although this is another matter) concerned only those new states in eastern Europe that emerged from the aegis of the old empires.

Any mandate of protecting minorities, not to mention the right of such minorities to self-determination as a last resort if the protection failed, was not predictably applicable to the empires of Western Europe, such as France or the United Kingdom. James Headlam-Morley, a leading British policymaker, for instance, vehemently expressed his refusal to allow the League of Nations to seize a sovereign state in the name of the protection of minorities. As he observed, "at first there was, so far as I recollect, a proposal that there should be inserted in the League of Nations some general clause giving the League of Nations the right to protect minorities in all countries which are members of the League. This I always most strongly opposed . . . for it would have involved the right to interfere in the internal constitution of every country in the world. As I pointed out, it would give the League of Nations the right to protect the Chinese in Liverpool, the Roman Catholics in France, the French in Canada, quite apart from the more serious problems, such as the Irish."[11]

Certainly the Irish were one of the most serious problems the British had to handle during and after World War I. Ireland was, in fact, the only exception of a partially triumphant secessionist movement boosted within the border of a victor of World War I. Though undeniably a territory of colonial settlement, indeed the origin of British colonialism,[12] the Irish question was never treated either as a decolonization process nor did the idea of self-determination play barely any role in the events starting off with the 1916 Eastern Rising, which certainly, despite the brutal repression that the British power dispatched against the Irish rebels, contributed to discrediting Britain's reputation as a liberal state and revealed that British imperialism was not so distant from the German one in exercising violence and abuses.

Among the scarce opportunities in which self-determination was expressed in the course of the Irish cause, there might be mentioned, for instance, the allusions to such a principle entailed in a speech delivered by Lloyd George to the House of Commons on April 16, 1918 in which the prime minister announced Irish conscription in order to obtain manpower to face up to the German 1918 Spring offensive in the Western front as a quid pro quo for Home Rule.[13]

Once the Great War was concluded, the Irish Free State's independence resulted from the democratic strength of the movement (expressed in the overwhelming success of the Irish republican party Sinn Féin in the 1918 British general election), the weakness of the United Kingdom after the armistice with Germany, and a succession of harsh conflicts such as the Anglo-Irish War and the Irish Civil War. The path taken by Irish secessionism was not wrapped up by any sort of international legal legitimacy even though it was developed within one of the most supposedly consolidated democracies of that time and a founder of the League of Nations.[14] In this fashion, it might be additionally remarked that even Woodrow Wilson denied Sinn Féin its demand that Ireland should be debated at the Versailles peace conference, such an issue remaining internal to the British Empire.[15]

In fact, the creation of the Irish Free State, together with Icelandic independence from Denmark during the Nazi occupation of the metropolis in 1944, represented the last secession that occurred in western Europe until the present,[16] a circumstance that, on the one hand, reveals, with the exception of the time encompassing the German expansion during World War II, the robustness and the cohesion of the western European states during the twentieth century and, on the other hand, confirms the lack of transcendence of the narrative on self-determination as a device to face up to the challenges posed by the minority nations of that area even though the right to self-determination was primarily designed to be applied in the European continent.

Though the aftermath of World War I marked the beginning of the decline of the empires of western Europe, Britain and France's triumph in the conflict, together with the circumstance that the United States was not prone to cause any serious breach with its European Allies, led to the de facto cancellation of the self-determination doctrine(announced only a few months before) to arrange the national conflicts emerging within the borders of the western European states.

Nobody would have fought and won a war with such a degree of sacrifice in lives and resources to attend afterward passively to the fragmentation of their own political community. Such a process would be reproduced again in the period immediately after World War II, with the difference that then the conception of a supranational European regional structure to prevent internal disintegration would be needed.

II

As late as 1941, in the middle of a still uncertain World War II, Winston Churchill, who besides President F. D. Roosevelt had reiterated his commitment to self-determination as a general standard for governing territorial changes in the Atlantic Charter, denied, nevertheless, the application of the proclaimed self-determination principle to the colonial peoples dominated by the British.[17] The Atlantic Charter only aimed to restore "the sovereignty, self-government and national life of the states and nations of Europe under the Nazi yoke." Again, self-determination was only conceived in continental Europe toward the enemy.

Shortly before, in the summer of 1940, when France was occupied by the German troops, also the Nazis pondered in their turn to play the card of the people's right to self-determination in order to debilitate French nationalism. The total defeat of France would not only in this way be achieved by the partition through the assignment of territories to the Reich and the setting up of an authoritarian government in Vichy, but also by encouraging minorities such as the Bretons to claim for their self-government in alliance with the new masters. Also when an eventual assault across the English Channel was envisaged in August 1940, a nationalities policy was designed in Berlin to tackle with the capitulation of the United Kingdom grounded on detaching Scotland from the United Kingdom and unifying Ireland. It was, as Mazower observed, a vision of securing German hegemony in the west of Europe through the same means that the French and the British had tried to do in central and eastern Europe after 1918.[18]

But the plans concerning the minorities within France (not to mention the prospects on the United Kingdom, which was not defeated) never went ahead and, in fact, the outcome of the war with the liberation of France and the recognition of its status as a victor power left the minorities in a very weak position, disregarding the performance of their cadres during the German occupation, and entered into the postwar era with scarce possibilities of unfolding a project of national emancipation.

Circumstances such as the one represented by nationalities within France after the conflagration and their role during the German New Order (that indeed may be extensible to other territories in Europe) may allow us to understand the comprehensive hostility shown by western European governments during the second half of the twentieth century to assume any kind of recognition of the right to self-determination within their European borders.

Other considerations might be made about what happened with the European possessions on a worldwide scale. A victorious but exhausted British empire after the war effort, for instance, had to contemplate its fragmentation by giving up most of its overseas dominions. That was the point in which the right to self-determination, in spite of its general formulation, was restrictively interpreted as a guide aimed to organize the decolonization of "saltwater" territories but without projection into the spaces that western European states considered their mainland.

The struggle to retain the European petty nations in the metropolitan western European states matched with the global trend to restrict the interpretation of the right to the people's self-determination to the territories since then ruled by a colonial power as regulated in Chapters XI, XII, and XIII of the United Nations Charter. The self-determination processes arranged in the decades that followed World War II concerned the dominions that western European countries had mainly in Asia and Africa as was provided in the Resolution adopted by the United Nations General Assembly 1514 (XV) of December 14, 1960, whose title was explicit enough: *Declaration on the Granting of Independence to Colonial Countries and Peoples*. The latter was so regulated in spite of the fact that the principle of the self-determination of the peoples was likely to be recognized regarding *all* the peoples in article 1.2 of the United Nations Charter and such general encompassing of the right to self-determination was confirmed by Article 1 of both the International Covenant on Civil and Political Rights, and the International Covenant on Economic, Social and Cultural Rights adopted by the United Nations General Assembly in December 1966.

The reluctance to attribute the right to external self-determination to the sub-state nations (which in the interwar time might be associated with the national minorities) would mark, nevertheless, the United Nations General Assembly Resolution *26/25 (XXV)* of 1970. From the recognition of the principle of self-determination entailed in this resolution it might be inferred that any claim on the people's self-determination able to dismantle the territorial unity of an existing sovereign and independent state would only be admitted in the cases in which the government representing the whole people belonging to that territory discriminated on grounds of race, creed, or color (no mention, again, is included regarding discrimination on the ground of nationality).

The general attribution of the right to self-determination to "all peoples" that, after the United Nations Charter, was reproduced in the 1966 International Covenants on Civil and Political Rights and on Economic, Social and Cultural Rights did not prevent, either, the restraint of the scope of such a right's applicability.

The representatives of the states that are part of this international law *corpus* on the right to the people's self-determination and the mainstream international law scholars see the right to external self-determination in the form of secession as an exceptional option allowed by international provisions limited to the cases of colonization, foreign occupation and domination, and oppression of minorities particularly addressed to repair (according to the Resolution *26/25 [XXV]* of 1970) discriminations grounded on race or religion (but not on nationality). In addition, the case of decolonization is restrictively interpreted as well: from the Resolution *1514 (XV)* of 1960 it could be extracted that only the colonized peoples geographically separated (and ethno-culturally different) from the country that administers them would hold a presumption to implement the right to self-determination in the form of secession (or integration or association with another independent state). Such a group of communities would certainly include those territories that appeared in the list of the United Nations as trustees, mandates, or any other form of administration by another power but also the so-called "saltwater" colonies in allusion to the oceanic distance that separates the metropolis from the territory that seeks to be transformed into an independent state.[19]

At any rate, sub-state nations with territorial continuity with the parent state, even though the former might be considered on social, ethnic, cultural, linguistic, or historic grounds a different people (or a different nation) from that which constitutes the demographic majority within the parent state are excluded from enjoying any presumption of applicability of the right to self-determination understood as a right to secession. Even though it is not clear what makes the "saltwater" territories (the factor of territorial discontinuity) the key element that allows a political community to be considered a "colony" and, consequently, a holder of the right to self-determination in its external fashion, the trend that is likely to dominate within the western European democracies in different *fora* (that is from their representation before the United Nations to the European Union institutions) is that the national minorities inhabiting within the western European states *are not colonies* in the sense provided by international law.

That something does not fit into an interpretation of the right to self-determination in its external dimension centered on the cases of decolonization of "saltwater" territories is revealed by the fact that from the five cases in which the doctrine on self-determination is most prominently developed by the International Court of Justice only one is clearly related to a decolonization context.[20] Even in that case, which concerned the secession of Namibia from South Africa, it was not a matter affecting a "saltwater" colony but a territory that presented continuity with the colonial power (see International Court of Justice Advisory Opinion of June 21, 1971, *Legal consequences for states of the continued presence of South Africa in Namibia [South Western Africa] notwithstanding Security Council Resolution 276 [1970]*). Regarding the cases on Western Sahara (International Court of Justice Advisory Opinion of October 16, 1975, *Western Sahara*) and Eastern Timor (International Court of Justice Judgement of June 30, 1995, *Case Concerning East Timor [Portugal v. Australia]*) although both had been "saltwater" colonies administrated by Spain and Portugal respectively, the self-determination claim was not held before the former colonial powers but before their contiguous neighbors that had invaded them (mainly Morocco in the case of Western Sahara [though Mauritania did also control a part of Western Sahara's territory] and Indonesia in the case of East Timor).

The case of Kosovo it is still more illustrative. Kosovo's declaration of independence represented a breakup from Serbia though the International Court of Justice analyzed the declaration on Kosovo's independence according to the legal framework provided by the United Nations Security Council resolutions that established an international administration over the territory after the offensive that NATO launched in 1999 against Serbia in order to stop the attacks against the Kosovar population. However, aware of the consequences to the stability of the existing states that the opinion on Kosovo's independence might represent, the International Court refused to handle the questions posed before her through the doctrine of self-determination (and, particularly, did not delve into the question around the idoneity of serious human rights breaches in conferring a right to external self-determination in the form of secession)[21] and limited the analysis developed in the opinion only to Kosovo's circumstances, avoiding any general statement on the compatibility between independence declarations and international public law.

Observed more closely, the five cases before the International Court of Justice in which the right to self-determination played some role in the court reasoning (even to deny its influence, as the court did in the advisory opinion on Kosovo) were to be sure related to an aggression and an occupation (or at least an attempt at that) by a surrounding power (not by a geographically distant metropolis), which is what usually has happened in the relationship between national majorities and sub-state nations in the formation of most of the western European nation-states.

Nevertheless, western European powers, two of them such as Great Britain and France holding veto power in the decision-making processes before the United Nations Security Council, have usually managed to elude any interpretation of the right to self-determination able to destabilize the hegemony of the majoritarian national communities within their respective states. In spite of the fact that both European powers acceded, for instance, to recognize Kosovo's unilateral independence at instances of the United States' geopolitical interests in Eastern Europe, the limited scope of the above-mentioned International Court of Justice advisory opinion on Kosovo's declaration of independence precisely allowed such western European powers to keep the doctrine of self-determination away from the context of territorial occupations within Europe.

One recurrent argument to exclude the European sub-state nations from the self-determination narrative was grounded on the idea that the violent acquisitions of the European territories that lie at the origins of the formation of modern western European states happened in the distant past (from the absorption of Provence by the French Monarchy through the destruction of the Cathar heresy in the late twelfth century and early thirteenth century, to the crushing of the Jacobite rebellion in the Scottish Highlands by the middle of the eighteenth century) but it is not clear, aside from the interests showed by the western European state-nations in staunchly preserving the territorial unity within their European borders, why the passage of time evaporates the actions against violent invasions when there is territorial continuity, while the "saltwater" that separates the metropolis from the overseas colonized territories blocks any limitation of period.[22] At any rate, such European nations that had built a global empire would never passively accept the dismembering of the state that represented the core of their national being for the sake of which their nationals had fought and won so many wars.

III

The limited interpretation of the right to self-determination of the peoples in the sense of excluding the national minorities coexisting within the European states was stretched until the decolonization processes that burst out in the 1970s.

In the case of Portugal, the withdrawal from its colonies was accompanied by the collapse of one of the last authoritarian regimes in western Europe, a circumstance that opened the door to the admission of Portugal to European Community membership a few years later. With some decades of delay, given the parenthesis of the dictatorship, Portuguese adhesion to the European project demonstrates the closed link between European integration and the loss of an empire.

In the same way as happened in Spain, the Portuguese authoritarian regime lead by Antonio de Oliveira Salazar until 1968 (and Marcelo Caetano in the beginning of the 1970s) was possible because of the backing of the United States, eager to find allies for the West's anti-communist umbrella.[23] United States support to Portugal in the Cold War strategy included the preservation of the Portuguese overseas empire at a time when other colonization adventures such as the British one or the French one were collapsing. Although the U.S. government was in principle supportive of anti-colonial movements in Africa, it overlooked Portuguese repression in Angola in order to avoid the fall of such territory into the hands of communist influence through the Cuban participation in the conflict.

However, wars spreading in the Portuguese dominions in Africa made the situation unsustainable in the mainland.[24] Portugal's defense of its colonial holdings was expensive and bloody. The spiraling inflation brought on by the oil crises put the regime of Marcelo Caetano and his colleagues on the ropes. The grievances of junior officers and their families, unable to subsist on already low wages further reduced by inflation, were now shared by a rising generation of businessmen frustrated at their rulers' incompetence and who understood that their country's future lay in Europe and not in Africa.[25]

Precisely the left-wing elements within the Portuguese army opposed colonization and were the ones who boosted the revolution in April 1974 (the so-called "Carnation Revolution") and forced Portugal's democratization. General António de Spínola, who was appointed to head the junta and shaped a provisional cabinet with centrists and socialists, soon announced plans to offer the African colonies full self-determination. Within a year the colonies, in spite of a chaotic retreat by the army and the opening of civil wars in some places like in Angola, were almost all independent (the exceptions would be the enclave of Macao and, as we shall see, East Timor, invaded in 1975 by Indonesia).

The anti-imperialist soul of the Portuguese revolution, which had motivated the young and leftist officials to withdraw from the African conflicts and to seize power in the metropolis, also embedded the text of the 1976 Portuguese constitution being one of the constitutional references in recognizing the people's right to self-determination and the right to insurrection to all forms of oppression (article 7.3 of the Portuguese Constitution). In a similar vein, article 7.2 of the same text provides that

> Portugal shall advocate the abolition of imperialism, colonialism and all other forms of aggression, dominion and exploitation in the relations between peoples, as well as simultaneous and controlled general disarmament, the dissolution of

> the political-military blocs and the setting up of a collective security system, all with a view to the creation of an international order with the ability to ensure peace and justice in the relations between peoples.

But the "abolition of imperialism," "colonialism," or the recognition of "the right to the people's self-determination" according to the wording of the Portuguese constitution followed the path marked by the international law common interpretation and was not attributed, of course, to the territories considered "mainland" by the same Portuguese constitutional system.

To them, in the Iberian Peninsula what ruled was the principle of "unity" provided by article 6 of the Constitution ("the State shall be unitary") regarding to which "the State shall not dispose of title to any part of Portuguese territory or of the sovereign rights that exercises there over" (article 5.3 Portuguese Constitution). At most, some degree of autonomy is recognized to the Atlantic archipelagos of Azores and Madeira that, in spite of being organized through their own political and administrative statutes and self-government institutions (article 6.1 Portuguese Constitution), are also subjected to the principle of unity and not entitled to exercise a right of self-determination in its external dimension or, at least, neither Azores nor Madeira have no unilateral right to secession in the same extent that the Portuguese Constitution is likely to confer to the territories qualified as "colonies."

Unsurprisingly, the Azores had been the cornerstone of the United States strategic interests during the Cold War and had represented one of the main motivations that backed the participation of Portugal as a founder of NATO in 1949, disregarding the illiberal character of the Salazar regime. Military bases in the Azores may explain in terms of realpolitik why the right to external self-determination has been recognized by the Portuguese constitutional system to almost every distant possession of the former Portuguese empire except for those archipelagos. In fact, after World War II, the United States, rather than struggling for colonial direct acquisitions, developed a policy of controlling military and naval bases enclaves,[26] the fate of the Azores Islands might be described as a remnant of Portuguese colonialism under American consent. Remarkably, the famous meeting that gathered the United States president, George W. Bush, with those European partners that supported his project to invade Iraq (a decision that caused a shock within the European Union since it divided the member states on such a crucial issue in the moment in which there was the struggle to build a common external policy during the drafting of the European Constitutional Treaty) took place in the Azores on March 15, 2003.

Realpolitik interests also were involved in the opposite situation: that of the recognition of the right to self-determination of farther away territories such as East Timor, to the extent that it was Portugal, the former metropolis, the state that, as we have seen, invoked that right of the East Timorese before the International Court of Justice when the occupant power of that part of the island, Indonesia, concluded an agreement with Australia with the aim of exploring and extracting the oil resources that lay in the subsoil of the Timor Sea.[27]

The fate of giving up the former colonies of the empire would be at least compensated by controlling some of the raw materials sources existing in those territories in exchange for recognizing their right to self-determination in relation to other powers. Portuguese involvement in the East Timorese struggle for independence may be interpreted as an attempt to stretch Portuguese influence to a former colony in a context in which, differently from other European powers such as Britain or France, Portugal was too poor to develop a "neo-colonist" policy. Leaving aside considerations regarding the brutal Indonesian occupation of East Timor from 1975 (condemned by the United Nations Security Council), the fact is that the Portuguese government of António Guterres reasserted the Portuguese role in the world by eagerly taking advantage of the Indonesians' political and economic crisis that, by the end of the 1990s, was devastating the country at the time of the troubles and played some geopolitical cards to make the international community recognize a unilateral secession that it would be very hard to recognize in any other context (including those in which the occupation, as happened in East Timor, is deemed illegal and the occupants subject the local population to the most abhorred practices such as torture and massacres).

In 1999, thus, an agreement was reached between Portugal and post-authoritarian Indonesia, with the encouragement of the United Nations, for a referendum on the territory's future. The serious violence that followed the anti-Indonesian vote led to a period of United Nations administration that ended with independence in May 2002.[28] António Guterres would become, in 2017, the secretary-general of the United Nations and in August 2019 he proudly celebrated the twentieth anniversary of the self-determination referendum in East Timor from his post.

If in 1999, and on occasion of the East Timorese issue, Portuguese diplomacy obtained an international triumph, one of the most brilliant after the Portuguese empire's collapse, it was because Portugal had been strengthened as a nation through its entry into the European Economic Community (later the European Union) thirteen years before. The road to the European Union was satisfying the Portuguese prospects of economic development, prosperity, and political self-confidence by providing compensation for overseas losses.[29] "The empire is dead, long live the EU," wrote António de Figueiredo, a leading opponent of the Portuguese authoritarian regime and writer on Portuguese colonialism.[30] The European Union offered Portugal the chance to develop a new national identity whose primary orientation was continental and European but without relinquishing to regain, as the Eastern Timorese example reveals, economic, diplomatic, or cultural allegiances with its former imperial dominions.[31]

As with other former European empires, the Portuguese horizon within the European Union looked bright until the eruption of the 2008 crisis. However, after the crash, the financial bailouts, and the European Union seizing of the Portuguese economy, it is likely that Portugal is by 2019 politically recovering itself much better than other European countries, especially if we compare the Portuguese situation with that of its Iberian neighbor: Spain.

IV

The most discordant difference in treatment between "the colonies" and "the mainland" is provided in the western area of Europe by the Spanish constitutional developments, which are still in motion, as the Catalan crisis testifies, and are to some extent behind the existential crises overshadowing the European Union.

Spain had already faced up to the trauma of decolonization by losing the remnants of its American empire, the Philippines in the Pacific and the Caribbean islands of Cuba and Puerto Rico in the hands of the United States after the 1898 defeat.[32] The 1898 Spanish-American war is interesting given its metaphorical character: what was the beginning of the global rising of a new extra-European empire, the United States, marked the decadence of an old and European one, Spain.

Losing Cuba and Puerto Rico, at the same time, triggered the modern nationalisms within the Spanish Iberian territories, such as the Basque and the Catalan ones, which were severely repressed by the Spanish central authorities. If the minority nations within the Iberian Peninsula could not take profit of any imperial expansion (as, for instance, the Scottish did by the creation of the British Empire) and, on the other hand, they had to suffer the burdens of the territorial shrinking (by over-taxation as happened regarding to Catalonia) the secessionist solution began to be envisaged. No wonder in this vein that Catalan secessionism from Spain was outlined shortly after the Cuban crisis by the creation of the Catalan pro-independence flag, the so-called *Estelada*, inspired by the Cuban flag with its lone star (which at its turn was likely to be inspired by the Texas "Lone Star Flag" adopted with the establishment of the Texas Republic when that territory seceded from Mexico in 1836).

By the first half of the twentieth century, Spanish nationalism reacted to the challenges posed by the Iberian minority nations and attempts of democratization through authoritarianism and militarism. Given the circumstance that Spain was not involved either in World War I nor in World War II, the military cadres that seized power in different occasions (in 1923 through the coup d'état led by Miguel Primo de Rivera and from 1936 through the putsch that degenerated into a war and paved the way for Franco's dictatorship) had been trained and gained experience during the conflicts of decolonization. The military structure that had been operating in northern Africa against the conflict in the Rif in the 1920s (that had been disastrous for Spain) chiefly composed later, beginning with general Franco himself, the force that in 1936 rebelled against the Second Spanish Republic.[33]

It has been argued, aside from the fact that the 1936 military rebellion was partially motivated by the attitude of the Spanish conservative cadres toward the peripheral nationalist movements that were considered a threat to Spanish unity,[34] that the Francoist faction applied to the mainland the tactics of war and terror upon the civil population that they had rehearsed during their fight against the decolonization processes in Africa.[35] Under such a perspective, the so-called "Spanish Civil War," developed between 1936 and 1939, might be to some extent appreciated (among other conflicts) as the struggle of an army that had fought against the "external colonies" to annihilate the "internal colonies" remaining in the Iberian Peninsula.

During the second half of the twentieth century, however, the repression over the minority nations within the Iberian Peninsula dominions of Spain contrasted with the reaction of the Spanish central authorities toward the liberation movements experienced in some of the still retained overseas Spanish possessions. Despite some attempts within the Francoist government to assimilate such territories, the need to supersede Spanish international isolation after World War II forced the regime to accept the inclusion of some parts of Africa under its control to the process of decolonization provided by the legal system of the United Nations. That happened regarding the northern part of Morocco under the Spanish protectorate until 1956 when Morocco acceded to full independence including the former Spanish zone; Equatorial Guinea (independent in 1968) and Western Sahara (a territory that, together with the northern province of Ifni, was added by the United Nations to the list of dependent subjects entitled to the right of self-determination and, consequently, involved in a process of decolonization). It might be remarked, as evidence of the close collaboration existing between European former imperial powers, that when Morocco acceded to independence in 1956, the Spanish government struggled to retain the southern side of the former protectorate arguing that the strip bordering between Western Sahara and that former protectorate was not included in the territories assigned to Morocco. Spain defended its sovereignty upon the contested areas by military means with French support in a joint operation called *Ouragan* (Hurricane) developed by the first months of 1958 from which resulted, according to the Treaty of Angra de Cintra concluded between Morocco and Spain on April 1, 1958, the continuity of Spanish control upon the Ifni enclave.[36] It is interesting to notice that the supposed democratic Fourth French Republic, which had signed the treaty on the European Economic Community in Rome just a year before, had no objection in being involved shoulder to shoulder with the General Franco dictatorship in order to fight the decolonization cause.

In the case of Equatorial Guinea, the Francoist government at first tried to assimilate its dominions to the condition of a Spanish province (1959) in the same strategy that France had done in Algeria before. The situation, however, soon proved unsustainable given both the emergence of Guinean nationalist movements and the involvement of the United Nations in the question. The Francoist dictatorship agreed to celebrate a referendum on Equatorial Guinea's autonomy in 1963 and a new legal framework was passed in which a government and a territorial assembly were provided. The process toward full independence accelerated in the fall of 1967 through a conference in Madrid integrated by both Spanish and Guinean representatives that discussed the constitutional framework of the future state. Such a constitution was even passed by the means of another referendum and finally the independence of Equatorial Guinea was declared and recognized on October 12, 1968. Equatorial Guinea's secession thus became one of the rare examples in the history of the Spanish dominions in which the Spanish authorities agreed to separation. It is in this vein remarkable to notice that such a process happened *during Franco's military rule*. While, as we shall see, the 2017 referendum on Catalan self-determination was severely suppressed by the Spanish central authorities under *a supposedly democratic regime* (and several attacks were launched by the Spanish police and paramilitary forces to the poll stations) almost fifty years previously an authoritarian Spanish government had allowed the Equatorial Guineans first to vote in a referendum on the Constitution of the new state (August 1968) and then to declare independence with immediate recognition (October 1968).[37]

But in the case of Western Sahara, we find another example of a more benevolent treatment shown by the Spanish authorities toward pro-independence aspirations developed in Africa than toward the ones present in the Iberian Peninsula. By the beginning of the 1970s Spain, still under an authoritarian regime, accepted the decolonization solution proposed by the United Nations for Western Sahara. The colonial power passed a statute for the region conceived as a transitional regime until the territory acceded to full sovereignty and announced the holding of a referendum on independence. Nevertheless, Moroccan territorial ambitions triumphed, and finally dismantled the immediate plans for the constitution of a new state in the region. During the last throes of an agonizing Franco in November 1975, the Spanish government consented to hand over the territory to Morocco (and in a smaller proportion to Mauritania) ignoring all the resolutions of the United Nations, including an opinion of the International Court of Justice.[38]

The departure of the Spanish authorities from Western Sahara allowed a Moroccan column of soldiers and civil volunteers (in a move called the Green March) to proceed to the occupation of the territory, in an operation that is still a matter of dispute in the United Nations. The Western Sahara question has not still finished well regarding the respect to the right of the people's self-determination but that was not as a consequence of the opposition of the former colonial authority, which in spite of the authoritarian character of the regime showed some willingness to carry out the United Nations mandates, but mainly as the result of the invasion triggered by the Western Sahara African neighbors: Morocco and, to a much lesser degree, Mauritania.

By the beginning of the 2020s, Western Sahara was involved in a complex diplomatic operation by which the United States under Trump's presidency recognized Moroccan sovereignty over the disputed territory in return for Morocco's normalization of ties with Israel. The material background of Moroccan thirst of domination over Western Sahara was chiefly defined by the richness of the mineral resources available in this jurisdiction, including an immense tellurian site located in the Atlantic ridge 240 miles from the Western Sahara coast which eventually might foster a new conflict with the former colonial power in that region, Spain, since the estimated 2,600 tons of tellurium discovered are also 250 miles in south-west direction from the island of Hierro, in the Canary archipelago. The Canary Islands, nowadays an Autonomous Community within Spain (and, as happens with the Madeira and the Azores Islands under Portuguese sovereignty, an ultra-peripheral region of the European Union) were involved in a decolonization dispute during the years, by the second half of the 1970s and the beginning of the 1980s, in which the Spanish constitutional regime as a liberal democracy was being defined.

V

Indeed, Spain as a unitary nation had emerged weak from the Francoist regime and Spanish nationalism was afflicted by a decided lack of reputation on the international scene, given the brutal repression against both dissident opposition and national minorities that the authoritarian state apparatus had displayed for decades.

Franco's authoritarianism, however, had not been actively fought by the members of the European Communities, rather the contrary. As Fernando Guirao convincingly argued, the governments of the Six (Nine in the 1970s) facilitated, via the European Communities, the subsistence of the Franco regime. From 1950 to the mid-1960s, the founding members of the European Communities avoided every sign of discrimination against Spain. By the mid-1960s the Six even fostered Spanish exports, which would provide the necessary resources to finance Spanish development and, thus, to ensure the anchorage of the dictatorship. And by 1970, even an agreement between Spain and the European Economic Community was concluded in which Spanish agricultural commodities and manufactures obtained a generous access to the Common Market without reciprocal access for the producers from the European Economic Community to the Spanish market, let alone that the Francoist authorities were not required to pay any specific price in terms of democratization nor domestic decentralization.[39] Somehow, the connivance stemmed by the European Communities with Franco's authoritarianism constituted a precedent lying behind the indifference shown by the European Union institutions when territorial claims within Spain erupted once such a state supposedly had already transformed itself into a liberal democracy.

Both the French and the German Federal Republic governments actively supported the Spanish transition in spite of the fact that it was controlled by the political and economic powers that had played a relevant role under Franco's regime. The most prominent powers within the European Communities were reluctant to experience a rupture led by leftist forces in the fashion as the one that had erupted in Portugal by 1974. European authorities in western Europe, always supported by the United States under both the Ford and Carter administrations, accepted a process toward a Spanish Constitutional democracy led by a head of state in the figure of King Juan Carlos I that had been appointed by the dictator and by conservative governments integrated by ministers coming from the previous regime apparatus.

On the other hand, regarding the Spanish leftist spectrum, Western powers opted to strengthen the social-democrats to the detriment of the communists, who had been the most solid opposition group during the dictatorship. A key moment during the transition was defined by the communist leadership's acceptance of the transition process in exchange for legalization of the Communist Party, though their final electoral outcomes were more meager than expected. By contrast, within the context of that stronger Western international support, the Spanish social-democrats obtained an overwhelming electoral victory by 1982, which represented the first peaceful transfer of power from the right to the left since the times of the Second Republic. Through the social-democratic government performance in that atmosphere of political stabilization for western Europe, the integration of Spain in the supranational structures of that area were culminated; Spain's accession to NATO, which had been concluded by a conservative government in 1981, was confirmed in 1986 through a referendum. In the same year of 1986 Spain also acceded to the European Communities.

VI

As was happening in the rest of Europe from 1973, Spain was severely hit by the economic crises. The oil shock caused unemployment, impoverishment, and inflation (averaged around 16 percent per annum in the 1970s) in a particularly intense fashion within an economy that was vulnerable to the price rise of raw materials.[40] Inflation soaring triggered also the increase of public deficit and the drop of business profits. The decrease in business margins, together with the deterioration of their expectations, had an immediate effect on productive investment and job creation. The progressive loss of the colonies, in a process that was at that time culminating with the loss of the African possessions, contributed to make the access to such resources still harder.

By Franco's death in 1975, thus, Spain was besieged by all sorts of threats, economic collapse was looming, the remnants of the colonial adventures were being concluded, and the transition to democracy after the death of the dictator was full of uncertainties. The national minorities coexisting within Spain, and harshly repressed in their political, linguistic, and cultural manifestations under Franco's regime, found their opportunity to claim for decentralization and self-government. The Spanish national center was weak and the political elites in Madrid had to offer some concessions in order to avoid an escalation of conflicts (which on the other hand persisted in the Basque Country through the armed strategy that the military group ETA had been deploying since the last years of the dictatorship).[41]

The building of a plurinational system in a democratic Spain did not, however, take long. Spanish nationalist hard-liners promoted a coup d'état in 1981 that, even frustrated, instigated the Spanish majoritarian national parties to trigger a regressive movement in the decentralization process, a movement that, in fact, relied on the generalization and the equalization of autonomy across all the Spanish territories diminishing thus the national characters of particular communities such as Catalonia and the rest of the Catalan speaking territories (Valencia and Balearic Islands), as well as the Basque Country and Navarra, Galicia, or the Canary Islands.

The Spanish government of the transition, led by Adolfo Suárez, in order to consolidate the international credibility of the democratic initiative that it was supposed to trigger, opted to recognize some degree of political autonomy and some cultural rights to the other nations beyond the Spanish one. In the case of Catalonia, furthermore, Suárez, a conservative politician that came from the Francoist apparatus, sought both in Catalan nationalism and in the re-settlement of the autonomous Catalan government through the figure of the former Catalan president, Josep Tarradellas, a way to contain the rise of the left parties that had won in the region the first Spanish democratic general elections held in June 1977.[42] In short, the Spanish government, committed to transform Spain from an authoritarian regime to a liberal democracy, recognized some sort of national pluralism because it *had no other alternative* if the provision of some legitimacy, both at the internal level and at the international level, was to be achieved by the new regime.

Nevertheless, the obvious intention of admitting some autonomy and political recognition to the national minorities (and, in fact, the whole process of the Spanish transition to democracy) was to strengthen the cohesion within Spain and prevent any secessionist claim. The recognition of political autonomy to the Spanish sub-state nations entailed in the Constitution was very cautious and never represented a challenge to the Spanish nation's sovereignty. The limited recognition of national differences within Spain and the evolution of what had to be a state defined by national pluralism into a mere administrative decentralization was in the beginning justified by the need of sending the diehard nostalgic supporters of Franco to the political fringes, but it soon became evident that the struggle for a strong central Spanish state was in the agenda of the Spanish political mainstream and that any centripetal trend would be stopped as soon as the debilities of the transition were superseded.

VII

The aversion to any political recognition toward sub-state nations by the bulk of the Spanish political system was indeed already overshadowing the building of the Spanish constitutional text. When it was leaked to the press in November 1977 that the constitutional draft enshrined the term "nationalities" to refer to those bodies to which the right of autonomy was recognized, representative parts of the political and military establishment strongly disagreed with the solution adopted by the drafters particularly with the inclusion of the term "nationalities," even though it was outlined in contrast with the term "nation," which was only attached to Spain.[43]

The conservative groups considered that the constitutional drafters had gone too far in the mentioning of another political subject beyond the central state. The debate around the decentralization of Spain before, during, and after the constitution-drafting process had to coexist with a spread of discontent among the military, to the point that the menace of a military coup cropped up several times during the Spanish transition until a coup d'état was effectively perpetrated in 1981. The right to political autonomy for "nationalities and regions" was admitted but only under the condition of stressing "the indissoluble unity of the Spanish Nation" with the subject of sovereignty placed solely in the Spanish people as a whole. This compromise was distilled in article 2 of the Spanish Constitution, which, in a winding and strange wording, provided that

> the Constitution is based on the indissoluble unity of the Spanish Nation, the common and indivisible homeland of all Spaniards.

The idea of such emphasis in stating the principle of political unity aimed to cut off any future interpretation able to bestow some sovereign attributes to another "nation" different from the Spanish one and, in that way, opening the door to legitimize some sort of secession (which was considered by Franco's followers to be a worst-case scenario). Such a narrow legal interpretation of the term "nation" regarding the concept of sovereignty fueled some decades later the Spanish central authorities' strategy in repressing the Catalan demands for organizing a referendum on self-determination. But, by the end of the 1970s and the beginning of the 1980s, Catalonia was not considered the main threat to Spanish national unity, since the Catalan political actors and the Catalan citizenry backed in a majoritarian fashion the 1978 constitutional framework.

The main concerns for the Spanish central authorities during the Spanish transition were, on the one hand, the terrorist conflict triggered by the Basque left nationalists and the armed force ETA and, on the other, the struggle for independence of the Canary Islands, which while lacking social support gained some international support through Algeria in considering that said territory, in front of the African coast, was not "mainland" but a colony in the same way as Western Sahara and, thus, that it deserved recognition of the right to self-determination.[44] After all, differently from the Basque or the Catalan cases, the Canary Islands are a "saltwater" territory according to the definition outlined in international law in pointing out the geopolitical situations able to be covered by the right to external self-determination.

VIII

The Canary secessionist struggle, nevertheless, was by the beginning of the 1980s already reduced through an intense diplomatic campaign sponsored by the Spanish government both in relation to Algeria (the same state that was supporting the West Saharan pro-independence armed groups against Morocco) and in relation to the United African Organization, which finally accepted Spanish sovereignty upon the Canary Islands, even though they are geographically located in Africa. The Spanish government managed to avoid the access of the Canary Islands to the United Nations list of dependent and nongoverned territories and thus blocked the road to vindicate a rearrangement of the Canary Islands self-government grounded on the context of a decolonization process.[45]

The tiny movement for the Canary Islands self-determination (el *Movimiento por la Autodeterminación e Independencia del Archipiélago Canario*, MPAIAC, The Movement for the Canary Archipelago Self-determination and Independence) ended the 1970s very divided and with its leader, Antonio Cubillo, disabled after an attack that he suffered in Algiers in April 1978, which was believed to have been planned and perpetrated by the Spanish secret services.

If the Spanish government saw the menace represented by the Canary Islands pro-independence movements vanishing, a very different conclusion might be reached about the Basque Country, which until the end of ETA and its armed fighting activity in October 2011 was the main concern in the aim of preserving Spanish national unity. The 1980s and the 1990s were the decades in which ETA attacks reached their peak with massive murders causing hundreds of victims in the 1980s, and more selective targets among politicians and the military and police forces of Spain in the 1990s. In the nineties, too ETA military pressure was accompanied by an intense social mobilization organized by the Basque left nationalist cadres, including street fighting, that made the Basque social division more profound. By the beginning of the twenty first century, even though the ETA armed strategy had already been debilitated as a consequence of different successful police operations against the ETA leadership, the Basque nationalist political branches were entrenching their popular support and preparing the ground for a leap forward in the political status quo that, as we shall see, was partially contained through Spanish commitment to European integration.

IX

Once the Spanish transition to democracy took shape with the approval of the 1978 Constitution and accession to the European Economic Community in 1986 was achieved, the democratic Spanish government sought in the European space formed by liberal democracies the coverage for strengthening the national unity that had been questioned during the last throes of the dictatorship and the aftermath of Franco's death. The eighties, when the negotiations for Spanish integration within the European supranational structures were developed and finally successfully concluded, were a time in which ETA's mortal victims may be counted around forty per year (in 1980 alone, ETA killed almost one hundred people).

European integration played a key role in the Spanish struggle to face up to ETA's challenge. The involvement of other European countries in the fight against the Basque armed group had begun with France in 1984 when an agreement on counter-terrorism collaboration between the Spanish and the French government had been reached. But Spanish integration in the European space made such collaboration more intense with the signing of new agreements (such as the one concluded between Spain and France in 1987, a year after the entering into force of the Spanish Treaty of Adhesion to the European Economic Community), which sought to implement the measures concerning the establishment of a people's free movement zone that was already outlined by the 1986 Single European Act.

Since the European freedom of movement area was being consolidated during the following years with the entering into force of the Schengen Agreements, also was being strengthened the collaboration between European states' authorities on criminal matters and against terrorism, as was demonstrated by the Justice and Home affairs common policy designed in the 1992 Treaty of the European Union. The initial French cooperation displayed before 1992 was partially motivated because there are Basque regions within French borders as well (and such Basque territories under French jurisdiction had become a sort of safe harbor for ETA members) but with the Treaty of the European Union, the shaping of a common area on repressing terrorism was extended to other European Union members.

The approximation between the Basque leftist nationalists, some of which had been involved in the armed activities, and the moderate and conservative segments of the Basque political establishment, led to the Lizarra agreement concluded on September 12, 1998, following the path of the Irish Good Friday Agreement (which had been adopted in April of the same year). The Lizarra agreement among the Basque nationalist forces inaugurated a political strategy devoted both to overcoming violence and to creating the framework for exercising the right of the Basque peoples to self-determination. The agreement was followed by an ETA truce (September 16, 1998) to promote, as read the text of the agreement, "Euskadi's nation-building within the democratic institutions."

In spite of the fact that ETA broke such a ceasefire sixteen months later (November 1999), the Basque political roadmap for self-determination was carried on at the institutional level; in 2003, the Basque government reached an agreement within the Basque parliament to start the process of amending the 1979 statute of autonomy in order to establish a sort of "associated state" to Spain (*Estado asociado*) vested with sovereign powers. Juan José Ibarretxe, at the time the Basque prime minister (*Lehendakari*) for the conservative nationalists, el *Partido Nacionalista Vasco* (Basque Nationalist Party) assumed a self-determination program shared with the leftist nationalists.

From Lizarra and throughout the development of the so-called Ibarretxe plan of the Basque statute amendment (2003–2005), the Spanish government intensified its campaign before the European institutions to get their support against any Basque secessionist attempt. To that aim, the September 11, 2001, jihadist attacks suffered by the United States had helped, fostering collaboration among the Western democracies in the fight against terrorism, and particularly, the adoption of several counterterrorist framework regulations within the European Union Council, which were sought to be applied against the Basque armed group as well. As happened in other parts of the world, the fight against the global jihadist threat worked as a proxy to besiege local armed activities.

The struggle against the high-scale conflict was complemented with the struggle against the political dimension of the Basque national aspirations. Besides the counterterrorist measures, the Spanish central institutions struck against the Basque nationalist cadres banning the Basque leftist nationalist parties *Euskal Herritarrok*, *Herri Batasuna*, and *Batasuna* (2002) and all the parties considered successors to the mentioned political forces. Such prohibition was confirmed by the European Court of Human Rights (ECtHR Judgment of June 30, 2009, *Batasuna and Herri Batasuna v. Spain*), which considered that no right of the Convention was violated with the measure adopted by the Spanish supreme court in declaring illegal the Basque leftist nationalist parties and ordering their dissolution.

In parallel with the Basque political effort to create a Basque quasi-independent "associate State," the Spanish government took advantage during the reshaping of the European Union through the drafting of the so-called European Constitutional Treaty. The Basque challenge perpetrated by the "Ibarretxe Plan" instigated the Spanish government, at that time led by the conservative José Maria Aznar, to look for assistance among the EU member states peers. In that hour, in which fundamental reforms at the European constitutional level were glimpsed, the struggle displayed to repress internal secessions in the EU member states "mainland" reached its peak.[46] The European Constitution draft, at Aznar request, finally included a clause, article I-5, that represented the keystone in the intention to armor the European Union member states national unity against the internal defiance launched by minority nations. According to this provision,

> The Union shall respect the equality of member states before the constitution as well as their national identities . . . it shall respect their essential State functions, including *ensuring the territorial integrity* of the State [exmphasis added].

From the point of view of the European Union institutions, thus, "ensuring the territorial integrity" was a specific element of the "national identity" of the member states in a way regarding to which the European Union was not allowed to intervene even in facing up derogations to European Union law.

But following a more intrusive reading of article I-5 of the Constitutional Treaty, European Union institutions were encouraged to actively support such measures adopted by a member state to crush any attempt at territorial partition.

As is well known, the Treaty Establishing a Constitution for Europe was in the end rejected since neither the French nor the Dutch citizenry voted for it in the respective referenda held in 2005. However, the provision on "ensuring the territorial integrity" of the member states was maintained in the amendment to the Treaty on European Union (TEU) established by the Treaty of Lisbon signed in December 2007 (article 4.2 TEU), which is currently in force. For authors such as Piris,[47] who follows a reading of the provision more committed with the preservation of member states' national unity, article 4.2 TEU would make illegal any recognition facilitated by any member state if the secession of a piece of a territory of the other associate had been achieved through a unilateral declaration against the constitutional rules of the rump state.

Such article 4.2 TEU, however, had finally no influence in the way of tackling the Basque secessionist movement since it declined at the beginning of the 2010s. At the political level the Basque nationalists lost the Basque government for the very first time since the reestablishment of the autonomy, mainly as a consequence of banning the successors of the Basque leftist nationalist parties in the Basque parliamentary elections held in March 2009. When the Basque Nationalist Party acceded again to the autonomous government from the 2012 elections through the *Lehendakari* (Basque president) Íñigo Urkullu, any project related to transforming the Basque Country into a sovereign entity fell from the political agenda. The reason for this turn was partially that the armed conflict had also ceased. ETA had definitively declared the end of its activities in autumn 2011, and the negotiations around the dismantling of the organization and the treatment of ETA's members remaining in prison was a priority issue for Urkullu's government.

The welfare, even in times of economic crises, provided by the Basque special fiscal system through which the bulk of the fiscal resources collected by the Basque authorities remain in Basque territory instead of being transferred to Spanish central powers (the so-called *Concierto Económico*) might additionally explain the lukewarm efforts showed by the Basque political class to push forward independence in the last cycle.

The presence of Article 4.2 TEU in the European system of governance marked, instead, the European institutional reaction and that of the EU member states to the biggest secessionist crises that Spain had in the twenty first century: the Catalan claim for independence.

X

In the opposite direction to the developments experienced in the Basque Country, the Catalan claims for secession have been from the outset presented in a strictly pacific and democratic way. In fact, the Catalan vindication for recognition and major self-government began in 2003 around the same time in which the Basque struggle declined. Accordingly, the structural measures that the member states were negotiating at the European level were also promoted by the conservative Spanish government of Aznar with an eye on the Catalan question. Nevertheless, the conservatives lost the 2004 Spanish general elections and the socialists, led by José Luis Rodríguez Zapatero, were more prone to hear the Catalan prospects for reforming their self-government. In 2006, precisely, one year after the outright rejection of the Ibarretxe plan by the Spanish central legislature, the Catalans amended their Statute of Autonomy (*Estatut d'Autonomia*) with the support of the socialist majority in the *Cortes Generales*.

Contrary to the Basque attempt to create the "associate State," the changes in the Catalan basic law did not *prima facie* represent a direct clash with the Spanish Constitution but only pretended to obtain a major recognition of the Catalan national character, to entrench the Catalan powers transferred to the Catalan self-government and to improve the financial system in order to limit the "solidarity" contribution. However, after the enactment of the *Estatut* by the Spanish parliament and its ratification by the Catalan citizenry in a referendum, the conservative People's Party, then in the opposition led by Mariano Rajoy, challenged the constitutionality of the new Catalan statute before the Spanish Constitutional Court.

After four years of deliberation, in June 2010, the Spanish Constitutional Court finally issued the decision on the Statue of Catalonia.[48] The Court nullified fourteen provisions of this statute and interpreted another twenty-seven provisions in accordance with the constitution. The decision, thus, undermined the aims and the basic structure of the statute's amendment.[49]

It has been stated that the Spanish Constitutional Court ruling on the Catalan statute was a main factor in triggering the Catalan claim for full independence.[50] Shortly after the ruling, on July 10, 2010, a huge rally was organized in the streets of Barcelona against the court's judgement and demanding respect for the will of the Catalan people expressed in the statute's referendum ratification. But after a new failed attempt of the Catalan government to reach an agreement with the Spanish government (at that time again in the hands of the conservatives under the leadership of Mariano Rajoy) at least on fiscal matters, hundreds of thousands of people gathered in the streets of Barcelona for the 2012 Catalan national day (on September 11) directly claiming for independence. Popular pressure forced the Catalan president of that time, the nationalist Artur Mas, to call for elections under the commitment of holding a vote on secession that was held under the form of "popular consultation" on November 9, 2014. In autumn 2015, new elections were held to the Catalan parliament in which the pro-independence forces won, obtaining the overall majority of seats in the parliament with an explicit secessionist platform (with 72 of 135 total seats). Such majority, at that time led by a new Catalan president, Carles Puigdemont, decided to hold a referendum on the independence of Catalonia which, despite the suspension of the Catalan referendum bill by the Spanish Constitutional Court, was celebrated on October 1, 2017.

The referendum of October 1 awoke to a fierce storm by the Spanish police at polling stations causing more than nine hundred people to be injured and produced terrifying images that scandalized the international public in the West. In spite of such enormous pressure, including the closing of 14 percent of the polling stations, the confiscation of thousands of votes, and the repeated cyber-attacks caused by the Spanish forces, Catalan people voted in a turn out that reached 43.03 percent of enfranchised citizens (the final outcome was of 2,020,144 YES votes for independence against 176,566 NO votes with 65,715 being void or blank). Spanish reaction was brutal and included serious violations of human rights that have no comparison within the European Union space and the Western area of liberal democracies. But worse were going to be the things to come. Since the majority that voted in the referendum backed the independence, the majority of the Catalan parliament declared the independence of Catalonia on October 27, 2017, but the Spanish government seized the Catalan autonomy, imprisoned eight members of the Catalan government and two leaders of grassroots pro-secession groups (who were charged with crimes of both sedition and rebellion), and forced the rest of the Catalan government and the president of Catalonia to go into exile.[51]

On October 14, 2019, the political and social leaders that organized the 2017 Catalan self-determination referendum were found guilty of sedition and misuse of public funds and were sentenced to nine to thirteen years of prison. (This is nearly the same punishment that, according to the Spanish Criminal Code, murders or rapists deserve. The Spanish judiciary, with its decision, thus, sent the message that threatening the Spanish national unity by a referendum is worse than killing and raping.)

The democratic character of the Catalan process to independence and the continuous support of this political aim by a majority of the Catalan people (to the extent that the pro-independence forces renewed their parliamentary majority both in the elections held on December 21, 2017, and on February 14, 2021, with the threshold of more than 50 percent of the popular vote backing Catalonia's independence being surpassed in the latter) was no concern for the European Union authorities. The territorial integrity of one of its members was at stake. The European Commission and the European Council only considered that the Catalan challenge in organizing a referendum violated the Spanish Constitution (such as the Spanish Constitutional Court interpreted the clause of the "indissolubility union of the Spanish Nation" provided by article 2 of that text) and consequently they decided not to be involved in the Spanish Catalan crises in spite of the fact that other values of the European Union, such as human rights and democracy itself, were threatened by the Spanish government reaction. Article 4.2 of the Treaty on the European Union urged "to respect" the territorial integrity of a state had been fully applied, and the Catalan question was officially considered at the supranational level a mere Spanish "internal" matter.

XI

The European Union Treaty, and particularly the indifference of the European authorities towards majoritarian secessionist movements endorsed by an interpretation of article 4.2 TEU, undermined, thus, the right of the people's self-determination (and more precisely the right of the European ones) as announced by Wilson at the end of World War I. Also contradicted is the idea of the people's self-determination enshrined in the United Nations law, and, specifically, as interpreted by the International Court of Justice when such body stated, ironically regarding a former territory of Spain, Western Sahara, that the right of self-determination "requires a free and genuine expression of the will of the peoples concerned" (which would include the right of that people to be consulted on "their political future").[52] The Catalan people, at least from the Spanish Constitutional Court ruling on the Catalan Statute amendment in 2010, is not more a people able to freely decide on its political status because considering such claim may cripple the real principle that inspired the creation of the European Union: the preservation at any cost of the member states' European "mainland."

European Union authorities and its member states' governments turned a cold shoulder to the Catalan secessionist claims when they burst out in October 2017, though they were expressed through a referendum, by pacific means, and with the endorsement of the overall majority of a democratically elected parliament. However, the point still not completely clarified is if the European Union authorities would allow the repression exercised by the Spanish state apparatus against Catalan secessionism to the degree of endangering basic human rights and democratic values theoretically recognized to all the European citizens (including, thus, the Catalans).

In the beginning, the European Union consented the crushing of the Catalan people's "free and genuine expression of its will" by the Spanish authorities. For instance, when two electoral candidatures to the European Parliament spearheaded by the former Catalan president, Carles Puigdemont, and the former Catalan vice president, Oriol Junqueras, gathered between them more than two million votes on May 26, 2019, they were not granted access to the seat in the parliament from the moment of their election. Since they were in exile or in prison, they were not allowed to implement the requirements established by Spanish electoral regulations in order to obtain the credentials as euro parliamentarians. Spanish authorities argued that Puigdemont, Junqueras, and the other Catalan leaders involved in the electoral process had, among other formalities, to swear an oath to the Spanish Constitution in front of the electoral administrative body even though those were elections to the European Parliament in which any European citizen from any other nationality may concur in Spain. The European Parliament supported in the first stance the Spanish's authorities' position and the parliamentarian condition of Puigdemont, Junqueras (and that of a third Catalan pro-independence politician elected to the European Chamber, Antoni Comín) *was denied* in the summer of 2019. The momentary outcome of such developments was that more than two million voters did not enjoy representation in the supposed stronghold of democratic values, the European Parliament, an abnormality never seen since the establishment of the elections to the chamber in 1979.

Such a trend of blindly supporting the abuses of the Spanish judiciary, nevertheless, was likely to change with the ruling rendered by the Court of Justice of the European Union (CJEU) on December 19, 2019, concerning a question raised by the Spanish supreme court on the scope of the parliamentary immunity of the former vice president of the Catalan government, Oriol Junqueras. Oriol Junqueras at the time of the European Court's ruling had been sentenced to a thirteen-year term of imprisonment and declared out of office, but when he had been elected to the European Chamber he was being judged and he had been maintained in provisional detention.[53]

The European Court concluded that Junqueras enjoyed immunity from the moment that the results of the elections were declared and that the Spanish supreme court would have had to authorize his release in order to accomplish his parliamentarian function and eventually asked the European Parliament to waive immunity. Even though the Spanish supreme court did not release Junqueras because it considered that the European court ruling was not applicable once he had been sentenced, the European court considerations benefited the other two former members of the Catalan government that were in exile and that had been elected members of the European Parliament: Puigdemont and Comín (together with Clara Ponsatí who as a consequence of Brexit and the extension of the number of members of parliament [MPs] from other states to occupy the seats left by the British also joined the chamber on February 2020). The European Parliament immediately changed the previous decision on banning their access to the status of members of the parliament and delivered the credentials to Catalan pro-independence candidates. However, the Spanish supreme court did not release Oriol Junqueras from prison since it considered that he was already convicted by the judgment issued on October 14, 2019 (a few months before the European Court of Justice decision) and the punishment of disqualification for office that the judgement provided together with the thirteen-year term of imprisonment had already canceled the parliamentary immunity. From the European Parliament it was argued that the chamber could not interfere on the concerned state's judiciary interpretation of the European Court of Justice execution of its rulings and accepted that Junqueras lose his condition as a parliamentarian, as dictated by the Spanish supreme court.

In March 2021, in a different vein, the majority of the European Parliament accepted to lift the immunity of Puigdemont, Comín, and Ponsatí at the Spanish supreme court's request in order to proceed with the European arrest warrant that the Spanish authorities issued to Belgium where Puigdemont and Comín resided (they did the same to Scotland where Ponsatí had gone into exile). Though irregularities tarnished the procedure to waive the immunities of the Catalan members of parliament (such as the lack of impartiality of both the president of the parliamentarian commission on legal affairs and the speaker of the report who already had shown a fierce opposition against the Catalan cause) and the relevant number of MPs opposed the measure (to the extent that never before the request for authorization to trial parliamentarians had gathered such a number of votes against, 248, in the mentioned chamber) most of the members of the biggest groups present in the European Parliament around the conservative, liberal, and social democrat families aligned themselves with the lukewarm position of their national governments on the Catalan question.

The maintenance of Spain's territorial integrity, regarding to which all the national governments saw a safeguard for their own national integrity, became not only a basic political principle to maintain European Union stability but also a raison d'état for all its members. In the alluded context, the attitude of the German Liberals, Christian Democrats, or some Social Democrats was particularly significant; they voted to lift Puigdemont's and the other Catalan separatists' parliamentary immunities in spite of the fact that the German tribunals themselves had refused to extradite Puigdemont to the Spanish judiciary on the similar charges on which the Spanish supreme court had grounded the request to authorize the MPs trialing before the European Parliament.[54] In contrast to the traditional commitment of the German representatives with international law, the German MPs in the

European Parliament that supported the Spanish judiciary intention to waive Puigdemont and others' immunity also refused to recognize the relevance of the United Nations bodies' opinions concerning human rights guarantees in which it was appreciated that the detention of some of the Catalan leaders in prison had been arbitrary and that they had to be immediately liberated.[55] By authorizing to proceed with the arrest warrants against the Catalan politicians, most of the German parliamentarians (as the rest of their colleagues that supported the request of the Spanish judiciary) accepted the possibility to send parliamentarians, elected with more than one million votes, to a judicial system that was limiting human rights, according to the United Nations. No wonder that (the following episode took place before the European Parliament vote on Puigdemont's immunity) Russian's foreign affairs minister, Sergei Lavrov, during a meeting in February 2021 with the EU High Representative Josep Borrell (a Catalan but nonetheless vehemently opposed to the Catalan pro-independence movement) of having "double standards" in assessing the courts decisions' accordance with human rights and the rule of law. While the EU High Representative went to Russia to claim for the release of the Russian opposition leader Alexei Navalny, the Russian Minister for Foreign Affairs Lavrov cited the case of the Catalan pro-independence leaders as examples of politically motivated court decisions within the European Union space that disguise the resolutions of international bodies such as the United Nations Human Rights Committee or the United Nations Working Group on Arbitrary Detention.[56]

On the other hand, envisaging that some backlashes from the Spanish judiciary against the Catalan pro-independence movement were not compatible with the liberal democratic consensus within the European space, the Parliamentary Assembly of the Council of Europe passed in June 2021 by an overwhelming majority of votes a report elaborated under the leadership of the representative Boriss Cilevičs examining the prosecution displayed both by Spain and Turkey against politicians for statements made in the exercise of their mandate. In the mentioned report, the Parliamentary Assembly of the Council of Europe invited the Spanish authorities, among other questions, to release from prison the Catalan politicians convicted for their role in the organization of the October 2017 referendum and the related peaceful mass demonstrations, to drop extradition proceedings against Catalan politicians living abroad (three of them covered by immunity as EU parliament members), to drop the prosecutions of the lower-ranking officials involved in the 2017 referendum, and to refrain from requiring the Catalan politicians to disown their deeply held political opinions in exchange for a more favorable prison regime or a chance of pardon. The pardons, partially affecting the nine politicians that had been in prison as a consequence of the events in the fall of 2017, were issued by Pedro Sanchez's Spanish government the day after that

Cilevičs' report was adopted. But in spite of the fact that the alluded Catalan leaders were released from prison, the pardons were not extended to their disqualification from office.

In summer 2022, the United Nations Human Rights Committee found that Spain violated the political rights of former Catalan government and parliament members by suspending them from public duties prior to a conviction following the independence referendum in 2017. According to the committee, the decision of the Spanish judiciary to charge the applicants (the former vice president of Catalonia, Oriol Junqueras, and three former ministers, Raül Romeva, Josep Rull, and Jordi Turull) with the crime of rebellion, which led to their automatic suspension prior to a conviction, was not foreseeable and therefore not based on reasonable and objective grounds provided for by law. Such a suspension from public duties of the Catalan politicians, concluded the committee, violated article 25 of the International Covenant on Civil and Political Rights since it unreasonably restricted the right to be elected at genuine periodic elections.[57]

Another assertive resolution on the Catalan case emphasizing the harsh repression of the Spanish authorities against the Catalan pro-independence movement from the United Nations Human Rights Committee was that concerning the suspension of the former Catalan president, Carles Puigdemont from his public duties rendered on May 15, 2023.[58] According to the United Nations Human Rights Committee, the Spanish supreme court's decision to suspend Carles Puigdemont once he was in a position to renew his presidential mandate through the pro-independence parliamentarian majority resulting from the December 23, 2017, elections violated Puigdemont's right to political participation, which is "the essence of democratic government."

The United Nations Human Rights Committee remarked the bar of "reasonableness and objectivity" that represented suspending a MEP (member of the European Parliament) on "the bases of public and peaceful" acts. Though European Union governments were reluctant to recognize the distortions on the democracy that the Spanish authorities' backlash as a response of the Catalan 2017 challenges represented, the United Nations bodies on human rights protections were clear in stating that deposing Catalan MEPs contradicted the will of the Catalan people freely expressed through the results of the elections.

XII

Despite the fears that an eventual Spanish territorial collapse aroused within European political instances, the Catalan exile in Belgium, most of whose members also became MPs in the European Parliament, obtained relevant endorsements for their cause in the judicial instances.

The parliamentarian immunity of the three Catalan exiled MPs, the former Catalan president, Carles Puigdemont, Antoni Comín, and Clara Ponsatí was provisionally reestablished by May 2022 since the Court of Justice of the European Union considered that they had the risk of being detained, as happened to Puigdemont when he traveled to Sardinia for a conference in September 2021.[59] That resolution of May 2022 annulled a previous order of the General Court of the EU that had dismissed precautionary measures for the three politicians while the merits of their appeal against the decision of the European Parliament to accept the requests issued by the Spanish judiciary in order to lift the parliamentarian immunity was reviewed.

On January 31, 2023, the Court of Justice of the European Union issued a ruling on Lluís Puig Gordi, former Catalan minister of culture exiled in Belgium since October 2017, that would also have implications to the rest of the Catalan exile based in the mentioned country targeted by the European arrest warrants issued by the Spanish judiciary (including again the former Catalan president Carles Puigdemont, Antoni Comín, and Clara Ponsatí).[60] In August 2020, the Brussels Court of first instance determined there would be a risk of human rights violation should Lluís Puig be sent back to Spain and refused the surrender. This was confirmed by the indictment chamber in January 2021. In turn, the Spanish supreme court introduced a preliminary ruling request to the CJEU challenging the Belgian refusal. In its January 31 decision, the CJEU eventually sided with the Spanish supreme court and ruled that cooperation should prevail. It nevertheless left the door open for national courts to refuse to execute future European arrest warrants in the Catalan case, as these courts have consistently done so far.[61]

With that ruling, the CJEU essentially performed a balancing act slightly softening its traditionally strong pro-cooperation approach. While it recalled the importance of mutual trust that underpins the European arrest warrant scheme, and the need to apply that device in a unified manner, it also underlined the necessity to respect fundamental rights in the application of the European arrest warrant. More specifically, the court noted that, in principle, no additional grounds for refusal can be added by national courts. However, the court also stated that European Union member states can, in exceptional circumstances, refuse execution of a European arrest warrant to ensure respect for the requested person's fundamental rights focusing especially on the issue of right to a fair trial before an independent and impartial tribunal previously established by law. In the *Puig* ruling, the court recounted its two-step approach developed in previous rulings to determine whether the requested person was at a real risk of human rights violations. But, in the Puig case, beyond the possibility of refusing a European arrest warrant by giving account of systemic and generalized deficiencies in the member state that issues the order, the Court of Justice of the European Union outlined the possibility for the national courts to refuse to execute a European arrest warrant when those deficiencies affect "an objectively identifiable group of persons to which the person concerned belongs."[62]

The CJEU is, in short, creating a new standard in order to appreciate systemic human rights violation against a national minority within a member-state, a member-state that, differently as happens regarding other jurisdictions besieged by democratic and rule-of-law general flaws, may reasonably work as a constitutional democracy except when one issue is concerned: when a sub-state national minority challenges its territorial integrity.

Decisions at European judicial level combined with resolutions stating human rights violations against a national minority both at the Council of Europe level and at the United Nations' bodies level may have relevant consequences for Spanish national sovereignty. Basically, they might question if Catalans have the government resulting from their free will expressed within a democratic framework, or if the current Spanish democratic status is unable to ensure such a correspondence between the Catalan people's will and their political status. In other words, the question is if the right to self-determination, disregarding the definition that is conferred to such expression in international law,[63] is respected in the case of Catalonia. If not, if even belonging to a space grounded on human rights, democracy, and rule of law, as the EU is supposed to be, such principles are violated, the possibility to claim the exercise of the right to self-determination for that sub-state European nation might remain open.

XIII

The Catalan case is relevant to my remarks since it has been transformed into one of the main battlefields within the union among the zeal of the states to preserve their national unity at any cost and with the coverage of the supranational institutions and the concern of preserving the supposed founding values of the EU as proclaimed in article 2 of the Treaty on European Union: the respect for human dignity, freedom, democracy, equality, the rule of law, and respect for human rights, *including the rights of persons belonging to minorities.*

The doubt is how long may the European Union be resisted as an organization grounded on such values having in its heart a place wherein a political community cannot decide by democratic means in which political form its people want to be organized. The real purpose of the states that created the European Communities (or later integrated as the European Union) relied on entrenching themselves as nations without risking the continental peace, but it will be intriguing to know how the European Union may endorse the nationalistic aspirations of its member states without sacrificing such peace.

While the dilemma shall be confined within Spain (being the Catalans or the Basques) European Union authorities and their member states' governments may adopt a cynical gesture and turn a blind eye to Spanish repression without concern for how harsh it is, an attitude that has been prevalent among the European institutions at least until the mentioned ruling of the Court of Justice of the European Union on December 2019 concerning the scope of the European immunity of the former Catalan vice president imprisoned by the Spanish judiciary.

But if the conflict between the maintenance of member states' privileges in relation to nations and national minorities stretches everywhere else in the continent and is accompanied in abolishing democratic decision-making procedures in some territories and by encroaching human rights able to discriminate *among* European citizens, the danger will fall upon the very essence of the European Union and it may precipitate its end. After all, the Spanish treatment toward Catalan secessionism resembles that with which the former empires treated the inhabitants of their overseas possessions but since such dominions have been mostly vanished for Spain and for most of the other European member states, the Catalan crisis has emerged as an experiment regarding to what extent a European nation-state could apply *imperial politics* within its "mainland" borders to its *own* citizens.

In short, with the Catalan-Spanish confrontation we have witnessed the first example in the twenty-first century of deployment of imperialism by *a European state toward European citizens*, something achieved with the tacit consent of the European Union institutions, let alone the consent of the other European member states' governments.

XIV

The authoritarian turn experienced in Poland or Hungary have shown that neither the European institutions nor the governments of the states that compose the organization have been really willing to take effective actions to prevent the crises of the democratic and liberal values concerning one of the member states. But the Catalan challenge has even made clear that the encroachment of democracy and human rights is not even denounced by the agents of the European governance when the territorial integrity of one of the European state-nations is at stake.

At least, regarding Poland or Hungary, the Commission had frequently denounced violations to the rule of law, to the division of powers, or to human rights supposedly perpetrated by Hungarian *Fidesz* agents or by *Law and Justice*'s Polish leaders and even occasionally it had threatened to begin the procedure entailed in article 7 of the Treaty of the European Union by which the rights deriving from the application of the European treaties may be suspended to that member state responsible for "a serious and persistent breach of the values referred to in article 2 of the Treaty on the European Union." No similar statements have been pronounced, however, by European institutions concerning Spain even though in its prisons there are Catalan leaders, even according to some United Nations bodies, punished as a consequence of their political ideology.

The axiological architecture that justified the foundation of the union entailed in article 2 of the Treaty on the European Union surrenders before the struggle to avoid the national disintegration of one of the former empires. The fall of a European power, even in the case of a middling power such as Spain, might represent such a great deal of political and economic changes that it might lead the union into complete disarray. In order to imagine the impact that Catalan secession would have for the European system, we only need, for example, to think of the economic consequences that would represent the loss of a region that contributes almost 19 percent of Spanish gross domestic product (GDP) for a state that in 2021 owed more than 1,360 billion euros, most of them to private or public European lenders. Obviously, those European powers that have exercised what I call "a capitalist occupation" over Spain, beginning with German lenders, would not show any interest at all in allowing the constitution of a new sovereign entity that would put at risk the loans that they had been granted and that from the secession of a region onward (in the absence of an agreement that is not likely to happen in case of a unilateral independence) should be paid by the rump state.

A similar chaos might be predicted, in the case of Catalonia's independence, regarding the bond purchasing programs that for almost a decade the European Central Bank has executed, which have enabled the financial sustainability of the Spanish sovereign bonds and the superseding of the euro crises. Spain's bankruptcy as a consequence of the rupture of a region that, on the other hand, represents more than 2 percent of the European Union GDP (comparable to that of Greece), might drag other member states into a spiral of financial crashes and would probably threaten the survival of the euro itself. Watched through the lens of such dangers it appears as less surprising the lack of enthusiasm of the German European MPs in defending the parliamentary immunity of their Catalan pro-independence colleagues, or the persistent silence of the Commission on the Spanish abuses against a national minority (which, on the other hand, should have been protected according to the European treaties as well as the allusion to such groups in article 2 of the Treaty on the European Union left somewhat clear).

European postwar history has revealed that the European powers had in the end agreed to withdraw from most of their former overseas possessions, but they are capable of bringing the European project of liberty to ruin if they see the European core of their national being menaced by the exercise of the votes and the rights that the union supposedly proclaimed to defend. The Catalan process expressed the European Union's contradictions, and those of the "nostalgic empires" that formed the association, at their peak and contributed to the loss of legitimacy before other superpowers who do not need to appeal to democratic values in order to ensure their internal cohesion. The silent consent of the European Union institutions on the repression of the Catalan pro-independence citizenry and political representatives by the Spanish authorities demonstrates not only that there is not a common European concept of citizenry but also that there are privileged European citizens, those belonging to a demos constituted in a nation-state, able to triumph over national minorities. In other words, the European Union confers full coverage to those nations that have formed a state in order to punish with impunity other national groups that inhabit within the same state.

By affirming that secessionist claims from a European member state are an "internal affair," even when human rights are clearly violated, European Union authorities are expressing that they renounce to act as a supranational organization able to shape a common political space. If integration does not come at least through the equal recognition of human rights to the whole European citizenry that means that there is indeed no project at all able to tie together the different European peoples and that the path for progressive disintegration is probably open.

If we revisit, on the other hand, the vicissitudes that led to the recognition of the European citizenry in the 1992 Treaty on the European Union concluded in Maastricht, we will realize that such a European citizenry has been always conceived as attached to the citizenry of the nation-states in a way that, as the Catalan process has revealed, if the claim is precisely grounded on shaping a new state and, consequently, to forge a new citizenry detached from the citizenry of the rump state, it is likely that such a national group loses all the liberties that until that moment had been recognized to them as Europeans.[64]

The point here, however, is that the collapse of the European system of rights regarding a particular national group does not take place once such community has reached full independence (by considering, for instance, that the separation from a member state is tantamount to a break up with the European membership) but that the rights of a national minority *qua* Europeans may be suspended and infringed without qualms by the central state *during the process* developed by the national minority to found a new state. Put differently, a national minority within a European member state may see the fundamental rights of its members protected as Europeans only as long as they do not question their condition of nationals of that member state.

Catalans can only be Europeans in terms of rights as long as they do not question their condition as Spanish nationals. But when the Catalans focus their political struggle in being Europeans *as Catalan nationals* then the Spanish authorities have free rein to treat them as if the system of human rights provided for the European citizens would not be applicable to them. From the point of view of civil liberties, thus, the Catalans that support the ideal of Catalonia's independence *are not Europeans* as may be inferred from the silence that the Spanish abuses displayed during the Catalan process have deserved among the European authorities.

If Europe had some opportunity to build a sense of identity able to transcend national identities, that was the ideal of human rights. Indeed, according to some specialists on human rights history such as Samuel Moyn, the circumstance that the human rights movement catalyzed by the middle of the 1970s was partially due to the European struggle to search for a common identity outside the Cold War terms.[65] The phenomenon was also fueled those years when western European politicians, journalists, or intellectuals (even those that had embraced socialist ideals in the past) began to receive the Soviet and other eastern European dissidents fleeing from communist dictatorships and, consequently, losing their trust in achieving any tangible welfare through the performance of real socialist regimes.

But if you have political prisoners in the heart of western Europe as happened with the Catalan pro-independence leaders[66] and you let one of the European nation-states crush the human rights of the members of a sub-estate *European* nation, the whole construction of a common identity supposedly integrated by defending a scope of liberties for *all* the European citizens begins to totter. And lacking identity also means lacking a common political horizon and, at the end of the day, lacking political sense.

European institutional acquiescence in the obliteration of the human rights of European citizenry as a consequence of a nationalistic fight erodes one of the main pillars upon which Europe could have built its future after the age of the Empires. Probably, the conflict between Catalonia and Spain might be read as a sort of sequel of decolonization processes but developed within the "mainland" of a European nation-state, Spain, which, perhaps not casually, was also, given several historical reasons (the early loss of the bulk of its overseas colonies, the internal conflicts such as the so-called Spanish Civil War solved through an authoritarian pattern, the Spanish lack of involvement in both of the twentieth-century global confrontations) the least nationally and socially cohesive and the least egalitarian of the former western European empires.[67]

Hard contradictions within the European Union in its approach to the crises that affect the nation-states, and particularly the "nostalgic empires," that composed it may indeed represent the previous stage of instability and disintegration both at the national and supranational level as was envisaged in the developments that surrounded Brexit that we shall analyze in the next chapter.

NOTES

1. See Adam Tooze, *The Deluge: The Great War, America, and the Remaking of the Global Order, 1916–1931* (New York: Penguin Books, 2014), 108–15.
2. See Vladimir Ilyich Lenin, "The Right of Nations to Self-Determination," in *Lenin's Collected Works. Vol 20. December 1913–August 1914* (Moscow: Progress Publishers, 1972). First published 1914.
3. Erez Manela, *The Wilsonian Moment: Self-Determination and the International Origins of Anticolonial Nationalism* (Oxford and New York: Oxford University Press, 2007), 19–53.
4. See Pau Bossacoma Busquets, *Morality and Legality of Secession: A Theory of National Self-Determination* (Cham: Palgrave Macmillan, 2020), 153–54.
5. Antonio Cassese, *Self-Determination of Peoples: A Legal Reappraisal* (Cambridge: Cambridge University Press, 1995), 19.
6. Norman Gordon Levin, *Woodrow Wilson and World Politics: America's Response to War and Revolution* (New York: Oxford University Press), 247.
7. Tooze, *The Deluge*, 120.
8. Quoted by Inis Lothair Claude, *National Minorities: An International Problem* (Cambridge: Harvard University Press), 81.
9. Mark Mazower, *Dark Continent. Europe's Twentieth Century* (New York: Vintage Books, 2000), 51–64. First edition 1998.
10. See Bossacoma Busquets, *Morality and Legality of Secession*, 165.
11. Quoted in Mazower, *Dark Continent*, 56.
12. Tooze, *The Deluge*, 108–115.
13. Stephen Hartley, *The Irish Question as a Problem in British Foreign Policy, 1914–1918* (New York: Palgrave Macmillan, 1987), 178.
14. Luke McDonagh, "Losing Ireland, Losing the Empire: Dominion Status and the Irish Constitutions of 1922 and 1937," *International Journal of Constitutional Law* 17, no. 4 (October 2019): 1192–1212.
15. Hartley, *The Irish Question*, 172 and 191.
16. To such a list it could be added Malta's independence from Britain in 1964, which would indeed be more adjusted to the pattern of exercising the right to the self-determination than the Irish and the Icelandic precedents. But in spite of the fact that the Maltese archipelago is situated in the middle of the Mediterranean Sea (in an area, thus, that would well be qualified as "Western Europe"), its secession was

rather developed in the midst of the decolonization processes that affected some of the former British overseas' dominions in the second half of the twentieth century.

17. Churchill's statement is mentioned by Edward R. Stettinius, *Roosevelt and the Russians—The Yalta Conference* (Garden City: Doubleday & Company, 1949), 244.

18. Mark Mazower, *Hitler's Empire: Nazi Rule in Occupied Europe* (London and New York: Penguin, 2008), 109.

19. Bossacoma Busquets, *Morality and Legality of Secession*, 159–67.

20. International Court of Justice Advisory Opinion of June 21, 1971, *Legal Consequences for States of the Continued Presence of South Africa in Namibia (South Western Africa) Notwithstanding Security Council Resolution 276 (1970)*; International Court of Justice Advisory Opinion of October 16, 1975, *Western Sahara*; International Court of Justice Judgement of June 30, 1995, *Case Concerning East Timor (Portugal v. Australia)*; International Court of Justice Advisory Opinion of July 9, 2004, *Legal Consequences of the Construction of a Wall in the Occupied Palestinian Territory*; International Court of Justice Advisory Opinion of July 22, 2010, *Accordance with International Law of the Unilateral Declaration of Independence in Respect of Kosovo*.

21. See International Court of Justice Advisory Opinion of July 22, 2010, *Accordance with International Law of the Unilateral Declaration of Independence in Respect of Kosovo*, para. 83.

22. Bossacoma Busquets, *Morality and Legality of Secession*, 162.

23. Ian Kershaw, *Roller-Coaster: Europe 1950–2017* (London: Allen Lane/Penguin Books, 2018), 42–43.

24. Elizabeth Buettner, *Europe after Empire: Decolonization, Society, and Culture* (Cambridge: Cambridge University Press, 2016), 190–210. See also Ricardo Ferraz, "The Financial Costs of the Portuguese Colonial War, 1961–1974: Analysis and Applied Study," *Revista de Historia Económica/Journal of Iberian and Latin American History*, October 20, 2021. Available at https://cambridge.org/core/journals/revista-de-historia-economica-journal-of-iberian-and-latin-american-economic-history/article/abs/financial-costs-of-the-portuguese-colonial-war-19611974-analysis-and-applied-study/31B3C7ADFAAB352A4D4EBAF0BFB7E3CA.

25. Tony Judt, *Postwar. A History of Europe Since 1945* (London: Penguin Books, 2005), 512–13.

26. Mark Mazower, *Governing the World. The History of an Idea* (London: Allen Lane, 2012), 252.

27. See International Court of Justice June 30, 1995, *Case concerning East Timor (Portugal v. Australia)*.

28. Norrie McQueen, "Portugal. Decolonization without Agency," in *The Oxford Handbook of the Ends of Empire*, eds. Martin Thomas and Andrew S. Thompson (Oxford: Oxford University Press, 2018), 174.

29. António Costa Pinto and Nuno Severiano Teixeira, "From Africa to Europe: Portugal and Europe Integration," in *Southern Europe and the Making of the European Union, 1945–1980s*, eds. António Costa Pinto and Nuno Severiano Teixeira (Boulder, CO, and New York: Social Science Monographs and Columbia University Press, 2002), 3–40.

30. António de Figueiredo, "The Empire Is Dead, Long Live the EU," in *The Last Empire: Thirty Years of Portuguese Decolonization*, eds. Stewart Lloyd-Jones and António Costa Pinto (Bristol and Portland, OR: Intellect, 2003), 127.

31. Buettner, *Europe after Empire*, 209.

32. On such Spanish colonial enclaves see Josep Maria Fradera, *Colonias para después de un imperi*. (Barcelona: Edicions Bellaterra, 2005).

33. See, among many other works on Spanish colonialism over Morocco, María Rosa de Madariaga Álvarez-Prida, *Marruecos, ese gran desconocido: Breve historia del protectorado español* (Madrid: Alianza, 2013).

34. Carme Molinero and Pere Ysàs, *El règim franquista. Feixisme, modernització i consens* (Vic: Eumo, 1997), 10.

35. Gemma Torres Delgado, *La virilitat d'Espanya a l'Àfrica: Nació i masculinitat al colonialisme al Marroc (1880–1927)* (Catarroja: Editorial Afers, 2020).

36. See Juan B. Vilar, "Franquismo y descolonización española en África," *Historia Contemporánea* 30 (2005); 129–58, 146.

37. See Gonzalo Álvarez Chillida and Rosa M. Pardo Sanz, "La independencia de Guinea Ecuatorial: El hundimiento de un proyecto neocolonial (Septiembre de 1968 a Mayo de 1969)" *Hispania* 82, no.270 (January–April 2022) 201–32.

38. See International Court of Justice Advisory Opinion of October 16, 1975, *Western Sahara*.

39. Fernando Guirao, *The European Rescue of the Franco Regime, 1950–1975* (Oxford: Oxford University Press, 2021), 13.

40. See Mark Mazower, *Dark Continent. Europe's Twentieth Century* (New York: Vintage Books, 2000), 329.

41. On the building and the evolution of the Spanish territorial organization through Autonomous Communities, see Eliseo Aja, *El Estado Autonómico: Federalismo y hechos diferenciales* (Madrid: Alianza, 1999).

42. Jordi Pujol, *Memòries (1930–1980)* (Barcelona: Proa, 2007), 318–19.

43. Bonifacio De la Cuadra and Soledad Gallego-Díaz, *Crónica Secreta de la Constitución* (Madrid: Tecnos, 1989), 42–45.

44. Xavier Casals, *La Transición Española: El voto ignorado de las armas* (Barcelona: Pasado y Presente, 2016), 435–57.

45. Such a list of Non-Self-Governing Territories is available at https://www.un.org/dppa/decolonization/en/nsgt.

46. Cristina Hermida del Llano, "Reflexiones sobre el Tratado por el que se instituye una Constitución para Europa," *Anuario de Filosofía del Derecho* 21 (2004): 287–312, 296.

47. Jean-Claude Piris, "La Unión Europea, Cataluña y Escocia (cuestiones jurídicas sobre recientes tendencias secesionistas en los Estados Miembros)," *Teoría y realidad Constitucional* 37 (2016): 101–34, 111.

48. Spanish Constitutional Court Decision 31/2010 of June 28, 2010.

49. On the Catalan 2006 statute approval process and the 2010 Spanish Constitutional Court Ruling, see Hèctor López Bofill, "The Limits of Constitutionalism: Politics, Economics, and Secessionism in Catalonia (2006–2013)," in *Constitutionalism*

and the Politics of Accommodation in Multinational Democracies, ed. Jaime Lluch (Houndmills: Palgrave Macmillan, 2014), 70–85.

50. Jordi Muñoz and Raül Tormos, "Identitat o càlculs instrumentals? Anàlisi dels factors explicatius de suport a la independència," *Papers de Treball Centre d'Estudis d'Opinió*, April 2012. Available at https://ceo.gencat.cat/web/.content/30_estudis/03_publicacions/Papers_treball/2012_04_04_papers_treball_identitat2.pdf.

51. On this process, see Hèctor López Bofill, "Hubris, Constitutionalism, and 'the Indissoluble Unity of the Spanish Nation': The Repression of Catalan Secessionist Referenda in Spanish Constitutional Law," *International Journal of Constitutional Law* 17, no.3 (July 2019): 943–69.

52. International Court of Justice Advisory Opinion of October 16, 1975, *Western Sahara*, para 55 *in fine* and para 64. See Antonio Cassese, *Self-Determination of Peoples: A Legal Reappraisal* (Cambridge: Cambridge University Press, 1995), 128; and James Crawford, "Self-Determination of Peoples. A Legal Reappraisal. By Antonio Cassese," *American Journal of International Law* 90, no. 2 (April, 1996) 331–33, 331. See also United Nations Assembly Resolution 1541 (XV) of December 14, 1960, Principle IX.

53. Case 502/19, *Junqueras Vies* [2019] ECR.

54. Schleswig-Holstein High Court, Aus(A) 18/18 (20/18) (July 12, 2018).

55. See, for instance Opinion 6/2019 (Spain) adopted by the Working Group on Arbitrary Detention at its 84th session A/HRC/WGAD/2019/6.

56. See "Russia Cites Catalan Independence Issue after EU Demands Navalny's Release," Catalan News, February 5, 2021, https://www.catalannews.com/politics/item/russia-cites-catalan-independence-issue-after-eu-demands-navalny-s-release.

57. See decision of the United Nations Human Rights Committee regarding the Communication No. 3297/2019, CCPR/C/135/D/3297/2019 adopted on July 12 2022.

58. Decision of the United Nations Human Rights Committee regarding the Communication No. 3165/2018, adopted on May 15, 2023.

59. Order of the Vice-President of the European Court of Justice, May 24, 2022, in Case C-629/21 P(R) *Puigdemont and Others v European Parliament*.

60. European Court of Justice Judgement January 31, 2023, Case 158/21, *Puigdemont and Others* [2023] ECR.

61. See Sibel Top, "Explosive Case: Cautious Ruling: The CJUE Prudently Favors Cooperation in the Puig Case," *EJIL: Talk! Blog of the European Journal of International Law*, February 20, 2023. Available at https://www.ejiltalk.org/explosive-case-cautious-ruling-the-cjeu-prudently-favours-cooperation-in-the-puig-case/.

62. Case 158/21, *Puigdemont and Others* [2023] ECR (*para.* 102).

63. I have explored the applicability of the right to self-determination in its external dimension to Catalonia under international law parameters in Hèctor López Bofill, "Catalonia: The Right to Self-Determination and the Consent of the Governed," in *Constitutional Law and the Politics of Secession*, ed. Antoni Abat Ninet (London and New York: Routledge, 2023).

64. Joseph Weiler, *The Constitution of Europe: 'Do the New Clothes have an Emperor?' and Other Essays on European Integration* (Cambridge: Cambridge University Press, 1999), 324.

65. Samuel Moyn, *The Last Utopia. Human Rights in History* (Cambridge and London: The Belknap Press of Harvard University Press, 2010), 8.

66. See "Criminal or Martyr? Prisoner Poses a Political Dilemma for Spain," *The New York Times*, May 4, 2021. Available at https://www.nytimes.com/2021/05/04/world/europe/spain-catalonia-independence-prisoner.html.

67. See Michael Albertus and Victor Menaldo, *Authoritarianism and the Elite Origins of Democracy* (Cambridge: Cambridge University Press, 2018), 7.

Chapter 2

The Split of the Metropolis

I

The Catalans, citizens of a peripheral nation in Spain, were not aware enough of the consequences of breaching European integration's foundational agreement grounded in the principle "giving up the overseas empire in exchange for armoring the mainland." But in the case that the rule is unknown not by the periphery but by the center, by the main nation constituted in a state, then the price to pay might be well the disintegration of that state. In the present, the implosion of a metropolis is represented, as it has been recognized by many analysts by the process of political fragmentation concerning the United Kingdom as a result of Brexit.[1]

Somehow, Brexit reopened the Pandora's Box of the ancestral and recurrent clashes between the Anglo-Saxon world and what has been called "the Celtic periphery" of the British Islands.[2] The voters that backed the withdrawal of the United Kingdom from the European Union in June 2016 probably did not know much about how the United Kingdom acceded to said organization. If the Brexiteers had turned their gaze upon the origins of their state's integration into Europe, they would have realized that it was accomplished while the United Kingdom was facing up to the most serious challenge affecting its "mainland" territorial integrity since the establishment of the Irish Free State, namely, the so-called Northern Ireland Troubles.[3]

Among other factors that traced the difference between the situation by the end of the 1960s and beginning of the 1970s and the one that erupted in the aftermath of World War I, it might be underscored that in the south part of the Irish island, Britain still preserved the empire while during the Northern Ireland Troubles most of the empire's former territories had already created their own sovereign entities. It is probably not causal that the Northern Irish question reignited (and something similar might be observed, as we shall see, regarding the reemergence of Scottish nationalism) at a time in which the United Kingdom overseas' possessions had been dismantled through the process of decolonization. As we have pointed out in previous chapters concerning Belgium, Portugal, or Spain, it is when the resorts of the external domination fail that the *metropole* turns into the discussions around the coexistence of its own internal national minorities.

Indeed, the United Kingdom had by the 1970s lost the bulk of its colonies and dominions in more or less convulsive procedures.[4] The Middle East mandates (including Palestine and the fierce conflict that the British withdrawal supposed in that region) India, Pakistan, Burma, the possessions in the Malay Peninsula, Egypt, Sudan, enormous extensions of territories in both west and east Africa and so on—everything was gone—and while enormous pieces of territories were being divided from the motherland, the British institutions still thought that they could cope with the situation without the aid of any other power.

Great Britain consented in detaching most of such large areas that constituted its overseas empire because direct dominion on them was not profitable.[5] To withdraw from the formal rule upon such countries while maintaining devices to ensure that British corporations would still trade with the new independent states (and would retain privileged access to the natural resources found within those territories) made more economic sense. In most cases it was, thus, cheaper both to make business and to have political influence through local elites than exercising direct rule and, eventually, to finance a coercive power able to fight against the rebellions triggered by the movements for national emancipation. "Territorial occupation" would be replaced by a more efficient "capitalist occupation."

Such economic considerations were particularly relevant for an old European power that was exhausted after coping with two world wars in forty years. But one thing had been faraway African or Asian possessions, and the other thing was a piece of land close to Great Britain in which a substantial part of the population had strong identity ties with the national center of that state. Northern Ireland was different, and any economic consideration would not mitigate the trauma of leaving loyal British citizens at the mercy of a Republican and Catholic majority within a unified island.

II

It has been controversial to specify from the perspective of historians why Great Britain was not involved in the European integration project from the outset. A thesis developed by Milward argued that British national strategy saw few advantages in focusing its economic relations in western Europe during the immediate postwar given both that the British assets were largely extra-European and that commonwealth markets still played a predominant role in the British tariff preference policy.[6]

British economic postwar policy was, on the other hand, aligned with that of the United States with the aim of creating a one-world economic system through the Bretton Woods agreements framework. The extensive British armed forces, their ability to build and deploy nuclear weapons, and the special military alliance again with the United States developed within NATO also gave few incentives for the United Kingdom to wage for a European common policy within the security field.

Such geopolitical and economic parameters made Winston Churchill encourage the European states to forge a European Federation but to *refuse* that the United Kingdom should become an integral part of it.[7] For Churchill the priority of Britain's policy was the commonwealth and then the "English-speaking world" (within which the United States was paramount but also encompassing Canada and other dominions).[8] Western Europe only figured in the third place of what should be, according to Churchill, British economic and military interests. Ironically, the Brexit vote in the 2016 referendum, apart from a chauvinist fundamental aversion to European supranationality, was motivated by the idea that the former privileged system of trade developed within both the commonwealth and the former empire territories could be regained in order to compensate the loss caused by the divorce with the European Union.

The British Empire's decline experienced by the end of the 1950s as a result of the empire's disintegration nonetheless forced a reconsideration of Churchill's vision that, in another sense, had been also shared by Labour politicians until then. The Macmillan government launched Britain's first application to join the European Economic Community only in 1961, propelled by shifts in British trade toward advanced industrial European markets and away from primary commodity-producing economies of the commonwealth. But this first membership application would meet the same fate as the second: the reluctance of General De Gaulle in allowing Britain's integration in the European project and the consequent French veto to Britain's adhesion (so, it is not surprising that when De Gaulle left office in April 1969, the prospects of widening the European Community to include the United Kingdom improved sharply).[9]

But it was the British internal crisis, and particularly, the territorial crises and the sense of weakness that overshadowed British politics from the end of the 1960s (combined with the unexpected election victory in June 1970 of the Europhile conservative Edward Heath) the main factor that explained the interest of the British society in belonging to the club that had been formed on the other side of the English Channel.

After all, among the Western countries that grew higher economically between the 1950s and the 1960s, Britain recorded the least remarkable outcome in comparison with its continental competitors.[10] While West Germany rates rose at high levels, Britain, losing its empire and handicapped in terms of economic efficiency given the outdated methods of production, the country's huge debts and scarce investment, declined. Economic problems linked to the separation of the outer colonies threatened the harmony in the inner empire. That was the moment to look at Europe in order not to make war (as had been usual) but to trade, to grow, and, in that way, to ensure the unity of the British nation-state.

III

Showing some similarities with the events developed in French Algeria, the crises caused by secessions concerned the heart of the British nation-state when, from 1968, problems spread within a territory considered a part of the metropolitan area: the Six Northern Counties of Ireland inhabited by a majority of British Protestants.

After four decades of relative peace from the partition of the island, the conflict between Northern Ireland Republican Catholics and Protestant Loyalists communities escalated. The end of the 1960s saw many episodes of violence, with hundreds of deaths.

As every summer, in August 1969 the loyalist order known as the "Apprentice Boys" organized a parade in Derry to commemorate the failure of King James II's Catholic forces in their attempt to take the town when in 1688 a group of thirteen apprentices shut the gates (such an event was considered crucial by the Protestant community to frustrate Derry's siege, which would finally be concluded in August 1689). Usually, the parade participants finished the celebration climbing the walls and launching pennies upon the streets and houses of Bogside, the Catholic suburb that laid below.

But in 1969 the provocation did not go unanswered, and fierce rioting broke out when the Catholics hurled stones, nails, and marbles fired by slingshot. As the battle reached a critical point, in which the unionist police forces were also involved fighting against Bogside Republican residents, British prime minister Harold Wilson took the decision to deploy the British army in Derry in a movement that would represent the first direct intervention of the London government in Ireland since the Republic's independence.

The British military presence, in the beginning conceived to act as a neutral force to come between both fighting communities, only made things worse. The Irish Republican Army reorganized with the split into the "Provisional" and the "Official" factions in a way that the "Provisional" one embarked itself in an armed struggle to defend the Catholic community against the British forces.

Following the killing of a British soldier in February 1971, the British government introduced internment without trial, a movement that radicalized still more of the Catholic community since they perceived that they had been flagrantly discriminated against in the authorities' struggle to restore order (all of the more than three hundred initial detainees were Catholics). As it was described by the European Court of Human Rights in dealing with a complaint lodged by the Republic of Ireland against the United Kingdom in which the massive human rights violations in Northern Ireland were denounced, what happened in Northern Ireland was in fact a latent civil war between the Protestant and Catholic communities.[11]

Violence, nevertheless, reached one of its peaks when on January 30, 1972, the British 1st Battalion Parachute Regiment killed thirteen unarmed civilians and injured more than fourteen who were marching peacefully in what was known as "Bloody Sunday." The point that I would like to observe here is that such an orgy of murders happened only seven days after the British prime minister Edward Heath signed the accession treaty to the then European Communities (on January 22, 1972) and just at the beginning of a dark year of fights that left 146 members of the security forces and 321 civilians killed.[12] Among other compelling causes, the United Kingdom needed integration into a supranational organization as a proxy to contain a confrontation in Northern Ireland that was evolving savagely against British interests.

When from 2003 the wave of eastern European countries coming from former communist regimes began to enter the European Union, they had previously been required to respect a criterion concerning human rights that the United Kingdom certainly had not fulfilled in 1972 when it was accepted among the European club. Brutal as it might sound, it was indeed when Edward Heath's government consented to delve deep into a human rights crisis in Northern Ireland in order to maintain the state's territorial integrity that the United Kingdom was welcomed by its European peers.

IV

Europe had been on the background of the Northern Irish conflict's explosion and would be again somehow present in its pacification. Unlike the Algerian case, however, in which given the recent foundation of the European Communities no direct involvement of European instances was perceived, the role of the European institutions was more active in the Northern Irish question, at least from the point of view of "back door" diplomacy.

As has been admitted by different actors, the European Union membership of both the Republic of Ireland and the United Kingdom facilitated the design of the agreement.[13] George Mitchell, for instance, a United States senator who performed as a mediator in the forging of the agreement stated, almost twenty years after the deal was concluded and on occasion of the Brexit negotiations, that the European Union played a part in thawing relations between the Republic of Ireland and the United Kingdom, which enabled the Northern Ireland peace process.[14] Literally, Mitchell, whose participation in the matter also shows the prominent patronage of the United States in fostering Northern Ireland peace under the Bill Clinton administration, declared, "I don't think the European Union was essential in the [Good Friday Agreement] talks themselves, but I believe the talks would never have occurred had there not been a European Union."

The European Union provided a coverage by which the political status of the post-conflict Northern Ireland would not be so controversial; given the European Union common membership an agreement on a single space of free movement of people, goods, and capital in the contested territory (as well as the recognition of an equal status and consideration for inhabitants in Northern Ireland regardless of their national identity or their religion) might be possible to broker.

As we have seen, in spite of the scarce recognition of the right to self-determination within a Western European context, the Good Friday Agreement became one of the rare examples that referred to a European "metropolitan" territory in which such a right was explicitly admitted.[15] But some reasons to justify such an exception might be found; after all, if we had defined the European project as an endeavor to strengthen the member states as nation-states within a common continental framework, it may be concluded that the 1998 agreement ensured benefits for both the United Kingdom and the Republic of Ireland, actual benefits for the United Kingdom in terms of pacification and potential benefits for the Republic of Ireland in the case that an Irish national majority expressed their will to join the Republic, a reunification which, at any rate, would happen within the same area of economic relations and equality of rights established by the European Union.

V

The Northern Irish question reignited, however, when the national center of the United Kingdom decided to break with the European Union. In the 2016 referendum the British, and particularly the English among whom the option for withdrawal clearly won, exercised *their right* to self-determination and their right to unilaterally secede from the European Union without being aware that such gesture may put the United Kingdom metropolitan unity at risk. Notice, in this vein, that whereas a sub-state region is deprived of any right to secede from the perspective of both domestic and international law, according to article 50 of the Treaty on European Union (TEU), a member state may unilaterally withdraw from that organization without an agreement and following only their constitutional rules.[16] Brexit is a good example of that point; even though article 50 of the Treaty on European Union provides a procedure to reach an agreement establishing an ordered withdrawal from the union, leaving such an organization may be effective if no agreement is reached and may only depend upon the will of the member states' sovereign institutions as was on the verge of happening when British prime minister Boris Johnson played with the possibility of breaking up without a deal (a detail that demonstrates that in spite of any cosmopolitan and globalized discourse, from the legal point of view sovereignty is still located within the states and, specifically, within the constitutional rules regulating such states).

At any rate, the 56 percent of the 2016 Brexit referendum voters in Northern Ireland opted for Remain. Surveys suggested that 85 percent of Catholics voted Remain compared with 40 percent of Protestants, and 88 percent of those identifying themselves as nationalists voted Remain, compared with only 34 percent of those identifying as unionists.[17] Such a majority of Remain votes was likely to understand that the withdrawal from the European Union may threaten the advantages that European freedoms (such as the free movement of people, goods, and capital within the island of Ireland) have provided to the peace process, stability, and reconciliation.

The fear was more intense as soon as the British government made it clear that, in the words of the prime minister of that time, Theresa May, "Brexit means Brexit" and, consequently, leaving the EU meant leaving both the EU single market and the Customs Union as well. However, perhaps aware of what the reappearance of a hard border dividing the island of Ireland might represent, Theresa May, while seeking the EU-UK deal in 2018, opted to leave things concerning the application of EU regulations in Northern Ireland basically untouched, at least during the transitional period with the possibility of extending the particular status of the territory even beyond.

Avoiding a hard border dividing the island that remembered the conflict and militarization of "The Troubles" was an aim at any cost to be reached because, as we have explained, Northern Irish citizens may always exercise the right to self-determination recognized to them by the 1998 Good Friday Agreement according to which any change in the constitutional status of Northern Ireland "can only be made with the consent of the majority of its people" placing a "binding obligation" on both the United Kingdom and Irish governments to respect and give effect to their decision.[18]

In spite of the struggle to balance all the interests in play, the draft on Brexit negotiated by Theresa May was overwhelmingly rejected in the House of Commons on of January 15, 2019. Such an episode was considered one of the most humiliating parliamentary defeats of a British government ever (which would only be the prelude of other parliamentary defeats suffered by May's government in the first half of 2019) and would reveal how entangled was the aim to make compatible the withdrawal from the union with domestic territorial and political stability.

One of the main factors responsible for May's parliamentary debacle was precisely the vote coming from the Northern Ireland Unionist MPs of the Democratic Unionist Party (DUP) which, albeit supporting the British government, rejected the prime minister's plan for withdrawal precisely because such a plan foresaw a "backstop" arrangement that would effectively place Northern Ireland under the scope of the European Union single market and Customs Union. The "backstop" solution was qualified by the Irish unionist leader, Arlene Foster, as a European Union "annexation" of Northern Ireland.[19] According to her, such an arrangement would not be temporary and would perpetuate the EU regime within the whole island.

No wonder, thus, that after parliamentary rejection of May's proposal the question of the Irish border represented one of the most burning issues of the Brexit agenda. The immediate reaction of the prime minister was to reopen the negotiations on Northern Ireland's status in order to gain the support of the DUP MPs and the hard-liner pro-Brexit *Tories*, who were terrified by the prospect that any part of the United Kingdom might remain within the European Customs Union.

May's struggle in breaking the Brexit deadlock included the possibility of replacing the backstop in Northern Ireland by *rewriting the 1998 Good Friday Agreement*,[20] a movement that represented an almost uncrossable line for the rest of political actors. The British nationalist hubris on the complete separation from the European Union was going to lead May's government to endanger the main device that had ensured peace in Northern Ireland during two decades. But instead of causing the collapse of the 1998 agreement, what collapsed was May's government itself. May's parliamentary weakness and the discords within the British government itself on the manner by which the prime minister had conducted the process paved the way for May's nemesis and her succession by Boris Johnson. Johnson, however, would also find in the Irish "backstop" a hard nut to crack.

Johnson's arrangement for Northern Ireland was indeed not substantially different from that proposed by May. The main change was provided by recognizing that *de jure* Northern Ireland remained within the United Kingdom (not the EU) Customs Union. But instead of threatening the Good Friday Agreement, Johnson sought political understanding with other figures involved in the peace process mentioned in the agreement, such as the Irish Taoiseach.

Resulting from conversations with the Irish Taoiseach, Leo Varadkar, it was emphasized that the differentiated treatment on the region concerning the application of EU law to keep the Irish border open could only be abandoned if the regional parliament would decide so (or if a future arrange supersedes it). Such proposal, consequently, took into account the right of self-determination of the Northern Irish people as provided in the Good Friday Agreement.[21] Despite the safeguards clinging from the Good Friday Agreement, the Irish border's remaining openness to traffic and trade and the new economic border between Britain and the European Union placed squarely in the Irish Sea earned the criticism of the Irish Unionist MPs of the DUP. The Irish unionists continued to suspect that leaving Northern Ireland open to cross-border traffic and trade with the Irish Republic (and, consequently with the European Union) would represent the first step to the political unification of the island and the permanent validity of EU law on Northern Ireland soil.

In the first instance, Johnson succeeded in passing the bill on the new agreement between Great Britain and the EU with the modifications on the Irish backstop but failed to fast-track a bill on the Agreements' approval before October 31, 2019, which had been announced by the prime minister as the deadline for achieving Brexit. However, Johnson called for general elections in December 2019, in which he obtained a resounding victory, and the Brexit bill was finally approved by the commons in January 2020.

The withdrawal of the United Kingdom from the European Union was finally consummated on January 31, 2020, though a transition period was in force until December 31, 2020, during which the United Kingdom remained in the European single market. Attached to the so-called Withdrawal Agreement, the special arrangement concerning the position of Northern Ireland was codified in the Protocol on Ireland/Northern Ireland, which entered into force once the transition period expired and began to be applied on January 1, 2021. Such a particular regime on Northern Ireland would be developed within the framework of the new relationship between the European Union and the United Kingdom traced in the European Union–United Kingdom Trade and Cooperation Agreement.

The principle of consent stemming from the Good Friday Agreement on deciding any change regarding the status of Northern Ireland evokes, thus, the main axis of the Northern Ireland Protocol to the extent that some of the commitments entailed in such provisions (as, for example, the *de iure* remaining of Northern Ireland in the United Kingdom customs territory while creating a *de facto* customs border in the Irish Sea) might be reviewed by a simple majority vote of the Northern Ireland Assembly at the end of the four years' initial period of the Protocol's application (article 18 of the Protocol on Ireland/Northern Ireland). That is, the vote of the Northern Ireland Assembly on the Protocol shall take place at least once before the end of 2024 and the United Kingdom has to provide the opportunity for democratic consent in the region for any subsequent period of the Protocol's application.

Though the agreement on the Northern Ireland Protocol might be qualified as "the best of both worlds" (that means the best opportunity for Northern Ireland in the context of both the Republic of Ireland's European membership and the United Kingdom's European membership abandonment), the truth is that the unique circumstances of a territory characterized by the "quantum" situation of being and not being in the European space at the same time is not experienced without tensions. Joseph Weiler would associate the final outcome reflected in the Northern Irish Protocol and the circumstance for the United Kingdom to having to deal with "a customs border run through its sovereign home territory" as an imposition that would resemble that of punished Germany with the Treaty of Versailles after World War I.[22] By the end of the "period of grace" bestowed upon traders and retailers in order to adapt themselves to the special customs regime created by the Protocol, in April 2021, a wave of violent riots expanded in several Northern Irish towns evoking, thus, the dark memories of the times that preceded the Good Friday Agreement. On the other hand, the prospects toward a Republican unification of the island increased once Sinn Féin obtained an overwhelming electoral victory in the elections to Northern Ireland's autonomous government in May 2022, changing the traditional balance of power in the region according to which the presidency of the government was exercised by the unionists and the vice presidency by the Irish nationalists. The majority gathered by Michelle O'Neill's option represented the opportunity for the very first time since the 1998 devolution for a Republican to access to the regional presidency and, probably, to advance toward the exercise of the Northern Irish self-determination by calling for a referendum concerning the political status of the territory. Nevertheless, months, and even years, went by with the Democratic Unionist Party blocking O'Neill's accession to preside the Northern Ireland regional government as would be expected for the political party that has won the elections. As it is constant, even in an old traditional democracy such as the one in the United Kingdom, regarding any movement from which a territorial disruption might occur, democracy is set aside without any big concerns. Something that would not be tolerated without a cataclysm at a "national" level, like jeopardizing access to office of those that have won elections, is treated with contempt regarding a "regional" government when the majority is won by those that threaten the unity of the state.

VI

Prime Minister Boris Johnson's response to the 2022 electoral victory of Sinn Féin and to the process of Northern Irish unionist minoritization (who in turn opted for blocking during months the constitution of a regionalist government) had profound consequences for Brexit's architecture and the relationship between the United Kingdom and the European Union once the withdrawal was consummated. The British government, backed by the conservative majority in the parliament, announced the possibility to unilaterally break up with that Northern Irish protocol that established a customs border in the Irish Sea. Such was a predictable movement by United Kingdom authorities in the path to gain independence from Europe and to elude as long as possible the domestic territorial consequences of the European divorce. After all, the United Kingdom had not won two world wars in order to tolerate a loss of control within its political borders through the configuration of different trade areas (and thus leaving Northern Ireland virtually inside the European single market). Facing up to the payment of the millions of euros in fines imposed by the European jurisdiction was a lesser evil (at least under the vision of the British political elites) than attending helpless to the fragmentation of the state.

After Liz Truss's brief and chaotic premiership, Rishi Sunak's government contributed to the pacification of several United Kingdom political and economic issues among which the brokering of a new deal on Northern Ireland with the European Union authorities in February 2023 occupied a prominent place. The so-called "Windsor Framework" essentially provided a special status for that territory in which checks over customs coming from the rest of the United Kingdom were reduced. The "Windsor Framework" envisaged two "lanes" for goods arriving in Northern Ireland from Great Britain: a green lane for goods that will remain in Northern Ireland and a red lane for goods that may be sent on to the European Union. On the green lane, product checks would not be displayed. Regarding the red line products, measures to reduce extra costs and delays as a consequence of the checks would be adopted. The idea was, according to Sunak, to confer on the region the unique advantage of frictionless trade with both the single market and with the rest of the United Kingdom, transforming Northern Ireland into one of the most "exciting" destinations for foreign investment.[23] On the other hand, the 2023 deal on Northern Ireland also emphasized the role of the Northern Ireland Assembly to object to any change of European law able to be applied in the region as a consequence of its special situation regarding the European single market. The so-called "Stormont break," though the threshold to introduce such an objection that the United Kingdom should convey to the European Union authorities in order not to implement the European Law rule in Northern Ireland, reflected in the track of the self-determination principles a special consideration toward the representatives of the Northern Irish people. The fierce opposition against the "Windsor Agreement" between the United Kingdom and the European Union on Northern Ireland coming from the Northern Irish Democratic Unionist Party and some dissidents among the conservative ranks did not jeopardize the approval of the agreement in the United Kingdom parliament.

At any rate, as we have seen, the normative framework both designed by the Good Friday Agreement and by the Northern Irish Protocol to Brexit reframed through the "Windsor Agreement" seemed devoted to ensuring that the Northern Irish population could decide on a reconfiguration of the Northern Irish constitutional status being within the Irish Republic or, in an opposite direction, within the United Kingdom. Another matter was that if such decision, which may eventually lead to a united Ireland or to a removal of the customs border in the Irish Sea, would be grounded on a consent "freely and concurrently given," or if they would rather be surrounded by pressures able to undermine the fairness, transparency, and deliberation supposedly attributed to any democratic process.

Encroaching the normative framework agreed to by the European authorities did not nonetheless look like the most respectful resolution to not only the "free will" of the Northern Irish people but also the principle of the rule of law. In the latter case, as happened in the Johnson/Truss era, the shortcomings of enforcing international law when one part feels confident enough to fail in respecting the commitments without consequences became also evident.

The Northern Irish question within the context of Brexit and the Protocol affecting such a territory reveal, in sum, the quantum of free political participation and the adscription to international commitments that a liberal democracy might bear if their authorities do not wish to see the political unity that they defend at the stake.

VII

The decade of the 1970s was horrendous for the United Kingdom. Besides the peaks of bloodbaths experienced as a consequence of the Northern Irish crisis, the British had to cope with an economic crash, partially derived from the global oil shock and the American decision to modify the international monetary system, but to a large extent rooted in local causes.

Balibar identifies in the crisis unchained by the beginning of the 1970s (to which he adds the consequences of the cultural transformations provided by the 1968 revolts) a process of structural change in the developments of

European integration that would be, among other issues, expressed in the 1973 first European Communities' enlargement with the entry of the United Kingdom, Ireland, and Denmark to the group.[24] The economic constraints that were hovering over the United Kingdom in such a context were particularly acute and extended themselves well beyond the UK accession to the European supranational organization: the lack of industrial modernization and the lack of investment caused inefficiency that could only be dealt with by drastic measures leading to high unemployment rates.

The United States' decision to let the dollar off the gold standard in order to finance the Vietnam War and, afterward, the Organization of Petroleum Exporting Countries (OPEC) crises that led to the combination of inflation with slow growth, had had devastating consequences for the British balance of payments and for sterling's stability.

By 1975, the year in which the United Kingdom European Communities membership referendum was held, the UK inflation rate was 24.24 percent. After Harold Wilson's unexpected resignation in March 1976, a bitter leadership struggle pitted the Labour left-wing against the more moderate cadres in which the new prime minister, James Callaghan, was ascribed. The leftists in the cabinet pushed toward increased protectionism, exchange controls, and domestic reflation even if this meant moving against the powerful City of London.[25] Such a situation was unsustainable; around this time government spending was out of control as public expenditure soared to 46 percent of gross domestic product (GDP). Investors became convinced that the pound was overvalued and that the government might devalue. A large-scale sale of sterling began, which rapidly lost value against the dollar. In spite of further efforts to reduce inflation, the pound continued to lose value, reaching a record low against the dollar in June 1976. The United States treasury secretary agreed with officials in the International Bank of Settlements that the pound was undervalued. He offered to partially fund a stand-by loan of $5.3 billion to support the pound. He insisted, however, on repayment of the loan by December 1976. Proposals for further cuts in expenditure and tax increases to reduce the budget deficit were debated in cabinet in July. By September 1976, Britain had already drawn heavily on the short-term loan, and it was apparent that a loan from the International Monetary Fund (IMF) would be necessary to fund repayment.

As pressure on the pound continued, the government approached the International Monetary Fund for a loan of $3.9 billion in September 1976. This was the largest amount ever requested of the fund at that time, which needed to seek additional funds from the United States and Germany.[26] The IMF negotiators demanded heavy cuts in public expenditure and the budget deficit as a precondition for the loan. Callaghan and his Chancellor of the Exchequer Denis Healey acceded and Labour's left-wing representatives in the cabinet capitulated. The defeat for the British left, the unions, and the British working class led, in fact, to the capitalist reconstruction not only in the United Kingdom but also in the West under the form of neoliberalism refusing the postwar social corporatism.[27]

VIII

Also, the loss of the overseas empire, as we saw falling into pieces in the decades of the 1950s and the 1960s, had its economic impact from the end of the sixties and besieged the British economy in the seventies. The metropolis had lost uncountable resources in the form of markets and sources of raw material extractions (as, for instance, the extraction of oil in the Persian Gulf when the British left territories that had been under their protectorate); and the finding of additional sources nearer Great Britain (as was the case of North Sea oil), did nothing but boost Scottish nationalism, which began to demand a political recognition that would allow the Scottish population to enjoy the revenues provided by the black gold. The overseas empire was being extinguished while the other nations within the metropolis arose by pacific means (as the Scots) or by violent means (as the Republican Catholics in Northern Ireland).

The Scottish question was precisely the issue that pushed the Callaghan government into the abyss when the devolution powers to a Scottish Assembly provided by the 1978 Scottish Act were repealed in a referendum.[28] Callaghan, given the disaster in Scotland and the background of the strikes against his economic policy crossing the country in the winter 1978–1979, was challenged by a motion of no confidence that he finally lost, leading to the general elections of May 1979, with a landslide won by the Conservative Margaret Thatcher. But Thatcher's promises of economic growth through her liberalization program were far from being accomplished during the first years of her administration. Although inflation fell, unemployment rose over three million while the inefficient British manufacturing industry was being dismantled.

However, with Thatcher's government besieged by the meager economic results of her policy and by the violence unleashed in Northern Ireland, something came to rescue her: the Argentinian invasion in April 1982 of the disputed Falkland Islands, in the south Atlantic. Thatcher, refusing to submit to Argentinian aggression, led Britain to war and sent troops that successfully retook the Falklands. In the age of the extinction of overseas empires, the United Kingdom engaged itself in an old-fashioned imperialistic conflict that allowed it, among other things, to mute domestic problems.[29]

The fact that Thatcher's government was fighting against the authoritarian Argentine military regime provides legitimacy to her adventure, but such episode also shows that the former empires would be allowed to embark upon colonial-style expeditions reminiscent of other ages in order to entrench the political cohesion within the metropolis, including, as in Northern Ireland, the internal national cohesion toward the claims posed by minority nations.

The Falklands war baffled much of European public opinion, but the European Communities, as was foreseeable, did nothing to avoid Thatcher's struggle to restore Britain's national pride after years of depression. After all, the European integration project had been conceived to make the European nation-states great again.

IX

Prime Minister David Cameron called for the referendum that led to Brexit in 2016 because he had previously attempted a successful experiment of that sort: the referendum on Scottish independence held on September 18, 2014.

The prime minister thought that he could convince a majority of the British citizens to remain in the European Union as he had persuaded a majority of Scottish ones that opted to remain in the United Kingdom. Unfortunately for those that wished to maintain the status quo, the continuity of the economic crises in the Eurozone's southern members (which pushed lots of workers from those countries to go to Britain in search of an employer) together with the fear of the avalanche of refugees fleeing from the war in Syria, dissuaded most of the voters that Cameron needed to support the continuity of the United Kingdom within the supranational organization.[30]

Things had gone differently a couple of years before Brexit regarding the Scottish question. Indeed, the 2014 referendum, agreed between David Cameron and Alex Salmond in the terms of the so called "Edinburgh Agreement" of October 15, 2012, was able to strengthen the union since it represented the democratic evidence that the Scottish people were part of that political community because they wanted to be. The right of the people's self-determination had been exercised giving to Great Britain the rare honor within the European Union of managing the question of the state's sovereignty in a democratic way. The Scottish, thus, in spite of predictions based on the latest polls, on September 18, 2014, voted against independence (55 percent against, 45 percent who voted for separation). Stability triumphed.[31]

However, in the wake of the Scottish decision, it could already be discerned, despite miscalculations made in respect of the issue, that *the rest of the Union's citizenry* would *also* like to vote in order to "freely decide on its political status," and that such a political decision concerning all the British on the belonging or not to the European Union would foster the emergence of internal divisions grounded in national identities. As we mentioned, England (joined by Wales) voted convincingly for Brexit in the June 2016 referendum, while Scotland recorded the highest Remain vote (62 percent) of the four United Kingdom constituent territories.[32]

In an analogous way to Winston Churchill doing his best to win the war against the Axis and to retain the British possessions overseas, David Cameron thought it possible to entrench the agreement with the European Union through the Brexit referendum in order to make stronger the ties between the different parts of the United Kingdom. As happened to Churchill, however, the final result of the contest on Europe led to the internal split (the empire splitting from 1945 onward while the threat of a split in the "metropolis" began in 2016).

Only hours after knowing the Brexit referendum outcome, the Scottish first minister Nicola Sturgeon, leader of the Scottish National Party (SNP), suggested the possibility of holding a second referendum on Scotland's independence. Such an initiative looked like it would count on the support of the European Union authorities as was shown by the immediate meeting that was organized shortly after the Brexit referendum between Sturgeon and the president of the EU Commission, Jean-Claude Juncker.

However, if Scottish nationalism refrained in the Brexit referendum aftermath from its intentions of celebrating a new secessionist vote, it was because their electoral results in the 2017 United Kingdom general elections (although the SNP maintained its position as the third-largest party in the House of Commons) were modest. The SNP decline in the 2017 elections was partially due to the fact that the Labour Party, led by Jeremy Corbyn, regained some of the support that had benefited such a political force until the question of sovereignty began to dominate the Scottish political agenda through the SNP hegemony by the first decade of the twenty-first century. Scotland's independence struggle was likely to lose priority both in Sturgeon's and the SNP's discourse expecting which would be the final status of the United Kingdom when Brexit would be fulfilled. But shortly after, in the same way that May's parliamentary defeat on her 2018 agreement proposal precipitated the crisis on the Irish border, it soon also encouraged the claim for a second referendum on Scottish independence.

In fact, even a few days before the parliamentary vote on May's Brexit plan, and foreseeing its collapse, Nicola Sturgeon announced that she would not let Scotland be dragged out from the European Union against its will and that as soon as the first phase of the Brexit process were concluded she would explain her preferred timetable for organizing the new popular consultation on secession. Though Sturgeon admitted that the Scottish National Party would join the campaign for another referendum across the UK to stop Brexit (an idea which at that time circulated among the circles of the British political opposition), she began to work with the aim to organize a second referendum on Scottish independence aside from the Brexit developments.[33]

In April 2019 Sturgeon announced before the Scottish legislature that the second referendum on independence should be held by 2021; but in that year the world was still fighting with the COVID-19 crisis, and the adoption of such a decision on sovereignty had to wait.[34] Instead, what took place in May 2021 were new elections to the Scottish Parliament, which were overwhelmingly won again by the Scottish National Party, only two seats short of the absolute majority that would be reached with the support of another pro-independence force: the Scottish Greens. In sum, pro-independence options resulting from the 2021 elections gathered 72 seats from 129 and more than 50 percent of the popular vote. As soon as she knew the electoral outcome, Sturgeon insisted in pushing ahead with the draft of the second referendum bill. It was not clear, however, if the United Kingdom government would allow a vote on Scotland's secession again.

X

Already in the general elections of December 2019, when the Scottish National Party, differently as what had happened in the 2017 general elections, obtained a remarkable result (by gaining 8 seats and entrenching with 48 seats its third position in the House), and Sturgeon had seen in her party's success a renewed call for a second independence referendum, Boris Johnson expressed his opposition by arguing that the question had already been concluded at least for a generation after the pro-independence option defeat in 2014.

During the 2021 campaign for the Scottish Parliament elections, the British prime minister argued additionally that in times of pandemic it would be "irresponsible" and "reckless" to be still speaking on a new Scottish secessionist vote.[35] When later the pandemic subsided by summer 2022, Boris Johnson's successor, Liz Truss, in the wake of her appointment, was even more defiant against the Scottish initiative by stating that there would be no second independence referendum on her watch.[36] According to Truss, the Scottish Independence Referendum Bill was not legal and would be invalidated if passed by the Scottish Parliament, since when Westminster devolved power to Scotland, it did not include "the ability to hold valid referenda to break up the Union." However, the Scottish demand for a second independence referendum was still vigorous, while Liz Truss's mandate became the most ephemeral among the ones performed by any British prime minister given the economic chaos in which her economic plan on reducing taxes for the highest incomes sunk the union by October 2022. Brexit would still undermine the governability of the United Kingdom, both from the territorial dimension and the economic dimension, for a long time.

In order to tackle the negative response to a second independence referendum expressed by the United Kingdom's successive Conservative governments, Scottish authorities referred the question on the powers held by the Scottish Parliament regarding the ability to organize referenda to the United Kingdom Supreme Court. Somehow, the path resembled at that point the developments experienced by the Catalan demands on a deciding vote regarding the region's political status, only that in the Scotland–United Kingdom dispute, given the refusal of the central authorities to agree with a referendum, it was not the judiciary that intervened on the United Kingdom's government request to repress any secessionist movement (as happened in Spain) but the initiative departed from Scotland with the perspective to ascertain if the Scottish Parliament had the authority to go ahead with a referendum on sovereignty disregarding the United Kingdom's authorities opposition. The question was, to summarize, if Scotland retained some original powers according to the United Kingdom constitutional system including that of deciding on its political status.

The answer that the court provided was nonetheless negative.[37] According to the Supreme Court, holding a referendum on the question of whether the union between Scotland and England should be terminated was of the utmost importance for the whole Kingdom.[38] From that reasoning, as appreciating that the whole Kingdom would be affected by the Scottish Parliament initiative, the court concluded that issuing a bill regulating such a referendum by the Scottish Parliament would go beyond the scope of the powers recognized through the 1998 devolution.[39] Such a conclusion would not be changed by the fact that the proposed bill on the Scottish independence referendum would organize an advisory consultation since the mere expression on the view of the electorate on that issue, which on the other hand would be displayed on a formal and official character, would have decisive political consequences relating to the European Union and the United Kingdom Parliament.[40]

The Supreme Court did not estimate either the additional arguments in favor to recognize the Scottish Parliament powers on issuing a bill on the Scottish independence referendum provided by the Scottish National Party regarding the right to self-determination in international law.[41] In the same fashion as the Canadian Supreme Court did in assessing the recognition of an eventual right of the Quebec to secede unilaterally,[42] the British Court stated that the self-determination of the Scottish people was respected through the internal arrangements promoted in a system of devolution founded on the principle of subsidiarity.[43] According to the United Kingdom Supreme Court, the Scottish situation was far from being comparable with that regarding colonialism or foreign occupation that was described by the International Court of Justice to ground the right to create an independent state through the right of self-determination under international law.[44] Keeping some analogies with the considerations that the Spanish Constitutional Court developed regarding the Catalan initiative to hold a consultation on independence, the United Kingdom Supreme Court solution would be also arguable on its reasoning concerning the right to self-determination in its external dimension. Indeed, it is difficult to see to what extent a people can freely decide on its political status (as the International Court of Justice defined the right to self-determination)[45] if it cannot hold a referendum on the matter of sovereignty without the consent of the representatives of *other* people.

In sum, the Supreme Court judgment on the Scottish independence referendum bill represented an additional example of the profound hostility that the central instances of the former western European empires show when there emerges the possibility to lose control upon a territory considered part of the metropole. Among the political resonances of the Supreme Court judgment and the legal stalemate on the Scottish question that it represented might be remarked Nicola Sturgeon's resignation as Scotland's first minister in February 2023, perhaps unable to push for a secessionist response despite the broad democratic support her government had.

Though Sturgeon's successor, Humza Yousaf, once appointed, stated that the path to independence remained open, months passed by without detailing which process would be adopted. The new Scottish leadership was likely to retake Sturgeon's idea of a "de facto referendum," counting the votes to the Scottish National Party in a regular election as a vote for independence. Already the Catalan regional elections in 2015, which were presented by the pro-independence supporters as a kind of plebiscite on the secession matter, showed however the shortcomings of this kind of strategy particularly if the center, as predictably would occur in Great Britain as happened in Spain, refuses to consider the consequences of a vote for secession in parliamentary elections (let alone that parliamentary elections make it difficult to discern if the citizenry vote for the territorial question or also vote for a given party because of other issues).

In any process of independence, confronting the opposition of the center, even while obtaining clear parliamentary majorities, is not enough to progress toward full sovereignty. Central authorities make indeed democracy irrelevant when questioning the territorial integrity of the state. If there are no majorities supporting the pro-independence side, then secessionism lacks legitimacy (as happened by the Scottish pro-independence defeat in the wake of 2014 referendum). If the pro-independence movement is likely to win, then the central authorities block any democratic initiative to make such a majority visible. Secessionism, the change of regime that represents the creation of a new sovereign entity, relies on factors that go far beyond the outcome of fair elections.

XI

In the context of continuous crises following the Brexit vote and the effective withdrawal from the European Union, the English response to any Scottish unilateral movement was not likely to be handled in the same gentle terms as were received the proposals that led to the referendum in 2014.

Adam Tomkins, a Tory member of the Scottish Parliament and law professor at University of Glasgow, wrote a column for *The Spectator* just before the 2021 Scottish regional elections in which he argued that the Spanish example in repressing Catalan pro-independence movement might inspire the United Kingdom government in its attempts to quell demands for a new Scottish plebiscite.[46]

Indeed, a United Kingdom out of the political and economic European structures would find enormous difficulties to overcome Scotland's departure. Brexit triggered the democratic struggle for independence within United Kingdom's constituent nations but, at the same time, it instigated the center, and particularly England through the British institutions, to impede Scottish independence (or the unification of Ireland) as a matter of life and death.

Within the European Union, Scottish independence would not have had the same consequences for the rump United Kingdom, especially if the new sovereign Scotland had joined the European Union within a reasonably brief time. Goods, capitals, and people would circulate under the same vault within the island and between the island and the continent. What's more, following the tacit principle according to which European integration works as a safeguard against secessions from "mainland" European Union members, the United Kingdom would have counted with the support of the EU authorities in discouraging the peoples of the British constituencies to leave (as, in fact, they did during the days that preceded the 2014 Scottish referendum on independence when the president of the European Commission, Jose Manuel Barroso, went to help David Cameron and stated that joining the EU would be "extremely difficult" for an independent Scotland).[47]

But the situation would presumably be harder to manage for Britain if, to the political and economic shrinkage derived from Brexit, had to be added the shrinkage left by Scottish independence and the Northern Irish detachment reducing, thus, the United Kingdom to England and to some appendix like Wales (in which pro-independence positions were also soaring, though more slowly).

England's perspectives would probably be tough in a world where the departure of the "interior colonies" would not be compensated by the return of any of the former "external" ones. Colonies and dominions of the previous centuries, to begin with the United States, would probably have no incentives to establish a privileged political and economic relationship with a tiny part of an old empire. In the turmoil of the Brexit crisis, while the May government was agonizing and replaced by Boris Johnson (and the British establishment of the whole political spectrum had no idea about how to get out of the mess), Sturgeon's proposal on holding a second independence referendum was received with indifference. It would be nonetheless rare that English nationalism would passively accept the separation of a territory that would confirm the irrelevance of an entity that once possessed 23.9 percent of the world's land surface[48] and, indeed, Johnson's successors more aggressive tone against the Scottish consultation, as much as the United Kingdom Supreme Court reference on the Scottish bill regulating an independence referendum, confirmed such a different approach within the British central institutions regarding secessionist ambitions.

XII

Without Scotland and without Northern Ireland, there would arise some doubts on the continuity of the "United Kingdom" itself as the same international law subject. The "United Kingdom of Great Britain and Northern Ireland" would not probably be the same state without "Northern Ireland" nor the "northern part of Great Britain," let alone the numerous issues that would have to be negotiated such as (in a similar fashion as what happened during the Soviet Union's extinction) which subject would hold the seat in the United Nations Security Council (associated to the veto power regarding the adoption of resolutions within that body) or which subject would retain the arsenal of nuclear weapons.

Whatever would happen, any secessionist process from the United Kingdom would be developed in a sphere *not covered* by the European Union. In that case the main thesis of this essay could thus be maintained, namely, that the European Union works shoulder to shoulder with its nation-states members to avoid any secession within their borders. However, when the secession takes place within a state that has asserted its will of divorcing from the union (as Britain did) the European instances cancel their commitment on protecting such state's unity and leave its political establishment to its fate.

As Brexit loomed on the night of January 31, 2020, the European Commission building in Brussels appeared illuminated with a huge message in which it could be read "Scotland loves Europe" (or "Europe loves Scotland" depending on the line that you began to read). The Scottish first minister Nicola Sturgeon, on Twitter, interpreted from that message that the European Union Commission "appears to have left a light on" for Scotland.[49] Although later it was discussed if "Europe loves Scotland" (or vice versa) was or was not an operation that had been paid for by the Scottish National Party, such circumstance does not detract from the point that in order to illuminate the European Commission building in Brussels, you have to count at least some complicities among the European Union officials.

In conclusion, in the case that Scottish independence would be materialized that experience would occur *outside* the European Union. It would not be a matter of a territory that once belonged to the union that after secession from a member state is menaced with the suspension of European freedoms (as occurred in Catalonia or in pre-Brexit Scotland). Post-Brexit, Scottish secession would be a matter of the previous secession of a member state from the European Union that paves the way for the emancipation of non-statehood nations. If things would evolve in that direction, the Brexit referendum, from the perspective of defending the integral territory of the existing state, would be appreciated by the historians as a singular case in which the turkeys had submissively voted for Christmas.

XIII

Against all predictions, however, the United Kingdom reacted relatively well by the first challenge that it faced as a split-off entity from the European Union: the COVID-19 crisis.

Though by the first months of the shock in spring 2020, Boris Johnson's government's management of the pandemic was catastrophic, as in many other parts of the world (underestimating the threat to health or trying not to jeopardize economic activity by naturally reaching herd immunity), the fact that the most advanced developments of the COVID-19 vaccine in terms of manufacturing and supply were located in Britain set the United Kingdom among those states with the highest vaccination rates globally (the British population vaccination rates by the first months of the vaccination campaign in 2021 were only comparable to those of one of the most promising new powers of the time: Israel).

In contrast, the European Union made its endemic crisis more acute by a disastrous organization of the vaccine distribution. European continental actors were incapable of producing their own vaccine in the first stages of the fight against the virus and, what was worse, the centralization of powers assumed by Brussels in order to supply the vaccine among the member states was shown to be inefficient and tarnished by corruption scandals and delays.

The plurality of confronted national interests within the European Union blocked the performance of the European Union authorities regarding the challenge to health systems. Some of the member states' governments, given such conditions, began to purchase and to develop their vaccination campaigns outside the channels provided by the European Commission (which in some case included the purchasing of the vaccine from geopolitical adversaries such as Russia).

In summary, the British success concerning the vaccination against COVID-19 and the superseding of the social and economic consequences of the pandemic vis-à-vis the European Union's failure reaffirmed the British political mainstream, and even a part of the British citizenry that had voted for Remain, in the right decision that leaving the European Union had represented.

Through the fight against COVID-19, the United Kingdom rediscovered its condition as a great power in a global context, whereas the European Union was wiped off the map. In technology for creating the vaccine and ensuring its supply, Britain placed itself again at the same level as, or even higher than, the big ones: the United States or China. The nostalgia for the reemergence of the former empire that had induced many British people, and particularly many English people, to vote for Brexit in 2016 was less "nostalgic" and more "real" by defeating the virus and reassuming normality. British national confidence, even despite Boris Johnson's political disarray and scandals, increased somewhat.

In economic dynamism and military terms post-Brexit United Kingdom, aside from occasional declines, had produced more relevant outcomes than the remaining European Union countries. When analyzing some data comparing the United Kingdom and the European Union the former emerged as the leader, with a wedge that continued to widen. Germany, Spain, and the Netherlands had, for instance, two cities each among the Europe's top 20, the United Kingdom had five and some rankings considered London the world's top city.[50] The capital invested in London was almost three times as much as that of the next placed city within Europe, which was Berlin.

Brexit was also good for high-tech companies, especially high-tech service providers, because the United Kingdom was able to give itself a tailor-made regulatory system for such a new industry. This required deviations from the European Union regulation in several fields, including data protection. The United Kingdom, on the other hand, benefited massively from the presence of the City of London, and from the financial technological sector as an important source of technical innovation.[51]

Post-Brexit United Kingdom also reasserted itself as a military power. It participated in the frontline regarding the two geopolitical hot spots recorded by the beginning of the 2020s: China's besieging of Taiwan and the Russian invasion of Ukraine. In the Pacific, Britain joined the United States and Australia in forging a new military alliance (AUKUS) in order to enable Australia to gain access to nuclear-powered submarine technology with the intention of preventing China's expansion in the region. In eastern Europe, the United Kingdom provided armament to the Ukrainian authorities within the framework of a firm military policy that contrasted with the hesitating support to that country shown by other European NATO partners and particularly by Germany.

XIV

Nevertheless, with the same speed in which it seemed that the United Kingdom reassumed some kind of new splendor in overcoming the challenges posed by the pandemic, it fell, just few months later, into a profound decadence. By the fall of 2022, coinciding with the time in which Queen Elisabeth II passed away, the incumbent prime minister of that time, Liz Truss, led Britain to an economic nightmare in which the worst fears around Brexit, in terms of public indebtedness, inflation, labor shortage, and problems in the supply chains, were reignited. Such a crisis, even with an occasional British military or technological resurrection within the global sphere, was not likely to be the best scenario to contain the centripetal tendencies derived from the British internal national plurality.

Aside from the Irish context, much more defined in its traditional relations with Britain through structures of harsh domination, the possibility to participate in a worldwide empire had contributed to tame Scottish nationalism and helped to tie it to a common unitary enterprise.[52] No wonder, in that sense, that the decadence of the British empire (that, as we have seen, in the 1960s and the 1970s of the twentieth century coincided with the raising of the British interest to join the European Communities) overlapped with the Scottish demands for home rule, first, and for fully fledged independence, later.

As long as the United Kingdom moved within liberal coordinates to deal with nationalisms, retaining the different peoples within the union would rely on the attractiveness of belonging to a wider polity associated with a successful "postmodern" reformulation of the British Empire. Such possibility would not even be incompatible with a kind of confederation resulting from Scotland's accession to full sovereignty or Irish reunification (both movements developed within the global system determined by the Anglosphere that would include some other commonwealth territories and would hold strong ties with the United States or even with India). The possibilities of consolidation of such a revisited British empire would, furthermore, depend on the progressive shipwreck of the European Union that would, for instance, make the Scots lose any interest in joining a project lacking in enthusiasm or future. It was not very clear which was the national horizon envisaged by those British citizens that voted for Brexit in 2016; but, at any rate, the withdrawal of the United Kingdom from the European Union on January 31, 2020, unsettled the assumptions of the European integration narrative and raised crucial questions on the *finalité* of the European Union project.[53] Indeed, it was quite hard to see, within the context posed by the British decision to leave, how a process could be reached of "ever closer Union" if one of its more powerful members opted to break ties with the rest.

However, the liberal premise in dealing with the sub-state territorial claims by the British central powers was precisely what was at stake once the union experienced the biggest drop in living standards on record sending British earnings in 2023 back to the levels of 2013.[54] The refusal of the successive British Conservative governments to agree on a second Scottish independence referendum and the United Kingdom Supreme Court judgment of November 23, 2022, denying that the Scottish Parliament had the power to pass a bill on that referendum suggested a ruder approach to Scottish nationalist aspirations than the one that David Cameron expressed when the latter suspected that the secessionist option, given the political coordinates of that moment, would be defeated in the polls.

Nicola Sturgeon's response to the 2022 Supreme Court judgment declaring that holding a Scottish referendum on independence is a matter that has ultimately to be decided by the parliament of the United Kingdom relied on making every election in Scotland a plebiscite on the question whether that country has to be sovereign or not. Such an approach placed Scotland in the same position that Catalonia had in 2015 once the Spanish Constitutional Court prohibited any unilateral consultation on Catalonia's independence without previously amending the Spanish Constitution,[55] and subsequently the Catalan authorities of that time decided to transform the elections to the regional parliament into a plebiscite on independence. But, as we explained, the Spanish central authorities opted to repress by force a new attempt of organizing a secessionist referendum and even indicted and convicted some of the Catalan leaders while others went into exile. The illiberal response prevailed in the relationship between Catalonia and Spain in the same vein that could be envisaged that would define the relationship between Scotland and the United Kingdom if the Scottish authorities pushed ahead for a movement of national emancipation backed by a majority of the Scottish population and without the British central authorities' consent.

Both Scotland and Catalonia cases reveal, in conclusion, how the supposed liberal democracies evolved from how the "nostalgic empires" react when there erupts a clamor by the majority of a population for full sovereignty within their European borders: by transforming into something probably different from a liberal democracy.

NOTES

1. See, for instance, Nicola McEwen and Mary C. Murphy, "Brexit and the Union: Territorial Voice, Exit and Re-Entry Strategies in Scotland and Northern Ireland," *International Political Science Review*, March 12, 2021. Available at https://journals.sagepub.com/doi/full/10.1177/0192512121990543.

2. See Niall Ferguson, *Civilization: The West and the Rest* (London: Penguin Books, 2012), 105.

3. David McKittrick, *Making Sense of the Troubles: The Story of the Conflict in Northern Ireland* (New York: New Amsterdam Books, 2002).

4. Elizabeth Buettner, *Europe after Empire: Decolonization, Society, and Culture* (Cambridge: Cambridge University Press, 2016), 23–73.

5. See, among many others, Peter Cain, "Was It Worth Having? The British Empire 1850–1950," *Revista de Historia Económica/Journal of Iberian and Latin American History* 16, no. 1 (March 1998) 351–76; Niall Ferguson, *Empire. How Britain Made the Modern World* (London: Penguin Books, 2004), 294.

6. Alan S. Milward, *The United Kingdom and the European Community. Vol. I: The Rise and Fall of a National Strategy, 1945–1963* (London: Whitehall History Publishing in association with Frank Cass) 1–9. On that point, see also James Ellison, *The European Rescue of Britain*. In *Alan S. Milward and a Century of European Change*, eds. Fernando Guirao, Frances M. B. Lynch, and Sigfrido M. Ramírez Pérez (New York and London: Routledge, 2012), 455.

7. "United Europe," Cabinet note by Mr. Churchill, November 29, 1951, NA, CAB 129/48, C (51) 32.

8. See Buettner, *Europe after Empire,* 72.

9. Tony Judt, *Postwar. A History of Europe Since 1945* (London: Penguin Books, 2005), 212.

10. Ian Kershaw, *Roller-Coaster: Europe 1950–2017* (London: Allen Lane/Penguin Books, 2018), 141.

11. See European Court of Human Rights Judgment of January 18, 1978, *Ireland v. United Kingdom*.

12. Judt, *Postwar*, 466.

13. See Elizabeth Meehan, "Britain's Irish Question: Britain's European Question? British-Irish Relations in the Context of European Union and the Belfast Agreement," *Review of International Studies* 26, no.1 (January 2000): 83–97; Nikos Skoutaris, "What's in an Irish Border? Brexit, the Backstop(s) and the Constitutional Integrity of the UK," *DCU/Brexit Institute. Working Paper* 2, February 24, 2020. Available at https://papers.ssrn.com/sol3/papers.cfm?abstract_id=3543514.

14.See George Mitchell's interview in the BBC, "Good Friday Agreement 'Wouldn't Have Happened without EU,'" December 29, 2017. Available at https://www.bbc.com/news/uk-northern-ireland-42412972.

15. See points 1 (i) and 1 (ii) regarding the Constitutional Issues of the 1998 Good Friday Agreement between the Government of the United Kingdom and the Government of Ireland: "The participants endorse the commitment made by the British and Irish Governments that, in a new British-Irish Agreement replacing the Anglo Irish Agreement, they will: (i) recognize the legitimacy of whatever choice is freely exercised by a majority of the people of Northern Ireland with regard to its status, whether they prefer to continue to support the Union with Great Britain or a sovereign united Ireland; (ii) recognize that it is for the people of the island of Ireland alone, by agreement between the two parts respectively and without external impediment, to exercise their right of self-determination on the basis of consent, freely and concurrently given, North and South, to bring about a united Ireland, if that is their wish, accepting that this right must be achieved and exercised with and subject to the agreement and consent of a majority of the people of Northern Ireland."

16. See Pau Bossacoma Busquets, *Secessió i integració a la Unió Europea* (Barcelona: Institut d'Estudis d'Autogovern, 2017), 16.

17. See John Garry, Brendan O'Leary, and John Coakley, "How Northern Ireland Voted in the EU Referendum—and What It Means for Border Talks," *Queen's Policy Engagement*, April 28, 2017. Available at http://qpol.qub.ac.uk/border-talks-brexit/.

18. Article 1.1 of the First Protocol to the Draft Agreement on the withdrawal of the United Kingdom of Great Britain and Northern Ireland from the European Union and the European Atomic Energy Community, as agreed at negotiators' level on November 14, 2018.

19. "DUP leader prefers no Brexit deal to EU 'annexation' of Northern Ireland," CNBC, October 13, 2018. Available at https://www.cnbc.com/2018/10/13/dup-leader-prefers-no-brexit-deal-to-eu-annexation-of-northern-ireland.html.

20. See "May Considering Amending Good Friday Deal to Break Brexit Impasse," Reuters, January 21, 2019. Available at https://www.reuters.com/article/uk-britain-eu-may-idUKKCN1PE0W2.

21. Skoutaris, "What's in an Irish Border?," 10 and 18; Colin Harvey, "The Irish Border," in *The Law and Politics of Brexit, Volume II: The Withdrawal Agreement*, ed. Federico Fabbrini (Oxford: Oxford University Press, 2020), 156.

22. Joseph Weiler, "Brexit, the Irish Protocol and the 'Versailles Effect.'" *Blog of the International Journal of Constitutional Law*, September 7, 2021. Available at http://www.iconnectblog.com/brexit-the-irish-protocol-and-the-versailles-effect/.

23. See Philipp Stephens, "The Meaning of Rishi Sunak's Northern Ireland Deal," *Encompass*, March 2023. Available at https://encompass-europe.com/comment/the-meaning-of-rishi-sunaks-northern-ireland-deal.

24. Etienne Balibar, "The Rise and Fall of the European Union: Temporalities and Teleologies," *Constellations* 21, no. 2 (June 2014): 202–12.

25. Mark Mazower, *Governing the World. The History of an Idea* (London: Allen Lane, 2012), 346.

26. Kershaw, *Roller-Coaster*, 271.

27. Kevin Hickson, *The IMF Crisis of 1976 and British Politics* (London: I.B. Tauris, 2005).

28. More exactly, even that the proposal was supported by 51.6 percent of the votes cast an amendment to the Scottish Act had provided that the devolution would only be passed if it counted on the support of at least 40 percent of the total registered electorate. Since the turnout was of 64 percent, the final outcome represented only 32.9 percent of the registered electorate.

29. Buettner, *Europe after Empire*, 75–77; and Ashley Jackson, "Empire and Beyond: The Pursuit of Overseas National Interests in the Late Twentieth Century," *English Historical Review* 122, no. 499 (December 2007): 1350–66.

30. See Hellen Thompson, *Disorder. Hard Times in 21st Century* (Oxford: Oxford University Press, 2022), 2–3.

31. John H. Elliott, *Scots and Catalans. Union and Disunion* (New Haven, CT, and London: Yale University Press), 243–48.

32. Together with Scotland and Northern Ireland, the Remain vote was also prevalent among the citizenry of some dependent territories of the British Crown, which participated for the very first time in a United Kingdom–wide referendum such as Gibraltar. See McEwen and Murphy, "Brexit and the Union."

33. "Sturgeon to Set Out Indyref2 Plans Even If Brexit Extended," BBC News, January 17, 2019. Available at https://www.bbc.com/news/uk-scotland-scotland-politics-46905024.

34. "Sturgeon Outlines New Scottish Independence Referendum Plans," *The Guardian*, April 24, 2019. Available at https://www.theguardian.com/politics/2019/apr/24/sturgeon-outlines-new-scottish-independence-referendum-plans.

35. "Boris Johnson Dismisses 'Irresponsible' Scotland Referendum as SNP Majority on Knife-Edge," *The Independent*, May 8, 2021. Available at https://www.independent.co.uk/news/uk/politics/boris-johnson-scottish-independence-referendum-snp-b1844159.html.

36. See "Liz Truss: No Second Scottish Independence Referendum 'On My Watch,'" *The Telegraph*, July 22, 2022. Available at https://www.telegraph.co.uk/politics/2022/07/30/liz-truss-no-second-scottish-independence-referendum-watch/.

37. See *Reference by the Lord Advocate of devolution issues under paragraph 34 of Schedule 6 to the Scotland Act 1998* [2022] United Kingdom Supreme Court 31, Judgment November 23, 2022.

38. Ibid., para 79–82.

39. Ibid., para 83.

40. Ibid., para 78.

41. Ibid., para 84–91.

42. See (CA) *Reference Re Secession of Quebec* (August 20, 1998), No. 25506 (S.C.C.), para 138.

43. *Reference by the Lord Advocate of Devolution Issues* [2022] UKSC 31, para. 90.

44. Ibid., para 89.

45. See chapter 1, XI, above.

46.Adam Tomkins, "Why We Need a New Act of Union—and What to Put in It," The Spectator, April 20, 2021. Available at https://www.spectator.co.uk/article/why-we-need-a-new-act-of-union-and-what-to-put-in-it.

47. "Independent Scotland 'Would Find It Extremely Difficult to Join EU,'" *The Guardian*, February 16, 2014. Available at https://www.theguardian.com/politics/2014/feb/16/independent-scotland-extremely-difficult-join-eu.

48.Mary E. Townsend and Cyrus H. Peake, *European Colonial Expansion since 1871* (Chicago, IL: Lippincott, 1941), 19.

49. Nicola Sturgeon (@NicolaSturgeon), "The EU Commission Building in Brussels Tonight (and If You Look Carefully You'll See That They Do Appear to Have Left a Light on for Us!)," February 1, 2020, 7:17. Tweet. Available at https://twitter.com/NicolaSturgeon/status/1223369787260260354.

50. See the AFAR ranking (September 21, 2021). Available at https://www.afar.com/magazine/best-cities-in-the-world; and the Best Cities ranking (visited on January 24, 2022). Available at https://www.bestcities.org/rankings/worlds-best-cities/.

51. Wolfgang Münchau, "Unicorns Everywhere," *Euro Intelligence*, December 12, 2021. Available at https://www.eurointelligence.com/column/unicorns-everywhere.

52. Elliott, *Scots and Catalans*, 121.

53. See Federico Fabbrini, *Brexit and the Future of the European Union: The Case for Constitutional Reforms* (Oxford: Oxford University Press, 2020), 1.

54. See "Britain in Lost Decade for Living Standards as Incomes Crash and Jeremy Hunt Squeezes Public Finances by £55bn," *I* (online news source), November 17, 2022. Available at https://inews.co.uk/news/politics/britain-in-lost-decade-for-living-standards-as-incomes-crash-and-jeremy-hunt-squeezes-public-finances-by-55bn-1979903.

55. See Spanish Constitutional Court Decision 42/2014 of March 25, 2014.

Chapter 3

Divisions

I

During the last stages of World War II, Italy's territorial integrity was in danger, and still would be for more than a decade after the war. Italian national unity was, indeed, young and fragile. By 1945 there had not passed even a century since the Italian troops got into Rome after the withdrawal of the French army caused by Napoleon III's collapse at Sedan against Prussia (1870). Some territories such as Trieste and Trento would not be annexed into the Kingdom of Italy until the aftermath of World War I as a consequence of the Austrian defeat.

Beyond the Italian protectorates in Somalia and Eritrea arranged from the 1880s and the 1890s, in the twentieth century interwar period, colonialist adventures were triggered in Africa at Mussolini's initiative by unifying the already Italian possessions in Libya under a single colonial entity (1934) and by fighting and occupying Ethiopia in a war of aggression (1935–1937) that revealed the ineffectiveness of the League of Nations in maintaining peace and avoiding the expansionist ambitions of the Axis powers before the outbreak of World War II.

Fascist Italy also showed expansionist ambitions within Europe with the invasion of Albania and the annexation of the Dalmatia territories, to which would be added some possessions in Yugoslavia and Greece resulting from the Axis performance once World War II started and despite the initial Italian reverses in the war against Greece in autumn 1940.

With the Allied landing in Sicily in July 1943, nevertheless, and the further attacks launched against the Italian peninsula, it soon become evident that it was Italy's metropolis itself that may be divided by the military operations. Italy, thus, also shared similar developments regarding the colonialist question with other western European powers that after World War II would contribute to the foundation of the European Communities, only that during the war and the years that preceded it the colonial overseas expansionism was combined with an attempt of intra-European imperialism (though to a lesser degree than that fostered by the Third Reich in Germany) and that the Allied invasion on Italian mainland territory already by 1943 made evident the ease with which the core nation of a former imperial European power might burst into pieces.

II

On the afternoon of July 22, 1943, advanced units of the American army entered Palermo. Throughout the city, a proclamation signed by the "Committee for Sicilian Independence" appeared on many walls. It asked the Allies to permit the formation of a provisional government that would conduct a plebiscite to determine Sicily's future status. The committee proclaimed the Savoy dynasty dead and asserted that Sicily deserved independence and sovereignty.[1]

Sicilian secessionism had existed in the post–World War I period and in the Fascist era, but already prior to the Allied assault, it had developed an intense political activity as the foundation of the Committee for the Independence of Sicily (*Comitato per l'Indipendenza della Sicilia*, *CIS*) in the Autumn of 1942 testifies. It was, nevertheless, following the Armistice of Cassibile of September 8, 1943 (according to which the Kingdom of Italy surrendered to the Allies), when the movement gained presence and support. At that time, Italian central government was still weak, and the Allies military authority expressed some tolerance at the idea of a fully sovereign Sicily. After all, Sicilian pro-independence activists, coming from very different political views (from revolutionary socialists to right-wing aristocrats, and that without leaving aside those members that maintained close ties to the Mafia) had helped the Allies to land in Sicily and to consolidate their military position.

In spite of the political pluralism that defined the pro-secessionist movement, the fear surrounding the American and the British political strategists of an Italy engulfed by communism was not in the spring of 1944 completely unfounded. If such a scenario had the scarcest possibility to crystallize, they were not thus particularly opposed to answer with an independent Sicily erected as an anti-communist bastion. Geopolitical interests were not at first sight opposed to an eventual partition of the Italian sovereignty, which was effectively envisaged while the fight between the Axis and the Allies was developed within the scenario of the Italian Peninsula.

The British prime minister, Winston Churchill, was on the other hand not eager to handle Italy in the same way as France was being treated: that is, recognizing Italy as a victorious power of the conflagration instead of considering it a loser as a former member of the Axis. Italy, according to the British plans, had to be punished and any measure supporting its national dismemberment, as Sicilian independence represented, was a movement to some extent observed with complacence from Whitehall. The anti-communist crusade together with the will to humiliate those who had sided with the Third Reich overlapped in the interest of advancing in the direction ambitioned by Sicilian secessionists.

As the war drew to a close, however, the tables turned. At least, the Americans and the British did not explicitly reject support of Sicilian separatists until the fall of 1944 when political hostility in the island had escalated and the Italian central government required a clear statement in order to combat separatist propaganda. It was precisely in the fall of 1944 that the members of the Sicilian Independence Movement (which had replaced the disbanded *Committee for the Independence of Sicily* in the previous Spring) pressed by its most radical elements and fearing that the consolidation of the Italian central authority would deprive them from reaching their final political aims, decided to create an armed branch, the EVIS (*Esercito Volontario per l'Indipendenza della Sicilia*, Volunteer Army for the Independence of Sicily). The EVIS would clash several times with the troops sent by the Italian government, causing the death of some of its leaders.

After World War II, a negotiation was opened: a special autonomy was offered to Sicily expressed in the Statute of Autonomy still approved under King Umberto of Italy in May 1946, that is, Sicilian autonomic status was established even before the creation of the Italian Republic and the approval of its constitution in December 1947 (the Sicilian Statute would be ratified under the Republican regime by Parliamentary vote in 1948). According to the agreement that led to Sicilian Autonomy, the United States would maintain their military presence in Sicily and the EVIS would be dismantled. The agreement between the Allies, the Italian central authorities and the more moderate cadres in Sicily meant that the Sicilian pro-independence movement would be sent to the political fringes. But some memories of the time in which the island functioned without almost any referent in the central government remained.

It has been stated that the Sicilian Mafia was involved in the negotiations on Sicily's Autonomy to the extent that one point of the concealed part of the agreement relied on the recognition of a direct link between the organization and a member of the Christian Democratic political staff (an agreement that the Mafia considered infringed as late as by 1992 when such breach led to the murder of Salvatore Lima, the contact that the Mafia had had in Italian politics at that time). In spite of the disbanding of EVIS as a consequence of the recognition of Sicilian Autonomy in 1946, some of the most radical agents of the armed movement did not agree with the decision and carried on with their activities until they were arrested, integrated into the Mafia as common criminals, or were killed, as happened with the bandit Salvatore Giuliano in 1950.

III

The stagnation of the front in the middle of the Italian peninsula and the Axis counterattack fostered the division of Italian national unity as well in the north through the formation of the German puppet state, the Italian Social Republic, also known as the Republic of Salò.

After the Allied invasion of Sicily in July 1943, the Grand Fascist Council with the support of King Victor Emmanuel III overthrew and arrested Mussolini and appointed General Badoglio as prime minister, who negotiated the armistice with the Allies. The Germans, however, aware of the negotiations of the armistice, sent at that time troops to seize control of northern and central Italy and launched a spectacular operation to liberate Mussolini from his captivity in the mountains of Abruzzo. After being moved to Bavaria to meet with Hitler, Mussolini was urged to go back to Italy in order to lead a new Fascist state created under German control.

The Republic of Salò was, somehow, a consequence of the weakness shown by the Italian inner resistance too inclined to the left in order to deserve resolute military and financial aid from the Western Allies that were fighting in the southern part of the Italian peninsula.

By contrast to what happened in the relationship between the Allies and the Italian partisans, Mussolini's Italian Social Republic was both militarily and economically thoroughly dependent on Germany. The Allies' progress was contained through deployment of the German army in central Italy and, particularly around Rome (a circumstance that explained why in spite of the fact that the Italian Social Republic declared Rome as its capital, the regime headquarters were placed at the town of Salò).

Rome and the front line was directly controlled by the German army and a direct German rule was also de facto established in other northern regions formerly attributed to the Italian Republic, such as the German-speaking territories of South Tyrol including Trento, Bolzano, and Belluno (incorporated into Germany's *Reichsgau Tirol-Voralberg*) and some other territories that before World War I had belonged to the Austro-Hungarian Empire, with both German-speaking and Slavic-speaking influence, such as Udine, Goriza, Trieste, Pola, and Fiume, which were incorporated into *Reichsgau Kärnten*. The real German dominion upon the mentioned areas of South Tyrol and the Adriatic coast during the time of the Italian Social Republic would make their integration in the post–War Italian Republic more complicated and some of them, such as Pola and the major part of Istria's peninsula territory, would be placed after the war under Yugoslavian sovereignty.

The events in Pola were especially dramatic after the war; the city had an Italian majority and a large proportion of the city's inhabitants (28,000 of its 32,000 inhabitants), which were forced to emigrate to the Italian Peninsula between December 1946 and the immediate aftermath of the signing of the Paris Peace Treaty in February 1947. Through that Treaty, Pola was granted to Yugoslavia and would remain in that Federation until Croatia's independence in 1991. The ethnic cleansing that, as we previously saw, would contribute to the European postwar stability would be founded on experiences as those recorded against the Italians in some territories of the former Yugoslavia.

In sum, several conflicts overlapped in Italy during the last years of World War II, all of them threatening Italy's national unity. There was the conflict between the Allies and the Axis, but beneath the formal war other wars were being developed;[2] there were national wars, civil wars, and class wars.[3]

There was a civil war between the Fascists and the partisans, most of the latter committed to communism and social revolutionary ideals. For the partisans there were at least three simultaneous reasons for fighting: firstly, to drive the Germans out of the peninsula; secondly, to defeat the Fascists; and, lastly, to bring about a social revolution. But there was also a clash between secessionist movements and the Italian central authorities (as the one that we mentioned regarding Sicily), which also deserve attention since they still mark Italian political dynamics until the present day.

Indeed, regionalism had already focused a relevant part of the discussions on the Constituent Assembly: the Catholics declared themselves in favor and the exponents of the Marxist left were much more cautious, despite partially changing their attitude from mid-1947. Being aware of the challenge that a strong regionalism supposed for the state's cohesion, the exponents of the pre-Fascist political class, such as Orlando or Croce, were nevertheless openly hostile to any decentralized impetus.[4]

Although eventually the partial autonomy of the regions obtained definitive recognition in the 1948 Italian Constitution, including the possibility to establish regional councils, regional competences were strictly circumscribed in the constitution, and objects falling under the exclusive legislative power of the state were clearly determined.[5] As ultimate instance, a Constitutional Court was created (established in 1953 and operative from 1956), which besides the power to decide on the constitutionality of the laws of the state, has the attribution to resolve both conflicts between central state and regions and disputes between regions. The Constitutional Court performed important functions for the emergent republican state in Italy, and it served partially to rectify conventional weaknesses of Italian statehood.[6] This became manifest for instance in the fact that the court played a key role in countervailing tendencies toward fragmentation and regional centrifugal movements in Italian politics.[7]

IV

Without being as sharp as the Sicilian case, secessionism also was present by the end of the war in Sardinia and such conflict also evolved in the beginning of the new Republican regime to the negotiations for a special autonomy in the island.

In the contemporary era, an ambivalent attitude toward Italian unity has always been present in Sardinia; on the one hand, by the beginning of the eighteenth century, Sardinia was transferred to the Kingdom of Savoy and, consequently, would belong to the political entity that boosted the creation of the Italian state in the nineteenth century. But, on the other hand, Sardinian people have all this time persistently shown aspirations to self-governance.

The last years of World War II also saw a resurrection of Sardinian nationalism, which afterward was responsible for Sardinia's designation as a special region in the Italian Constitution, passed in 1947. Temporarily satisfied by this concession, Sardinians gravitated away from the Sardinian Party of Action (*Partito Sardo d'Azione*), Sardinia's main nationalist party, but nationalism regained support from the 1960s onward.

By the 1970s, repackaged in cultural and anti-colonial terms, Sardinian nationalism embraced not only continuity and increased support for federal-style devolution and regional autonomy but also at times support for outright independence, which included by the first half of the 1970s some flirting with armed struggle.[8] The fact that more than a half of the military facilities built in Italian territory are based in Sardinia has strengthened for Sardinian nationalism the impression according to which the island rather than being voluntarily attached to Italy, has been an object of domination.

By the end of the 2010s the autonomist *Partito Sardo d'Azione* again dominated the Sardinian political landscape, though detached from its original left-leaning orientation and rather supporting a liberal conservative program. Some parts of the former leftist branch of the Sardinian Party of Action contributed to form other political groups bent on the independence cause.

In some episodes, however, the state apparatus has answered the Sardinian self-government demands through police and judicial means, as when in 2006 it launched a great operation with more than fifty people indicted and ten people detained, charged with terrorism, that also derived in the seizing and the dissolution in 2015 of the Sardinian pro-independence political party *A Manca pro s'Indipendèntzia* (to the Left for Independence) showing, thus, that Italian centralist forces have also handled Sardinian separatism repressively, even in recent times.

The minority character of the Sardinian pro-independence cause, at least formally counting with much less support than other comparable nationalist movements within Europe such as the Catalans or the Basques, has not undermined the perception among the inhabitants of the island to be considered as a case of "internal colonialism" such as the one that we mentioned in the introduction of this contribution. Such a situation of domination is nevertheless blurred by different political and social conjunctures.

On the one hand, national minorities are plural within the island, it is not only that there might be identified a Sardinian nationalism but also that there remain further national sensibilities, such as the ones embodied by the Catalan-speaking minority in the city of Alghero. On the other hand, the circumstance that Sardinian conservative nationalism had reached some agreements with the Italian nationalist right expresses something about the internal streams of national pluralism that might be illustrated by the fact that Sardinian conservativism came to terms easier with Salvini's *Lega Nord*,[9] which in turn politically grew by defending northern Italian interests rather than pure Italian centralist nationalism.

The paths of national minorities are diverse and winding but are always suspicious toward the desire of control, domination, economic exploitation, and social uniformity triggered by the imperial center.

V

Identity-based conflict, particularly in the north, made Italian postwar constitutional arrangements complicated. The 1946 Austrian and Italian agreement, also known as the Gruber-De Gasperi agreement provided some solutions for German-speaking South Tyroleans and avoided in a first instance South Tyrol's reunification with Austria.[10] But, in spite of the fact that the new Italian republic included South Tyrol in the list of autonomous regions with special status and that linguistic rights for the German-speaking minority were recognized (as was established in the Gruber-de Gasperi agreement) a campaign of Italianization boosted during the following decades by the Italian government increased the tension between ethnic groups and led to a short phase of organized ethnic violence that even deserved two resolutions of the General Assembly of the United Nations.[11]

The situation only became more stable a decade later when the Italian Parliament passed, through a constitutional statute, a range of policies agreed, after an arduous negotiation, between the Italian government and the *Südtiroler Volkspartei* (SVP) as representative of the German-speaking community in the region.[12] Although the Austrian Republic did not join both the European Union and the Schengen agreement on the free movement of people until 1995, the 1946 Gruber-De Gasperi agreement already foresaw some provisions related to grant the free movements of individuals and goods between both sides of the border that divided the Tyrol, creating a sort of a pre-EU freedom of movements area that would anticipate the ideals of European integration.[13]

VI

The end of World War II also finished with Italian expansionist dreams at the expense of France. While the French Third Republic regime had been collapsing as a consequence of the German attack perpetrated in the north, Fascist Italy had declared war on France on June 10, 1940, and launched an attack through the Alps with the intention of annexing some of the territories that the Kingdom of Piedmont had relinquished to the French during the Italian unification in the middle of the nineteenth century, in exchange for French military aid for the campaign.

Of that territorial loss, Nice had been Mussolini's most appreciated jewel to be reconquered in the 1940 offensive. The regaining of Nice has been indeed one of the most recurrent ambitions for Italian nationalists since the nineteenth century. However, by 1940, the strength of the Italian attacks through the Alps had been so disappointing that they only ensured the occupation of Menton and no other important location was claimed to be annexed to the Kingdom of Italy in the Franco-Italian armistice signed on June 24, 1940. In spite of the fact that great parts of Provence had been targeted by Mussolini's regime, only when Germany occupied most of the Vichy government jurisdiction in November 1942 was the Italian army willing to take control of Toulon, all of Provence to the River Rhône, Savoy, and, finally, Nice. Even Corsica fell temporarily into Italian hands. Such stretched Italian dominion upon French territories was, nevertheless, ephemeral, since the Italian surrender to the Allies in September 1943 after the Allied invasion of Sicily and the southern part of the Italian Peninsula caused the seizing of the Italian occupied zones in France by the Germans.

The collapse of the Italian Social Republic by the spring of 1945 was also accompanied by troubles in some of its western regions bordering with France that also endangered the continuity of Italian sovereignty in the postwar arrangements. Not surprisingly, the Aosta Valley, for instance, an Alpine mountainous region in northwestern Italy in which French and Franco-Provençal are also spoken, gained its special autonomous status shortly after the war, by constitutional law passed in February 1948. Also in the case of the Aosta Valley, consequently, the origin of decentralization and structures of self-government is related to the tangible possibility of that territory's detachment from the political entity that was being created.

VII

Aside from the South Tyrol question and the French border regions, other parts of northern Italy had been before the conclusion of World War II, and in the immediate years that followed it, on the verge of escaping from Italian control. There were conflicts between Italian nationalists and other nationalisms such as the Slavic ones, both Slovenian and Croatian, in which social questions between Tito's communist partisans and Italian Fascists were involved as well.

The disputed territories under Yugoslavian influence were at the center of the turmoil and, in fact, some of them, such as the aforementioned case of the Istria peninsula, fell definitively into the hands of Tito's regime. Some territories in Dalmatia, such as the city of Zadar, had already been absorbed by the Fascist puppet state of the Independent State of Croatia from the fall of 1943 and afterward occupied and retained by the Yugoslavian partisans. And, in the Adriatic coast, there was of course the question of Trieste; the Yugoslav Army, on the one hand, and the Allies, on the other, had occupied this territory by the beginning of May 1945, inaugurating a dispute that would mark the first steps of the Cold War.

The United Nations had to intervene through a resolution that called for the creation of a Free State in Trieste and in the region surrounding it.[14] In this resolution it was planned to arrange a self-government framework for the territory but it worked de facto under military occupation divided in two zones: the zone A, which included the city of Trieste, administered by British and American forces; and the zone B, encompassing the north-western part of the Istria peninsula, administered by the Yugoslav Forces.

It was not until 1954, through the London Memorandum of October 5, that the international interests derived from the Cold War context hammered out a compromise that led to the return of zone A and the city of Trieste to Italian sovereignty (zone B and some villages in the municipality of Muggia that had been part of zone A, would fall into the Yugoslavian side).[15]

The outlining of the Italian borders after the war would not, thus, be established until the incorporation of Trieste in 1954,[16] six years after the approval of the Italian Constitution in 1948 and three years after the conclusion of the Treaty of European Coal and Steel Community in 1951, the embryo of the European integration project.

Postwar Italy was anemic, with both the wounds of the war and the emergence of the disputes between the capitalistic world and the Communist bloc developed on the other side of the Iron Curtain making its territorial integrity tremble. However, western European cooperation through the establishment of common institutions and a common economic space (and later, a common political space) would come to rescue this nation at the crossroads.

VIII

The fragile situation that Italy had to tackle by the end of World War II was superseded by an unexpected spirit of unity that embedded the main Italian political actors involved in the fight against Mussolini and the final triumph of the Allies against the Axis.

Already under the monarchy, and when the war was not over, a government of national unity was formed embracing parties from the Christian Democrats to the Communists. The Communists had played an important role in the resistance against fascism and were the cornerstone of the guerrilla against Mussolini's Italian Social Republic in the north during the closing months of the conflict.

Communists were in position to rehearse a Marxist revolution through the grassroots governments that they had created in key areas. However, when their leader, Palmiro Togliatti, returned from exile in March 1944 instead of repudiating the king and triggering a complete change of regime, he decided to join the government of national unity postponing the final constitutional configuration of Italy at least until the defeat of the Nazis.[17]

Togliatti was well aware that Stalin had conceded Italy under the Western Allies sphere of influence in exchange for Soviet hegemony in some parts of eastern Europe. He did not wish to see Italy entangled in a civil war between the Left and some Western Allied power of the sort that was being developed at that time in Greece with the clash between Communists and the conservative forces directly supported by the British army.[18] From another perspective, both Togliatti and Stalin saw the Italian Communist Party strong enough as a result of their leading role in the resistance as, in the same strategy that Moscow had designed for French Communists, to maintain the goal of reaching power through the parliamentary game.

With the Communists' acceptance to participate in the Constituent Assembly called by King Umberto in June 1944, it was clear that the decision on the final regime in Italy should wait until the approval of the constitution. In the critical moments in which Italian national fragmentation was a real danger, and disregarding the tensions within the Allies that soon would split in the Cold War, the Italian Left, including its most radical part, saw the need to work shoulder to shoulder with the Christian Democrats to design the foundations of the new regime. National unity prevailed momentarily over social revolution.

Such struggle for national unity also undertook another challenge when before the drafting of the Constitution a decision on the monarchy had to be adopted. Instead of following the criterion of the Communist and Socialist representatives in the provisional government according to which the monarchy might be abolished without referendum, the Christian Democrats convinced the other members of the government to call for a conscious act of the People's popular sovereignty in order to confer legitimacy to the new Republic.

Understanding that some parts of southern Italy remained strongly monarchist, the Christian Democrats claimed successfully for the organization of the referendum in order to ensure national unity that, after all, was the main aim of the commitment between the major parties (the Christian Democrats, the Communists, and the Socialists) to trigger the constitution-making procedure. Creating a republic was, in fact, an existential constituent decision previous to all other issues handled in the Constituent Assembly. However, the outcome of the referendum held on June 2, 1946, won by the Republicans with some 54.3 percent of the votes cast against 45.7 percent for the Monarchists, did not conceal the strong division between the north of Italy (Republican) and the south (Monarchists) in a fracture that would be expanded to other matters in the following decades of the new regime.[19]

National unity around the creation of a new constitution did not last long. Even before the conclusion of the Constituent Assembly the Christian Democrats, led by De Gasperi, maneuvered in order to expel the Communists as soon as possible from the government. They counted with the backing of the United States, which as long as the conflict with the Soviet Union was looming, was eager to financially aid the reconstruction of the European countries that had fallen under their influence (including those countries such as Italy which the United States had just fought in the war).

The loans already received from Truman by the beginning of 1947 (which would be only a precedent of the American aid that would be known as the Marshall plan passed a year later) allowed De Gasperi to strengthen his position in a moment when according to a CIA report, "[t]he greatest danger to the security of the United States is the possibility of economic collapse in western Europe and the consequent accession to power of Communist elements."[20]

De Gasperi used the American financial support precisely as the CIA suggested: to block the advance of the Comintern's dependent actors in Italian politics. With the support of the Democratic Socialists on the Left and anti-Fascist conservatives on the Right, De Gasperi finally dismissed the Communists from the cabinet in May 1947, but the wide range of anti-Fascist forces, included the Marxists, persisted on working on the drafting of the new Republican Constitution, which was finally enacted on of December 22, 1947.[21]

IX

The beginning of the Cold War buried definitively the collaboration between the former opponents to Mussolini's regime and the mirage of national unity. The storm of the Communists in Czechoslovakia's democratic institutions perpetrated in February 1948, just some weeks after the Italian Constitution had entered into force (January 1 of that year) instigated the Christian Democrats and the rest of the Italian parties, backed by the Western Allies, to square off against the Marxists.

In the dramatic general elections of April 1948 the Christian Democrats (following an electoral campaign waged by the U.S. State Department and the CIA) won the elections with a comfortable margin, gaining the absolute majority of seats in both the Chamber of Deputies and the Senate. De Gasperi led a coalition formed by the Christian-Democrats and other center-right parties but the divorce with the Left, and particularly with the Communists, resurrected an atmosphere of social confrontation that would mark Italian politics for the rest of the century.

By spring 1948 the fracture between the Communists and the other parties, particularly the Christian Democrats, nevertheless reached a critical point. After the fall of the Berlin Wall in 1989, there emerged different historical evidence indicating that the danger of an Italian civil war in 1948 had been imminent; according to some versions the militants of the Italian Communist Party were prepared, if necessary, to seize power by means of military insurrection.[22]

It was likely that the Communist leader Togliatti had some reserves to get into an outright war against the opposing political camp. Togliatti remarked in a letter sent to Stalin that in case of going ahead with the rebellion the Italian Communist Party would need the support of the Yugoslav army and the other forces of other Eastern European countries in order to maintain its control over Northern Italy since the anti-Communist side would be supported by the combined forces of the United States, Great Britain, and France. The harsh tensions between Tito's Yugoslavia and the Soviet Union throughout1947 and 1948, which culminated in the expulsion of Yugoslavia from the Cominform, also advised, in the eyes of Moscow, against any military involvement of the Yugoslavian armies in the Italian theater.

Stalin, thus, responded to Togliatti by not using "armed insurrections for any reasons" to seize power in Italy. Any movement in Italy, located within the

British-American sphere of influence, would have to wait. There would be, thus, no open civil war but the evolution of Italian politics after 1948 would not be deprived of agitation sometimes degenerating into raw violence.

X

A polarized political system means a weak state, and such circumstances made De Gasperi see clearly that Italy had to entrench its alliance with its neighbors overshadowed by similar threats.

The Schuman Declaration, by which the French foreign minister Robert Schuman on May 9, 1950, proposed to place French and German production of coal and steel under a common High Authority, seemed a good opportunity for that aim. Whatever the opinion that the creation of the High Authority may deserve for the Italian coal and steel industry (and, for instance, the Italian Ambassador in Paris, Pietro Quaroni, judged it very negatively), De Gasperi had the intuition that European integration would endorse the democratic and economic reconstruction of Italy, as well as the strengthening of his government vis-à-vis the hard Communist opposition.

It was remarkable, from another perspective, that all six foreign ministers who signed the 1951 Paris Treaty founding the European Coal and Steel Community were members of their respective Christian Democratic parties and some of them were confronting with the pressure of the Communists in their own countries as happened in France.

As we have seen with other examples, also in Italy, Europe counted less in the birth of the European Communities. The priority was the fight against the Soviet Union and the Eastern bloc, the restraint of the internal Communist threat and, above all, the consolidation of the Italian nation-state through the expansion of the markets that would bring prosperity and would provide the funds to sustain the welfare needed to dissuade radicals from revolution or from war.

The Soviets, at their turn, perfectly identified that the European Communities were a device for the self-preservation of its capitalist member nations. That may explain why shortly after the conclusion of the Rome Treaty in 1957 the Soviet government already began a concerted effort with each individual member state of the community to determine the treatment that would be reserved for Soviet and eastern European products in the light of the construction of the Common Market.[23] Threats of retaliation were carefully calibrated and some of them even lay behind some institutional crises that the European Communities had to deal with, such as French President de Gaulle's attempt to boycott the European Council by recalling French representatives in that body in response to the commission's proposals regarding the Common Agricultural Policy and other issues. But, at the end of the day, the spectacular economic growth that accompanied the first decades of the European Communities' existence contained the political effects of the divisive struggles fostered by the Communist bloc.

XI

The Cold War, thus, masked the profound divisions within Italian society. There were territorial divisions (as the one mentioned between the north and the south on the Republican or Monarchist form of government revealed in the 1946 referendum), social divisions (as shown in the political contest between the Christian Democrats and the Communists), national divisions (such as the ones expressed by the struggles for greater autonomy in South Tyrol or in Sicily), and division between the state and other organizations whose actions were grounded in physical coercion, such as the one represented by the Mafia. But the need to contain the influence of the Socialist world (beginning with the Yugoslavian particular path to Socialism, which bordered with the Italian regions) covered most of the internal tensions. Both the United States' financial aid and military presence helped to keep the veil of pacification and gave to the Christian Democrats a prevalent position to control Italian postwar politics at national level.

However, the Italian Republic, between its origins and the collapse of Communism in eastern Europe in 1989, had to face up to at least two harsh political crises: the first happened in 1960, when the Fernando Tambroni government took office with the support of the neo-Fascist Italian Social Movement, and the second in the midst of the oil crises of the 1970s, with the political violence that was carried out in the campaigns of the Red Brigades and other militant factions.

When in March 1960 the Italian Liberal Party withdrew its support from Antonio Segni's government, the President of the Republic, Giovanni Gronchi, and after several failed proposals, entrusted the formation of a new executive to Tambroni. Surrounded by a very hostile atmosphere from the conservative media against any openness to the Left, the only votes that Tambroni's Christian-Democratic single-party government could obtain came from the far-Right, a circumstance which almost led the country to civil war.[24] Indeed, several demonstrations and riots spread across Italy during the spring and the summer of 1960, leaving dozens dead and injured. Tambroni's government permitted the Italian Social Movement to hold its national Congress in Genoa, which had been one of the capitals of the Italian Resistance against Fascism. The Left answered to such an initiative with a large demonstration heavily suppressed by the police, a violent intervention that would be reproduced in Reggia Emilia, Rome, Palermo, Catania, or Licata, showing to some extent the percolation of the Italian far-Right within the security forces. Both Tambroni and his interior minister, Spataro, minimized the mortal victims resulting from the repression arguing that they were fighting against the menace of those that were seeking to destroy "the free institutions." Both the domestic and the international repudiation to a government sustained by the Italian Social Movement was dragging the country to a chaos of such proportions that in the end Tambroni had to resign by mid-July 1960.

But the clashes experienced in the 1970s would be even more shocking though a more pacific tone surrounded the Italian political establishment. On that occasion, the upheaval precisely exploded when both the Right and the Left were searching for solutions in order to surmount the radical divisions that were corroding Italian society in which also converged some of the tensions globally displayed between the Western world and the Communist bloc.

After the Communist Party obtained an historic gain with 34 percent of the vote in the 1976 Italian general elections, the leadership of the Christian Democrats embodied in the figure of Aldo Moro, struggled to gradually involve the Communists in governmental policies in order to moderate their aims. Moro deemed that was crucial to broaden the democratic support for measures designed to handle the social and economic crises while the Italian Communists, through Enrico Berlinguer's initiatives, distanced themselves from the Soviet influence in a movement that made cooperation between the two political forces possible and digestible for the Christian-Democratic bases.

Both superpowers nonetheless, the United States and the Soviet Union, strongly opposed the rapprochement between the Italian Communists and the Christian Democrats. The United States feared that the cooperation between Communists and the Christian Democrats might have allowed the former to gain information on strategic NATO military plans. On the other hand, the Soviets considered the potential participation by the Italian Communist Party in a cabinet as a form of emancipation from Moscow.

In spite of such pressures the operation crystallized in the shape of a government led by Giulio Andreotti that would count with the votes of the Communist representatives in parliament. On March 16, 1978, nevertheless, just when Aldo Moro was on his way to a session of the Chamber of Deputies (where a discussion was to take place regarding a vote of confidence for Andreotti's government that would have, for the first time, the support of the Communist Party) Moro was kidnapped by the Red Brigades and, after agonic negotiations, killed fifty-four days later.

XII

As we have seen, conflicts between the Italian majority and the linguistic, cultural, and national minorities led to commitments from the very beginning of the postwar Italian Republic, (or even before as in the case of Sicily) and outlined the recognition of regional self-government through the special statutes. Regionalism was indeed associated with the weakness that marked the Italian state central authorities by the end of World War II and was consequently envisaged as an alternative to territorial rupture and a safeguard against the emergence of smaller sovereign entities.

The social confrontation between the Right and the Left, and particularly between the Christian-Democrats and the *Partito Comunista Italiano* (PCI) also defined regional developments to the extent that ordinary regions had to wait for their implementation until the moment that the PCI revealed some shortcomings in its struggle to assault power. Only after the moment in which the risk of civil war began to be dogged would the Italian center-right accede to expand self-government to those fifteen ordinary regions.

The Christian Democrats feared that the Communists and the Socialists would be bound to win control of the Regional Councils in Emilia Romagna, Umbria, and Tuscany creating thus a "red belt" stretching across the center of Italy.[25] Only the split between the Communists and the Socialists, the participation in the national government by the latter under the Christian-Democrat leadership of Mariano Rumor and the isolation of the Communists left the door ajar for the federalist generalization (though still with a low degree of self-government recognized to the territorial entities). If initial regionalism was a concession to national minorities, regionalism in the 1970s was an attempt to pacify social conflict.

The disruption that Italy experienced in the 1990s as the consequence of the disintegration of the Cold War status quo and the loss of strategic value of the country as a frontline against Communism also had strong repercussions concerning territorial organization. The evaporation of the traditional parties also represented the appearance of new options, some of them proposing territorial centripetal solutions to overcome the crises of governance. Maybe the most prominent example of that trend was the proliferation of pro-autonomist parties in northern Italy that by 1989 converged in the *Lega Nord*. The reliance on that regionalist federation by the Italian New Right parties (notability Berlusconi's *Forza Italia*) triggered a profound constitutional amendment in a federalist sense by 2001, not without first having to overcome the secessionist challenge that the *Lega Nord* launched against the leftist government in Rome by declaring the independence of the Padania region in September 1996.

In a similar fashion as to what had happened during the foundations of the Republic, the concern for adopting devolution schemes of political organization only arose given the political fragility of the central actors, but differently from the territorial confrontation that burst out in other European Union member states, particularly in Spain regarding the nationalist movements within it. In Italy the concession for more autonomy was likely to dissolve pro-independence vindications and contributed to the pacification of the political system. Even the *Lega Nord*, as I will remark, evolved from northern Italian economic separatism to a stronghold of Italian far-Right nationalism.

XIII

With the mentioned dramatic exceptions represented by the Tambroni and the Moro episodes, the Italian political system, due to its crucial role in providing stability in Europe between the two Cold War poles and American political and financial endorsement, conveyed a certain continuity in its pillars, at least expressed in the Christian-Democratic predominance and the gradual moderation of the majority of actors on the Left.

Things, however, dramatically changed from the fall of the Berlin Wall in 1989 in a manner in which the inner confrontations between different parts of Italian society that had been more or less silenced from the postwar years (and had been frozen by the geopolitical urgencies of the United States and its allies) emerged again.[26] Italy (aside from German reunification) was probably the most affected state in western Europe by the events that had exploded with the end of the Iron Curtain.

The lifting of the veil showed, in the first stance, the general corruption of the entire Italian political system. Some politicians from all the main parties at the highest level were strongly suspected of collaboration with the Mafia, including the former Socialist prime Minister, Bettino Craxi, and the once almighty Christian-Democrat leader and several times prime minister, Giulio Andreotti.

By May 1992 magistrates in Milan issued the first official warnings to leading figures in both dominant parties that they were under investigation for corruption. At virtually the same moment, the motorcade of Giovanni Falcone, the prosecutor who had become a symbol of determination to root out the Mafia in Sicily, was blown up in an ambush outside Palermo. Hit by these two thunderbolts, the political establishment that had dominated the country since World War II suddenly tottered. Over the next months the Milanese magistrates unleashed a blizzard of further investigations against the political class and its business partners, a scandal dubbed by the press "Tangentopoli" or "Bribesville."

Within little more than a year, Craxi had fled to Tunisia (where he died some years later) and Andreotti was charged as an accomplice of the Mafia. By the autumn of 1993, more than half the members of the Senate and Chamber of Deputies had been served notice that they were under suspicion for corruption and a referendum had abrogated the system of proportional representation that had elected them.[27] The Christian Democratic Party, the Socialist Party, and the Liberal Party were all dissolved by the end of 1994. The Communist party, victim of an identity crises unleashed by the collapse of the Soviet bloc, had already been disbanded by 1991.

Party politics had to begin almost anew and that was the moment in which the populists, the radicals, and the politicians claiming for the revival of differentiated national identities found their opportunity.

Turbulences and secessionist trends in Italian politics were once more contained by European substantial reforms coined by the Treaty of the European Union concluded in 1992, though Europe's transformation had been from Italy conducted by a political elite (to begin with Craxi and Andreotti under whose mandate as an Italian prime minister the treaty had been signed) that were on the verge of being expelled from the system and replaced by cadres much more skeptical on the Italian role in European integration (from Berlusconi and Bossi in the 1990s to Salvini in the 2010s).

The traditional Italian political establishment sought in the commitment to Europe a way to strengthen national cohesion, but the immediate outcome of the series of choices made in the 1980s and early 1990s on the track of a greater European union provided an external constraint upon the nations' developments (and particularly upon its political economy) that would precipitate, besides the collapse of Communism, the ruin of its leaders.[28]

Germany invoked the European change to convince the Allies that the German national resurrection represented by reunification would be mitigated given the German integration in a "more perfect Union." If in the German case the strength of the union was designed to dilute national consolidation, in situations like the Italian one, the European move toward integration saved the nation-state from political default at the cost of finishing with the parties that had ruled the country from the immediate postwar period onward.

Populism was indeed not unknown in Italian politics before the advent in the 1990s of Berlusconi, Bossi, or Fini (a strand that would even be more remarkable later with Salvini, Meloni, or the *Movimento 5 Stelle*) but according to some authors was already rooted from the outset of Italian postwar constitutionalism.[29] The participation of members of *the Common Man's Front* (*Fronte dell'Uomo Qualunque*) in the work of the National Constituent assembly gives a good account on that point and the references within the constitutional text to concepts such as "majority," "people," or even "democracy" itself helped to build a counter-narrative of the Italian Republican developments.

But the cascade of crises experienced from the 1989 fall of the Communist bloc in eastern Europe to the 2008 economic slump and its sequels were what laid the ground for Italian populism to be a majority phenomenon, both in the Right and later, with the *Movimento 5 Stelle*, in the Left.

After the 2018 general election, Italy became not only the first European member state in which two self-styled populist forces obtained the majority of votes (*Movimento 5 Stelle* and *Lega*) but also the only example of two populist movements that, although having very different agendas and voting constituencies, ruled *together* in a coalition.

XIV

The evaporation of the old Italian political system did nothing but make more acute the divisions between the economically advanced north of Italy and the inefficient, poor, and subsidized south. It is from that time that there emerged a sort of economic nationalism focused on the electoral success of the *Lega Nord* (Northern League) led by Umberto Bossi, who demanded more autonomy for the Italian northern regions and an end to subsidies for the south.[30]

The *Lega Nord* joined forces with the man of the moment, the also northern tycoon Silvio Berlusconi (who nevertheless presented an Italian national right-oriented movement, *Forza Italia*) and concurred together in northern Italian districts in the general elections of March 1994 under the alliance named *Polo delle Libertà* (Pole of Freedoms). In order to win the elections, however, Berlusconi formed another electoral alliance in the central and southern provinces: the *Polo del Buon Governo* (Pole of Good Government) with the heirs of Fascism, The *Alleanza Nazionale* (National Alliance) led by Gianfranco Fini. Berlusconi did not ally with Fini's party in the north because the *Lega Nord* did not want to join the neo-Fascists.

The consequence of such pre-electoral moves was that Berlusconi's Party, *Forza Italia*, would be able to participate in the elections with two parties that were not allied to each other. The *Polo del Buon Governo*'s success in the Mezzogiorno including the neo-Fascists, expressed several contradictions given the historic account of the Italian north-south dialectic that we have already seen. In spite of the fact that southern territories were the ones first liberated by the Allies (while Mussolini remained in his northern German's puppet state, the Italian Social Republic), the southern Italians, maybe nostalgic for a return to authoritarianism, sought to supersede the crises of the traditional parties by backing an ultra-conservative option that included Mussolini's successors. On the other hand, the discursive attacks coming from the *Lega Nord* to the South had not prevented the southern Italians from voting for an option that they knew that in case of victory, as happened, would form government with the ones that blamed them and even launched accusations not free of resonances of ethnic hate.

XV

Similar peculiar alignments would be somehow reproduced in the aftermath of the 2018 general elections when the successor of the *Lega Nord*, rebranded simply as the *Lega* (the League) that had been triumphant in the north concluded a government coalition with the *Movimento 5 Stelle* (Five Star Movement), which had obtained a sweeping victory in the southern provinces; the *Movimento 5 Stelle* formed a government with those that the southern Italians that voted for them repudiated. At least in 1994 the national centrality of Berlusconi's figure blurred the Italian territorial division expressed in electoral terms. But in 2018, once Berlusconi began to be definitively displaced from the stage of Italian politics in which he had been influencing for almost twenty-five years, the political cleavage between the north and the south was more dramatically expressed in the Italian electoral outcomes map, which was clearly colored with the blue of the *Lega* in the north and the yellow of the *Movimento 5 Stelle* in the south.

Italian territorial integrity, nonetheless, given the northern and southern antagonism, had to suffer another shock in the 1990s with the declaration of Padania's independence. The shaky rightwing coalition of Berlusconi, Bossi, and Fini had fallen apart when the leader of the *Lega Nord*, Umberto Bossi, left the coalition arguing that the electoral agreement had not been respected. Bossi was preparing a more northern-identitarian turn as a political proposal, and for that aim he had to get rid of the ties with an Italian National Right that included the parties consolidated in the southern provinces. After a brief technocratic government headed by Lamberto Dini, who had replaced Berlusconi as prime minister shortly after Bossi broke the alliance, snap elections took place in April 1996, which were won by the left coalition, the Olive Tree (*L'Ulivo*) led by Romano Prodi.

One of the reasons of the Right's defeat in these elections was related to the fact that Bossi and his *Lega* had run alone in the contest obtaining a remarkable result in their northern strongholds. Encouraged by the *Lega*'s momentum, despite the defeat of the rest of the Italian right, Bossi managed to orchestrate a rebellion against the New-Left Italian national government. The *Lega* established a shadow parliament at Mantua and a Padanian Liberation Committee, in saucy imitation of the Resistance Committee for the Liberation of Upper Italy, of 1943–1945. On September 15, 1996, after a whole series of "happenings" along the length of the river Po (which valley coins the term "Padania" though the territory of that entity included areas that might be associated to northern Italy more or less coinciding, ironically, with Mussolini's Italian Social Republic), Bossi arrived in Venice to declare Padanian formal independence.

However, given the lack of both social support and cultural background of such separatist movement and the symbolic character of the declaration (in fact, the Italian government was loath to react against the initiative by repressive means since it was not considered a real challenge to Italian territorial integrity), Bossi's movement was by all sides quickly interpreted as a trump to negotiate a greater decentralization in favor of the Italian northern regions, beginning by reducing the transfers to the subsidized south. Prodi's government reacted to Bossi's challenge by underpinning again Italian's unity with the European cement; the single monetary union to which Prodi had just decided to be firmly committed would leave little room for the *Lega* secessionist dreams. No serious struggle to split Italy by convincing the European chancelleries that Padania, in contrast with the southern Italian regions, would fulfil Maastricht's convergence criteria on monetary union, would succeed, and European governments would close ranks in defense of Italian sovereignty. Padania would not be recognized by anyone, but Bossi's secessionist gamble would not be lacking in fruits.

The immediate aftermath of the Padania crisis revealed what would enshrine the basic lines of the *Lega*'s future political strategy until the present: influencing the Italian national government by creating a strong political movement in the right-wing in order to benefit the Italian northern regions *within* the Italian constitutional framework. Bossi was indeed quite successful in achieving this objective, to the extent that he became Minister of Institutional Reforms and Devolution in some of the subsequent Berlusconi governments and struggled, from that position, to strengthen the regions' power and to design a fiscal reform under federal parameters. The plan, however, could not be implemented, particularly the questions concerning the enhancement of the regions' fiscal autonomy and the decrease of the fiscal dependence on the national level. The disruption caused by the financial crises from 2008 triggered rather a recentralization on decisions regarding public spending.

XVI

Berlusconi's fall into disgrace in Autumn 2011, being due to the criminal prosecution in which he was involved or being because of the refusal of some

European powers to cope with the Cavalieri's insolence and his total lack of skill to face up to crises, made some cadres of the *Lega* realize that they were in a perfect position to lead the resurrection of a right-wing political movement but under the condition according to which such a political stream had to be engaged with an Italian *national* project.

The *Lega* was also committed from its first times with another major issue that would have important consequences in the building of its political identity: the fight against immigration. Under Bossi the *Lega*'s rejection of immigrants encompassed not only European Union outsiders (in the 1990s the wave of immigrants that landed on the coasts of Italy were spearheaded by eastern Europeans and, particularly, by the nationals of a former Italian colony: Albania) but also the southern Italians that went to northern Italy in search of a better future.

In the 2010s the *Lega*'s anti-immigration discourse was nonetheless focused on the refugees from northern Africa and the Middle East that were crossing the Mediterranean (from another former Italian colony: Libya) in usually dreadful conditions. The opposition to immigration from outside the European Union, and particularly to the Muslim immigration from the southern and the eastern coasts of the Mediterranean, required the transformation of the *Lega*'s anti-migration ideology from Italian northern regionalism to an Italian centered nationalism, a task that Matteo Salvini accomplished with an outstanding appeal for the majority of Italian voters.

Salvini fulfilled the gap that Berlusconi had left on the Right and, at the same time, understood that he could challenge neither the European mandates on immigration nor the financial restrictions on deficit and public debt through a territorially fragmented Italy as the one that Bossi conceived in the 1990s with his Padania.

Paradoxically, Salvini, the leader of the *Lega* from 2013 (and between 2018 and 2019 minister of interior and strongman of the Italian government) realized that he could not get into a confrontation with the European Union from a territorially fragmented state as has been Italy from the end of World War II. Setting up the clash in such a position would have been too risky given, for instance, the United Kingdom's experience in which the betrayal of the European integration principles would be able to endanger the national territorial unity. Consequently, Salvini, coached by the renewed mainstream of his party, evolved from an active member of the Young Padanians Movement seeking for Padania's secession in his twenties to a fierce Italian nationalist as soon as he acceded first to the leadership of the *Lega* and then to the Italian government's office as minister of the interior in his forties.

The Italian experience expressed in Salvini's assault to power hatched in the summer of 2019 may be deemed as the political aftermath of the failure of the equation "the strength of the Nation-States depends on the strength of the European integration" that had been more or less awkwardly operative until the 2008 economic crisis. In Salvini's ideology, the welfare of the Italians, the maintenance of the status quo that somehow had provided prosperity to the people, would be from the crisis onward only possible by ignoring the values of the European Union: ignoring the macroeconomic mandates to ensure the euro's sustainability but also the core European values related to human rights and human dignity.

The latter might explain Salvini's (and his *Lega*'s) position on the issue of immigration, which would be shared and even improved by Meloni's *Fratelli d'Italia*. It was not precise to state that Salvini or Meloni refused immigrants. Their struggle relied rather on creating a perpetual second class of citizens who could be exploited as a labor force by the Italians in order to maintain their standard of living. Boosting the fear of an immigrant invasion and closing Italian harbors to avoid the immigrants who had been rescued by the humanitarian ships that had been crossing the Mediterranean from landing on the coast was also an electoral strategy in the short run; for instance, by 2019, the *Lega* from the north had to be voted also in the Italian southern regions (that before voted for the *Movimento 5 Stelle*). If northern leaders pretended to gain hegemony in the whole of Italy, attacking illegal immigration might provide them with the electoral success they so coveted.

XVII

Salvini's operation by the end of the summer of 2019, nevertheless, was frustrated when his strategy of breaking with the *Movimento 5 Stelle* in order to call for elections turned against himself. The political leadership of the *Movimento 5 Stelle* maneuvered to get rid of Salvini from the government while reaching an agreement with the Social-Democrats of the *Partito Democratico* to form a new government under the same prime minister that had headed the previous coalition between the *Lega* and the *Movimento 5 Stelle*: Giuseppe Conte.

If in France the alienation of the immigrants from such regions, and the alienation of the descendants of those immigrants, had been considered a failure of the Republican system, in Salvini's and Meloni's Italy such alienation was precisely the final horizon; after all, if the basic division in Italy was that confronting the Italians against the immigrants, the other disputes that had been lacerating Italian politics for decades (the northern Italians against the southern ones or the Italians from the Left against the Italians from the Right) were easier to conceal.

A strategy like the one that Salvini or Meloni represented, however, could not be achieved in the first instance without a direct confrontation with both the European Union and the other member states. That may be consolidated only if the majority of the states' governments are controlled by leaders (as the experience in the eastern Europe countries gathered around the Visegrád group showed) with similar pretensions.

The legal foundations in order to introduce a cleavage between Italians (extended at most to other European citizens) and non-European immigration and tracing a framework of domination by one of the communities upon the other had been already perceived by invoking doctrines echoing those developed in Poland or in Hungary. As in such states, the Italian legal apparatus, beginning with the judiciary and the Constitutional Court, had adhered to the so-called doctrine of "constitutional identity" in order to avoid the primacy in the application of European Union law. In its January 2017 preliminary reference to the Court of Justice of the European Union, for instance, the *Corte Costituzionale*[31] asked the Court of Justice of the European Union to revisit its previous *Taricco* judgement[32] expressing its conviction that this "would be applicable only if compatible with the constitutional identity of the member state, which it is for the competent authority of that state to assess."[33] Though no specific clash between the Italian nationalistic program embodied in the protection of core elements of its constitutional system and the European Union legal framework emerged, the Italian Right and far-Right had repeatedly expressed their intentions to reassert the national sovereign concerns upon the European values as the ones mentioned in article 2 of the Treaty on European Union.[34]

In short, if the Italian reactionary political elements had been able to cover their political targets by embracing the notion of a national constitutional identity in order to avoid the European commitments, that was because the moderate ones, including the agents of legal interpretation, had anticipated such an outcome, which is none other than turning into a fundamentally discriminatory society, distinguishing between nationals and non-nationals in their access to rights and goods.

The Italian case in the version first delineated by Salvini's *Lega* and then by Meloni's *Fratelli* revealed a stage in which the ones that in some moment of the past had been colonized by the European imperial powers (as in the Middle East or North Africa) were forced to abandon their homes given the circumstances of wars and poverty only to be displaced into some European territory where they are expected to be subjected and economically exploited. Such a situation may be well qualified as another sort of "internal colonization" in the heart of a European Union member state derived from a catharsis of imperial nostalgia that, considering the background of Italian history we have explored, rather might be interpreted as a past that never was.

XVIII

As noticed, the European integration process was not primarily conceived nor developed to provide cohesion within Europe but to provide cohesion within the European nation-state that emerged from war and disintegration.

Both the foundation of the European Coal, Iron and Steel Community and the Common Market Community have produced a great deal of literature but less commented has been the role of the third ground of the original design of European integration, namely, the European Atomic Energy Community (Euratom), which has been crucial in the both the aims of creating a thriving common European economy and of providing cohesion for the nation-states that composed the new supranational experiment.

The other treaty signed in Rome on March 25, 1957, besides the European Economic Community, is the Euratom Treaty, which allowed those that had lost the war (such as Germany and Italy) to share the nuclear power that was being produced by those that had appeared as winners of the contest (France) and, consequently, to share the benefits of economic growth sustained through access to cheap sources of energy. Such an intention was somehow derived from article 1 of the Euratom Treaty whereby it was declared, "It shall be the aim of the Community to contribute to the raising of the standard of living in member states and to the development of commercial exchanges with other countries by the creation of conditions necessary for the speedy establishment and growth of nuclear industries." The accelerated raising of the "standard of living" among the population of the community's member states was, thus, proclaimed as one of the most relevant aims of integration according to both the first version of article 2 of the treaty establishing the European Economic Community and to the mentioned article 1 of the Euratom Treaty.

An operation of that kind was particularly profitable to Italy, which was not rich in other natural sources of energy, such as the coal shared in the European Coal, Iron and Steel Community. Aside from this point, as a loser of the war, an independent production of nuclear power by Italy, if someone had consented to transfer the technology to the Italians to do that, would have been always seen with suspicion by the Western Allies (not to mention if that technology had been provided from the other side of the Iron Curtain).

A western European supranational institution would, thus, from 1957 onward, organize the dissemination of technical knowledge and investment transfers in order to encourage the construction of basic facilities required for the development of nuclear energy. France as the single nuclear power in the area would lead the consolidation of nuclear energy in the rest of the members of the communities, ensuring thus through economic success and the welfare of the citizenry the political stability of those countries. It would be through atomic technology that France would maintain a pole of influence over other European partners independent of the Cold War's turbulences that confronted the Atlantic world defined by the U.S.-British alliance against the Soviet Union and its satellites.

The French prominence in the system explained French governments' willingness to support the approval of a treaty concerning atomic energy cooperation. The government of the Fourth Republic sought through the Euratom Treaty, and given the establishment of de facto French monopolies in the provision of some basic nuclear materials, to subsidize French nuclear development both on civil and military facilities.[35]

At any rate, even though the outcome of the Euratom was in the end more modest than the one that the French had aimed for (because some other European partners did not want to be detached from the British and the U.S. uranium supplies), at least it provided the first and maybe the most complete example of Europeanization of techno-scientific research, especially in the field of nuclear fusion developed from the very beginning in a European common space.[36]

It is true that comparing with the original pretensions attributed to the founders of the European integration process, that is, promoting European unity through nuclear energy, the final result of the Euratom project became modest.[37] The mentioned distrust by the other member states of French motives in supporting Euratom and the growing environmental and safety concerns about nuclear energy, eventually resulted in the marginalization of the treaty.

But there might be traced some effects of the European nuclear power framework that did not completely fall into irrelevance, particularly after the oil crisis in the 1970s that ended the abundance of imported oil. Indeed, the 1973 crises made more evident the need to safeguard Europe with autonomous sources of energy. As in the previous time of economic growth, in facing the problem of fossil energy shortage given the reduction of supply concerted by the producer countries, France reinvigorated its nuclear energy policy: the French prime minister, Pierre Messmer, announced a huge nuclear program aimed at generating all of France's electricity from nuclear power and boosted the installation of fifty-six reactors over the next fifteen years. But France's developments in nuclear power were also exploited by other members of the Euratom and the Common Market Communities, Italy remarkably, which was eager to purchase French energy without paying the costs of building its own nuclear plants. Even though the Italian government worked on a plan on energy devoted to lowering the country's dependence on fossil fuels by making huge investments in the nuclear energy sector, between 1970 and 1980 there was ordered the construction of only one reactor, that of the Caorso power plant, which was completed in 1978.

Given the Euroatom, the postwar Italian governments had not been very concerned in building nuclear reactors. The lack of interest on the subject was still more acute once the electricity sector was nationalized in ENEL's hands during the 1960s. The trend of avoiding the production of its own nuclear energy was maintained in Italy even during the oil crises of the 1970s and during the 1980s when, following the Chernobyl disaster in 1986, it was decided to phase out the existing nuclear plants.

In spite of the fact that during the 2000s the Italian government adopted strategies toward the revival of nuclear power, in June 2011, following the Fukushima nuclear accident, Italian voters decided through referendum to cancel the building of any of the nuclear power structures that had been conceived in the previous years. The intense seismic activity experienced in the Italian peninsula (the same problem that had hindered the nuclear power projects in Japan) advised against the construction of nuclear plants. If that concern on promoting the establishment of nuclear facilities in a territory frequently devastated by earthquakes had called for restraint in yielding to nuclear power had been already present from the first stages of the nuclear power developments, the Fukushima accident in 2011 decisively contributed to cancel any plan in that regard.

However, if an economy with scarcity of energetic resources, such as the Italian one, can grow without nuclear power, it is due to the fact that part of its energy *is imported* in the framework of the single market. At least around 10 percent of the electrical energy imported by Italy has nuclear origins: it comes from France in the system that Euratom had designed. The luxury of setting aside nuclear power, in the same way as Germany planned to do after the Fukushima episode, was viable only as long as said economy belonged to a single market in which nuclear power is produced by others.

XIX

Only recently, Italy has become a relevant producer of renewable energy in a way that may help to overcome the traditional Italian power deficit. Solar energy production accounted for around 8 percent of the total electric production in the country by the middle of the 2010s. Bioenergy, wind power and geothermal power also have made an important contribution to Italian energy demands. In a similar fashion as what had happened in Spain, nevertheless, the transition from nuclear and fossil-fuel energy to renewable power, particularly given the boom in solar installations deployed by the first decade of the twenty-first century through government incentives, represented a financial burden that lay in the background of the Italian banking crisis and the sovereign debt crisis that were corroding the Italian economy, particularly from 2010 onward.

The problems of the Italian banks were still far from being solved by 2020. Europe's most dangerous stock of public borrowing—some 1.5 trillion euros ($1.7 trillion)—was concentrated on the balance sheets of banks in Rome and Milan transforming the Italian debt, combined with poor growth, into one of the most pressing issues for European economic development.[38]

War in Ukraine starting in February 2022 showed the urgency to be less reliant on Russian gas and oil supplies. The Italian imports of Algerian gas through a pipeline crossing Tunisia and reaching Sicily (named as the Enrico Mattei pipeline in remembrance of the man who struggled to strengthen economic and cultural ties between Italy and African developing nations),[39] leaving aside the environmental problems that represent grounding a power supply system on carbon sources, are not enough to cover Italian energy demands, let alone to compensate an eventual ban on all Russian gas imports in eastern and central Europe, such as the one that was announced a few days after the invasion of Ukraine by the Russian troops.

The Greenstream pipeline departing from Libya and supplying gas also through Sicily is not sufficient either to cover European energy needs and, on the other hand, such a route is also threatened by political instability and the civil conflicts perturbing Libya from the times of the fall of Gaddafi's dictatorship in 2011. On the other hand, France's hegemony in European nuclear power production induced their governments to be reluctant to promote the consolidation of a continental gas supply network coming from the south of Europe. After all, France pressed the European Commission to include nuclear power within the group of "green" energies in the strategy of leaving behind carbon-based sources of energy, and much more damaging for the cause against climate change, such as gas and oil.

In summary, the struggle to fight against the energy deficit partially led to an enormous public debt that, at the same time, is able to threaten not only Italian stability but also the stability of Europe. The Italian strategy in externalizing in the European Union all sorts of problems that oppress the country (in this case energetic and economic) might have its limits—or not—and they might indeed be the limits of the European Union integration project itself.

XX

One attempt to cover Italian economic inadequacies already occurred by designing the European Monetary Union. The lukewarm Italian involvement in inspiring the architecture of European integration had some exceptions by the decade of the 1980s, notably represented, on the one hand, by the reform of the treaties conceived in the so-called "Spinelli Project," which would influence the elaboration of the Treaty on European Union.

The Italian hosting of the June 1985 Summit of the Presidents and Prime Ministers at Milan revealed at its turn to be also decisive in pushing for a substantive amendment of the treaties' structure. Before the astonishment of Eurosceptic figures such as Margaret Thatcher, with the intention to supersede the divisions between the members that gambled for a great leap ahead in the federalization of Europe and the ones, led by the United Kingdom, that hold the maintenance of the status quo, the Italian premier and chairman of the meeting, Bettino Craxi, proposed for the first time in the ten-year history of the European Council of heads of state or government, *to vote* and, thus, to take by majority the decision to convene or not an intergovernmental conference to amend the treaties.[40]

The extension, within the Council of Ministers decision-making process, of qualified majority instead of unanimity in a wide number of areas, and the consequent removal of the ability for a single state to block progress, counted indeed among the major novelties in the resulting reform of the treaties that crystallized from the intergovernmental conference voted in Milan and gathered in December 1985: the Single European Act. Such a document would anticipate some of the characteristics that would define the structural reform entailed later in the 1992 Treaty on European Union entrenching the shift in the balance of power away from the member states toward the community institutions.[41]

Another remarkable Italian contribution to the governance of the European Union that was being founded at that time was represented by the 1989 Report by Tommaso Padoa-Schioppa's on Economic and Monetary Union, which would also lay the basis for the Maastricht Treaty. Prime Minister Andreotti would propose at the last minute of the Treaty on European Union negotiations to add an automatic deadline of 1999 into the draft in order to implement the single currency (to the consternation of both the British and the Bundesbank).

As suggested, British reluctance to European integration soared during these years of Italian initiatives. Thatcher had expressed her disdain against the Italian political staff by the inclusion of qualified majority voting in the Milan episode and would become even more exasperated by the economic integration measures that the Italians envisaged. No wonder Thatcher, regarding whom the steps toward the European changes prepared, among other factors, the grounds for her resignation from office, stated that "if I were an Italian I might prefer rule from Brussels too."[42] Through such a sardonic comment, the former British prime minister, expressed that the Italian proneness to be directly subjected to a European supranational power was understandable given the Italian weaknesses as a nation-state, no less the Italian flaws as an economic power considering, in Thatcher's views, that the Italian elites had seen in being tied to the single currency the horizon to overcome their domestic economic precariousness.

The path to the euro, however, and the need to fulfill the convergence criteria established in the Treaty on European Union and in the related protocols, soon proved to be disastrous for Italian political stability. The previously mentioned decomposition of the traditional Italian political cadres, beginning with one of the main figures behind European reform initiatives such as Craxi, took place during the process of the Maastricht Treaty ratification.

If it was not enough with the political turmoil the participation of the Bank of Italy in the European Exchange Rate Mechanism, by September 1992, following unprecedented speculative attacks, was suspended with the ejection of the lira from the monetary system.[43] Such a disarray forced the Italian government to seek the way to restore the confidence of the markets by adopting a package of measures in order to reduce fiscal imbalance, debt, and to control the inflation that fostered still more a social discontent already exacerbated given the cascade of corruption scandals.

XXI

By the second decade of the twenty-first century, the opacity of the Italian banking system and the failures of the Italian economy still persisted. It had already been symptomatic that even on the brink of the economic collapse that represented the sovereign debt crisis at the beginning of the 2010s, and considering that the Italian system had been one of the most affected public debt systems through one of the highest bond yield surges in Europe between 2011 and 2012, the Italian government, unlike what happened in places such as Greece, Cyprus, Ireland, Portugal, or Spain, *never* asked for a bailout by the European Financial Stability Fund or its successor, the European Stability Mechanism.[44]

Without bailout Italy was not subjected to the same level of scrutiny in applying the austerity measures that had been required of the other European member states in order to gain access to loans, though the weaknesses that hovered over the Italian economy, such as high debt-to-GDP ratio, the increasing and volatile costs of servicing debt and the slow economic growth, were as worrying, if not more so, than in other southern European states such as Spain. On the other hand, the austerity package foreseen by the technocratic Italian government led by Mario Monti passed with the intention to trim the debt was very contested both at social and political level and poorly implemented, since the electoral results of Monti's coalition in the 2013 elections were catastrophic, and he had to resign.

However, and in spite of such sinister perspectives, Italy eluded default and, consequently, so did the whole of Europe.

Even before the official activation of the asset purchase programs by mid-2014, the European Central Bank provided cheap refinancing and liquidity boosts to some European member states with its "long-term refinance operations" that already by 2012 were qualified as a "quantitative easing program by the back door,"[45] to which Italy appeared to be one of the chief beneficiaries. At face value, the measure permitted the containment of the calamitous Italian bond yield surge and paved the way to the sustainability of Italian debt without any additional aid, while the transition to the implementation of the official purchasing of securities program (which would also benefit both the public and corporate sectors in Italy).

Mario Draghi became Italian prime minister by February 2021, leading again a technocratic government similar to the one led by Monti almost a decade before and with the Italian economy pressed by similar unresolved challenges that Monti handled (maybe even worsened by the economic and social disgraces that the eruption of the COVID-19 pandemic represented). Nevertheless, Draghi's response as an Italian prime minister was similar to that which he had promoted as European Central Bank president: to involve the European Central Bank system in concealing the Italian economic lack of sustainability, beginning with that of its banking system.

By 2022, the European Central Bank still held 30 percent of the Italian debt (not to mention the unknown Italian public debt held by the Italian banks under the coverage of the European Central Bank) allowing the maintenance of the Italian sovereign bond to moderate yield rates.[46] Ensuring the political and national cohesion of the third economy in the Eurozone (and preventing its fall) through monetary policy has been from 2011 to the present a priority for the European authorities, leaving aside the claims coming from the German political and economic elites and from the German Federal Constitutional Court regretting the loss of competitiveness of German corporations and the sacrifice of the German savers in order to allow the economic continuity of one of its biggest member states.

As usual, the European Union institutions, this time through the European Central Bank measures, came to the rescue and preservation of the nation-state. But as some observers pointed out, there was no way to see trajectory whatsoever for Italy to generate the degree of productivity growth needed to render its foreign debt sustainable.[47] The only way to avoid disaster was for the European Central Bank to support Italian debt forever. By the beginning of the 2020s, nevertheless, it was already rather illusory to believe that it was possible to indefinitely pump money in order to satisfy Italian financial urgencies without endangering at the same time the entire monetary union.

XXII

Apart from the previously mentioned remarkable exceptions, and despite the popular majority adhesion to European Federalism that arose during the 1980s, Italy did not play a major political role in the building of European integration (at least in correspondence with the weight of the state within the European project in demographic and economic terms).

We have seen Spinelli's idealistic approaches that influenced in the reforms experienced in the European Single Act and in the Treaty of Maastricht, the coup that orchestrated Craxi in the 1985 summit in Milan introducing the majority vote in the European Council, the Italian contributions in the reforms of the treaties that would take place on the road to the creation of the European Union or the Italian participation in the design of the single currency.

We could also add to such innovations more secondary ones developed previously, by the first years of the communities, that have become of the utmost importance within the institutional framework of the European Union. Such is indeed the case of the preliminary ruling before the Court of Justice of the European Union; such a procedure, entailed in the former article 177 of the European Economic Community, was likely to be inspired in the *questione di costituzionalità* before the Italian Constitutional Court and translated by the Italian jurist Nicola Catalano to the European court's mechanisms to examine the compatibility between European and member states' law.[48]

However, rather than being involved in the decisions that would define the European fate, the Italian establishment were prone to use and to exploit first the communities, and later the union, to manage (and eventually to surmount) the challenges that had been besieging Italian national cohesion. If there is a nation-state "rescued" by European integration in Milward's terms, although such operations had been more or less hidden, that is Italy.

European institutions, on their part, had been many times profoundly concerned about to which extent Italian domestic problems might be able to destabilize the entire continental political and economic structures. Corruption and widespread cronyism within Italian public administration, regional inequality, macroeconomic disorders, and the Italian energy deficit and nontransparent banking system have been perceived as endemic risks all the time able to poison the entire European governance. When things looked serious for Italy, the European powers, sharing complicities with the Italian elite, did not hesitate to wipe out the uncontrolled Italian rulers in order to impose a technocratic solution directly connected with Brussels or with the European Central Bank headquarters in Frankfurt am Main.

As the former governor of the Bank of Italy, Guido Carli, wrote, "[T]he European Union represented an alternative path for the solution of problems which we were not managing to handle through the normal channels of government and parliament."[49] In other words, Italy benefited from the democratic deficit of the European Union institutions to enforce a mandate against its national structures of representation. The state was to be constrained by the European Union to put its house in order.[50]

The move described above was clearly given in three situations during the last decades: the first, when the judicially besieged Berlusconi and, given his inoperative way to handle the economic crises, the European establishment in connivance with the Italian one forced his resignation in November 2011 and replaced him with Mario Monti's technocratic executive.

The second, as we have highlighted, when in August 2019 an equally dangerous Mateo Salvini, who had no intention of respecting European limits either on deficit or on public debt, was on the verge of precipitating snapshot general elections to entrench his majority. The European powers blessed the removal of the *Lega* from the government and the formation of a new one through the coalition between the *Movimento 5 Stelle* and the social democrats.

But there would be another third movement in this fashion not long after the previous one when in the winter of 2021, in the midst of the COVID-19 crisis and the fall of the Conte government, another technocratic coalition was formed around Mario Draghi as prime minister. Such coalition was supported by a large majority of the Italian Parliament, including the *Movimento 5 Stelle*, the *Lega*, the still surviving Berlusconi party *Forza Italia*, the *Partito Democratico*, the centrist *Italia Viva*, and the leftist *Articolo Uno*. The shock that was looming had to be of big proportions to the extent that even Salvini had to relinquish his political roadmap and support Draghi's initiative through the involvement of the *Lega* in the government.

XXIII

Italy is a good example to envisage how the European integration project had been obliged to absorb the problems created by the nation-state' chaos. As we have seen, in the case of energy output and public borrowing, Italian political and economic cadres used the union as a receptacle to externalize their crises.

The union, however, was not likely to cope with a generalized political and economic default concerning more than one of its biggest members. Until the present the strategy both at the European level of governance had been grounded on the attempt of diverting problems, trying to solve them in a selective manner step by step, or simply blinding the eye (as happened with the Italian banking system) to initiatives that make corruption, unfair extraction of resources, and cronyism still more acute. The big crash might precipitate if patchworks are not enough to cover a chain reaction of economic and political crisis in Italy as its epicenter combined with other desperate moves from other nation-states stubbornly determined to ensure their cohesion through plundering and abuse.

On the other hand, regarding territorial cohesion, European integration worked as somewhat of a double-edged sword. The European support entrenched Italian unity both through providing funds for the most impoverished southern Italian regions and, particularly after the establishment of the single currency and the design of the European Central Bank, by ensuring financial coverage to attenuate the escalation of the Italian bond yield, to palliate the deficits in energy demands and, in short, to prevent a general default of the Italian banking system. However, the single market, economic integration, and the free movement of goods, services, and capitals meant that the wealthier and more industrialized north of Italy strengthened its economic attachment to the northern European economies (and particularly to the German one) rather than to the *Mezzogiorno*. From an economic point of view, and in terms of possibilities of economic growth, the European Union contributed thus to Italian territorial division. The latter might explain the recurrent discourses in northern Italy pledging for economic (and even sometimes political) separation from the Italian south and, in a more moderate fashion, a discourse on the "differential regionalism" (*regionalismo differenziato*). The "differential regionalism," though outlined by the Italian Constitution itself and somehow inherited from the origins of the Republic's formation after World War II, was in the last decades developed (and leaving apart the discussions on the powers of the regions during the COVID-19 pandemic) to define mechanisms favorable to the northern regions in order to contain transfers of resources to the south.[51]

Finally, the entrenchment of "internal colonization" was not only a hallmark of those European member states that had lost vast overseas empires. Also the ones whose colonial adventures were scarce and late, such as the Italian case with its imperialistic episodes in Libya, in Ethiopia or in Somalia, apart from its European expansionism before and during World War II, practiced several forms of internal looting with European coverage: repression of centripetal trends boosted by regions and minority nations, social regression, and, in more recent times, anti-immigration crusades (with the unconcealed aim of ensuring unity among Italian nationals at the expenses of the extra-European aliens) give good accounts on such initiatives toward domination and authoritarianism in order to protect national identity and the social and economic welfare of its members.

XXIV

In a similar direction as the movements experienced in France, though much anticipated, the economic *diktat* provided by the European integration around the single currency also precipitated in Italy the evaporation of the political center.

As pointed out, the first shock wave came in 1992 with the collapse of the traditional parties that had been involved in Italian governance from the conclusion of World War II. That was the time in which Silvio Berlusconi founded a brand-new party on the shoulders of his media empire and joined with the heirs of fascism and the northern regionalists to stop the heirs of the Communists (it was hard to accept by the West that the fall of the Berlin Wall would represent that the Italian left, once closely tied to Moscow, would accede to power).

But, paradoxically as it might sound, Berlusconi's defenestration in 2011 (given his fiscal frivolities within the agonic context of the sovereign debt urgencies) was the starting point of a new cycle leading to political extremism. Monti's technocratic government designed a labor market reform and adopted fiscal discipline measures that only contributed to polarize both the society and institutional politics. The *Movimento 5 Stelle* won the largest single party share of vote in the Chamber of Deputies in the 2013 general election, a success that required the center-left and center-right groupings, plus the small centrist party created by an electorally humiliated Monti, to form a government. That grand coalition sought to navigate between the external need for the European Central Bank support and the domestic political need to put some resistance to fiscal surveillance by the Eurozone institutions.

A continuous political and economic turbulence forced the appointment of the young mayor of Florence, Matteo Renzi, as prime minister by February 2014. But the reaffirmation of the European Central Bank support through the massive bond purchase required new reforms of the labor market and new fiscal discipline measures that ignited the society through large demonstrations and a general strike. The loss of a constitutional referendum in December 2016 was the straw that broke the camel's back for Renzi's government, with an already harshly deteriorated popularity given the economic impositions coming from the Eurozone institutions.

As discussed above, when the elections came in April 2018, the only plausible government was the one constituted by the extremes: the Euroesceptic Five Star and the *Lega* under the premiership of the non-elected law-professor Giuseppe Conte. After a brief period of coalition between the *Movimento 5 Stelle* and the Democrats once the *Lega* retired from the government, the center was likely to resurrect with the new grand coalition led by Draghi.

But such a struggle to refrain the extremes proved to be impotent once the September 2022 elections elevated Giorgia Meloni and her party *Fratelli d'Italia* at the head of a right-wing populist and nationalist coalition (also integrated by the *Lega*, *Forza Italia* and other minor parties) making of the Italian government the first one in western Europe dominated by the most radical elements of the far-right since the end of World War II. Meloni's government was formed almost exactly one hundred years after Benito Mussolini's assault on power through his 1922 *Marcia su Roma*.

XXV

The 2022 clash between Russia and Ukraine left Italy in an ambivalent position. On the one hand, the previous Italian complicity of the *Lega-Movimento 5 Stelle* government with Putin's regime, particularly with some elements such as Salvini, generated some distrust among the Western allies once Russia launched a general offensive to instigate the overturn of the Ukrainian government and to extend its control upon the eastern and southern territories of Ukraine. In that sense, Salvini's popular regression within the landscape of the Italian Right might be interpreted as a punishment after having received the favors of the Kremlin.

But, on the other hand, regarding the deprivation of the Russian sources of energy that hurt the economies in northern and central Europe, Italy emerged as a relevant replacement for Russian oil and gas given its nearness with the Algerian and Libyan deposits, apart from the more recently discovered gas reserves in the eastern Mediterranean between Cyprus and Israel.

Projects of improving the gas capacity in existing pipelines and of building new provision channels from Greece soon appeared as an alternative to elude the block in the east caused by Russian aggression and the subsequent sanctions against Putin's regime agreed among the European governments, though the completion of such projects revealed would take time in bearing any fruit.

In the long run, the creation of a new energy network having the Italian peninsula as a hub might even minimize the chronic energy flaws that, as we have seen, have hindered Italian economic activity. But in the short run it was not possible to count on Italy as a new gateway in safeguarding European energy supplies, and the crises overshadowing the European economy as consequences of war and inflation also affected Italian politics.

The above-mentioned Enrico Mattei gas pipeline, the main gateway of Algerian gas penetration into the Italian peninsula was by 2022 only able to transfer around 34 billion cubic meters of natural gas of those 76 billion cubic meters that Italy consumed. The Italian energy deficit was, by the beginning of the war in Ukraine, still there.

The lack of nuclear power plants made the dream of Italian energy self-sufficiency still more difficult to attain, not to mention any idea of becoming an energy-exporting power. The increase in the costs of production considering the rise in the prices of commodities also widened Italy's trade deficit.

In a different fashion, a new energy horizon grounded on the multiplication of gas and oil pipelines from the eastern Mediterranean would not reduce the problem of returning the debt that was not going to be solved in a scenario marked by the need to satisfy Germany's demands grounded on containing inflation, raising interest rates, and reducing the European Central Bank purchases of debt belonging to southern European states. Colossal energy infrastructures have to be financed in one way or another, and the Italian debt burden coming from the previous sovereign debt crisis was still strangling the Italian administration's margin of maneuver. The incompatibility between Italian and German interests in monetary policy given an inflationary perspective might lead the European monetary authorities, in a different sense to what happened in 2012, to abandon Italy to its luck and, thus, to aggravate the Italian debt crisis to the extent of making more realistic the possibility of its default. European monetary authorities, in other words, shall be at some point forced to choose *between antagonistic national interests* creating thus new tensions in European political and economic governance.

XXVI

Economic uncertainty led to political uncertainty and Draghi's governmental coalition became by July 2022 the first government of a major European Union economy to collapse (in parallel to the collapse of the government of another western European power though already outside the union: that of Boris Johnson in Great Britain). The *Movimento 5 Stelle* opposition to Draghi's plan to tackle inflation and energy costs triggered the process that concluded with the prime minister's resignation. There was an attempt to salvage the coalition, but it definitively failed when Draghi lost the backing of both the *Lega* and Berlusconi's party *Forza Italia*. Meloni's far-right party, which had never joined Draghi's government, appeared on the first instance to benefit from that *débâcle*, but there was also delight within the Russian regime watching the Italian turmoil at the worst moment for the European struggle to launch economic sanctions in retaliation for the invasion of Ukraine.

Italian economic interests were simply not pleased in cutting ties with Russia since from 2012 to 2021 the total value of Italy's exports to Russia had been equivalent to 8.2 billion euros per year on average. This amount had been much higher than that of countries such as Spain (2.1 billion on average) and France (6.1 billion). Much of the damage concerning European sanctions against Russia affected strategic industries for the Italian economy: the textile sector, the food sector, and that of machinery production. Once in power, however, Meloni firmly placed Italy within the ranks of the Western opposition to Russia's aggression and frequently expressed her government's staunch support to Ukraine in its military effort. The political and diplomatic theater somehow silenced the economic and trade fluxes flirting at some point with Western (and European) geopolitical adversaries.

Once the admirer of Italy that, as were many other northern Europeans, Lord Byron was, he wrote that in Italy "there is, in fact, no law or government at all; and it is wonderful how well things go on without them";[52] but in modern times, and particularly after World War II, things would not be so wonderful for Italy as Byron described if it had not been for the law, the order, and the financial support that the European framework has provided for the survival of that nation-state. And there are no safeguards that all such tenets will be maintained in the near future.

NOTES

1. Monte S. Finkelstein, *Separatism, the Allies and the Mafia: The Struggle for Sicilian Independence, 1943–1948*. (Bethlehem, PA: Lehigh University Press, 1999), 36.

2. See Keith Lowe, *Savage Continent: Europe in the Aftermath of World War II* (London: Penguin, 2013; first edition 2012), 272; Tony Judt, *Postwar: A History of Europe since 1945* (London: Penguin, 2005), 33–34.

3. Claudio Pavone, *Una Guerra civile: Saggio storico sulla moralità nella Resistenza* (Turin: Universali Bollati Boringhieri, 2006).

4. See Giacomo Delledone, "La resistenza in Assemblea Constituente e nel testo costituzionale italiano del 1948," *Historia Constitucional* 10 (August 2009): 217–41. Available at http://www.historiaconstitucional.com/index.php/historiaconstitucional/issue/view/12.

5. Alfonso Tesauro and Ginevra Capocelli, "The Fundamentals of the New Italian Constitution," *Canadian Journal of Economics and Political Science* 20, no. 1 (February 1954): 44–58, 48.

6. See Chris Thornhill, *A Sociology of Constitutions: Constitutions and State Legitimacy in Historical-Sociological Perspective* (Cambridge: Cambridge University Press, 2011), 332.

7. Malcolm Evans, "The Italian Constitutional Court," *International and Comparative Law Quarterly* 17, no.3 (July 1968): 602–33, 603.

8. Antoni Abad Ninet and James A. Gardner, "Distinctive Identity Claims in Federal Systems: Judicial Policing of Subnational Variance," *International Journal of Constitutional Law* 14, no.2 (April, 2016): 378–410, 394.

9. The *Partito Sardo d'Azione*'s secretary general, Christian Solinas, concluded by 2018 an electoral agreement with the *Lega Nord*, which paved the way for Solina's appointment as a member of the Italian Senate and later for his accession to the presidency of the region.

10. On the Gruber-De Gasperi Agreement and, generally, on the evolution of the status of the South Tyrol within Italy, see Vito Breda, *Constitutional Law and Regionalism: A Comparative Analysis of Regionalist Negotiations* (Cheltenham and Northampton: Edward Publishing, 2018), 79–88; and Elizabeth Alber, "Qualified Autonomy versus Secessionist Discourses in Europe: The Case of South Tyrol," in *States Falling Apart? Secessionist and Autonomy Movements in Europe*, eds. Eva Maria Belser, Alexandra Fang-Bär, Nina Massüger, and Rekha Oleschak Pillai (Bern: Stämpfli Verlag, 2015), 275.

11. General Assembly UN Resolution 1497 (XV) of October 31, 1960, and General Assembly UN Resolution 1661(XVI) of November 28, 1961.

12. Constitutional Law no. 1 10.11.1971 (n 60).

13. See Annex I and Annex III, of the Austrian and Italian Agreement of September 5, 1946.

14. United Nations Security Council Resolution 16 of January 10, 1947, on the approval of the Statute of the Free Territory of Trieste.

15. On the Free Territory of Trieste, see Maura Elise Hametz, *Making Trieste Italian, 1918–1954* (Woodbridge/Rochester: Boydell Press, 2005); and Bogdan C. Novak, *Trieste, 1941–1954: The Ethnic, Political and Ideological Struggle* (Chicago, IL: University of Chicago Press, 1970).

16. In fact, the territorial claims over the former Free Territory of Trieste would not be stopped until the conclusion of the Treaty of Osimo signed in 1975 by Italy and Yugoslavia.

17. See Bruce Ackerman, *Revolutionary Constitutions: Charismatic Leadership and the Rule of Law* (Cambridge, MA, and London: Belknap Press of Harvard University Press, 2019) 131–50; Gianfranco Pasquino, "Italy's Transition to Democracy: 1943–1948," in *Transitions from Authoritarian Rule: Southern Europe*, eds. Guillermo O'Donnell, Philippe Schmitter, and Laurence Whitehead (Baltimore, MD: Johns Hopkins University Press, 1986), 60.

18. Mark Mazower, *Dark Continent: Europe's Twentieth Century* (New York: Vintage Books, 2000; first edition), 228.

19. Indro Montanelli and Mario Cervi, *Storia d'Italia: Volume IX: 1943–1948* (Milano: Rizzoli Editore, 2006), 306–17.

20. Quoted by Judt, *Postwar*, 95.

21. See Bruce Ackerman, *Revolutionary Constitutions: Charismatic Leadership and the Rule of Law* (Cambridge, MA, and London: Belknap Press of Harvard

University, 2019), 146–47; Paul Ginsborg, *A History of Contemporary Italy: Society and Politics, 1943–1988* (London: Penguin Books: 1990), 103.

22. See Victor Zaslavsky, *Lo Stalinismo e la Sinistra Italiana: Dal mito dell'Urss alla fine del communismo 1945–1991* (Milano: Mondadori, 2004), 84–85; Vladislav M. Zubok, *A Failed Empire: The Soviet Union in the Cold War from Stalin to Gorbachev* (Chapel Hill, NC: University of North Carolina Press, 2007), 76.

23. Giuliano Garavini, *After Empires: European Integration, Decolonization, and the Challenge from the Global South, 1957–1986* (New York: Oxford University Press, 2012), 64.

24. Paul Ginsborg, *A History of Contemporary Italy: Society and Politics, 1943–1988* (London: Penguin, 1990), 256–57; Mazower, *Dark Continent*, 312.

25. Aldo Cassuto and Muriel Grindrod, "The Regional Experiment in Italy," *The World Today* 26, no. 7 (July 1970): 305–12, 306.

26. Paul Ginsborg, *Italy and Its Discontents: Family, Civil* Seeciety*, State: 1980–2001* (London: Allen Lane/The Penguin Press, 2001), 251.

27.Perry Anderson, *The New Old World* (London and New York: Verso, 2009), 282.

28. Ginsborg, *Italy and Its Discontents*, 251.

29. Giuseppe Martinico, "Between Mimetism and Parasitism: Italian Populism in a Comparative Perspective," *European Public Law* 26, no.4 (2020) 921–40, 921.

30. Ginsborg, *Italy and Its Discontents*, 178.

31. Italian Constitutional Court Order n.24/2017, of January 26, 2017.

32. Court of Justice of the European Union Judgement Case C-105/14 *Taricco* of September 8, 2015.

33. Italian Constitutional Court Order n.24/2017, of January 26, 2017, para. 7; see on that resolution Federico Fabbrini and András Sajó, "The Dangers of Constitutional Identity," *European Law Journal* 25, no. 4 (July 2019): 457–73, 459.

34. Roberto D'Alimonte, "How Populists Won in Italy?," *Journal of Democracy* 30, no.1 (January 2019): 114–27.

35. Andrew Moravcsik, *The Choice for Europe: Social Purpose and State Power form Messina to Maastricht* (London: UCL Press, 1998), 105.

36. Barbara Curli, "Italy, Euratom and Early Research on Controlled Thermonuclear Fusion (1957–1962)," in *Nuclear Italy: An International History of Italian Nuclear Policies during the Cold War*, eds. Elisabetta Bini and Igor Londero (Trieste: Edizioni Università di Trieste, 2017), 59.

37. Giandomenico Majone, *Dilemmas of European Integration: The Ambiguities and Pitfalls of Integration by Stealth* (Oxford: Oxford University Press, 2005), 6.

38. Giovanni Salzano, Demetrios Pogkas, and Ben Sills, "Why Italy's Debts Are Europe's Big Problem," February 3, 2019. Available at https://www.bloomberg.com/graphics/2019-italian-banks/.

39. Marcello Colitti, *Energia e sviluppo in Italia: La vicenda di Enrico Mattei* (Bari: De Donato, 1979).

40. Van Middelaar, *The Passage to Europe*, 104.

41. Derek W. Urwin, *The Community of Europe: A History of European Integration since 1945* (London and New York: Longman, 1993), 231.

42. Margaret Thatcher, *The Downing Street Years* (London: HarperCollins, 1993), 742.

43. Marco Bassetto, "Fiscal Policy and Price Stability. The Case of Italy, 1992–98," *Chicago Fed Letter* 233, December 2006. Available at https://www.chicagofed.org/publications/chicago-fed-letter/2006/december-233.

44. On the bailouts affecting Cyprus, Greece, Ireland, Portugal, and Spain, see, among an oceanic literature, Adam Tooze, *Crashed: How a Decade of Financial Crises Hanged the World* (New York: Viking, 2018); and Pierre-Olivier Gourinchas, Philippe Martin, and Todd Messer, "The Economics of Sovereign Debt, Bailouts and the Eurozone Crisis," *CEPR Discussion Papers*, 14891, June 2020. Available at https://papers.ssrn.com/sol3/papers.cfm?abstract_id=3628214#./

45. See David M. Henningsen, "The Origins of Italian Sovereign Debt Crisis," *Claremont McKenna College Senior Theses*, Paper 379, May 2012. Available at http://scholarship.claremont.edu/cmc_theses/379, 9.

46. See Alvise Lennkh-Yunus, "Italy: Bond-Buying Shift from ECB to private Sector Requires Policy Flexibility, Political Stability," *Scope Ratings*, June 15, 2022. Available at https://www.scoperatings.com/ratings-and-research/research/EN/171430.

47. See, for instance, Wolfgang Münchau, "When Did We Lose the Fight," *Euro Intelligence*, January 23, 2022. Available at https://www.eurointelligence.com/column/when-did-we-lose-the-fight.

48. Vera Fritz, *Juges et avocats généraux de la Cour de Justice de l'Union Européenne (1952–1972): Une approche biographique de l'histoire d'une révolution juridique* (Frankfurt am Main: Vittorio Klostermann, 2018), 62.

49. Guido Carli, *Cinquant'anni di vita italiana* (Bari: Editori Laterza, 1993), 435.

50. See Ginsborg, *Italy and Its Discontents*, 243.

51. See Lorenza Violini, *Una forma di stato a regionalismo differenziato? Percorsi e argomenti per l'attuazione dell'Art. 116, III comma, Cost* (Torino: G Giappichelli Editore, 2021).

52. 2 January 1821, *Byron's Letters and Journals*, Vol. 8 (Cambridge, MA: Belknap Press at Harvard University Press, 1977), 55, quoted by Anderson, *The New Old World*, 278.

Chapter 4

Revenges

I

France achieved something brilliant: after being defeated, humiliated, and conquered by Germany in 1940, and after having established a regime that actively collaborated with the occupant during more than four long years, it appeared as a winner of the war beside the United States, Great Britain, and the Soviet Union.

Though the French did not attend the Yalta conference, in that meeting it was decided that France would be considered an Allied power and that it would take control of some territories in Germany. French representatives would be integrated in the Allied Control Council, the governing body called to exercise supreme power in Germany. Rhineland-Palatinate, the Saar, Württemberg-Hohenzollern, Baden, the district of Lindau, and even a part of Berlin fell under French dominion. The Saar would be constituted as an independent state under a French protectorate in 1947 and would remain in such condition until the first of January of 1957 when it became a new German *Land* after a referendum in 1955 in which most of the population voted for integration into Germany, and that was reflected in the Luxembourg agreements of 1956. France, in sum, *exercised a kind of colonization of parts of Germany*, among them some territories at the heart of the coal extraction zones and the steel industry.

The French authorities had already taken control of the coal and steel resources in the Ruhr basin after World War I, a history somehow that would be repeated by the end of the second global conflict. But when it began to be clear that Germany, at least the western part of it, would become a federation with higher degrees of sovereignty under the 1949 German Basic Law and that the Allies would not rule directly any longer, the French authorities sought to retain at least some influence upon the German steel industry and the raw materials extracted in the parts of Germany that the French controlled, which were essential for French industry itself.

Not surprisingly, one of the architects of the creation of the European Coal, Iron, and Steel Community, Jean Monnet, had been in charge of the modernization plan for the French economy, and it was from that position that he recognized the importance of solving France's permanent coal deficit.[1] Indeed, French occupation of parts of Germany ensured the provision of German coal, but what would happen if the Germans would gain some degree of sovereignty? What would happen, in short, after the French "*decolonization*" of German territories?

In spite of the fact that the French authorities were delighted with Germany's total submission (they would back any proposal prone to annihilate German industry and to block any kind of political development toward the creation of a German Federation), such a situation would not last long.[2] As is well known, the threat of the Soviet Union's power changed the perspective of the two other Western Allies, the United States and Britain, to face up to the problem of the postwar German status.[3] From the Allied London Conference of 1948–1949, both the British and the Americans would support the economic and political development of Germany.[4] After all, west Germany was the frontline in the fight of the Cold War and, under the Anglo-American vision, could not fall into Stalin's circle of influence.

The alternative of a neutral, unified, and demilitarized Germany (inspired in the decisions adopted on Austria) though rhetorically announced by both sides, the Western Allies and the Soviet Union, was not really desired anywhere, and still less in Paris. The holding of eastern Germany by Stalin, indeed the cornerstone of the Communist policy in Central Europe, also defined the United States' priorities in which were included the provision of financial aid to entrench the market economy in western Germany and the setting up of a German federation with a national level of governance vested with centralized powers.

The juncture did not look good for the French; it seemed their country was going to have to face a resurgent Germany in the framework of a liberal integrated Europe, funded by U.S. dollars, and thus be forced to renounce their claims.[5] The new German Federation would become a liberal democracy with which the French had to interact for its own sake, a situation that finally would instigate the French authorities to agree in arranging a common institutional framework with their eternal enemy.

II

The first step of European integration, the European Coal and Steel Community, was thus France's attempt to somehow retain the control of the German steel industry and German coal production after the withdrawal of the direct rule upon the German *Länder*, rich in such resources. In exchange, West Germany received the first recognition as a sovereign entity after its defeat in World War II and a consideration as an equal subject among the other signatories of the treaty concluded in April 1951.[6]

Both France and Germany renounced some powers, transferring them to a common entity, the High Authority of the European Coal, Iron, and Steel Community, in order to gain more power as nation-states. The European Coal, Iron, and Steel Community Treaty would contain virtually all the rules that the member states deemed necessary for the smooth operation of the common market regarding those commodities that would be afterward extended to the architecture designed by the 1957 Treaty of Rome, namely, the prohibition within the community of all import and export duties (or charges having equivalent effect) the prohibition of all measures discriminating between producers, purchasersx, and consumers and the prohibition of state aid and restrictive practices.

Whatever the European founders had in mind regarding their goals for political integration, it was clear from the beginning that the measures to achieve such goals would acquire a modest, technical, and chiefly economic fashion. The only exception would be envisaged by the signature of the European Defense Community Treaty in 1952, which was likely devoted to pursue political ends by openly political means but, as we shall see, the collapse of that treaty in August 1954 would finish with such a direct path to a scenario resembling a European fully fledged federal union.[7]

The European Coal, Iron, and Steel Community was, as Alan Milward remarked, a *nationalistic project* conceived as the product of a national diplomacy maneuver.[8] French policy makers were able to translate their domestic ambitions into an original and lasting European framework.[9] Jean Monnet, again, was not only one of the most revered figures in the early history of the European Community and of European federalism but also, and primarily, a central figure in the postwar reassertion of France as a nation-state.

Monnet's aim, in the same way as the intention surrounding the rest of the figures of the French postwar diplomacy, was to restore his country as a major national force by creating an integrated area in western Europe able to dispatch structures of political and economic domination. French European integration boosted in the beginning of the 1950s was a matter of French nationalistic elites and not a movement promoted by idealistic European federalists, only confined at that time to fringe political groups.

The nationalistic character of the origins of European integration in France is revealed by the supports that the project inspired among some of the French cadres that had been involved in the Vichy collaborationist regime. As we shall more profoundly develop in the next chapter, the differences between the economic conception that the Nazis had for western Europe in their New Order and the postwar creation of a customs union and a free movement space for goods were not so distant between each other as the caesura of the fall of the Third Reich might lead us to think.

Some French agents with a prominent role under the occupation as businessmen or as Vichy officials would be later involved as servers of the European Communities. After all, the French *Comités d'organisation* among the entrepreneurs and industrialists created under the German occupation mirroring the German economic groups in order to interact with them would be similar and sometimes composed by the same people that would later handle the negotiation of the European Communities foundational treaties.[10]

Although many of the French economic elites were suspected of collaborating with the German occupiers and of having become unworthily enriched between 1940 and 1944, only a few of them were effectively punished through nationalizing the companies' assets. Among such companies might be highlighted the famous nationalization-sanction of Renault factories: the owner, Louis Renault, was arrested for collaborationism in September 1944 and the provisional government seized the factories and nationalized them in January 1945.[11] However, the long time that the company was in public hands did not finally prevent it from being privatized in 1990 (under a socialist majority) and thus to be regained by the French capitalist structures that were maintained in spite of the nationalization waves experienced first by the end of the war and, in a second stage, by the Socialist and Communist coalition once François Mitterrand acceded to the presidency and before the Socialists succumbed to developing the liberal policies that would define their economic performance by the end of the 1980s.

Disregarding the disenchantment that some elements of French conservativism and the far-Right experienced toward European integration, particularly after Algerian independence and more intensively by the liberal turn that marked the European project from the 1970s and 1980s, by the time of the Schuman Declaration and the ulterior signature of the treaties, such former collaborationists welcomed the initiative of a closer continental union given the affinities that it had with the German New Order. They were interested in such horizon of regaining grandeur for the "Old Nations of Europe" and to trace a third way between the Soviet Union's communism and American capitalism that might be found in a sort of *corporatism* in which there echoed remembrances of the Vichy authoritarian regime.[12] Former totalitarian allegiances were, thus, behind such an eclectic mix of Social Democratic and Christian Democratic visions that would define the European postwar nations and the creature that they would together conceive: the European Communities.

III

The consolidation of the Eastern bloc and the beginning of the Korean War in June 1950 had forced the Americans to focus their military capacities in Asia and triggered the need to organize an army in western Europe beyond the already existing NATO. The idea of cementing integration through a military supranational organization began to take shape.

The Americans themselves, given the threats in the context of the Cold War, encouraged the European governments, and particularly the French, to raise such forces in order to build a parapet against any possible attack from the other side of the Iron Curtain. But the plan required the rearming of Germany, and that was seen with reluctance by the former enemies of Germany, the British and the French.

The British never participated in the European Defense Community project, but in the beginning the French government of René Pleven, convinced by the idea that it was not Germany that was going to be rearmed but a supranational institution, changed its initial opposition and finally allowed the approval of the EDC Treaty by the National Assembly. In the midst of the colonial wars, such as the one fought in Indochina, nevertheless, the solution of the European army provided by that organization would still be highly controversial in France for a couple of years. The elections of June 1951 were won by the right-wing parties, which were hostile to the European army and, from then onward, to find a majority in the assembly to ratify the instrument became a very difficult task. Those opposed to the European Defense Community began to fight the initiative relating the creation of the army with nationalistic principles; as the old Radical Édouard Herriot, argued, "the army is the soul of the fatherland";[13] and, in this vein, it was likely to be inconceivable to transfer military power to an abstract instance beyond the nation (both discussions and arguments that would be reiterated many years after as long as the European Union progressively assumed political powers).

In the end, most of the Right, fearing the threats against French national sovereignty that according to them the European army may represent, but also most of the Communists and, decisively, half of the Socialists, voted against the ratification of the European Defense Community Treaty and the European common defense project was wrecked definitively in August 1954. That session in the National Assembly happened only a few months after the defeat of the French army at Dien Bien Phu in which "the soul of the fatherland" had received a decisive strike that would anticipate the fate of the colonialist adventures.

IV

But from the ashes of the Defense Treaty something revived in favor of closer European integration: the willingness to provide technology for the peaceful use of nuclear power in Europe, which would lead to the creation, as we explained, of a European Atomic Community followed by the establishment of a common European market to sustain economic growth, an aim that was chiefly sought by Germany in its struggle to strengthen the links with western Europe and its international recognition.

Nevertheless, what is not very widely known among the public is the German willingness to be committed with the French government in a joint program of nuclear weapons production.[14] Despite the depressive precedence of the European Defense Community, the last governments of the Fourth Republic understood that France needed a defense capacity that was independent from the United States and the United Kingdom. French authorities shared the opinion according to which in the times of Cold War such defensive capacities required the development of a nuclear weapons program. In the same fashion they saw that, though having the materials and the know-how to proceed, they lacked the financial means to achieve that goal.

The creation of a powerful nuclear arsenal required the involvement of a wealthier partner among which, by the end of the 1950s, and in spite of the whole stock of French grievances and mistrust, Germany appeared as the most favorable candidate. Aside from Germany's economic resources, the point was that the German government had repeatedly shown its interest in also being covered by nuclear protection against the Soviet threat (a coverage that, with the help of the French, would be provided in an independent way from the United States–British alliance). Again, the Soviet shadow helped to heal the wounds between the old visceral enemies.

The French intention to exercise a de facto monopoly on the provision of uranium in order to subsidize the military plans was in the background of the negotiations that led to the Euratom Treaty. The Euratom thus was straightforwardly related to the French and German *national* interests on developing a system of defense grounded on nuclear weapons and able to consolidate a third nuclear power between the Soviet Union and the U.S.-British system.

However, the French hope of establishing through the Euratom a common European facility for isotope separation and a monopoly on the provision of uranium was finally rejected by the Germans due to the pressures of German industry, which preferred to deal with the United States and Britain. The French only obtained a symbolic result: a centralized European uranium supply agency that somehow watered down the ambitions of the initiative.

The conclusion of the treaty did not discourage Mollet nor Adenauer, either, from moving ahead with the secret planning of nuclear weapons production (the French governments themselves were developing a nuclear weapons program in secrecy since the Faure government). Yet, the project on the Franco-German collaboration in the use of nuclear power for military purposes was, in the end, terminated when De Gaulle entered office, essentially because France was soon able to complete alone a national nuclear weapons program and that national-centered solution was obviously the one preferred by the general at a time in which French grandeur had to swallow bitter pills.

V

Indeed, the European Common Market was being designed as an exception to the economic global ideal that both the United States and Great Britain had conceived to rule the capitalistic world through the 1944 Bretton Woods agreements and, afterward, through the General Agreement on Tariffs and Trade (GATT).

The capitalist restraint that the European Coal, Iron, and Steel Community and the further Europe Common Market would represent would provide substantial benefits for France and Germany alike and would entail consequences in the postwar general economic landscape and in the balance of power, but the continental economic structure was a clean departure from the liberal project called to embrace the non-Communist sphere of influence.

France had signed the Bretton Woods Agreement on December 1945 on the understanding that it would only participate in the multilateral system when its economy had been reconstructed and modernized.[15] But through the European Common Market, the special economic regime aside from global liberalization took longer. The European customs union and the European free movements of goods, as well as some European economic policies such as the Common Agricultural Policy, would be exceptions to the general plan of liberalization conceived by the Bretton Woods and GATT systems. Hayek himself, who remained in America during the first stages of the European Communities, would come to the conclusion that the European economic organization was too *dirigiste*.[16] After all, if the European project was indeed a mechanism conceived to strength the nation-states that composed it, it was no wonder that, from an ordoliberal point of view, it had been besieged by the same flaws that Hayek had denounced regarding the nation-state policies before World War II, namely, that electorates within the nation-state were perpetually subjected to redistributive temptations able to encroach the rights of property in the name of democracy.

Nevertheless, at the end of the day, and despite the strong opposition and the fatal predictions coming from the ordoliberals, the European exception that began to be formed aside of the global economic architecture traced by the IMF/World Bank and GATT systems encouraged the European Golden Age of economic growth until 1973.[17] Success, thus, disavowed the distinguished (and grumpy) liberals.

Hayek had not been alone in his criticism of the emerging European experiment: the German-speaking economic theorists in Germany itself or in Switzerland also watched with some distance the economic evolution of the European supranational entities that were being designed. Although some of such figures were close to Ludwig Erhard, Adenauer's economic minister (1949–1963) and afterward the German chancellor to whom is attributed a relevant role in the consolidation of the postwar German miracle (1963–1966), they could not prevent West Germany's strong commitment in the shaping of the mentioned European exception to the liberal global order.

The European Common Market liberalized the economies of its members within the European space but, as the Common Agricultural Policy notoriously revealed, *was rigidly protectionist* toward the liberalization process of the global economy and particularly toward the Atlantic area dominated by the United States and its dollar but also toward agriculture producers of the Global South. As the neoliberal economist Wilhelm Röpke commented on the European Common Agricultural Policy when it was passed in 1962, such initiative was "the most grotesque system of price-fixing, subsidies, and artificial purchasing arrangements that had ever been created in a modern industrial economy."[18]

It must be said that the European continental exception had been *consented* by the United States' authorities themselves in order both to ensure economic growth in western Europe and to strengthen European welfare and political stability enough to contain the impetus of the Communist model in a border area of the Cold War theater. Even before the first episodes of European integration, article 24 of the GATT, concluded in October 1947, already foresaw the limited scope of its provisions toward regional customs unions or free-trade areas, which would later allow adjusting the European Common Market emergence with the GATT system.

In short, American politico-military imperatives, in the global conflict represented by the Cold War, trumped commercial calculation without the slightest difficulty. Eisenhower, for instance, informed Pineau that the realization of the Treaty of Rome would be "one of the finest days in the history of the free world, perhaps even more than winning the war."[19]

As the decades went by, the strain between the global economy and the shared tariff wall and the subsidized agriculture that the European Union represented (and that the neoliberals predicted) would grow and would become more difficult to manage, at least for European interests. Continental Europe (Britain had been another matter, given Margaret Thatcher's radical liberal regime) rediscovered neoliberal doctrines by the dusk of the Soviet bloc and they easily became undisputed while the 1990s advanced and reached their peak in the so-called Lisbon Strategy, launched in March 2000 by the EU heads of state and government, whose aim was to make Europe "the most competitive and dynamic knowledge-based economy in the world."[20] But the outcome of such struggle was unequal among the member states and the abrupt deterioration of the economic climate caused by the 2008 Great Recession revealed the Lisbon Strategy's enormous fractures.

VI

The French economic developments of the last decades provide a good account of the complexities and contradictions of adapting the European economic system that had arisen by the early days of the Common Market to the imperatives of the liberal global age.

One of the factors that threatened the European Union as a space of economic prosperity and, particularly, the maintenance of economic growth and the sustainability of the welfare state in nation-states such as France in the twenty-first century, was the opening of the European Common Market to such a liberalized global order. That operation was, however, displayed mainly through bilateral free-trade and investment agreements between the European Union and third countries rather than relying on the framework of the World Trade Organization, which replaced GATT in the 1990s, and found several barriers to minimize the establishment of tariffs, particularly by the most advanced economies including the United States or the European Free Trade Association area.

As a member of the European Common Market first, and of the European Union after, France contributed to enhance Europe's power of bargaining in trade and investment agreements toward third actors within the global space. Somehow it might be stated that also French integration in the European framework of performance toward the world's economy benefited in the first instances French national interests. But the clash of the limited European free trade area (restrained by European common regulations and conceived to ensure a European [nation-states'] welfare system) with a liberalized global system would contribute to eroding the French economic privileges upon which the French political and social system was underpinned, and would lead the country to the different forms of crises and social uncertainties that are still on course.

There was a time, however, in which the western European powers led by France sought to make compatible European integration with the preservation of their respective empires. That time would not take long, but even in the face of the access of their former colonies to full sovereignty, there took place the attempt of maintaining at least streams of privileged trade between the new states and the old metropolis. Such a trend was particularly acute regarding the European older possessions in Africa and the struggle to build a single market between Europe and some African territories barred to the free trade principles that after World War II had been set up at the global level through the GATT.

The building of tariff walls around the members of the European Communities and their still present or former colonies in Africa was one of the last expressions of the colonization endeavor that began with the Berlin Conference of 1884–1885, in which the European powers expressed a common unity of action in usurping and plundering the lands and the raw materials of Africa. The privileged trade relations recognized from the European bloc to the newly created African states was no other thing than a move conceived from the European governments to perpetuate their influence upon their former dominions covered by a mask of aid for African development.

Regarding such cases in which formal decolonization had not still arrived during the signing of the Treaty of Rome in 1957, the expansion of the European market to the African colonies (including still Algeria) was a battle that the metropolis offered to the populations of those territories to distract them from their illusions of independence. Certainly, by 1957 France, Belgium, the Netherlands, and to a certain extent even Italy, still had overseas possessions, and those powers managed to include them in the new economic area (that encompassed, among other territories, French Overseas *départements*, the Belgian Congo, and Rwanda, Dutch New Guinea, and Italian Somalia).[21]

The financial aid that the French explicitly obtained for their colonies in the treaty was an additional argument exhibited by Paris to guard the status quo and even to strengthen the notion of *Eurafrique* under a different form of Empire.[22] To some extent, the foundations of the European Communities might be read within the framework of the last efforts of the old European *metropoles* to relaunch their imperial projects through economic and administrative rationalization programs.[23] In France, the *Fonds d'Investissement en Développement Economique et Social* were launched in order to revive the colonial economies.

But the escalation of the Algerian conflict and the independence processes that in the 1960s swept across Africa soon burst this late colonialism into pieces. As late as 1963, that is after Algerian independence, de Gaulle nonetheless still insisted in a form of association between the European Communities and the Association of the African states and Madagascar formalized in the Yaoundé Convention. Such an organization brought some fruits in terms of cooperation but worked rather as a mere mechanism for the French to maintain its post-colonial influence over the recently independent African states than as a common economic structure between Africa and a progressive integrated Europe.

On the contrary to the French, the Germans had no interest at all in Eurafrica since, according to the German minister of economic affairs and later Chancellor Ludwig Erhard, it "Europeanized the costs of empire" and threatened to recreate protectionist blocs that were of little use to a Germany that had already lost its African colonies by the aftermath of World War I and purchased only a fraction of its imports from the former French colonies.[24]

By the beginning of the 1970s, within the context of the détente between the United States and the Soviet Union, and the opening in Europe of a path of understanding with the Soviet bloc beyond the American interests, there emerged again, among some European actors, the willingness to foster commercial exchange with the recently independent African countries. At that time, while socialists and social democrats dominated much of the decision making in the European Community, the need to forge a new international partnership between a newly reorganized Europe and a newly cohesive South seemed morally right and strategically prudent.[25] The clout of an older vein of European thought, dreaming of a naturally symbiotic *Eurafrique* that would bring together the manufacturing Europeans and the resource-rich lands across the Mediterranean, revived in the horizon of the European political and technocratic minds that were planning the future of commercial flows.[26]

The remembrances of European domination of Africa through the form of privileged access to African raw materials and agricultural products into the European market would, indeed, persist until the first decades of the twenty-first century when the European Union was challenged before the panels of the World Trade Organization for the tariffs provided against the agricultural goods coming from Latin America in contrast with the treatment deserved by the goods coming from Africa. The nostalgia for empire was also present in some apparently more secondary questions such as the "banana legal wars" that confronted the World Trade Organization and the Court of Justice of the European Union, which began through an action that unsurprisingly was lodged by a German banana importer.[27]

By the 2010s and the 2020s, the progressive European withdrawal from Africa was replaced by an avalanche of Chinese investments devoted to controlling a wide range of natural resources and to shape infrastructures to ensure the flux of commodities. Soon the Chinese economic penetration turned out in political influence and military presence in order to protect the investments and even Russia, despite the problems that Putin's regime had to face up to at home as a consequence of the campaign in Ukraine, extended its arm upon the Sahel and was behind some coups d'état that caused the fall of governments in Mali and Burkina Faso, and undermined France's presence and legacy upon such countries.

VII

The aftermath of World War II represented the struggle to forge liberal democratic states in western Europe while, at the same time, treating the colonies with an iron fist. No wonder that from the perspective of the claimers for decolonization (some of them having believed in the promises delivered by the Western Powers during the war in order to recruit their support in the fight against Nazism) the European states were eager to foster plain aggression against their African or Asian dominions rather than standing for constitutional law and building a liberal order overseas.[28]

Toward the western European supranational structure that was being defined in the 1950s and the 1960s, the consideration of Algeria as a part of metropolitan France under the jurisdiction of the ministry of interior (already established in some parts of that territory from the nineteenth century) was not a minor circumstance: war and repression were displayed *in a European frame* and *in the name of a European nation*.

That's where the big trauma that the Algerian issue would represent for the French identity and for the idea of a supranational fate came from: a national identity grounded in the universal values of the Enlightenment was capable of destroying them in order to enforce its national supremacy upon others. The same that the Germans had done to occupied France a few years before was being done by the French in the fight against anti-colonial movements and, what was more shocking, it was not rare to find that the same far-Right elements that had collaborated with the Nazis under the German occupation were responsible for torturing and killing in some of the territories fighting for independence.[29]

By the end of World War II, masses of people gathered in the streets of Algeria to celebrate the sealing of Hitler's fate. In some towns, as in Sétif, Guelma and Kherrata, however, these victory celebrations evolved into violent protests by Arab demonstrators against French colonial rule, to which the French army reacted by killing thousands of people and destroying entire Arab villages. French military and civilian forces killed an estimated two thousand Algerians in the region of Guelma alone, or many more, depending on whose tally one follows.[30] Already, thus, at the time of the collapse of fascist regimes in Europe and the hour of Europe's liberation, European colonies experienced one of the bloodiest days in a way that the European powers made it very clear that they would not accept a radical change in the existing colonial relations.[31]

The conflicts for national emancipation would escalate and the French struggle to stop them, even with the alliance of other western European colonial powers, would lead to one fiasco after another. In spite of the circumstance that the extra-European context for the creation of today's European Union is often overlooked by commentators, the conclusion of both the European Economic Community Treaty and the Euratom Treaty in 1957 would be only explainable considering such defeats suffered by the western European empires in which their weakness had been sharply revealed. When French officials picked up their pens to sign these accords, the France that they represented was not a nation-state but an empire that they wished still to maintain.[32]

VIII

Soon after the loss of Indochina, maybe the next relevant episode of decolonization in which the French government had been involved was the debacle of the Suez Canal in the summer and the fall of 1956.[33] Indeed, some authors such as Küsters point to the Suez crisis as a defining event in the path of concluding the European treaties.[34]

As a response to the cut in American financial support for the building of the Aswan dam on the Nile, vital for Egyptian water supplies, the regime of Nasser, in July 1956, nationalized the Suez Canal Company, a joint British-French enterprise that had owned and operated the canal since its construction in 1869.

Britain and France decided then to send the matter to the United Nations, but the Soviet Union vetoed in the Security Council any action against Nasser. In this context, the former colonial powers decided to ignore the United Nations, going ahead with a military solution without even informing the American government of their plans.

The conspiracy also involved Israel, whose army had to occupy the Sinai Peninsula before Britain and France would launch air and sea attacks with the aim of taking over the canal occupied by the Egyptians. However, once the Israeli invasion went ahead by the end of October of 1956 and the British and French troops began an airborne landing in Egypt in November, the Soviets threatened with rocket attacks on the invaders even suggesting the possibility of using nuclear armament. The American leaders in their turn, President Eisenhower and his secretary of state, John Foster Dulles, reacted furiously against their Allies urging them to stop the attack immediately. The United States voted for UN resolutions publicly condemning the invasion and approving the creation of a UN peacekeeping force. The British, pressed by the huge loss of their currency reserves, already during the two first days of operation, agreed to a ceasefire without even consulting the French, which also shortly after consented to bring the attack to an end. By December 22, 1956, the Anglo-French Task Force finished its withdrawal and was replaced by the United Nations peacekeeping troops. The humiliation toward the former colonial powers was, thus, complete. It began to be clear that the imperialist era was something of the past, but France had still to face up to a more pressing challenge.

IX

The Algerian crisis escalated from the insurrection of the Algerian *Front de Libération Nationale* (National Liberation Front, or FLN) in the country's southern mountains on November 1, 1954. But if France had been involved in the Suez plot, it was chiefly due to supposed responsibility of the Nasser regime for training and supplying the FLN.[35] The Suez turmoil was, with the previous reversal in Indochina, the prelude of the disintegration of French imperial dreams, which caused, as a correspondence, a change toward French politics in Europe. It is no coincidence that the Algerian insurrection broke out in 1954, the same year in which the decisive defeat that General Giáp's army inflicted upon France's forces at Dien Bien Phu hastened the end of French rule in Vietnam.

Algerian revolutionaries saw in the Vietnamese victory six months after Dien Bien Phu their opportunity to get rid of the French colonial regime. Despite the declining support from the general public, the French Fourth Republic's authorities systematically refused to retreat from their overseas possessions.[36] They had poured vast military resources into a decade-long battle against Vietnamese independence generating large budget deficits and significant inflation, which would debilitate still more the metropole when handling the Algerian crisis.[37]

Such a succession of revolts and military disasters paved the way in France for the arguments supporting European integration as means of counter-weighting the influence of the great superpowers' dominance. The serial of losses that France was suffering left the country with no other option than to invest in the European project and shaping it into the service of France's goals.

The Germans also saw both in the French decline in the colonies and in European integration the opportunity to be rehabilitated within the Western alliance and to be treated as an equal partner. The Suez catastrophe gives again a good glimpse of this point: five days after the Suez expedition was launched on November 1, 1956, Adenauer arrived in Paris for confidential talks on the Common Market. He was in the middle of discussions with Mollet and Pineau, when Eden suddenly rang from London to announce that Britain had unilaterally called off the expedition, under pressure from the United States.[38] It is said that upon seeing the anguish of the French prime minister Guy Mollet after knowing the news, Adenauer did his best to comfort his host by arguing that Europe would be the way for the French to take their "revenge."[39]

A point that has been usually omitted in the analysis of European integration is to what extent the defeat in the 1950s and in the 1960s of the empires of western Europe, and particularly France's colonial defeat in Indochina and Algeria, contributed to eclipsing the German question and, indirectly, to paving the way for the conciliation between the Germans and those western European nations that had been occupied by them in World War II. A divided Germany in the postwar scenario was a secondary concern for those French governments (and also for the Dutch and Belgian governments entangled respectively in both the Indonesia and the Congo decolonization conflicts) that were witnessing the dissolution of their power in large parts of Africa and Asia.

Under such a perspective, it is not casual that De Gaulle's France concluded a treaty of friendship with Adenauer's West Germany in January 1963, not even a year after Algerian's independence was consummated in 1962. Not only were French fears toward Germany (or at least toward West Germany) vanishing in less than twenty years from the capitulation of the Third Reich, but even the leader of the French fight against the Germans, General De Gaulle, was admitting, through his understandings with Adenauer, that a Germany integrated in Europe was beginning to be perceived rather as a solution to the French post-imperial crisis than as a problem.

X

The largest colonial conflict of the century (at its height, the French army in Algeria numbered four hundred thousand; and probably as many Algerians died, in a war that uprooted nearly two million people)[40] precipitated a change of regime in France itself and the return of General De Gaulle. Not surprisingly, if Algerian secessionism had to be fought by assimilating the Algerian territory into the metropole, the resolution of the conflict through Algerian independence would require the displacement of one metropolitan constitutional framework (that of the French Fourth Republic) by another one (the presidential Fifth Republic of Gaullist inspiration).[41]

The new Republic was founded, with institutions—above all, a strong presidential executive—designed to give the country the firm political stability that was lacking in the previous regime. But the blatant disregard for all principles of constitutional law and natural basic rights inherent in the anti-liberal policies used in the colonial periphery landed like a boomerang at the point of origin, the French European mainland, and would begin to undermine the liberal order there:[42] it would lead to the collapse of a constitutional system and it would cripple the normative framework settled through the Fifth Republic for the following years as well. The rescission of constitutional norms and the growing militarization of all aspects of the state in the wake of emergency laws in Algeria led to an increasing politicization of the French army, which directed itself against democracy.[43]

It was not clear whether or not the transition from the Fourth Republic to the Fifth was the result of a coup d'état. The assumption of the powers by the De Gaulle was instigated by the seizing of powers in Algiers perpetrated in May 1958 by the military and right-wing extremists; they had felt betrayed by the parties of the Fourth Republic and considered the general the only figure able to cope with the Algerian nationalist insurrection.[44] From this point onward, De Gaulle played a clever double game using the threat of a military coup while having nothing to do with it and insisted in returning power through legal means.[45]

By the end of May 1958, General Massu in Algiers was ready to launch the seizure of government buildings in Paris by paratroopers while hundreds of thousands of citizens joined a rally in that capital orchestrated by the Communist party against the establishment of a dictatorship. Fearing both threats of the far-Right military and the revolution boosted by the far-left, the political establishment rushed through in investing De Gaulle as prime minister.

De Gaulle was finally invited by President Coty on May 29 to form a new government and on June1, the general asked the assembly for full powers and to draft a new constitution, a task that was undertaken during the summer of 1958 and fulfilled with the referendum for constitutional ratification held on September 28, 1958. This year, 1958, was the same year, and maybe it is easier through that observation to be aware of the parallel developments between both the domestic constitutional transformations and those displayed as a consequence of European integration, that the Treaty of Rome came into force.

Certainly, while all those events were occurring in continental France since Algerian departments were equivalent to those of Dordogne or Vosges, Algeria *was a part* of the European Communities. From 1958 and until Algerian independence in 1962 the European Economic Communities regulations for trade and social security extended to Algeria though it was not clear if it extended to the non-European Algerians, revealing, thus, an element of racism and Islamophobia shared by most European officials. Representatives of the Six, including, for the most part, French officials, viewed Algerian's ability to count as European as suspect and undesirable.[46]

Algeria's break up with the metropole, however, did not concede enough time to clarify such questions (among which might be also explored the geographical dysfunction likely to derive from including as a European territory a place on the southern shore of the Mediterranean that had a bigger land surface than any other member state). The fact was nonetheless that from 1976, when the European Economic Community and the independent Algeria signed the first of the different agreements of cooperation among them that would be displayed in the following decades, the *acquis communautaire* ceased to be applied in all its extent to that part of Africa and to its inhabitants.

XI

Although the French Fourth Republic appeared as a spectacular failure, floundering into the swamps of governmental instability and colonial disaster, the experience of that time showed another face that seemed more positive and able to endure beyond the political chaos.

It was in those years that the administrative structure of the French state was overhauled, and there took shape the technocratic pattern of administration and business that would not only dominate the French framework of ruling but that would also characterize the bureaucratic way of operating within the European sphere.[47]

It has not to be forgotten in that sense, for instance, that the French *grande école* of civil servants, the *École nationale d'administration* (ENA), was created in 1945 in order to consolidate the meritocratic technocracy that would organize the French administrative and political life struggling with the ephemeral life of the cabinets of the Fourth Republic of France.

Somehow the supranational instances that would be formed, beginning with the European Coal and Steel Community's High Authority, mirrored the structures of economic planning to supplement market mechanisms that were at the same time modernizing the French economy. No wonder that the architects of European integration such as Monnet and Schuman were embedded by a strand of market economy complemented by indirect planning that surrounded the French immediate postwar atmosphere and that would be transferred to the supranational administrations once they were created by the 1950s.

It was upon the bureaucratic apparatus of the Fourth Republic of France that both the state survived in spite of the decolonization challenge and that the incipient European administration found a solid ground that would define its activity until the present.

XII

De Gaulle grounded his political action through the pressure of the military and the violent context in the Algerian crisis, which led him to found a new constitutional structure centered in the presidential figure to supersede the national emergency. The fact that that movement was disguised through the clothes of the Fourth Republic's legality does not conceal its revolutionary, and to some extent authoritarian, character.

De Gaulle returned to power by playing with the threat of the far-Right at war for defending a French Algeria. However, the man called to save the dreams of French grandeur by ensuring territorial integrity would also be the man that would agree to the conditions for recognizing Algeria's independence.

France would lose Algeria's war and De Gaulle would certify it with his initiative in favor of peace and self-determination (which would cost him the wrath of the French extremists who had helped the general to bury the Fourth Republic).

Already in the fall of 1959 the French president made clear that he would offer the possibility for the Algerian people to decide on their political status, including the possibility to secede from France. That movement inspired fierce opposition among the French Algerian radicals.

From April 22–25,1961, the leading generals of the French army in Algeria (Maurice Challe, Raoul Salan, Edmund Jouhaud, and André Zeller) assumed power by staging a military putsch and brought France to the brink of war.[48] On Salan's backlash Carl Schmitt saw the paradigm of the partisan warfare in which besides the absolute enemy that the Algerian nationalist insurrection represented there was another enemy: France's own government and own commander, who was considered a traitor.[49]

The French army in Algeria, endowed with special powers to protect the state, threatened the existence of the French Republic itself, and the Paris government was forced to declare a State of Emergency in the European mainland that it had originally brought into being to quell unrest in Northern Africa.[50] Even after the putsch failed, the Secret Army Organization (*Organisation de l'Armée Secrète, OAS*) was founded, a body formed by dissident soldiers and political far-Right extremists that waged a campaign of terror both in Algeria and on the mainland.

In parallel, De Gaulle began in June 1960 negotiations with the FLN at Evian on Lake Geneva, which initially failed since both sides did not find a common ground.[51] The sequence of violent upheavals, nevertheless, was increasing; aside from the aforementioned military putsch in Algiers that decisively affected the morale and the international image of the French Army, in October 1961 the police, led by the former Vichy collaborationist prefect Maurice Papon, harshly repressed a demonstration in Paris in favor of peace: 11,538 people were arrested, seventy four were shot, beaten to death or thrown into the Seine, and sixty-eight disappeared in one of the least-publicized and most atrocious acts of mass violence in postwar western Europe.[52] The overwhelming majority of the Frenchmen and women began to be tired of a conflict in which many of their sons were serving. The inevitability, and desirability, of Algerian independence was being consolidated in public opinion.[53]

Negotiations at Evian went forward and finally De Gaulle obtained in March 1962 a ceasefire agreement with the FLN that led to the celebration of referendums on "Algerian independence in cooperation with France" both in Algeria and in metropolitan France. More than 90 percent of the voters gave their support in both territories to Algerian secession and independence was finally recognized on July 5, 1962.[54]

After independence, however, troubles and violence did not end: about 150,000 Algerians who had remained loyal to the French were killed by the FLN as were up to 10,000 French Algerians. The *OAS* was still active undertaking the mission of punishing those who had allowed Algerian secession including spectacular assassination attempts on the French culture minister, André Malraux, and De Gaulle himself. In February 1962 alone, *OAS* operatives and bombs killed 553 people.[55] In the early 1960s, thus, the Algerian independence war generated a significant level of armed conflict within Europe.

Meanwhile, thousands of such *pieds-noirs* were repatriated, creating a cleavage within French society that would have been aggravated by the migration of hundreds of thousands of Algerians in the following decades in search for more social and economic opportunities. Somehow, French metropolitan soil would bear witness to the conflict experienced in Algeria in other terms: Arab Algerians migrating to France both for economic and political reasons and constituting the largest foreign community in France by 1975 had to live together with the repatriated French Algerians who returned from north Africa between 1962 and 1965. The transfer of population from Algeria formed by such two groups, the former French settlers and the former Arab colonized population, would represent one of the major sources of conflicts that France would have to confront until the present day.

Indeed, no other European society had received such a large settler community from its colonial empire. A million *pieds-noirs* arrived, expelled from the Maghreb, with all the bitterness of exiles; and no other European society had received such a large influx of immigrants from the very zone once colonized: two and a half million *maghrébins*.[56] That combination was always likely to release a political toxin as it has done several times in recent decades.

France had emerged profoundly debilitated from World War II. The occupation and the Vichy Regime had left a trace of confrontations and contradictions and the Algerian crisis, as the coronation of the empire collapsed, would have added more disruptions to French confidence in its national unity.

XIII

The French Empire might have been dismantled through the vast territories, mainly in Africa, that followed the lead of the Algerian process and gained their political emancipation. But colonialism still persisted in the French rule of a wide range of dependencies around the world. The independence of Djibouti in 1977 did not finish with France's overseas possessions. Until today the French authorities still control the islands of Guadeloupe, Martinique, Saint-Martin, Saint-Barthélemy, Saint Pierre, and Miquelon in the Atlantic Ocean; the Reunion island, Mayotte, and the French Southern and Antarctic Lands in the Indian Ocean; the French Polynesia, New Caledonia, Wallis, and Futuna in the Pacific Ocean, and the French Guiana in South America, which is one-seventh the size of metropolitan France and which explains that it is Brazil, and not any other European country, the jurisdiction with which France shares the longest border. The French overseas' empire, thus, despite not being what it used to be, still exists.

Indeed, French territorial organization in the present still reproduces the same fictions of domination that characterized the colonial developments in the past. While archipelagos like New Caledonia were treated as non-self-governing territories according to the United Nations regulation and, consequently, with recognition of their right to external self-determination (three referenda on sovereignty have been held in New Caledonia in 1987, 2018, and 2020) the full integration in the French Republic of French Guiana in (a maneuver resembling that operated in Algeria) have prevented the debate around decolonization in that dependency. French Guiana, a part of the European Union overseas in which the Euro circulates (and even the drawing of French Guiana's surface appears on the Euro bills) is a remnant of a colonial age that the European authorities have normalized. The political status of that American territory within the European Union would be the one that would have defined Algeria if it had been retained by the French Republic.

Yet, why did Algeria become a sovereign state outside of the European Union and yet French Guiana is French territory within the European Union? Why is French Guiana not considered a subject on the self-determination issue while that is the case of New Caledonia or French Polynesia (in which the pro-independence parties won the regional elections in 2023)?

Why is the right to self-determination recognized for New Caledonia and not, as suggested, to Corsica? Is it because New Caledonia is further away than Corsica? Has the distance an argument sufficiently relevant (though used in international law) to determine which territories may access full independence and which cannot? The point, under our vision[57] relies on the interest of the French authorities to preserve a particular structure of domination upon a given territory and a given population, rather than a physical distance that would count on that existential analysis about what would be the more or less proximity with those elements concerning the French "core nation," namely, the ability of a given social/national group to exercise an imperial relationship upon others and to reproduce it over time.

As discussed before, Corsica played a crucial role in the events that contributed to configure the French Fifth Republic and represented a continuous focus of national tensions until the present. The island became a strategic enclave during Algeria's war of independence. Within the context of that conflict, a part of the French military attempted to depose the rulers of the Fourth Republic (an operation that would eventually evolve with the return of General De Gaulle) by gathering paratroopers in Corsica and preparing to launch an attack on Paris from that territory. De Gaulle's return refrained the most radical sectors of the army that completely opposed Algeria's emancipation, but finally Algeria seceded and a part of the French (and European population) that had been settled in northern Africa set up home in Corsica (eighteen thousand former settlers from Algeria in the Corsican eastern plains) as in other regions of the Midi characterized by the presence of other national minorities beyond the French one.

With the background of the northern African emancipation processes, the struggles from Paris to entrench Corsican assimilation, the presence of French radical nationalists coming from the parts of the defeated empire, the cultural and linguistic siege encouraged the Corsican movement of national emancipation from the 1970s. That contestation, similar to the paths that were being taken in Northern Ireland or in the Basque Country was at that time focused on military attacks. However, in spite of the progressive abandonment of the armed struggle, there were almost no concessions in terms of recognition for the Corsican national movement by the French central authorities. Corsican institutions were conceived with a greater degree of autonomy than other French regional collectivities, but their self-government was far from reaching the levels of decentralization adopted by some autonomous communities within Spain or by the Italian regions with special status (not to mention any accommodation of the different national, cultural, and linguistic Corsican particularities within an emphatic French monolithic national reality). Promises of greater autonomy and national recognition never went so far, even when the French government appeared to be committed to reforms as a bait to pacify the island after a turmoil. That happened, for instance, when riots erupted across Corsica after the pro-independence leader Yvan Colonna was attacked in prison on March 2022 and died as a consequence of his injuries weeks later; the courthouse at Ajaccio was assaulted by a crowd, which attempted to set it on fire, while other convulsions affected Bastia and Calvi. The President Macron offered some measures to reform the political status of the island but, as happened regarding other dimensions of Macron's policies, nothing tangible came from those plans announced by the French president.

The combination of allocating former European settlers in Algeria, Islamic immigration also from northern Africa in a landscape of sub-state nationalities was also extended in the southern part of mainland France. Social, religious, national, and economic cleavages were particularly intense in Occitania, a large region that did not deserve much interest for French central authorities from the point of view of investments and resources reallocation nor from the perspective of any linguistic and cultural recognition for national minorities (even in 2023, for instance, the public use of Catalan within the municipal council meetings in the towns in which that language is spoken was forbidden by the French Courts, arguing that French was constitutionally the only official language within the Republic). The ground was prepared in the Midi for harsh tensions confronting extreme French nationalistic groups (it was there where the far-Right obtained remarkable results) with both immigration of northern African origins and the mosaic of autochthonous nationalities.

XIV

In April 2002 a far-Right candidate, Jean-Marie Le Pen (a veteran of the Algerian War), qualified for the round off to the French presidential elections for the first time in the history of the Fifth Republic. Such an episode inaugurated the era in which most of the divisions concealed within French society since the end of World War II emerged in the form of increased electoral support for the far-Right party, the National Front (from 2018 National Rally, *Rassemblement national*).

The National Front was beginning to attract a public much beyond its initial base of nostalgic conservatives, and it was spreading among parts of the working class in the suburbs of the cities that once voted for the Left. Le Pen's electoral breakthrough came in 1984, a year after Mitterrand had abruptly jettisoned the social vision of the Common Program and embraced orthodox monetarism. It was such a turn on the Left that gave the National Front its opportunity, as it picked up increasing numbers of disgruntled voters that felt themselves abandoned by the French political establishment, including the Communist Party, which maintained support for Socialist Party governments despite the neoliberal discourse of the latter.

After the turbulent transition of the National Front leadership from Jean-Marie Le Pen to his daughter Marine Le Pen, the party enjoyed a series of electoral successes that lead it to win the 2014 and 2019 elections to the European Parliament and allowed Marine Le Pen in 2017 and in 2022 to also qualify for the second round of the presidential elections. Even though Emmanuel Macron defeated Marine Le Pen (as Jacques Chirac had done with Marine Le Pen's father in 2002) the far-Right represented by the National Front (or today the National Rally) appears as the most consolidated opposition not only to the French government but also to the fundamental principles of a French Republic integrated in the European Union. Somehow, Le Pen's movement (both father and daughter) has been making use of the French traumas around national unity to underpin its political influence.

The most immediate fear that has been invoked in order to gain electoral support is immigration and, particularly, the Islamization of France displayed, according to the far-Right imaginary, through the means of terrorism. As we saw, the immigration threat began to be perceived within French society precisely in the aftermath of the Algerian crisis: with the migration of hundreds of thousands of Algerians it seemed to some French people that French Algeria gave way to Algerian France.[58] But at that time the presence of the immigrants did not cause reluctance because of the Islamic religion that the newcomers professed, but rather because of the constant remembrance that the Algerians represented a war that France had lost.

Decades later the political and the cultural problem evolved into an economic and a social one, even existential. Poor unskilled French workers in the suburbs of the cities had to compete with the immigrant population from formerly French North Africa and their descendants who in spite of being French nationals found great difficulties assimilating. No wonder that fear would be maintained by the sustained support received by a party that had made the rejection of Islam and Arab people the core of its political message.

By the beginning of the twenty-first century, there may be told histories of social cohesion and successful integration (at a popular level, one may think, for example, of the winning of the Football World Cup in 1998 and 2018 by a multi-ethnic French national team); but there may also be strong signs of alarmism with the mentioned growth of the electoral success of the far-Right among the population belonging to all strata (especially, among low- and middle-class workers that once supported Communism and Socialism) while non-assimilated children and grandchildren of Arab Algerians had devoted themselves to nihilistic violence.

The socially deprived *banlieues* provided fertile soil for hatred to germinate, spawned by the barely concealed racism of a sizable sector of the population.[59] Examples of destruction and carnage were the 2005 riots in which both cars and public buildings were massively burned, and the wave of terrorist attacks unleashed from 2015.

In 2005, five months after the debacle of the Treaty Establishing a Constitution for Europe (which was rejected in the referendum that President Chirac had called to ratify it) an explosion of violence lacerated cities across France. Riots erupted in high-rise slums with high concentration populations of Maghrebin and African origin, bleak zones of racial dereliction and repression, where youth unemployment doubled the national average.[60] Night after night the insurgents torched cars in a pyre of social anger.

Almost ten years after the car-burning crises, on January 7, 2015, two gunmen entered the building in Paris of the satirical magazine *Charlie Hebdo* and opened fire with automatic rifles, killing twelve (including the editor in chief) and injuring another eleven people. The *Charlie Hebdo* events inaugurated a cascade of Islamist attacks:[61] on the evening of November 13, 2015, coordinated terrorist attacks were perpetrated in Paris in cafés, restaurants, outside the France football stadium, and in the Bataclan theater during a rock concert. The bombings and mass shootings left 130 people dead and hundreds injured. When a heavy lorry was deliberately driven into a crowd of people in Nice as they celebrated French National Day on the evening of July 14, 2016, another eighty-six people were dead and more than four hundred injured.

France suffered the horror of Islamist terrorism more grievously than other western European countries because the wounds of division and discrimination left by the decolonization wars (and most prominently the Algerian one) were still present. Some of the terrorists, though borne in France, were sons of northern African former colonial immigrants. France's crises developed over recent decades (whether in the form of Islamist terrorism beating in the heart of French cities or in the growth of the nationalist French far-Right exploiting the fears of the French home population toward the increasing migration from Northern Africa and Middle East) shows to which extent the violence that France has exported to other continents during the colonialist era could strike back in the metropolis.

The sense of alienation experienced by the descendants of immigrants from Northern Africa and the Middle East reached a breaking point in the summer of 2023. Violent riots erupted in the suburbs of French cities following the tragic killing of Nahel M., a seventeen-year-old who was shot by the police in Nanterre. Despite the significant deployment of security forces, the anger and violence exhibited by the demonstrators overwhelmed them for over a week. These protests clearly demonstrated a complete rejection of the French political system, irrespective of left or right affiliations.

The burning *banlieues* and peripheries served as expressions of the struggle faced by certain segments of the population in their quest to break free from a political, trade union, and media representation system. After enduring precarious living conditions for several decades, they no longer acknowledged the legitimacy or moral superiority of the political, media, or university elite. This emergence of a "counter-society" was not driven by any specific ideology or new agenda but rather represented the culmination of a deep-seated desire for retribution among those whose ancestors had endured the effects of colonization in Northern Africa and had been colonized again in the heart of metropolitan France.

XV

In addition, the colonial shipwreck, as happened regarding other former empires, had direct consequences for the French economy and the French standards of life that crippled the welfare of large sections of population. The prolonged French influence toward its former possessions during the decades following decolonization, and the maintenance of subordination by economic dependence of the new sovereign states, allowed the financing of the welfare structure that helped to mitigate social discontent by the end of the twentieth century. But the consolidation of the neoliberal realm in Europe together with the progressive economic emancipation of the regions once under French control (or their opening toward other non-European superpowers) experienced in the twenty-first century continued to debilitate still more the French economic and social cement.

While by the end of the 1990s, under the Socialist government of Jospin, the French debate revolved around the entrenchment of labor rights such as the reduction of working time to thirty-five hours per week, the 2000s began with crises in the French public finances given a deficit that surpassed the limits traced by the euro convergence criteria.

By 2002 and 2003 Germany was also breaching the macroeconomic rules established in the protocols attached to the Treaty of European Union with the aim of adopting the euro as a single currency. But, as we shall later see, although in both cases, the French one and the German one, the European Commission waived to open a procedure against such states for noncompliance with the deficit limits, Germany superseded the excessive deficit problem through the adoption of a package of economic measures that triggered economic growth and reduced public spending while the French budget deficit, instead, remained over 3 percent of GDP in the following years (with the exception of 2006 and 2007) and exploded until reaching 7.2 upercent of GDP by 2009 after the global crash of 2008.

The French budget deficit would exceed 4 percent and 3 percent of GDP until 2017, the only year in a decade in which it fell below 3 percent of GDP. The economic malaise corroded all the other French macroeconomic data: between 2008 and 2018 unemployment rose to worrying levels (from 7 percent to 9 percent, while in Germany unemployment declined in the same time from 7 percent to 3 percent), poverty grew, the debt climbed continuously as did the trade deficit (-3 percent of the GDP in 2016 and -3.5 percent of the GDP in 2017) while growth scarcely crept above zero. Consumer spending fell and tax revenue also declined.[62]

In the meantime, none of the French presidents elected between 2007 and 2017, neither the conservative Nicolas Sarkozy nor the socialist François Hollande, renewed their mandate for five additional years. Hollande became the most unpopular president in the history of the Fifth Republic. In December 2016 he became the First French president to announce that he would not be standing for reelection. Only Emmanuel Macron, in office from 2017, had the opportunity to be elected for a second term in 2022, but in order to gain some stability, and in spite of his background as a minister in Hollande's socialist cabinet, he had to form his own centrist party to compete against the growing far-Right of Marine Le Pen. Macron subsisted but the whole traditional party system of the Fifth Republic fell behind him.

Depriving France from the direct or indirect means of economic exploitation of vast parts of the Global South accelerated its political and social crises. Also, in the twenty-first century European integration was perceived as a salvation table with the aim of strengthening the French bargaining position toward other economic actors (as the different trade and investment agreements concluded between the European Union and a third party during the last decade reveal). But such a strategy ratified the reduction of the margin of maneuver in pursuing French national interests and, on the other hand, it was not clear that the benefits obtained by the European common external trade policy would be enough to stop the slump of the welfare structures that have until recently, despite the downturn that some of the above related events have caused, preserved cohesion within French society.

XVI

The French governments, both of the Fourth and the Fifth Republics, turned thus to European integration in search of a remedy to imperial disintegration and, specifically, in search of a way to supersede crises such as the Algerian secession that caused the arrival of thousands of people of different cultures and religions.

Nowadays, however, the European Union is seen, especially by the far-Right, as the main culprit allowing more immigrants from the former colonies to come (the far-Right claims are mainly centered against the arrival of Islamic immigrants from the Islamic world that once France dominated, that is, from northern Africa to Syria). Such a perception is in some way paradoxical because what the terrorist threat has caused is the consolidation of a state emergency situation that in fact contributes to the raising of barriers against the free movement of people that defines the European project.

The French political establishment that had to manage with terrorism, the Right under Sarkozy, the Socialists under Hollande, and the Center under Macron, developed a discourse on terrorism and immigration sometimes not very far from that of Le Pen, with the shocking evidence that the problem, rather than lying in recent immigrants, lies in the descendants of the immigrants who hold French citizenry. The values of the French Republic and public order have not been damaged by aliens but by alienated French who grew up within an Islamic framework.

As we have seen, until the Great Depression beginning in 2007–2008, the European Union had provided a degree of prosperity that had minimized the impact of such a range of social, cultural, and religious turbulences lacerating France. But, as we have emphasized as well, the European Union structure rather than triggering a fulfilled liberalization through the Common Market had allowed protectionist measures at the European scale. The latter was what happened in the case of the Common Agricultural Policy that, set up between 1961 and1966 as a condition of France's entry into the European Economic Community, replaced the subsidies provided by the state to the extent that France received by the 1970s up to 40 percent of the global European funds.[63] The point is if some of the traditional inefficiencies that have marked, and still do, the French economic system will be sustainable.

Macron's presidency emerged at the crossroads of those various contradictions that affected French economic shortcuts and French ethno-cultural pluralism. On the one hand, Macron represented a firmly pro-Europe strand, understanding that the imperial times were over and that France could only display its influence in the world within the framework of a strong Europe. Macron's gamble on a European army or a closer fiscal union certainly resembled the aspirations of the French leaders of the founding time, including De Gaulle, who sought in European integration the creation of a pole able to be independent of the tutelage of the United States and to compete in the global arena as a starring actor.[64]

On the other hand, however, from the 2007 to 2008 Great Depression onward, the European Union ceased to accomplish its former (and foundational) function of rescuing the European nation-states. The strength of the European Union toward other global actors within a liberalized global framework required the dismantling of the nation-state resorts that had conferred social equality but also inefficiency. France, which may be seen as the paradigm of a nation-state grounded on protectionist and noncompetitive principles within a space apparently liberalized (as the one provided by the European Single Market) would not probably survive by itself without the coverage of a supranational organization.

To some extent that was already perceived when the French citizenry refused to adopt the reforms entailed in the treaty establishing a Constitution for Europe, and with that decision the hopes for a leap forward in European integration vanished. But that refusal came in 2005, when the economic crash was likely still to be far ahead in the horizon and the political consequences of the failed experiment were smooth. A revival of French anti-Europeanism embodied in the far-Right options that Macron did vehemently fight might be conceivable given the resistance to adopt the liberalizing measures that the challenge to compete at the global scale requires and the social damages that such changes might represent in the form of inequalities exacerbated by religious and cultural cleavages.

Macron vacillated throughout his presidency in undertaking the removal of the inefficient burdens holding back the French economy because he feared a social collapse. Here comes thus the great contradiction that the Macron presidency confronted: how to entrench the French attachment to the European Union in the midst of reforms required by the European Union's authorities able indeed to deconstruct the devices conceived to ensure national unity through the appeal to social justice and the welfare of the citizenry.

At the end of the day, the reformist program to which Macron was committed from his access to the presidency in 2017 was stuck. In fact, Macron's presidency, supported in his first term by a large majority in the legislative chamber too, was unable to show any single progress in any defined direction. On the contrary, Macron's records of service were dominated by the hesitation in relation to the riots launched by the *gilets jaunes* in 2018–2019, to which the French government only ambitioned at least to contain the problem. The *gilets jaunes* revolt showed how difficult the euro can make democratic politics when the distribution of taxation is at the same time circumscribed by international capital markets and offshore banking. Macron sought to face the *gilets jaunes*' demands for more democracy and fewer taxes by opening a "great national debate" with citizens around the country in which he promised income tax cuts for the middle class and more provision for referendums.[65] He did not accomplish any of such promises. Demonstrations and protests were going to be even more massive and radical during Macron's second presidential term.

XVII

In the 2022 presidential elections, Marine Le Pen not only was qualified again for the second round as she had been in 2017, but she even obtained more votes than in the previous contest making Macron's margin of victory still narrower. The far-Right progressed from the meager 17.79 percent of the votes that Marine Le Pen's father, Jean-Marie, had obtained in 2002 against Chirac to the 41.46 percent of the votes gathered by Marine Le Pen in 2022. In 2022, still, another more radical conservative figure than that of Le Pen's, Éric Zemmour, obtained the fourth position in the first presidential elections round, while the leftist Jean-Luc Mélenchon finished third in the race leaving the candidates of the parties that had dominated the French political landscape, the Socialists and the Liberal-Conservatives rooted in the Gaullist tradition, agonizing with percentages of vote under 5 percent (the Socialist mayor of Paris, Anne Hidalgo had to settle for only 1.74 percent of the vote).

The 2022 French presidential elections showed, first, the total distrust of the majority of voters toward the previous references of the French politics, and second, the strong polarization and the profound cleavages existing in the French society only moderated by the agglutinating capacity of Macron to absorb votes in order to contain the far-Right and, finally, the growing disaffection toward the system expressed in one of the lowest turnouts in French presidential elections and the issuing of more than 6 percent of blank votes.

As we have seen, the dissolution of the French empire was correlative to the creation of a closer European Union. That may be noticed if we focus on the evolution of French foreign trade in the years that followed the conclusion of the European Economic Community Treaty: while the proportion of French exports to the former colonies fell from 30 percent to 10 percent in the period 1958–1970, its exports to Europe increased from 10 percent to 50 percent of the total.[66]

Rather than being competitive in foreign trade, the French economy thrived in a regional and limited liberalized market such as the one outlined by the European Common Market. What would nonetheless happen if the European Common Market lost competitiveness before the global liberalized market because of the national needs of its members? What if it is the European Union itself that is threatened in its competition against other global powers as long as the preservation of nonliberalized structures justified in the name of national cohesion are deemed as a priority?

XVIII

The spread of the COVID-19 pandemic and the lockdown measures contained momentarily the social protests but the health and economic calamities that the virus brought (causing France's worst recession since World War II with the GDP shrinking by 8.3 percent following the successive lockdowns) made Macron's government still more feeble and more dependent on European coverage through the 750 billion euro that composed the so-called "Next Generation EU" funds.

The French government was one of the most active ones in clamoring for a supranational solution to trigger recovery, and became the third most benefited member state from the initiative by collecting 11.7 percent of all the European subsidies, most of them being grants. But the slow management of the funds, and the delays caused both by the ratification and by the involvement of judicial instances such as the German Federal Constitutional Court (as has always happened concerning the implementation of any European policy) made uncertain the application of the funds, let alone the assessment of their effect according to the aims envisaged (both at the EU and at the national level) such as the digitalization and de-carbonization of the economy in order to overcome the crises. When the time came to receive and manage the aid, furthermore, war in Ukraine and its economic consequences overlapped the disasters that the pandemic had left.

The narrative on the European joint response to the COVID-19 challenge struggled to provide an assertion of the supranational institutions by fulfilling the two major gains that Jürgen Habermas deemed as the two big achievements associated to the integration process, namely, "governance beyond the nation-state" and the shaping of a "welfare system" for its citizens.[67]

But such a "welfare system" supposedly enlarged to the last corner of the European Union was not only never achieved but its failure was accompanied by the corrosion of the most developed national "welfare systems" among which the French one had stood out. Moreover, the lack of legitimacy of the union, which was one of the strong points in the French far-Right (and also in the far-Left) arguments, became more intense as citizens directly blamed the European authorities for this process of degrading their well-being.

During his presidential second term, Macron sought to implement the reforms requested to sustain the welfare state and to make the French economy more competitive. But the contestation toward such measures was even more intense than in the 2017–2022 mandate, particularly regarding the attempt to reform the pension system and the two-year delay in the retirement age. The last months of 2022 and the first half of 2023 experienced a succession of strikes and riots that paralyzed the country for weeks. Since Macron's party had lost the majority in the French Assembly in the 2022 legislative elections, he could not find majority support for his initiatives, and he had to pass the reform of the retirement age delay by decree. While the streets were burning, only nine votes coming from the moderate Right prevented Macron's appointed prime minister Élisabeth Borne from losing a motion of no confidence.

The unpopular economic reforms to entrench the Eurozone, together with the successive wave of crises affecting the French standards of living and undermining the welfare state (the COVID-19 pandemic, the war between Russia and Ukraine, which caused inflation to skyrocket) corroded the French political center. In spite of these difficulties, nevertheless, Macron's presidency still preserved the institutional framework and the French attachment to the EU, something that might not be taken for granted regarding his successors.

XIX

Such a decadence in the French standards of living happened in a society increasingly divided for cultural and religious reasons.

Even in the midst of one of the waves of the 2020 pandemic, Macron had to promote a legal structure to avoid the "separatism" that, according to the president, was beguiling the Republic. What, thus, was identified as a "separatist" backlash? Again, the main cleavage endangering French national cohesion came from the vision that brought those descendants of the peoples that had been colonized by the French empire in northern Africa or the Middle East who at some point during and after the decolonization processes migrated to the homeland.

The law that Macron announced in October 2020 was devoted to combat the Islamist struggle to create a set of values and loyalties alienated from the supposed promises of "equality and emancipation" of the French Republic. By trying to liberate the Islam in France from "foreign influences" and providing a range of resources to be invested in education and social problems the French authorities were likely to admit the disruptive effects that had represented the transfer of the same pattern of domination that was designed for the former colonies to the center of the Empire.

Macron's presidency was also precisely marked by the attempt to admit the French wrongdoings during Algeria's independence war. But, instead of assuming a clear responsibility toward both Algerian authorities and citizenry (which would concern as well some hundreds of thousands of Algerian Arab immigrants and their descendants inhabiting in France), the French president focused his plea for forgiveness regarding those Algerian Arab immigrants that *fought on the French side* in the Algerian war of independence and were abandoned to their fate.[68]

As occurred in any other western European power, France's representatives are still far from asking for forgiveness for *all* the crimes and sufferings that recent imperial performance had perpetrated against populations under their jurisdiction. Such an attitude would somehow be tantamount to recognizing the bloodbath that lies behind the origins of the *present* nation-state and would debilitate it both toward its external and, above all, its internal menaces.

The story of the present French Republic in the present stage of the evolution of the European Union is, in sum, another European example of the story of the progressive deterioration affecting the core of a Nation that once expanded itself on a global scale and that it is now experiencing its conversion into a white dwarf star.

NOTES

1. See Frances M. B. Lynch, "Resolving the Paradox of the Monnet Plan: National and International Planning in French Reconstruction," *Economic History Review* 37, no. 2 (May 1984): 229–43.
2. See Edmund Spevack, *Allied Control and German Freedom: American Political and Ideological Influences on the Framing of the West German Basic Law* (Münster, Hamburg, Berlin and London: Lit Verlag, 2001), 116.
3. Erich C. J. Hahn, "The Occupying Powers and the Constitutional Reconstruction of Germany (1945–1949)," in *Cornerstone of Democracy: The West German Grundgesetz 1949–1989*, eds. Erich C. J. Hahn, Detlef Junker et al. (Washington DC: German Historical Institute, 1995), 16.
4. Alan S. Milward, *The Reconstruction of Western Europe, 1945–1951* (London: Methuen, 1984), 468.
5. Ruggero Ranieri, "Unlocking Integration: Political and Economic Factors behind the Schuman Plan and the European Coal and Steel Community in the Work of Alan Milward," in *Alan S. Milward and a Century of European Change*, eds. Fernando Guirao, Frances M. B. Lynch, and Sigfrido M. Ramírez Pérez (New York and London: Routledge), 299–306.
6. Fernando Guirao, "Reflexiones desde la historia," in *¿Una Unión Europea en crisis? Reflexiones para un debate urgente*, eds. Fernando Guirao and Josep Pich, (Madrid: Catarata, 2019), 35–36.
7. Giandomenico Majone, *Dilemmas of European Integration: The Ambiguities and Pitfalls of Integration by Stealth* (Oxford: Oxford University Press, 2005), 4–5.
8. See Alan S. Milward, *The Reconstruction of Western Europe, 1945–1951* (London: Methuen, 1984), 470; and Milward, *The European Rescue of the Nation-State* (London and New York: Routledge, 2000), 17.
9. Ranieri, "Unlocking Integration," 307.

10. Dieter Gosewinkel, "Europe antilibérale ou anti-Europe? Les conceptions européennes de l'extrême droite française entre 1940 et 1990," *Politique européenne* 62, no. 4 (2018): 152–79.

11. Thomas Piketty, *Les hauts revenus en France au XXe siècle: Inégalités et redistributions 1901–1998* (Paris: Grasset, 2001), 137–38.

12. See, for instance, Maurice Bardèche, "Une nouvelle carte du monde," *Défense de l'Occident* 34 (June–July 1956): 3–10, 10.

13. Quoted by Gildea in Robert Gildea, *France since 1945* (Oxford: Oxford University Press, 2002), 18.

14. Andrew Moravcsik, *The Choice for Europe: Social Purpose and State Power from Messina to Maastricht* (London: UCL Press, 1998), 149.

15. Lynch, "Resolving the Paradox of the Monnet Plan," 231.

16. Perry Anderson, *The New Old World* (London and New York: Verso, 2009), 65.

17. Milward, *The European Rescue of the Nation-State*, 122.

18. Quoted by Quinn Slobodian, *Globalists The End of the Empore and the Birth of Neoliberalism* (Cambridge, MA: Harvard University Press, 2018), 191.

19. Quoted by Anderson, *The New Old World*, 18.

20. See Presidency Conclusions. Lisbon European Council. March 23 and 24, 2000. Available at https://www.consilium.europa.eu/ueDocs/cms_Data/docs/pressData/en/ec/00100-r1.en0.htm. Also Christopher Bickerton, *European Integration from Nation-States to Member States* (Oxford: Oxford University Press, 2012), 116.

21. Giuliano Garavini, *After Empires European Integration, Decolonization, and the Challenge from Global South, 1957–1986* (New York: Oxford University Press, 2012), 47.

22. Alfred Müller-Armack, *Auf dem Weg nach Europa* (Stuttgart: C.E. Poeschel, 1971), 119.

23. Martin Shipway, *Decolonization and Its Impact: A Comparative Approach to the End of the Colonial Empires* (Oxford: Blackwell, 2008), 51.

24. Slobodian, *Globalists*, 194–95.

25. Mazower, *Governing the World*, 312.

26. Garavini, *After Empires*, 231.

27. James Wiley, *The Banana Empires, Trade Wars, and Globalization* (Lincoln, NE: University of Nebraska Press, 2008), 125.

28. Fabian Klose, "Europe as a Colonial Project: A Critique of Its Anti-Liberalism," in *Anti-Liberal Europe: A Neglected Story of Europeanization*, edited by Dieter Gosewinkel (New York and Oxford: Berghahn, 2015), 48.

29. See Bertram M. Gordon, *Collaborationism in France during the Second World War* (Ithaca, NY: Cornell University Press, 1980).

30. Megan Brown, *The Seventh Member Stat:e. Algeria, France and the European Community* (Cambridge and London: Harvard University Press), 2.

31. Klose, "Europe as a Colonial Project," 50.

32. Brown, *The Seventh Member State*, 3.

33. See John G. Stoessinger, *The Might of Nations: World Politics in Our Time* (New York: Random House, 1962), 129–35.

34. Hanns Jürgen Küsters, "West Germany's Foreign Policy in Western Europe, 1949–1957: The Art of the Possible," in *Western Europe and Germany: The Beginnings of European Integration, 1945–1960*, ed. Clemens Wurm (Oxford and Washington: Berg, 1995), 69.

35. Elizabeth Buettner, *Europe after Empire: Decolonization, Society, and Culture* (Cambridge, MA: Cambridge University Press, 2016), 140–41.

36. Frank Giles, *The Locust Years: The Story of the Fourth Republic, 1946–1958* (London: Secker & Warburg, 1991), 5.

37. See Hugues Tertrais, *Le piaster et le fusil: Le coÛt de la guerre d'Indochine 1945–1954* (Vincennes: Institute de la gestion publique et du développement économique, 2002).

38. Anderson, *The New Old World*, 10.

39. Tony Judt, *Postwar: A History of Europe since 1945* (London: Penguin, 2005), 292.

40. Anderson, *The New Old World*, 141.

41. On this episode, see Georgette Elgey, *Histoire de la IVe République: La République des Tourmentes (1954–1959) Tome 3. La fin* (Paris: Fayard, 2008), 93–254; and Michel Winock, *L'agonie de la IVe République* (Paris: Gallimard, 2006).

42. Klose, "Europe as a Colonial Project," 60.

43. Pierre-Cyril Pahlavi, *La Guerre Révolutionnaire de l'Armée Française en Algérie 1954–1961: Entre esprit de conquête et conquête des esprits* (Paris: Harmattan, 2004), 62–64.

44. Winock, *L'agonie de la IVe République*, 116–23.

45. Gildea, *France since 1945*, 50–51.

46. Brown, *The Seventh Member State*, 6. On the Algerian status under the 1957 Treaty of Rome see also Megan Brown, "Drawing Algeria into Europe: Shifting French Policy and the Treaty of Rome (1951–1964)," *Modern & Contemporary France* 25, no. 2 (March 2017): 191–208.

47.Anderson, *The New Old World*, 140.

48. See Raoul Girardet, *La crise militaire française 1945–1962: Aspects sociologiques et idéologiques* (Paris: Colin, 1964), 200; and Pahlavi, *La Guerre Révolutionnaire de l'Armée Française en Algérie*, 99–108.

49. Carl Schmitt, *Theorie des Partisanen: Zwischenbemerkung zum Begriff des Politischen.* (Berlin: Duncker & Humblot, 2002; first edition 1963), 88.

50. Klose, "Europe as a Colonial Project," 59.

51. Judt, *Postwar*, 288.

52. See Gildea, *France since 1945*, 32; Klose, "Europe as a Colonial Project," 60; Mark Mazower, *Dark Continent: Europe's Twentieth Century* (New York: Vintage, 2000), 312.

53. Judt, *Postwar*, 288.

54. Gildea, *France since 1945*, 32.

55. Judt, *Postwar*, 289.

56. Anderson, *The New Old World*, 173.

57. Hèctor López Bofill, "Catalonia: The Right to Self-Determination and the Consent of the Governed," in *Constitutional Law and the Politics of Secession*, ed. Antoni Abat Ninet (London and New York: Routledge, 2023).

58. Gildea, *France since 1945*, 34.

59. Ian Kershaw, *Roller-Coaster: Europe 1950–2017* (London: Allen Lane/Penguin Books, 2018), 520.

60. Anderson, *The New Old World*, 191.

61. See Matthew Moran, "Terrorism and the *Banlieues*: The *Charlie Hebdo* Attacks in Context," *Modern & Contemporary France*, 25, no. 3 (April 2017): 315–32.

62. Kershaw, *Roller-Coaster*, 503.

63. Gildea, *France since 1945*, 100–101.

64. Stanley Hoffmann, "Obstinate or Obsolete? The Fate of the Nation-State and the Case of Western Europe," *Daedalus* 95, no.3 (Summer 1966): 862–915, 879.

65. Thompson, *Disorder*, 242–43.

66. Gildea, *France since 1945*, 100–101.

67. Jürgen Habermas, *The Divided West* (Cambridge: Polity, 2006), 43.

68. See "France Asks 'Forgiveness' for Its Abandonment of Algerian Harkis," *The New York Times*, September 20, 2021. Available at https://www.nytimes.com/2021/09/20/world/europe/france-algeria-harkis.html.

Chapter 5

Colonization within Europe

I

Europe is a continent that has defeated Germany in two world wars but that has borne German hegemony in the first decades of the twenty-first century through monetary policy.[1] In a similar fashion to what happened with the imperial powers that had withdrawn from their former overseas colonial possessions but maintained an indirect control upon them by economic means, the Federal Republic of Germany relinquished direct domination upon other European countries (and particularly upon the eastern European countries) in order to ensure its economic supremacy. German economic predominance in the continent, very acute during the 2010s, had sometimes been interpreted as a postmodern version of the disturbing old notions of German *Großraum*.[2]

Certainly, the traditional space for Germany to develop its expansionist plans had usually been eastern Europe. Some parts of eastern Europe were indeed considered a core region of Germany itself or territories over which the German Empire had some rights considering that they had been inhabited by German ethnic population for centuries. It is usually forgotten, even within the present Germany itself, that the Reich, until the beginning of World War II, entrenched itself until Lithuania's borders (including the Memel territory, annexed in 1939) or that the capital of Lower Silesia, Breslau (today Wrocław, in Poland) had been one of the largest cities within the German Empire mostly inhabited by ethnic Germans.

German population, on the other hand, had been present in many places in eastern Europe, and some of them had been Habsburg or Prussian subjects until the Central Empire's defeat in World War I. Those groups of ethnic Germans turned suddenly, and not without shocks, to be ruled by Czechs, Poles, Estonians, or Latvians. The latter situation supposed a never-ending source of conflicts by the 1920s (as was demonstrated by the fleeing of German refugees from Poland mostly to eastern Prussia on a big scale),[3] which partially motivated the national expansion of Germany to the east that would be later promoted by the Nazi regime.

The aspiration to build a real *Grossdeutschland* toward the east, an aim that during the interwar period was shared both by racially inspired German nationalists and by the republican Left,[4] became a taboo after 1989. As soon as there was envisaged the slightest possibility of the reunification of the German States that had been defined in the Cold War, renouncing the horizon of a Greater Germany was perceived as a fast track to facilitate the consent of the powers that had won World War II to tolerate the appearance of a single German polity.[5]

The impossibility to exercise territorial domination of eastern Europe instigated among German both public and private agents the project to develop forms of economic expansion in that area. Such a struggle, nevertheless, began to be thwarted when high-scale conflicts between Russia and its neighbors suggested that relying on economic dominance alone is insufficient to maintain any kind of political influence and, possibly, to ensure the continuation of economic prosperity itself.

II

Since a unified Germany, much later than its western European counterparts, was forged in 1871, it also entered into the overseas colonial contest. At that time, by the Berlin Conference of 1884–1885, most of the world's great masses of land and population had already been allocated and only some parts in Africa, in the Far East, and a few islands in the Pacific were still available for German imperial rapacity.[6]

It was precisely in the decade of the 1880s when there opened a debate on two visions around German imperial expansion: on the one side, there were those politicians, pressed by the German corporations' needs for raw materials, who argued for building a great world empire through the colonies that were on the verge of being occupied in Asia and Africa. From the other side, in which was situated Otto von Bismarck himself, Germany's destiny lay in shaping a grand project of continental integration, an empire by land.[7] It is told that before the displaying of the plans concerning an eventual German expansion in Africa, Bismarck observed that "my map of Africa lies in Europe." According to such a legend the chancellor pointed to Russia and then to the left, to France, and stated that "we are in the middle," arguing that the only question in which he was interested regarding the African scramble was to make the dissension between the rest of the European powers more profound in order to facilitate German's hegemony within the continent.[8]

But in contradiction to his words, Bismarck also fostered German expansion overseas. Between 1884 (when precisely Bismarck announced a protectorate over the bay of Angra Pequena, in what is today Namibia)[9] and the conclusion of World War I, the German empire extended claims and controlled territories between the British Cape territory and the southern border of Portuguese Angola. In Africa Germany's colonization, beyond the mentioned territories, included Cameroon, Togo, and Tanganyika as well. Additionally, the *Kaiserreich* ruled in the Shandong Peninsula in Asia and even possessed a part of New Guinea and some other adjacent archipelagos in the Pacific such as what to this day is still called the Bismarck Archipelago.[10]

It was in that time of the German colonialist adventure that the German authorities even had the opportunity to set in motion genocidal practices that thereafter they would organize at home: in the colony of the German Southwest Africa approximately eighty thousand individuals of both the Herero people and the Nama people were killed through battle, starvation, and thirst in the Omaheke Desert. In the following stage, individuals belonging to the Herero and Nama peoples also perished as the consequence of forced labor, malnutrition, sexual violence, diseases, and the medical experiments conducted within what would represent a German precedent of the *Konzentrationslager*.[11]

Europe would become from 1914 the main concern of German imperialism again, but the techniques of total warfare, racial extermination, and looting, would be tested overseas. Some of those who joined the ranks of the Nazi Party had had some experience in the German display of murderous racial policies in southwest Africa or Cameroon. Viktor Böttcher, for instance, the man that Hitler appointed as provincial governor of Posen in 1939, had been a civil servant in the German Cameroon. He was one of the many Nazi functionaries who sought "to perform in the east of the Reich the constructive work that we had once carried out in Africa."[12]

After Germany's defeat in World War I, such African, Asian, or Pacific colonies were lost, and the British and the French entrenched still more their respective empires, and any German overseas expansion project would have to be abandoned. Germany had been one of the last European empires to be involved in the Western enterprise of global domination and one of the first in losing its overseas possessions. For a later generation than those that had fought African peoples like the Herero or the Nama, it became clear that political, economic, and military hegemony had to be gained, as Bismarck had already suggested, in the first instance, against Germany's European neighbors.

III

The priority, as Hitler's obsessions clearly revealed from the outset of his political career, was continental Europe and, particularly, eastern Europe, which was seen as the natural courtyard of the German settlement.

While the social and economic consequences of conquering France and the rest of the countries in western Europe that fell in the late spring of 1940 had not really been planned by the Nazi leadership, the attack against the Soviet Union from June 1941, as previously had happened in Czechoslovakia and the occupation of Poland in 1939, implemented the core of the Nazi ideological principles.

Movements eastward had as a main motivation to take the control over an enormous land area able to provide both enough resources to make the German Reich economically self-sufficient and to build the Nazi project of a racist society in which the Germans (the ones that lived within the territories annexed and the ones that would be sent there after the military occupation) would dominate and exploit other peoples.

The *Lebensraum* doctrine (already present for a long time in German nationalist politics, though the Nazis were the ones who offered its most extreme version)[13] held that Germany required a wide territorial scope for its survival and that most of the indigenous populations of central and eastern Europe would have to be removed permanently (either through mass deportation, extermination, or enslavement) including Polish, Ukrainian, Russian, Czech, and other Slavic nations considered non-Aryan. The repopulation of those eastern areas with German colonists combined with elimination through starvation and assassination of broad layers of the autochthonous inhabitants had to allow the appropriation of a large amount of agricultural surpluses in order to feed ethnic Germans both within the Reich and within the new territories under the yoke of the Reich.

The Nazis, to sum up, aimed to transpose elements of other extra-European imperial projects onto the European continent. They tried to build their empire in Europe itself.[14] It is no wonder thus that Hitler described Russia as "our Africa."[15] "What Hitler was offering," wrote Hitler's biographer Ian Kershaw, "was a modernized version of old-fashioned imperialist conquest, now translated to the ethnically mixed terrain of Eastern Europe where the Slavs would provide the German equivalent of the conquered native populations of India and Africa in the British Empire."[16]

Even before the outbreak of World War II, the Nazis applied an extra-European colony-like regime to the first non-German territory that they conquered: the Protectorate of Bohemia and Moravia that corresponded with the rump Czech state left after the occupation of the German Sudetes in

October 1938 and that fell completely into Hitler's hands by March 1939. The legal framework that the Germans set up in Bohemia and Moravia was similar to the status that the French recognized, for instance, to Tunis or Morocco. Although the authorities of the Bohemian and Moravian protectorate enjoyed some degree of autonomy (with a president, a government, a militia, and an internal public administration) the power had to be exercised "in conformity with the political, military and economic rights of the Reich." The establishment of a dual system of law by which Germans of Czech citizenship were allowed to register automatically for citizenship of the German Reich while the rest remained nationals of the Protectorate also resembled practices of the European colonial powers in other continents, such as what happened with the division between French Algerians and Arab Algerians.[17]

IV

Although the domination and conquest of eastern Europe were the first of Hitler's ambitions, the astonishing conquest of western Europe by the *Wehrmacht* in the Spring of 1940, and particularly the control of France, produced for the Germans another concern beyond the crusade for obtaining land and wealth from the east: how to set up the unification of advanced capitalist economies, how to create a German-led trading bloc (which may be deemed as a closer precedent of the situation that afterward the European Union outlined).

Except for a brief moment after France's invasion, the rationalization of the interactions among capitalist economies only preoccupied German industrialists and bankers but was something of little interest for the core of the Nazi leadership. Only certain Reich ministries, such as the German Foreign Ministry (from which was sought a fast movement toward customs and currency union with as many European countries as possible) and the Economic and Armament Ministries,[18] had been concerned with the economic framework of collaboration between Germany and the western European occupied territories.

In spite of the relative indifference with which western Europe was likely to embed the Nazi strategy of domination upon the continent, it should be remarked, nevertheless, that the horizon envisaged in the mentioned instances maintained some analogies with the notion of European integration that would be developed after the war: namely, (1) the building of a big economic space ("*wirtschaftlicher Großraum*") with a customs union and (2) the recognition of free movement of goods, both grounded on legal equality. Somehow, thus, the European conception focused on economic issues organized under the expert criteria that was developed in the second half of the twentieth century was not so distant from that designed through the Europe of Occupation and Collaboration in which, for instance, the relationship between the German Minister of Armament, Albert Speer, and his French counterpart in Vichy, Jean Bichelonne, was so close and fruitful.[19]

The substantial difference between the Nazi New Order and the European Communities was, of course, that the former was not intended to establish a free market area according to liberal principles with the aim to provide economic growth and prosperity, but to subject the economies of western Europe to the interests of the occupant and, particularly, to implement the rationalization and the mandates of economic efficiency in order to fulfill the demands of the German war effort.

The collaboration between advanced capitalist economies in western Europe by the beginning of the 1940s was, thus, centered in serving *one* national interest instead of representing a confluence of plural national aspirations seeking to achieve an optimal economic outcome able to benefit all the agents involved, which is the supposed aim shown through the performance of the current European Union authorities.

V

The last stages of the war and its aftermath brought disastrous consequences both for the plan of colonizing and displaying Germany's rule of eastern Europe (whether direct or indirect through protectorates) and the ideal of the single market and the economic bloc under German dictates conceived for western Europe.

In eastern Europe the outcome was exactly the opposite of the one designed by the Nazi plan; not only did the ethnic Germans who had been living outside of the Reich's border before the war have to emigrate westward, but Germany also lost parts of its territory from before the war, which had been inhabited by a majority of ethnic Germans for generations.[20] That was the case of East Prussia, the port of Danzig, or the large territories of East Brandenburg, Pomerania, and Lower and Upper Silesia that were transferred to Poland (apart from a portion that the Soviet Union would keep for herself) as was outlined by Stalin, Roosevelt, and Churchill in their meetings first in Teheran (November-December 1943), then in Yalta (February 1945), and finally (with President Truman in the United States and British prime minister Clement Attlee replacing Roosevelt and Churchill respectively) in Potsdam in summer 1945.

With the former German territories mostly assigned to the new Poland, there was triggered the removal of almost 7 million Germans, to which should be added another 3 million removed from Czechoslovakia, and more than 1.8 million from other eastern lands, making a total of almost 12 million refugees (some authors estimate more than 14 million[21] and even more than 16 million if one includes removals from southern Europe)[22] in one of the hugest transfers of population that humanity has ever seen.[23] The massive migration of ethnic Germans westward from territories that they had inhabited for generations was, however, only one more of the catastrophes that the collapse of the Third Reich would bring to the German nation.

The total war, to which Joseph Goebbels appealed in 1943 after the first disasters of Stalingrad and El-Alamein, certainly led to the total defeat of Germany. *Der totale Krieg* created *die totale Niederlage*.[24] The disintegration of the Nazi regime represented, at least in the immediate aftermath of the war, the disappearance of German Statehood, its complete loss of political or military significance, and a landscape of physical destruction across the country that defies any description.

By May 7, 1945 at least 1.8 million German civilians had perished. One-third of the boys born to German families between 1915 and 1924 were either dead or missing. Among those born between 1920 and 1925, losses amounted to 40 percent.[25] Economic activity had been paralyzed (although not all the German industrial facilities had been completely devastated). There were no banks, no shops, no means of transportation. There was no sense of law and order, goods belonged to those who were strong enough to hold on to them, famine was widespread, and there was only survival.[26] Large parts of Germany had been reduced to "a rubble strewn wasteland in which the living often envied the dead."[27] At least 3.8 million of a stock of 19 million apartments had been destroyed, leaving 7.5 million people homeless. In the cities hit hardest by the bombing, losses in housing stock ran to 50 percent.[28]

When the Allies took control of the situation, they only allowed the creation of local and regional governments with no perspective of reestablishing anything that resembled a central German government. Even most of the *Länder* created in the first postwar years had no specific correspondence with the Weimar's regional organization. A *Land* such as Prussia, the biggest and the most powerful one, considered the source of German militarism and authoritarianism, ceased to exist because of a decision by the Allies.[29] As late as in winter 1948 the French, always obsessed about avoiding the resurrection of Germany, still opposed the British and American plans to establish a German central power and claimed for designing a confederation of small states able to confine the German people to a perpetual political marginality.

It may have been even worse for German interests. In order to crush the German nation for the longest possible time, in the last year of the war some powers on the Allied side were planning the full annihilation of Germany's industry and economy in what was known as the "Morgenthau" plan (since it was overseen by the United States secretary of the treasury, Henry

Morgenthau Jr.).[30] Only the ambitions of the conquerors upon the German resources that kept standing in spite of the bombing raids, and the rivalry that was quickly growing between the Western Allies and the Soviet Union, restrained the victors from proceeding with the total deindustrialization of Germany and the conversion of the country into a rural area.

The allocation of the occupied zones among the Allies, on the one hand, and the Soviet Union, on the other, was also in the track of dismembering Germany as a political entity. However, since the western part of the country became the front line in the battlefield of the Cold War, and a focal point in the competition between two economic and social systems, the British and the Americans gave up their plans for punishment and fostered, instead, the creation of a democratic German federation grounded in a free market economy within the *Länder* under their control.

Western Allies did not suddenly design a constitutional system characterized by fundamental rights, citizenry political participation, rule of law, and territorial division of power with the intention of entrenching a thriving economy because they were sympathetic or humanitarian toward the Germans against whom they had fought only a couple of years previously. They had no other alternative than pushing Germany toward a welfare state and an expanding economy if they wanted to face up to the challenge represented by the Soviet Union and Communism that had been already established in East Germany.

The communist threat is what really lies behind West Germany's rebuilding and the subsequent economic growth that was underpinned by the American aid that began to flow from April 1948. The need to prevent the spread of communism was also what lay behind the founding of the European Communities. If West Germany was not even allowed to trade with the eastern European territories that once had belonged to its jurisdiction, or that it conquered during the war, with whom would it go to establish economic relations? To whom was it going to send the goods that its industry was beginning to produce again?

The former western European enemies were, of course, and even in spite of the strong reluctance shown by the French, the only possibility to ensure Germany's social and economic leap forward. High value-added capital goods industries (machine tools, machinery, transport equipment, and chemicals)[31] needed a place to be sold and, by the same token, the resting German system of production was dependent on raw materials that were at the disposal of some other European power's colonies (though not for long since pro-independence movements were beginning to cause instability in those territories in such a way that raw material supplies would become more limited).

In that regard, while being true that what would be the future partners of Germany were going to be engulfed by colonial wars, which they were going to lose, at least they still retained territorial control upon their mainland European jurisdictions; something that could not be said about Germany. Indeed, West Germany's position was still more debilitated than that of its partners; it was not only that it had lost its "colonial" empire within Europe, but also what had been considered the core of its national entity had been amputated (transferred to Poland, to Czechoslovakia or even to the Soviet Union) and divided through the creation of the German Democratic Republic (let alone the restoration of Austria's independence).

By the time of its creation, in May 1949, the German Federal Republic was, essentially, a weak state on the eastern edge of western Europe[32] a situation that would mark as well West Germany's developing negotiations to outline any European organization and that would eventually prepare the ground for the success in the common enterprise of creating a stable political and economic pole. A strong Germany had led Europe to the most ominous conflicts. Maybe a weak one (shadowed by the Communist bloc) might provide tranquility and prosperity—this is what effectively happened.

VI

The postwar mood on the Soviet Union that stretched itself across western Europe and allowed for understanding between Germany and the other European partners somehow reproduced the perception that dominated Nazi rhetoric after the Third Reich's Stalingrad defeat, namely, that the fight by the German side also represented the fight for *Festung Europa*, the Fortress Europe against the Asiatic hordes. It was not surprising that the consolidation of such a narrative on the grounds of the project of European integration in fact allowed the transformation of convinced Nazis under Hitler into fervent Europeanists after the war.[33]

Present dangers helped to forget past atrocities and allowed the imagining of a common future with the former enemies. West Germany, once the great continental power, represented by its creation in 1949 the weakest among those weak elements in western Europe that would gamble to supersede the differences in order to push toward integration.

The rise of the Soviet Union, its progressive control of different states in Eastern Europe, beginning with the Communist seizing of Czechoslovakia in 1948, revealed the urgency to create and to strengthen the ties between the fragile pretended liberal democracies existing between the Elbe and the Atlantic following a trend that has traditionally marked the building of political unions: the *fear* toward an external and common enemy. There was not the spirit of conciliation that waivered the relationship between the German Federal Republic, France, Italy, Belgium, the Netherlands, and Luxembourg, not even the concern to ensure a standard of living for their populations but that fear to see the whole national, economic, and social system dismantled whether by a direct attack of forces coming from the other side of the Iron Curtain or by domestic crises opening an opportunity for local Communists in western Europe to assault the institutions (as was on the verge of happening in Italy).

Fear, real or imagined, was present in the foundation of the European Communities, and still represents the magnetic force that marks further steps in the integration process.[34] Even in the present, fear, of another superpower such as China,[35] of massive migration movements, of war in Ukraine, and inflation, or of whatever other cause that creates dependence among member states, appears as a possibility to reverse the centripetal inertia experienced in episodes as with Brexit.

The backlash within the western European landscape given the Communist emergence by the beginning of the Cold War was only a further sign of a more universal collective mechanism of self-protection that called for conciliation in order to confront an alien power judged to be superior and dreadful.

VII

Focusing on international trade regulated by common institutions was the only way left to such border lands of the Western world to develop their foreign policy. But if the Federal Republic authorities assumed the necessity of co-operating with others to ensure security, stability, and economic growth, it was because they were deprived from doing anything else.[36] There was, indeed, the proximity to the Soviets that instigated Adenauer's policy on the approach to the West. But there was also an additional and relevant factor: Germany's need to bury the stigmatization of its Nazi background.

The distrust expressed by French or British rulers toward the resurrection of a strong German military power embedded with expansive ambitions of domination would certainly hover over European developments even as late as the fall of the Berlin Wall in 1989. The opposition that at his time was encountered by Chancellor Kohl to Germany's plan of absorbing the territories that had belonged to the German Democratic Republic, coming from the French president, François Mitterrand, and from the British prime minister, Margaret Thatcher, would be only mitigated through the German commitment to integrate the political and economic developments of a united Germany into a Europe defined by a closer union. That commitment, expressed by Kohl on several occasions,[37] convinced Mitterrand, who also knew that the project of a reunified Germany inserted in the European Communities and in NATO was firmly backed by the administration of George H. W. Bush in the United States, but Margaret Thatcher who in fact was opposed to any political entrenchment of a European supranational institution, still in a gathering of the European Communities' leaders in Strasbourg on December 8–9, 1989, emphatically declared in front of Kohl and the others, "We have beaten the Germans twice! And now they're back again!"[38]

The German urgency to generate trust among its neighbors, to rehabilitate itself for the injuries caused to them in the past, had already decades before crucially influenced the decision to participate in both the creation of the European Coal and Steel Community (1951) and, a few years after, the creation of the European Economic Community (1957). The foundational treaties of what would later become the European Union represented the first stage in which the German Federal Republic was treated for the very first time since the defeat in 1945 as an equal partner within the framework of international relations.[39] Taking distances with socialism and reasserting a capitalist system within the framework of a market economy modulated by a system of rights would suppose a fundamental achievement to gain such recognition among the other Western partners.

VIII

The postwar constitutional constraints in West Germany somehow expressed the features that would be later translated to the building of the European project; West Germany was a precedent in restraining sovereignty for the sake of a wider international settlement (a divided and an occupied country had no other alternative than to abdicate from any ideal of legal and political supremacy grounded on a national ethos). It anticipated, in the same vein, the displacement of a radical constituent power depriving the German "People" the ability to give itself a constitutional framework[40] and, finally, it modeled an economic order defined by a free market economy whose excesses could be softened by some corporatist limitations but without democratizing the economy.[41] The history of West German postwar constitutionalism is therefore that in which the idea of a People as a constituent force is replaced by the rhetoric of constitutional rights guaranteed at the last instance by courts and also that in which the economic constitution is restructured in order to avoid political extremism.

At the end of the day, in a drift that would also be translated to the European sphere, West German legal and political development would provide a model in which the economy, insulated from democratic interference through a strong defense of property rights and the rule of law, would be viewed as the principal ground of authority for the constitution.[42]

According to the vision held by the ordo-liberal canon that triumphed within the political and economic cadres that would assume the reigns of the first German federal governments, individual economic freedom (under the coverage of the legitimacy of the protection of fundamental rights) would represent a barrier to popular radical constitutional changes. The European integration project would host the developments experienced in West Germany in the immediate postwar period according to which a program on the creation of "constitutionalism without constitution" would be implemented. Mirroring the German path, achievements grounded on the techno-legal apparatus of the European Communities eventually allowed the consolidation of a legal doctrine without political constitutional support, a normative structure able to constrain the supposedly anti-liberal tendencies of the unrestrained majority as the one that had been unleashed in the interwar period.[43]

Postwar West Germany, thus, would lay the ground for the main ideological strands that would be adopted at the European level able to be summarized in the following tenets:

1. a formally denationalized entity justified rather by its technical developments than by popular participation (though Adenauer's motivation to go ahead with European integration was defined, as we have seen in what happened with Monnet as well, by a nationalistic perspective which had in the assurance of Germany's equality vis-à-vis the other European partners its most immediate goal);
2. a decision-making process centered on the political and technical elites keeping a very diffuse connection with the citizenry;
3. a political organization founded on the rule of law at its turn defined by the specific allocation of powers derived from the *pacta sunt servanda* principle concluded among the partners;
4. a system in which economic liberties and their safeguarding play the main role; and
5. a political structure that finds its legitimacy mainly in economic success (as the evolution of West Germany demonstrated vis-à-vis its Socialist counterpart) rather than in democratic consent.

In this sense, the notion of "militant democracy," understood as a kind of device that would impede the modification of the constitutional pillars through democratic means (the mechanisms devoted to justifying democratic restrictions in order to "save democracy from itself") provides a good account regarding the liberal efforts to preserve the economic model designed through constitutional rules.[44]

More precisely, as Wilkinson observes, "militant democracy" was an expression applied, rather than to restrict democracy for its survival, to curtail mechanisms of popular participation in order to "serve" liberal and "neo-liberal" ends.[45] The "militant democracy" constitutional design provided in the 1949 German Basic Law permitted the prohibition of the Socialist Reich Party, considered the successor of the NSDAP, by the Federal Constitutional Court in 1952, but also paved the way for the prohibition of Germany's Communist Party in a maneuver that was consented to in 1957 by the recently founded European Commission of Human Rights within the framework of the Council of Europe, which backed West Germany's authorities decision by arguing that the dictatorship of the proletariat stage advocated by Communist doctrine in order to establish a political regime was incompatible with the rights enshrined in the European Convention on Human Rights.

By the time in which such resolutions were issued in the mid-1950s, that is between the conclusion of the Treaty of the European Coal and Steel Community and shortly after the signature of the Treaty on the European Economic Community, some of the questions concerning West Germany's role as a state were being resolved:[46] Germany's defense was being consolidated by the rearmament of the German military forces within NATO, control over West Berlin was likely to be ensured as well, and the Saar had been repatriated.

Germany's pro-Western alignment, which would be entrenched by the opening of the western European markets to German manufactures and the consequent economic growth, would prevent, according to Adenauer's strategy, any temptation to commit West Germany to the ideologies of the left including those proposals coming from the opposition of the Social Democratic Party concerning the so-called *Ostpolitik*. Within the European Economic Community, West Germany would politically reemerge from its ashes and would transform itself into a prosperous free market economy.

In this fashion such prosperity obtained within a capitalist free market economy decisively contributed to achieving the mentioned goal concerning German rehabilitation and to surmount the shock caused by the loss of the former German continental empire. In a different way, however, the constitutional technology outlined through militant democracy, the defense of property rights, and the constraints to popular intervention in pushing for radical changes anticipated the legal architecture that would foster another kind of German colonization within Europe: the economic one.

Such growth that West Germany led in Western Europe from the beginning of the 1950s allowed, among other things, *to forget* the previous physical occupation through military means displayed under the Third Reich, a forgetting that, as a collateral consequence, stretched a thick veil on the capitalist forces that were behind Germany's economic success within the new

European Communities framework. Indeed, in contrast to the massive expropriations experienced in East Germany with the Communist ascendancy, the property relations in West Germany, aside from the destruction caused by the war, *did not change* substantially.

West German economic development from the 1950s was surrounded by undeniable empirical evidence: from 1952 to 1958 its GNP expanded at a yearly rate of 7.6 percent in real terms and at a still robust rate of about 5 percent into the 1960s; workers' wages increased by 79 percent in real terms between 1949 and 1959. West Germany literally rose from the ashes as its cities and factories were rebuilt, exports soared, and the West German standard of living improved. But the idea of the West German miraculous reconstruction of its economic system to a great extent depended also on a political and cultural narrative whose definition not only involved the leaders of the conservative Christian Democratic Union/Christian Social Union but also a large array of political, economic, and social agents in America and western Europe. It was such a narrative founded on economic reconstruction and the ensuing growth of consumerism that provided a new sense of identity and helped to escape from the Nazi past's memories and moral burden.[47]

The West German legal order, however, basically maintained the prewar capitalist structures and that essentially meant that the ones that mainly contributed to German postwar growth were the ones that already controlled the means of production in the previous regime.

IX

The West German postwar order was founded by the distrust of the popular political involvement that had led to political polarization and finally to fascism and the destruction of the liberal order.[48]

The process of constitution drafting moved from a diffuse advocacy of relative political-economic pluralism toward a pattern of restrictive liberal consolidation. The ultimate character of the Basic Law of 1949, originally only intended to assume force as a provisional constitution until the united German people were able to establish a definitive supreme law, was specifically conceived as a remedy for the problems resulting from the Weimar Constitution. The Basic Law aimed at once to avoid the executive-led presidentialism and the reliance on emergency laws of the interwar polity and to highly restrict convergence between economy and state. In the latter case, it endeavored to reinforce the non-derogable status of singular basic rights, to limit the inclusionary allocation of material and corporate rights, and to give primacy to a catalogue of rights that reflected classical ideas of subjective liberties and defined the primary spheres of human liberty vis-à-vis state power.[49]

The interwar experience, thus, promoted an institutional design reliant on the strong moral guidance of constitutional, political, and economic elites.[50] Such a collective self-distrust, and the desire for collective self-commitment to liberal values, induced the West German postwar constitutional programs to be elite-led and elite-managed.[51] But who composed such elites pledging for the resurrection and maintenance of the liberal order shortly after the conclusion of World War II? Who was going to run the new West German constitutional democracy established in 1949?

A genealogical reconstruction of such capitalist forces that were in motion by the first years of the German Federal Republic might reveal their closer links that they maintained with the oligarchy that had been committed with the Nazi regime. The taboo that prevented to point out such continuities, or even identities, within West German postwar developments was later extended to the interactions that such German economic elites *displayed within the framework of the European Communities*.

Already having in mind the aim of creating a new political entity, the future West German chancellor, Konrad Adenauer, on May 5, 1946, spoke out against the denazification measures demanding that the "Nazi fellow travelers" be left in peace. The political leaders that were being envisaged for the new German beginning, thus, considered it more prudent to encourage silence on the social support that Hitler's regime had had while turning a blind eye to the presence of the same groups in postwar West Germany both in the public sector and in business circles.

Continuity defined the civil administration of the western zones first at territorial level and, after, at federal level. American and British attempts to break up German bureaucracy and replace it with a civil service of the Anglo-Saxon type met with no success. No judge, for instance, was condemned for involvement in the judicial terror of the Third Reich.[52] From the series of trials between 1945 and 1947 in which the Allied occupying powers in Germany prosecuted Nazis and their collaborators for crimes of war, crimes of war, murders, and other felonies committed in pursuit of Nazi goals, there only resulted in the western zones the conviction of around 5,000 people, of whom just under 800 were condemned to death and 486 eventually executed.[53] The bulk of Germans that had been actively involved supporting the Nazi regime, whether within the administration as civil servants or within the private sector, dogged the retribution.

Among such "Nazi fellow travelers," in the territories controlled by the Western Allies, were an important number of German bankers, industrialists, and businessmen, and some of them had supported the regime from the beginning. A wide range of figures and companies might be mentioned.

The chemical giant IG Farben, indeed one of the largest private companies not only in Germany but in the world, donated 400,000 reichsmarks shortly after Hitler's seizure of power on January 30, 1933, for the elections held on the following March 5 in which the Nazis sought to entrench themselves by wiping out their political opponents and gaining massive support among the voters (with scarce success since in the end that support in the 1933 March elections was much lower than the expectations held by the Nazi leadership). Among the other donors assisting Hitler in establishing his dictatorship at this preliminary stage of his seizing of power also figured the Deutsche Bank, the association of the mining industry, the organizers of the Berlin Automobile Exhibition, or a cluster of electrical engineering corporations including Telefunken, AEG, and the Accumulatoren Fabrik.[54]

German big industrial and technological corporations were crucial in the rearming that marked the regime between 1933 and 1939, boosting the recovery of the German economy from the global crises previously unchained in 1929. After the outbreak of the war in 1939, such economic agents also thrived through the raw materials and the workforce obtained in the territories occupied and controlled by the Reich.

By the last months of the conflict and, in spite of the general devastation of Germany, some productive structures survived the catastrophe, including some assets of the businesses that had supported the regime and had benefited from the mentioned cycle of conquest, exploitation, enslavement, and genocide. In the whirlwind of 1945, while the Allies were approaching from the west and the south—the same as the Soviet Union did in the east—the Third Reich's minister of Arms and war production, Albert Speer, worked to circumvent Hitler's instructions, the so-called Nero Decree, regarding the destruction of German industry in the territories that were going to fall into the hands of the enemy. Speer's struggles enabled to keep relatively safe, particularly in the west, some German industrial facilities that would be needed once the war was concluded. Physical destruction of industrial assets was quite limited, for Allied bombing had focused on the transportation infrastructure and civilian housing, and gross industrial capital in fact grew by a fifth between 1936 and 1945.[55] While in what was to become the German Democratic Republic the capital stock that had not been destroyed would be dismantled at least by 30 percent and private possessions would be expropriated by the Soviet authorities, in West Germany a relevant part of the industrial capacities would not only avoid annihilation but would remain in private hands.[56]

However, most of the business owners that lay behind the surviving industrial premises had been very close to the Third Reich authorities. It was not only that the punishment against capitalist Nazi supporters was from the end of the war light, but also that their engagement with the future Federal Republic would be crucial in order to have some perspectives of stability. As the Western Allies soon realized it was not in their interest to see the German economy crippled, still less with the Red Army in Berlin. The relevant part of the German capitalists that supported Hitler were thus going to play a prominent role in the Federal Republic and would also emerge as an important social agent in the reconstruction of the whole continent through a European integration process grounded on the principles of the market economy.

Even those that might have shown more personal distance toward the Nazi regime fully participated in the German war effort and were involved in the creation of the formidable German war machine that subjugated almost the whole continent. That was conveniently silenced, but the truth was that the total mobilization of labor and resources that the German expansion demanded would not have been possible without the full implication of German society at large, including the decisive contribution provided by the great majority of the economic elites. Nazism, in short, had spread deep roots within the country.[57]

In the aircraft procurement plans of the regime, for instance, were involved major German manufacturers such as the *Bayerische Motor Werke* (BMW) Junkers, Messerschmitt, and Heinkel, which worked in an agenda of rationalization and optimization dictated by the ministry of air and later by the single armaments authority that the aforementioned Albert Speer led. BMW, on the other hand, one of the Luftwaffe's main suppliers of aero-engines, was also one of the major companies that benefited from employing foreign workers, most of them in a regime of slavery. In September 1944 and in its Munich plants alone, BMW employed more than 16,600 foreign workers (they were housed in eleven dedicated facilities, including a prisoner of war camp and a subsidiary of Dachau concentration camp).[58]

X

But the German oligarchs were not the only ones that had shown commitment to the Third Reich. Another omitted topic in the postwar period was related to the fact that some of those German industrialists that regained their position after 1945 had had a close relationship with businessmen from France, Belgium, Luxembourg, or the Netherlands before and during the war. Everywhere small businessmen, bankers, and officials who had helped administer occupation regimes build the "Atlantic Wall" against an invasion of France, supply German forces and so forth were left in place to perform similar services for the successor democracies and provide continuity and stability.[59] The similar traces of continuity that might be found among German capitalism between the prewar and the postwar world, in sum, may be recognized among the rest of the western European economic elites that worked during the German occupation of their respective countries.

The same French or Dutch entrepreneurs that joined their German colleagues in the organization of the European Communities had only a few years earlier been involved in negotiations when the Nazi German Economics Ministry had talked about managing European cartels and output planning.[60] Monnet himself (the postwar *Commissariat Au Plan*, the President of the High Authority, the Companion of Honor, and the first Citizen of Europe) did not express any concern by having concluded deals with Friedrich Flick to sell chemical products in Nazi Germany.[61]

After 1945, the western European elites' collaboration with the Germans was conveniently forgotten passing in silence over the fact that German officials in most of Europe had not been overly troubled by resistance until late in the day.[62] For a long time, the links between the Third Reich and the western European industrialists, traders, or bankers, which planted the seed for the subsequent continental economic union, were suppressed and concealed. While true that the "Europe" of the *SS* was not the same of that of the Common Market (the specialists insist that the idea of Europe was of no use to Hitler and Goebbels and was even something that they despised or, at best, only used tactically),[63] the discourse of the Cold War and postwar western European alliance politics allowed the smooth recycling of the former supporters of the authoritarian regimes to the free market and liberal democratic faith. Somehow, the progress of the capitalist elites experienced by the establishment of the European Communities had been already envisaged under Hitler's empire.

XI

The above-mentioned Friedrich Flick, indeed, spearheads the list that entails the examples of industrialists involved in the Nazi regime that were later maintained under the West German Republic. Convicted as a war criminal in 1947, Flick was released three years later by the Bonn authorities and restored to his former eminence as the leading shareholder in Daimler-Benz. Flick became the richest person in West Germany during the Cold War and was one of the richest people in the world at the time of his death in 1972.

Senior figures in the incriminated industrial combines of IG Farben and Krupp (like Otto Ambros and Alfred Krupp) were also released early and reentered public life little the worse for wear. Otto Ambros, for instance, had made a spectacular career as IG's leading expert for synthetic rubber developing, therefore, one of the most cherished regime ambitions related to the building of an industry of artificial materials for the army industry that Germany, given the lack of an overseas empire, had great difficulties to extract and to import. By the late 1930s he was a member of the managerial board and chair of IG's Buna commission.[64] Arrested by the U.S. army in 1946, Ambros was put on trial at Nuremberg in 1948 and was found guilty of establishing and overseeing the slave-labor production system in the IG Buna Werke rubber plant at Monowitz, near Auschwitz, and sentenced to eight years' confinement. He was nevertheless released in 1951 and became an adviser to chemical companies such as W.R. Grace, Dow Chemical, as well as the U.S. army Chemical Corps and even to the German Federal Chancellor Konrad Adenauer, who did not hesitate to surround himself with some of the "Nazi fellow travelers" that, like Ambros, had composed the scientific intelligentsia of the Third Reich.

Following the same trend, by 1952 Fordwerke, the German branch of Ford Motor Company, had reassembled all its senior management from the Nazi years.[65] Harald Quandt, the son of Günther Quandt and Magda Behrend, who later would marry Joseph Goebbels, also ran with his half-brother Herbert Quandt the industrial empire inherited from his father after World War II. Günther Quandt, Harald's father, was arrested and interned in 1946 but was soon released in 1948 considering that even though he had accepted Nazi ideology, he supposedly had not taken an active part in crimes. Harald Quandt served as a lieutenant in the Luftwaffe and was captured by Allied troops in Italy but was also soon released in 1947. The Quandts, among other businesses, are owners of about 46 percent of the BMW vehicle manufacturing company until today, which, as we have remarked, was one of the major contributors to the German war effort in work substantially grounded on slave labor.

The owner of the clothing company that designed and supplied the Nazi uniforms from the 1920s, Hugo Boss, was only condemned to a fine of 100,000 German marks for being a supporter and beneficiary of National Socialism. Also from the textile industry, the support to the Nazis given by the Dassler brothers did not avoid them in the postwar period from making burgeoning businesses through their firms devoted to the production of sports clothing: Adidas and Puma.

Companies such as Siemens, Henschel, Volkswagen, Adam Opel AG, or Deutsche Bank, which also profited from slave labor during the Nazi era, carried on with their activity and even expanded from 1945.[66]

For its part, the chemical giant IG Farben, which had been formed with the fusion of different chemical companies such as BASF, Bayer, Hoechst, or Agfa, once the Allies seized the group after the Nazi defeat, was divided back into some of its constituent companies. The resulting companies after the division, though involved in the Third Reich's conquests and crimes, also became one of the main pillars of West Germany's postwar growth. Agfa, Bayer, and BASF still remain in business, with BASF being the largest chemical producer in the world and Bayer one of the largest pharmaceutical ones.

Hoechst, on the other hand, became Aventis Deutschland after its merger with France's Rhône-Poulenc S.A. in 1999. With the new company's 2004 merger with Sanofi-Synthélabo, an operation that was possible, through the free movement of capitals and workers between the European Union member states that the single market provided, it became a subsidiary of the resulting Sanofi-Aventis pharmaceuticals group.

By the beginning of the twenty-first century both public and private initiatives fostered the creation of independent commissions of historians to examine the role of different agents during the National Socialist era. As a consequence of one of such initiatives, the Independent Historical Commission headed by the University of California and led by the historian Saul Friedlander, found new ties with the Nazi regime. Among those revelations highlighted is the one that involved Bertelsmann, the international media and publishing giant, which produced under the Third Reich anti-Semitic material and Nazi propaganda, allowing the company to make huge profits.[67]

The Nazi intellectual cadres would not be alien either to the smooth transition toward the Federal Republic. Beyond the most well-known cases of philosophers such as Martin Heidegger, there were more concealed examples of accommodation into the new regime and more effective in the building of the new economic and social order: that was the history of Reinhard Höhn, a young sociologist and law professor under the Nazi regime that was considered the father of the intellectual *SS* arm: the *Sicherheitsdienst* (*SD*). Nevertheless, when times changed, Höhn founded the Harzburg Academy for Economic Leadership and became the management studies guru of 1950s West Germany.[68]

Continuity was also the rule among the legal profession. Through tacit coalition and active association, virtually all the lawyers who had practiced in the Third Reich were reinstated in public office and private law firms. There were hardly any abrupt breaks or dismissals. Like the rest of German society, jurists were reluctant to look back into the abyss.[69] The core of law faculties that from 1945 began to regroup were still formed by the same professors who had taught at the universities between 1933 and 1945.

The lines of continuity between the Third Reich and the German Federal Republic also affected the military. As long as the crises regarding Berlin and the German Democratic Republic recrudesced and the western Allies pushed for the Federal Republic's rearmament, whether within the framework of the failed European Defense Community Treaty or within the framework of NATO, Soviet propagandists remarked on the fact that several Nazi-era high commands were involved in the efforts to create the new West German army.[70]

In sum, most of the prewar economic powers, academic staff, civil servants, or even military personnel integrated decisively the constitutional movement that led to the 1949 German constitutional system and underpinned its consolidation. The legal framework there provided, especially on the point concerning the guarantees on liberal economic individual rights and the constraints to democracy, was designed to protect the interests of such elites.

The German Federal Republic was founded on both the aim to avoid political extremism through the new rhetoric of constitutional rights and the restructuring of the economic constitution in order to de-politicize the economy. Ordo-liberalism would become the dominant ideology in postwar West Germany, albeit in practice tempered by the practical implementation of the social market economy. The effects of such neo-corporatism prevented the alienation of wide strata of West Germany society and an eventual social revolution.[71] The immediate goal relied on competing with the Soviet occupied Germany where the action of Soviet authorities was focused on expropriating and finishing off the economic elites in order to erect a Communist regime. Committed Nazi capitalists and intellectuals remained in West Germany and became the seed of the subsequent economic and cultural take-off while East Germany stagnated. West Germany achieved from the 1950s its *Wirtschaftswunder* that crucially contributed to confer political legitimacy to the federation, but the adoption of such a path of economic success was partially possible through the "restoration" of pre-1945 that the Adenauer and Erhard governments consented.[72]

West Germany's postwar economic success was in a substantial part rooted in the individuals and the capital that had been active while the Third Reich displayed a colonization of Europe through the force of the arms. The German postwar economic colonization of the continent was, in other words, closely related to the previous Nazi imperialist era.

XII

As we have suggested, the redemption of former Nazi cadres in order to build the new liberal regime of the German Federal Republic was also extended to the creation of the European Communities and included fascist collaborationists from other places in western Europe.

Such a phenomenon was particularly visible in appointing technical profiles for the new supranational instances and, particularly, the legal staff involved in the formation of the Court of Justice of the European Community (first the body conceived to review the performance of the European Coal and Steel Community and, after October 1958, the Court of Justice of the European Communities, which unified the judicial supervision for the European Coal and Steel Community, the Euratom, and the European Economic Community).

In the context of the Cold War, it was likely that being converted to liberalism (though coming from a totalitarian past), or simply remaining a conservative and traditionalist, was a good credential to participate (and even to lead) the judicial apparatus of the European experiment. Those were times in which what mattered were not the misdeeds of the fascist past but rather the menace of the Communist present.[73]

As the historians Carbonell[74] and Fritz[75] have demonstrated, some of the profiles that formed the institutions of the European Coal and Steel Community, including the Court of Justice had not been, to say it lightly, hostile to the authoritarianism that had lost the war. After all, as we saw, the Nazi Order had played its part in bringing about the new postwar Europeanism.

The architects of the Common Market, despite some shadows hanging over Monnet himself, were usually characterized by holding impeccable anti-fascist and anti-Nazi records. Nevertheless, some of the key figures and advisers behind the scenes were not anti-fascists but wartime insider—French, Belgian, Italian, or German—who had served the Nazis, the French collaborationists, or the Italian Fascists but grown disillusioned with them.[76] It could be again appreciated regarding the European supranational institutions the traces of relationship between those involved in the Nazi Order and those committed to the building of the European Common Market.[77]

XIII

Let's take, for instance, the composition of the Court of Justice of the European Union, a body that has been qualified as "more powerful than any world equivalent" since, at least until recently, national courts of member states were generally willing to defer to its judgments.[78] By whom was the Court of Justice of the European Union formed in its origins?

The first member of the Court of Justice appointed by the German Federal Republic (then, as now, judges were appointed by member states) gives a good account of this transition: Otto Riese was a devoted Nazi who could only conceal his condition thanks to the circumstance that he spent the war in Switzerland as an academic. Riese became a member of the NSDAP's foreign organization in 1939 and retained his NSDAP membership well into 1945 while the regime was falling into pieces.[79] Given his political past, by 1947 Reise was suspended in his functions as law professor at Lausanne, but he was finally restored to his position after a few months and spent the following years writing academic contributions on comparative law and international law. Later he was called by the young German Federal Republic to serve as a judge in the federal court, but he was soon nominated by the German government to the post for the European Coal and Steel Community's

Court of Justice and he preserved this condition when that body became the Court of Justice of the European Communities.[80]

The fascist background was still more striking in the case of the Italian first president of the court: Massimo Pilotti. He had been deputy secretary-general of the League of Nations in the 1930s and advised Mussolini on what countermeasures to take to shield Italy from condemnations of the league for its imperial adventures in Ethiopia. During World War II, Pilotti headed the high court of occupied Ljubljana after Italy's annexation of Slovenia, where resistance was met with mass deportations, concentration camps, and police and military repression. Pilotti had the ability to escape from Ljubljana when the province was occupied by the Germans following the armistice between Italy and the Allies, and once he was in the country liberated from Fascist control, he was appointed general prosecutor at the Court of Cassation (where he performed leading the accusations against his former Fascist comrades). Given his experience in international law, the Italian government offered Pilotti a post first in the Permanent Arbitration Court and afterward the presidency of the European Coal and Steel Community's Court of Justice.

A dark past also encompassed some of the advocates-general attached to the nascent European Court: Karl Roemer, the German advocate-general, had spent the war in occupied Paris managing French companies and banks for the Third Reich. After the war Roemer acted as defense lawyer for the *Waffen SS*, charged with the responsibility for the massacre of the occupants of the French village of Oradour. Another advocate-general, Maurice Lagrange, had been a senior functionary in the Vichy government. Acting as a link-man between the judicial apparatus of the *Conseil d'État* and the political apparatus of the Council of Ministers, Lagrange was in charge of coordinating the first wave of persecution of French Jews. After the war Lagrange was chosen by the Americans to help in the democratization of the German civil service and by Monnet to draft the Treaty of the European and Steel Community.

These people were the legal intelligentsia behind the conception of the great principles that still organize the European Union legal order such as the direct effect principle or the primacy principle, which were envisaged in the first stage across the Court of Justice of the European Communities' jurisprudence. Indeed, the court radically transformed from its starting point the nature of the European Communities reshaping the balance of power along both the vertical and horizontal axes.[81]

In the leading Court of Justice judgments such as the 1963 *Van Gend and Loos*[82] and the 1964 *Costa-ENEL*[83] might be read both the name of Otto Riese acting as judge in the former case and the name of Maurice Lagrange acting as advocate-general in the latter. Though it seems that neither Riese nor Lagrange were very enthusiastic about the concepts respectively outlined in the mentioned resolutions (they argued rather for not breaking with the classic international law elements and, consequently, for avoiding the doctrines of direct effect and supremacy)[84] the point was that such former collaborators and sympathizers of the Third Reich and the Vichy regime composed the first tranche of the legal discussions that crucially marked the European constitutional evolution.

The legal activity of the Court of Justice to enforce the principles of supremacy and direct effect sought to impose "a specific legal order" in which a European norm would be situated at the top of the hierarchy of norms. That movement might be understood, in its specific genesis, not only as the translation of a political mobilization into the language of law, but also as the legal expression of the social autonomization of a specialized body of legal experts.[85] The pursuit of technocratic supremacy through both the law and the law's final adjudication suits well with authoritarianism and the disdain toward any solution adopted by a wider circle of citizens.

As it has been pointed out, the *Van Gend and Loos* and *Costa* resolutions represented the main avenue through which the European polity as an autonomous space would be defined, namely, Europeanisation through case law[86] or, more generally, the building of a "European Rule of Law" as a crystallizer of European integration aspirations. Focusing on the European Law allowed the ideological neutralization that turned many of the political issues raised by European integration into supposed matters of expertise inaugurating, thus, a trend that would embed the vicissitudes of the European supranational experience until the present.[87]

Somehow, the central position of a formal principle such as "the rule of law" and the postwar European narrative focused on legal integration as central structures of legitimacy contributed to make thicker the veil of amnesia on the disruptions suffered in the continent through the war as well as on those ones that were still ongoing. After all, within societies lacerated by harsh political confrontations and vulnerable to the external threats emanating from the context of the Cold War, trusting in a legal order guarded by a nascent body of technocrats was revealed as an effective cover to provide stability and economic development (legal certainty, as was envisaged in *Van Gend and Loos*, facilitated the growth of intra-community exchanges).

The "Europeanisation through case-law" also left the door ajar to introduce the figure of "independent" bodies, beginning with the Court of Justice of the European Union itself, and including also institutions such as the European Commission, which provided another formula of legitimacy on figures shielded to electoral pressures, which supposedly possessed a vision on the organization beyond the national interests.[88]

Biographies such as the ones concerning some of the first judges and advocates general of the Court of Justice of the European Union show to what extent from the outset of the European Communities the appeal to "independence" and technical capacities of some of those profiles might be conceived as meaning to diffuse the hard political commitments that those personalities maintained under the authoritarian regimes.

The presence of profiles coming from the Nazi engagement was not limited to the European court: it also concerned other institutions. Since the court was one of the less visible bodies, however, it was also the one in which the former political and legal careers were easy to hide (and that circumstance may explain why there were so many examples of the mentioned attitude).

Also within the High Authority of the European Coal and Steel Community, there coexisted, nonetheless, figures with a committed Nazi past. Such was, for instance, the case of Karl-Maria Hettlage, member of the High Authority between 1962 and 1967, who had been a close collaborator of Albert Speer, Hitler's architect and minister.

In sum, the construction of the free market coverage through the customs union or the economic liberties that would be able to trump upon national regulations with the aim to provide, as it effectively did, the impressive western European economic boom (and that would later decisively defeat its Communist rival) was, in a relevant part, a work of the accomplices of the authoritarian aegis that had previously defined the continent.

XIV

Beyond West Germany's leading economic performance within the European Communities, it was also remarkable that the Federal Republic became the western European industrial country that developed the most dynamic trade policy with eastern Europe during the Cold War.

The increase of trade between West Germany and the area of Soviet influence, and particularly, between the German Federal Republic and the German Democratic Republic began to take place in some significant terms after the 1960s, though they still represented a small amount of exchange compared with the flux of goods and capitals displayed between West Germany and the rest of the economies of the West.

By the creation of the Bonner Republic in 1949, the Cold War had already burst out (in fact, as we saw, the Federal Republic itself was a consequence of the increased tension between Stalin's Soviet Union and its former Western Allies) and West Germany had to respect the trade embargo measures against the Socialist economies dictated by Washington, which had been on the other hand provided by the Marshall Plan as a political requirement to receive the financial aid thereof conceived.

At the peak of the West's embargo during the Korean War, nonetheless, the legal basis for trading between West and East Germany was secured through an agreement on the monetary conditions for goods exchange that, once the conflict in eastern Asia concluded, allowed an increase in internal German trade.[89] That trade volume between both German Republics would not be very relevant for the Federal Republic (reaching an average of not more than 2 percent of the West German foreign trade volume), but it would be crucial for the German Democratic Republic in the sense that next to the Soviet Union the Federal Republic became East Germany's second most important trading partner for decades (internal German trade represented 10 to 11 percent of the German Democratic Republic's foreign trade).[90]

West Germany would be in those circumstances able to entrench from the 1950s the politically special character of the economic relations between the two German States, both in global international trade organizations such as the GATT, and in the context of the European Communities. The national background existing among the two German states attenuated the radical confrontation among the socioeconomic blocs and designed an exception on commercial relationships that would lead to some disputes between West Germany and its European partners (as would be expressed in the complaints of those partners regarding East Germany's farm products). At the end of the day, those burgeoning contacts between the two German republics would progressively define a privileged status of the German Democratic Republic toward the West that would be materialized after 1989 in the rapid access of the former East German territories in the European Communities through absorption into the German Federal Republic.

The collaboration between both sides of the divided Europe through the German states soon began regarding the issue of energy, with consequences that are still visible today. The lack of oil supply to western Europe became a more acute problem once France and the United Kingdom lost control of the Middle East as a consequence of the Suez crisis. To the astonishment and anger of the American politicians, western European governments broke the prohibition on Soviet oil imports. Italy, Austria, and West Germany already in 1958 began negotiations for a large-scale oil deal with the Soviet Union that would be reflected in the building of the Druzhba ("Friendship") pipeline, which took Soviet oil first to eastern Europe and then to central Europe.[91]

During the 1960s discoveries in western Siberia boosted the Soviet oil industry still further. In 1968, the Soviets completed an extension of the Druzhba pipeline to the Baltic coast, increasing export capacity to western Europe. Two years before, in 1966, the American commitment in Vietnam led the Johnson administration to put pressure on West Germany in order to obtain its financial support for the war. But the Washington strategy only succeeded in precipitating the end of Ludwig Erhard's Christian Democratic-Free Democratic coalition government and to pave the way for a grand coalition between the Christian Democrats and the Social Democrats that politically entrenched West Germany's accommodation with the Soviet Union already developed in energy issues.[92]

XV

The détente policy that had begun to be developed by the Nixon administration toward the Soviet bloc from 1969, though hesitant in areas that had concerned American-Soviet relations, was firmly reasserted by the West German chancellor, the Social-Democrat Willy Brandt, in what concerned the relations between West and East Germany (as well as between West Germany and the rest of the eastern European Communist countries). While the Adenauer governments (and the ones led by his Christian-Democrat successors) had always, at least formally, refused to recognize the German Democratic Republic, Willy Brandt abandoned the West German insistence upon the illegitimacy of that state and would acknowledge its undeniable facticity.

Between 1970 and 1974, Brandt and his foreign minister, Walter Scheel, negotiated and signed a series of major diplomatic accords within the framework of what would be known as the *Ostpolitik*; they concluded treaties with Moscow and Warsaw in 1970, recognizing the *de facto* existence and inviolability of the postwar intra-German and German-Polish frontiers and offered a new relationship between Germany and its eastern neighbors; a quadripartite agreement over Berlin in 1971, in which Moscow agreed not to make any unilateral changes there and to facilitate cross-border movement, and a Basic Treaty with the German Democratic Republic, a milestone of the intra-German rapprochement policy, by which Bonn, while continuing to grant automatic citizenship to any inhabitant of the German Democratic Republic who succeeded in coming to the West, relinquished its longstanding claim to be the sole legitimate representative of all Germans.[93]

The Soviet Union under Brezhnev's leadership achieved thus, what Khrushchev had failed to achieve ten years earlier: the opening to West Germany and the stabilization of West Berlin. Such a new frame of relations grounded in the détente was not deprived of dramatic moments, such as the episode in which the ratification of the Soviet-West Germany Treaty was in 1972 saved through a vote of confidence that Brandt won only by a two-vote margin, or when the conclusion of the treaty between the two German states required the resignation of the Moscow-Bonn dialogue's biggest opponent: Walter Ulbricht. The general outcome of the process, however, was an irreversible consolidation of a bridge between the Socialist world and a major capitalist economy.[94]

Indeed, trade policy and economic relations would represent the *Ostpolitik*'s pivot. West German exports to eastern European Communist countries would increase fourfold between 1970 and 1980, and the size of the loan borrowed by East Germany from its western counterpart also increased by the same time from 700 million deutsche marks to 3000 million.[95] The Soviet Union supplied oil, gas, and cotton to West Germany in exchange for German equipment, technologies, and much-coveted consumer goods.[96] It is from the time of the *Ostpolitik* triggered by Willy Brandt that there began to be amalgamated the lobbying around the Social Democratic Party and trade unions supporting a preferential relationship with the Soviet Union (and after with Russia) that offered a moderate and conciliatory position in the face of Putin's territorial ambitions displayed in the 2010s and the 2020s.

The West German and eastern Bloc rapprochement in the 1970s, nevertheless, coincided, in a similar fashion as was happening in Italy at the same time with the effervescence of activity of far-left armed groups.

While Brandt and his successor, the Socialist chancellor Helmut Schmidt, were delving into the political and economic exchanges with the Socialist bloc, including the German Democratic Republic between 1970 and 1978, the Red Army Faction and its ancillary offshoots pursued a strategy of deliberately random terror, assassinating soldiers, policemen, and businessmen, holding up banks and kidnapping mainstream politicians. The Federal Republic, even ruled by the leftist government that had opened channels with Brezhnev and Honecker, responded harshly to those aggressions.

The founders of the Red Army Faction, Ulrike Meinhof and Andreas Baader, were found dead in their cells while they were on trial or serving a life sentence for murder. Gudrun Ensslin had the same fate in midst of rumors that all of them had been executed by the state.[97] Détente and business between Capitalism and Communism were, thus, not incompatible with a violent clash in the terrorist underground, perpetrated by both revolutionary groups and the police and judicial apparatus.

XVI

The reemergence of tensions between the United States under the Reagan administration and the Soviet Union by the beginning of the 1980s did not alter West Germany's government's determination to reaffirm its system of economic relations with the European Socialist space. The hardening of American-Soviet tensions of that time led to several political controversies between West Germany and the United States rather than fracturing the West German eagerness to maintain their leadership in exporting goods and lending money to the Soviet sphere economies.

The Federal Republic was subscribed more than any other Western country to the strategy of close trade and capital entwinement with eastern Europe.

As the collapse of the Socialist area was approaching, West German banks became gradually more involved in supplying credit to the eastern European governments. The total foreign debt of eastern Europe grew from $95 billion by the end of 1981 to $158 billion on the brink of the fall of the Berlin Wall.

While the United States banks retired from investing in that part of the world more or less coinciding with the more aggressive policy toward the Soviet Union displayed under Reagan's presidency (American banks had been relatively active in eastern Europe during the 1970s), West Germany dramatically expanded its lending to East Germany, the Soviet Union, and other Communist regimes.[98] West Germany's involvement in eastern European financing would reach a peak by the crises of the Communist bloc in 1989 and the struggle to ensure democratization and market reforms.[99] But experiences of West German credit flowing eastward had already been crucial in the previous years and they were not attached to political and economic reform requirements.

East Germany, for example, faced a critical situation in 1982 when bankruptcy was expected. Declining Soviet support, rising interest rates, and the financial turbulences in Poland (derived from the political contestation) caused a "credit boycott" among the Western powers making it unaffordable for East Germany to finance its imports.[100] Nevertheless, West Germany went to the rescue of its Socialist counterpart through two loans contrived by, paradoxically, the conservative Bavarian prime minister Franz Joseph Strauss in 1983 and 1984, which released the German Democratic Republic from the acute debt crises.[101] It was likely that the money transferred from Bavaria that would allow the German Democratic Republic to restore its creditworthiness worked in reality as an investment to buy freer movement of people, information, and ideas.[102] In the long run, nonetheless, the Strauss loans contributed to consolidate East Germany's dependence on the western part of the nation. In avoiding changes concerning the economy and postponing political concessions, the Communist regime made its foundations weaker and its dissolution more likely.[103]

Following the line of what had happened in previous decades, in the 1980s relations between the eastern Bloc and West Germany continued to be marked by German investments in the energy sector. In 1981, for instance, the Soviet government struck an agreement with a German banking consortium led by Deutsche Bank to provide credit to build a new gas pipeline. The Trans-Siberian pipeline would run from the Urengoy gas field in the west Siberian basin to Uzhhorod in today's western Ukraine, where the gas was transported to central and western Europe. The Reagan administration opposed the Trans-Siberian pipeline, but in the end the Americans had to back down on the pipeline after the west Europeans agreed that no more than 30 percent of their gas imports would come from the Soviet Union.[104]

The picture of the relationship between West Germany and the eastern European area by the 1980s, on the one hand, already advanced the relevant economic sway that Germany would hold upon that eastern part of the continent in the years to come. But, on the other hand, it would also reveal the constant that would also define the German attitude once the country would be reunified, namely, strengthening the economic dependence of the eastern neighbors in relation to Germany but renouncing (with the exception of East Germany) any territorial vindication or any other form of direct political domination upon them.

XVII

West German trade and lending activity in eastern Europe before 1989, thus, had laid the groundwork for its progressive penetration in the economic systems and chains of production of some of the former Communist countries. But the Federal Republic's assistance to eastern Europe and particularly to the Soviet Union had by the time of the Socialist downfall other reasons and other goals. Whereas the United States rapidly endorsed German ambitions for reunification,[105] the Soviet Union, in spite of the economic and political crises that it was going through, was in principle still in position to veto the emergence of an enlarged Germany in the middle of Europe.

The Soviet leadership under Mikhail Gorbachev was in a very difficult juncture and not only because of his problems at home but also given the threat that for his own credibility it would represent to reverse his gamble for democratization and transparency through an authoritarian turn only to avoid the Germans achieving their political hopes. But the chancellor, Helmut Kohl, found a very effective way to persuade Gorbachev not to jeopardize the horizon of a united Germany: by paying the occupants of East Germany and ensuring the withdrawal of Soviet troops from German soil an approximate amount of 12 billion German marks plus an additional 3 billion German marks in interest-free loans.[106] German reunification might be deemed in that fashion the only example from 1989 in which the German European "economic colonization" would still have territorial consequences. The rest of money transfers executed throughout those years would not represent any further movement of borders in spite of the relevance of the amounts involved.

The financial support obtained by Gorbachev in 1990 would be complemented by 1994 through transfers from the German authorities to the Soviet Union (and latter Russia) that totaled around $71 billion.[107] When the cash of the assets held by the public authorities in the Soviet Union began to be distributed (in what was described as the most massive privatization in capital's history)[108] the unified Germany took the pole position in the bargain to obtain some of the benefits of their management.

The Russian gas industry, for instance, experienced in the 1990s and the 2000s a convulsive cycle of privatizations and re-nationalizations characterized by breathtaking managerial embezzlement and generalized corruption,[109] which nonetheless did not prevent the consolidation of Gazprom as the largest natural gas company in the world and the largest company in Russia by market capitalization.

But even before the dissolution of the Soviet Union, German companies concluded several agreements with the Russian gas industry, which basically were focused in ensuring the Russian gas supply for Germany while conducting German investment in technology for gas extraction in Siberia. Germany already enjoyed privileged access to Russian gas because there existed cooperation in the management of gas flows between the Soviet Union and the German Democratic Republic, mainly operated through Verbundnetz Gas AG, but the ambition to create a gas market "from Vladivostok to Lisbon" and to distribute the astronomical profits that such a business could entail, arose the interest of West German gas companies in strengthening their partnership with Gazprom and with the reshuffled Russian oligarchies that were behind the evolution of that company in the different stages.

Wintershall, a 100 percent subsidiary of BASF, created a joint venture with Gazprom in 1990 responsible for selling, transporting, and storing natural gas in Europe; and BASF Wintershall became the first foreign company to produce natural gas jointly with Gazprom in the Yamal-Nenets Autonomous Okrug. Ruhrgas AG, on the other hand, became in 2003 the largest foreign shareholder in Gazprom, owning about 6.5 percent of the company.[110]

During the fragmentation of the Soviet Union and the chaotically rapid privatization of its economy, the conclusion of a wide array of bilateral instruments depicted the legal framework to foster capital and trade flows among two powers (such as agreements on Good Neighborliness, Partnership and Cooperation [1990] on Cooperation in Labor and Social Policy [1990] on the environment [1992] on mutual help in times of national emergency [1992] and on cooperation in international road and air transport [1993] let alone the bilateral investment treaty between Germany and the Soviet Union signed in the last throes of the Cold War [June 1989, being the Russian Federation the successor once the Soviet Union vanished in December 1991]). Germany would, in turn, facilitate Russian integration in economically relevant multilateral treaties with the other members of the European Communities (such as the 1994 Agreement on Establishing a Partnership between the European Communities and Their Member States, and Russia) or the Energy Charter Treaty, which was originally aimed to integrate the energy sectors of Russia and eastern Europe into the European markets (and that would be later expanded to a global regulation on investment and cooperation in the energy industry).

Hence, by the middle of the 2000s, Germany would become the main exporter to Russia,[111] and the cooperation in energy matters between Russia and Germany would begin to be consolidated. German loans and investment would also flow, around $36 billion, to the Communist States of eastern Europe by the end of the Cold War contributing with such transfers to accomplish a double aim; on the one hand, the unified Germany would consolidate its economic dominance upon such territories and, on the other hand, money would help to mitigate Germany's eastern neighbor's fears of German irredentism.[112]

XVIII

After the fall of the Berlin Wall in November 1989, the process toward the reunification of Germany required the German authorities to accept that the country's eastern borders would never be modified.

Disregarding the circumstances of such territories' status before World War II, the strict condition posed by the Allies and the Soviet Union to recognize Germany's full sovereignty was that the German Federation would not be stretched beyond the line marked by the Oder-Neisse rivers at which the borders between Poland and Germany had been established at the end of the war.[113]

Somehow, the developments experienced as a consequence of the 1970s West-East détente policy in Europe had already anticipated the maintenance of the German borders as conceived in Potsdam by the aftermath of the war. The recognition of the German Democratic Republic by the West German government was partially possible by not questioning the German Democratic Republic's limits with Poland and Czechoslovakia, and such concern in avoiding borders was also present at the Conference on Security and Co-operation in Europe that had culminated in the Helsinki Final Act in 1975.[114]

Such an approach on the unified Germany's eastern borders was reasserted in article 1.2 and in the article 1.3 of the Treaty on the Final Settlement with Respect to Germany concluded on September 12, 1990 (also known as the Two Plus Four Agreement), which provided that the Federal Republic had to confirm the Oder-Neisse border with Poland in an international law treaty (it did it in the German-Polish border treaty signed on November 14, 1990) and that the united Germany had no territorial claims whatsoever against other states and would not invoke any claim of that sort in the future.[115]

The "Two plus Four" Treaty, the Unification Treaty, or even the Treaty between the German Federal Republic and Poland on the Eastern German border revealed the strong internationalist character that was surrounding the emergence of the new Germany somehow constrained by the safeguards that its neighbors required in order to consent to that movement of political unification.[116] The "German question," with all its echoes of 1937 borders and the Hitler era, had to be laid to rest,[117] and so was easily assumed by Kohl and the rest of the authorities in West Germany.

The culmination of that internationalism on defining the new federation was, obviously, Germany's commitment to European integration, as would be explicitly inserted in the new wording of article 23 of the Basic Law, also known as the "European Article." Legalism, the contention of the citizenry in the constitution-making process, or the integration of the united Germany in supranational structures ensured the achievement of the abduction of the territories from the former German Democratic Republic by the Federal Republic but at the same time reduced the political and economic margin of maneuver with which the new polity would count.

Deprived of territorial annexations, which had constituted the traditional German mode of dominating the continent since Bismarck's national unification, the institutions of the Federal Republic turned only to the possibility of exercising economic predominance upon the adjacent countries that would progressively be extended to other parts of Europe and, particularly, to southern Europe.

The preferred economic position held by West Germany by the end of the Cold War and, afterward, the German economic impulse from the second half of the 2000s (the latter culminated by the aftermath of the euro crises managed and led by Angela Merkel's government) generated, thus, a very different scenario to the one experienced in the zenith of the Nazi dominion of Europe.

The unified Germany renounced altogether to any eastward political expansion to the former territories of the Reich (or to Slavic inhabited areas) while it attributed the utmost importance to the mission of leading the coordination of a large European internal market both in western and eastern Europe (grounded on this time in the voluntary union of sovereign States and not in the consequence of a military triumph).

But replacing a project of direct domination by another of economic facture could be explained because the Germany that had been defeated in World War II had no other alternative. Somehow, the consequences of the total surrender in 1945 were still there in 1990 though, as we shall see, some German economic and political figures did their best to dodge such limitations and tested a more nuanced way to create stability and to promote channels of capitalist exchange between Germany and eastern Europe, including Russia, beyond the traditional forms of military occupation and colonization. Certainly, the post–Cold War Germany military lacked the most basic operational capacity: fewer than half of its tanks and a third of its fighter aircraft were fit for action in early 2018, and at the end of 2017 it did not have a single submarine in operational order.[118]

The German decline experienced from 2022 by the irruption Russia's general invasion against Ukraine introduced serious doubts of the effectiveness of such an economic way to influence in other polities without any political strategy grounded on rawer forms of coercion.

XIX

In the first stage after the fall of the Berlin Wall, the German Federal Republic had enough troubles in embracing the former German Democratic Republic. East Germany had been subjected to a communist Soviet Union satellite regime and had been, consequently, marked by a profound *décalage* in comparison to the social and economic conditions regarding the West. In the three years following unification, total transfers from western into eastern Germany amounted to the equivalent of 1,200 billion euros; and by the end of 2003 the cost of absorbing the former German Federal Republic had reached the staggering amount of 1.2 trillion euros.[119]

The first years of German reunification were, thus, full of sacrifices also for those of the west to embrace their brothers from the east and, particularly, such an effort was particularly acute for the rich *Länder* of the South like Bavaria, Baden Württemberg, or Hessen. They had to cope with those aforementioned enormous transfers of money to rebuild the devastated economy of the east, including the rebuilding of the new capital of the reunified Germany: Berlin.

For a culture educated under the parameters of "constitutional patriotism," the "patriotism" expressed by some of the richest West German *Länder* was rather moderate if we take into account that their governments did not hesitate in lodging an unconstitutionality appeal concerning the federal statute regulations on the finance balancing between the *Länder* and the federation (in a procedure at the end of which the German Federal Constitutional Court considered that the criteria outlined in the federal statute regulating the financial transfers between the different entities and the rules of fiscal balancing, including the establishment of a "German unity" fund, were too undetermined).[120]

Germany's European partners also did not escape from the burdens of subsidizing a former Communist country and its population. The German federal government chose not to raise taxes and decided to meet its commitments in relation to national unification through deficit. The Bundesbank, in order to prevent the inflationary impact of such a policy began steadily to raise interest rates that, at precisely the moment when the deutsche mark was being attached to the European single currency, impinged on the monetary stability of the European monetary system and caused unemployment and slower economic growth not only in Germany but in other European economies.[121]

Such a gigantic German public investment to the five new *Länder* and, generally, to the formerly Communist Eastern European countries, caused some macroeconomic shocks in western Europe such as the exchange rate crises erupting in September 1992, but some other actors found the way to transform such ruinous expenditures for the public sector into fabulous private gains.

XX

While the West German private investors were finding opportunities by buying, at bargain prices, the assets of some eastern European key corporations that had still been efficient under a Communist system, the German public sector experienced a financial stress situation by facilitating the political conditions, particularly in Eastern Germany itself, to promote such a capitalist expansion.

Though a historical reconstruction of German private investment in the former Communist countries is still pending, it might not be erroneous to think that the main agents of that enterprise were the *same* elite and its successors that had been dominating the economy within West Germany from the founding of the Federal Republic (we have already mentioned from where such capitalist elites came and to what extent they contributed to the underpinning of that constitutional democracy).

Given the circumstance that both in eastern Germany and in the rest of eastern Europe there were almost no compensations to the former owners as a consequence of the Communist taking over of lands, goods, or World War II's remaining industrial facilities, the movements displayed by the 1990s somehow might have represented a capitalist reoccupation by those corporations that were behind the Third Reich's expansion. In this time, however, the private performance was covered by the fiscal struggle that the German Federal Republic's authorities arranged in a democratic framework and that would not be cost free.

Indeed, problems within Germany concerning the so-called five-new *Länder* from the former German Democratic Republic had to be solved. After German unity, almost two decades had to pass in order to gain competitiveness for the German economy, to foster equality among the territories within the Federal Republic, and, in short, to become an undisputed economic power. Private West German businesses benefited from the opening of non-competitive markets in an operation that was basically financed by the public sector. In the same vein, the establishment of those German actors in other eastern European countries beyond the five-new *Länder* was coached by political initiatives orchestrated from the German federal government.

The first years of the twenty-first century were characterized by the German authorities' great struggle to reform a stagnant domestic labor market and to overcome an alarming public deficit that was hardly compatible with the implementation in such time of the European single currency. The benefits of the mentioned policy of liberalization (ironically planned under the supposedly leftist government of Chancellor Gerhard Schröder) only began to be perceived when the rest of Europe delved into the turbulent waters of crisis.

The liberal roadmap followed by Chancellor Schröder (called to energize the post-unification German economy) had its reward regarding the deployment of German capital in eastern Europe. Schröder would complete the story of the Russo-German gas and oil relations that I introduced above and that might symbolize the structure of capitalist interactions between Germany and that part of eastern Europe performing in the market economy.

XXI

The traditionally German sever Protestant ethic was not likely to be applicable to Schröder, who shortly after standing down from the chancellery was recruited by Gazprom as a head of the shareholder's committee in charge of executing the building of the pipeline under the Baltic Sea known as Nord Stream 1. Schröder had taken advantage of his last weeks in power to sign an agreement with the Russian government to construct that North European Gas Pipeline to take gas from Vyborg, near Russia's border with Finland, to Greifswald on the north-east German coast.[122] Criticisms did not deprive the former chancellor from spearheading the flow of German capital toward Russia in order to design the mechanisms of energy supply for central Europe.

Schröder's task was not without political counterparts including lobbying to support, or at least to justify, the Russian position in the long list of domestic and international crises caused by Putin's regime. The former chancellor carried on in his role, and even improved it, despite episodes such as war in Georgia, Crimea's annexation, or the allegations of Russian involvement in the poisoning of the regime's opponent, Alexei Navalny.[123]

In 2016 Schröder was nominated as chairman of the board of directors of the Nord Stream 2 project, an expansion of the original pipeline, in which Gazprom was the sole shareholder. In 2017 he was also nominated to serve as an independent director of the board of Russia's biggest oil producer Rosneft, a post to which the ex-chancellor was reelected in 2020. Amid the 2022 war in Ukraine, Schröder was even nominated for a post on Gazprom's supervisory board. Schröder's trajectory, to sum it up, embodies the structure of the capitalist relationship interwoven between Germany and Russia within the context of a unified Germany integrated in the European Union. Somehow, Schröder's performance embodied the long tradition of mutual dependences of a big bloc in Eurasia that in some periods have been expressed through trade and understanding (as under the 1887 Reinsurance Treaty or the 1922 Rapallo Treaty, not to mention the 1939 Soviet-German agreements).[124]

Schröder's work for Russian oligarchies is usually stressed, but less mentioned is that if the former chancellor had been involved in Russian energy corporations that was possible because German bankers and industrialists consented and promoted such developments in a dynamic of mutual enrichment by the Russian and German elites that goes beyond political conflicts and military tensions. Russia's regime has been able to play to destabilize eastern Europe in order to guarantee a zone of influence because the European Union and, particularly, reunified Germany provided the necessary stability to make economic relations thrive, although the majority benefited by said exchange mostly focused in the energy market were the elites of both systems, widening thus the gap of inequalities not only in Russia, as is commonly admitted, but also in Germany.

The decision on the Nord Stream 2 pipeline to enlarge Germany's provision of Russian gas was taken after the first Russian aggression upon Ukraine in 2014, once Putin's expansive ambitions were evident. The German reliance on Russian oil and gas was, thus, an active German choice, not only a matter of Schröder, and not even a matter concerning the German Social-Democrats; it was a meditated choice involving wide sectors of German society, which compromised German political discussion (still more considering that the Merkel government had decided to abandon nuclear energy).

Schröder's shadow concerning the economic relations between Russia and Germany and the consequent definition of Germany's political approach toward Putin's regime persisted, as an old remembrance of the Cold War's *Ostpolitik*, in the leadership of the Social Democratic Party. In the wake of the growing tension between Russia and the West as a consequence of Putin's plans of invasion of Ukraine, the next Social Democratic German chancellor after Schröder, Olaf Scholz, did his best to contain any possible European backlash against Russia. He did it even shortly before the hostilities broke out on February 21, 2022, when Russia recognized the independence of the self-proclaimed republics of Donetsk and Lugansk in the Donbass region and sent troops to those territories.

Scholz, well aware of the German energetic reliance on the Russian sources (and German economic reliance on the Russian market) warned of the consequences that severe sanctions against Russia might represent for the ones that inflicted them.[125] In that sense, Scholz made a call to be "prudent" in dictating sanctions, a moderate discourse oriented to avoid economic cataclysm that would cause a profound dispute with the Social Democratic government partners, the Greens, headed by the minister of foreign affairs, Annalena Baerbock, not very prone to be concerned by the shortcuts in the carbonized economy that she and her party sought to replace. Contributing, in the eyes of NATO and others of Germany's partners, to the scandalously lukewarm attitude on retaliation against Russia showed by Scholz, the head of the German Navy of that time, Kay-Achim Schönbach, even questioned Western views over Putin's intentions regarding Ukraine, adding that the Russian president "deserved respect." Schönbach was forced to resign but revealed to the world the dominant German vision on Russia and, thus, made more acute divisions within the European Union on that issue that in fact paralyzed, as it had been a constant in the history of that organization, the external action once it was time to face up to a political and military shock. In that fashion, Vide-Admiral Kay-Achim Schönbach recognized that differently from the fears that Russia awakened among most of its neighbors, including the former members of the Soviet Union, for twenty-first century Germany, Russia was closer to being considered a natural ally than an enemy.

XXII

Reluctantly, when the open war between Russia and Ukraine started, the German chancellor issued an order to halt the process of certifying the Nord Stream 2 gas pipeline. At the end of the day, nevertheless, among the first wave of sanctions against Russia issued by the West given Putin's initiatives within Ukraine's territory blocking the Nord Stream 2 project was likely the harshest. Yet, and ironically, such a severity not only represented damage for Russian's economy but a self-inflicted deep wound to the European Union's economy and particularly to the German one, both still not able to replace gas by renewable sources of energy in order to sustain their activity.

The lack of energetic independence has been revealed as the main deficiency in the German project of economic "internal colonization" of Europe. After all, in spite of the struggle against climate change and the discourses on green energy, oil and gas are still fundamental in both present economies and the building of systems of coercion. Oil still powers ships and aircraft, it is the energy source on which military power rests, it is crucial to distribute supplies in trucks across land and ships across seas. Petrochemicals that are obtained from oil are indispensable components of plastic and medical equipment.[126] Manufacturing, in short, is not still ready to be developed relying only on green energy, let alone if, in addition to reducing oil and gas consumption, nuclear energy is dispensed with, as Germany has tried to do.

Nowhere as in the relationship between Germany and Russia has it been more evident that Germany's foreign policy has been in function of its industrial-corporatist model. As Wolfgang Münchau once wrote, Germany pursued a neo-mercantilist foreign policy,[127] subordinated to the interests of its manufacturing industry. In times of manufacturing decline among advanced economies, Germany presented a manufacturing share of the GDP closer to 20 percent (in France, for instance, manufacturing only accounted by the beginning of the 2020s for 9 percent of the GDP) and that German manufacturing power was only possible thanks to the special relationship with Russia (and China) not to mention the effect of the Euro-area's crises, which raised Germany's competitiveness through an undervalued exchange rate.

The Russian regime preferred to renounce to business in order to satisfy its expansive political aims but Germany, still in search of its national project, saw, through the threat to its supply of energy sources, the undermining of its more mundane project concerning the struggle for economic wealth and welfare.

XXIII

Exercising an economic power means, however, exercising some sort of power. Given its past, Germany may have not chosen after reunification to become both a military and a territorially expansive empire as it was before 1945, but that doesn't mean that the German authorities have relinquished to exercise another sort of domination able to be tolerated by the powers that won World War II to which Germany was committed by the 1990 Two Plus Four Agreement.

The curious thing about watching the European developments of the twenty-first century in comparison with what happened in the 1940s with German imperialism is, firstly, the quiet resignation with which present Germans accepted the total loss of any prospect of territorial regains in the east of Europe (leaving thus clear the complete success of the ethnic cleansing policies against the Germans practiced by the Slavic peoples spearheaded by the power of the Red Army at the end of World War II). Secondly, in a different vein, the other particularity that might be appreciated in observing the evolution of both, the Europe in the 1940s and the Europe in the 2010s is the quiet resignation that in their turn embedded the attitude of the other European nation-states (including the eastern European ones) in accepting the unarguable German economic leadership that, even in the most turbulent moments of the sovereign debt crises between 2010 and 2015, was only contested, and not very harshly, by the Greek government of Syriza.

The dark conclusion of the latter comparison relies on the circumstance that, though by different means (military ones in the 1940s, economic ones in the 2010s) the Europeans fell into line and contributed to what the Germans demanded.

But, in contrast to the transition that Europe experienced from 1945, silence and cautious switching of sides were not needed for assuming the acceptance by the European elites of Berlin's diktat to manage the crises in the 2010s. The European political, economic and media top cadres from every nationality and from almost all the ideological spectrum offered the Germans their full collaboration in containing popular unrest while applying the policies of austerity required by Germany's oligarchies. The only clear opposition came, of course, from the British, given their recurrent attitude regarding the fight toward German direct or indirect hegemony: in 1940 by carrying on with the fight and in the 2010s by voting to leave the European Union.

Germany's economic hegemony upon Europe from the beginning of the 2007–2008 world economic crises and, particularly, from the 2012 Eurozone crises was also guided by nationalistic aims though the word "nationalism" was forbidden from the German mainstream political vocabulary. The horizon was not the dissolution of the German nation within an integrated Europe. It was rather a European integration controlled by Germany though concealed by the means of its credit-holder position. Grounding national goals only through economic requirements had nevertheless its limits, as was clearly perceived in both the political and economic German evolution experienced by the beginning of the 2020s.

Since the German Federal Republic did not translate its economic hegemony into a political one (while other European partners were strangled by deficits and debts) the lack of national initiative returned to Germany again in a form of an economic stagnation overshadowing its industry output, its banking sector, its consumer confidence, and its unemployment rate.

Not having determined which national project was held by German authorities had its costs. At the peak of the 2008–2012 economic crises, German authorities undermined European political integration, but they did not offer any assertive alternative for the continent to confirm German leadership in the entrenchment of a "closer" union. By 2020 in the midst of the COVID-19 crisis, and aside from the financial patches that the coveted Next Generation funds represented, no structural solutions were offered either. In 2022, the catastrophic consequences for Germany of the Russian general invasion of Ukraine even questioned the character of Germany as an economic power and threatened its ability to spearhead any advance regarding European integration.

XXIV

Such an horizon for a closer European union had already been jeopardized by the German Federal Constitutional Court when it stated, in its 2009 ruling on the Lisbon Treaty, that the transfer of powers to the European institutions could not go beyond the limits outlined by the German constitutional identity.[128] Once the crises of the southern European states' sovereign debt burst out in 2012, the German refusal of a common debt-issuing mechanism in the form of Eurobonds, as well as the strong opposition of the German elites to the European Central Bank programs of purchasing in secondary markets bonds issued by Eurozone member states[129] made it clear that the German political and economic establishment were engaged in a strategy to bully the Eurozone into submission.[130]

Instead of struggling for a common European solution grounded in a more profound integration, German authorities and German economic oligarchies were seeking a way to use Germany's formidable trade surpluses and their role as the main creditors within Europe to dictate political solutions to weak states that desperately needed a bailout. If the elites of a given nation have the chance to gain power at the expense of other more vulnerable nations, no doubt they shall launch the raid. That is precisely the movement that Germany showed after it recovered itself from the costs of reunification using its economic model reliant on large savings to play a non-cooperative game in the European monetary union.[131]

The judicial *coup de grace* against a European common monetary policy to relieve the southern European states from the pressure of the debt arrived in the midst of a new critical juncture as the one that represented the COVID-19 pandemic in the spring of 2020. Just when a new package of funds was discussed to support those member states, such as Spain and Italy, that have suffered most the effects of the health crises, the German Constitutional Court declared that the previous program of sovereign debt purchasing launched by the European Central Bank (Public Sector Asset Purchase Program) had been developed beyond the powers transferred to the European Union and that it had consequently encroached on the democratic principle, fundamental rights of political participation, and the German constitutional identity.

In its decision issued on May 5, 2020, the German Constitutional Court arrogated itself the power to control European Union law under the parameters of the German Basic Law and suspended the prevalence of the European decisions upon those stemming from the German authorities.[132] Specifically, in the dispositive part of the judgment it was stated that the German federal government and the *Bundestag* violated the German Basic Law by omitting to take appropriate measures against the European Central Bank's Public Sector Asset Purchase Program that was adopted without checking or explaining if it was in compliance with both European Union law and the principle of proportionality.[133]

The idea, in sum, was grounded on establishing an exception to the primacy of the European Law when the German Constitutional Court considered that it violated the core of German national interests. Particularly, the court declared that a previous judgment of the Court of Justice of the European Union[134] by which the European Central Bank's Public Asset Purchase Program was considered compatible with the European Union Law was, under the German Court's vision, *ultra vires* and not applicable in Germany.

Indeed, while other constitutional systems invoked the doctrine of the national constitutional identity as a justification to set aside the application of European Union law in different kinds of areas (we may also think about the success of such an idea on the national identity prevalence upon European Union law shown by some constitutional courts in eastern Europe)[135] Germany's *Bundesverfassungsgericht* appeared as one of the most fruitful bodies involved in the development of the referred doctrine on the national constitutional identity focused on monetary issues that may threat Germany's fiscal balance and Germany's economic interests altogether.

Every European member state used the constitutional identity doctrine at its convenience, but the German Federal Constitutional Court was likely to present such a contribution in a more neutral fashion through its analysis on constitutional powers and monetary policy than its counterparts in eastern Europe, which did not conceal the pure nationalistic character of their claims. The *Bundesverfassungsgericht* movement, however, was not deprived of such nationalistic concerns.

The above-mentioned decision of May 5, 2020, only executed the legal consequence already announced by the beginning of the saga of jurisprudence around monetary transactions, namely, the court's reservation of a right to decide whether a measure adopted by the European Union authorities (in that case by the European Central Bank) "could violate the constitutional identity of the Basic Law."[136] Through the defense of the German companies' competitiveness and the defense of German savers, the court envisaged, thus, a German *national* project, namely, to entrench the German economic hegemony even against the formal rhetoric of the federal government and the *Bundeskanzlerin* Angela Merkel, which given the COVID-19 problem, were in 2020 (and in a different vein as what had happened during the sovereign debt crises) supporting the gathering of European common funds to assist the countries most affected by the pandemic.

On July 21, 2020, however, the European Union member states finally reached a deal on the recovery fund to rebuild European economies ravaged by the health crisis. Even the austere northern and central European states managed from the total amount provided (750 billion euros) to assign at least 360 billion euros to loans, the rest, 390 billion euros, would be money borrowed by the European Commission on financial markets and distribute it as grants. The veto of the common issuing of debt, in the context of the fight against the recession, was likely to be cracked. But the so called "frugal" countries led by the Netherlands, worried about being indebted to fund the spending of the southern governments, ensured the establishment of political safeguards to control the distribution of the grants.

Besides the fact that any applying state would have to render a plan to spend the funds that needs the approval of the council through qualified majority, any single country might refer an objection on the management of the funds to the European Council able to block the payment. member states internal checks, as the one envisaged in Germany through the mentioned Constitutional Court resolution of May the 5, 2020, were able to threaten such major involvement of the European institutions to support economically the hardest hit European Union members by borrowing money in the financial markets.

At any rate, the Constitutional Court resolution of May 5, 2020, expressed that as long as the European politics would affect any issue considered vital by the national elites of a given state, the final decision on such issue would be placed in the member state, a circumstance that might generate new tensions every time that a recovery plan might be designed. Though, from another point of view, some celebrated the fund to fight against the effects of the COVID-19 as the start of a European fiscal union, it was hardly admitted that such a mechanism lacked any cyclical component and its value represented only 0.3% of GDP per year.[137] It was quite difficult to recognize which kind of advance toward fiscal and economic union such data might represent.

Well aware that consenting the exceptions to the European Union Law's primacy regarding Germany in fact contributed to justify other member states' deviations such as the challenges posed by the Polish Constitutional Court or the Hungarian one, the European Commission decided by June 2021 to send a letter of formal notice to the German Federal government for violation of fundamental principles of EU law (including the principles of autonomy, primacy, effectiveness, and uniform application of union law) as a response to the *Bundesverfassungsgericht*'s resolution of May 5, 2020.[138] The commission was particularly concerned about a subsequent German Constitutional Court's resolution (the Order of April 29, 2021)[139] in which even the German

Constitutional Court refused the complaints grounded on the claim that both the federal government and the *Bundestag* had not implemented at all the measures previously dictated in the May 5, 2020, resolution on the European Central Bank Purchases Program, the court persisted in asserting its power to check, according to the German Constitutional Law, the measures adopted by German authorities to ensure the proportionality of the monetary programs.

In December 2021, however, the European Union Commission decided to close the infringement procedure against Germany triggered by the German Constitutional Court resolution of May 5, 2020, trying to minimize the clash between German Constitutional Law and the European Union legal order.[140] According to the commission, the German federal government provided "very strong commitments" to infer that Germany would from then onward respect the principles of autonomy, primacy, effectiveness, and uniform application of union law as well as the values laid down in Article 2 TEU, including the rule of law. The commission also argued that the German government explicitly recognized the authority of the Court of Justice of the European Union, whose decisions were considered final and binding in a way that the legality of acts of the union institutions could not be made subject to the examination of constitutional complaints before German courts. But the real context of such an exchange between the European Union Commission and the German federal government with its "very strong commitments" was that the latter *did not bind*, according to the German Constitutional Law and the elementary principle of division of powers, the *German Constitutional Court*. Put it in another terms, whatever the concerns expressed by the German federal government or the German federal legislator, any measure adopted by the European Union institutions would eventually not escape from the German Constitutional Court's review according to the German *sovereignty* expressed in the fundamental law *supremacy* and legally articulated through the constitutional identity-*ultra vires* doctrine.

The revolutionary change that would represent the transfer of the final political authority from the member states to the European Union could not be solved through the fine print of the legal debate. In the episode of the European institutions and the German Constitutional Court tug-of-war regarding the European Central Bank Public Sector Asset Purchase Program the commission clung itself to the margin that the German federal government's act of restraint offered in order to pacify the union (and particularly to dissuade others in eastern and southern Europe from imitating the German Constitutional Court's gesture). But the tensions among the different national interests coexisting within the European integration process (eventually expressed through the opposition between the member states constitutional court's declarations and the European Union law primacy as interpreted by the Court of Justice of the European Union) have still a long way ahead to be surmounted.

XXV

The economic recolonization of Eastern Europe had already begun before the 1990 reunification. But the end of the Cold War suddenly created an arc of low-wage economies with skilled workers on Germany's borders.[141] German manufacturers outsourced production to central and eastern Europe in a way that the relocations of production within Germany's eastern neighbors flourished in the second half of the 2000s, after countries such as the Czech Republic, Hungary, Poland, or Slovakia had acceded to the European Union in 2004.

The European Union's eastward enlargement was developed with the enthusiastic support of the German authorities, who concealed their raw appetite for economic profits with the "moral duty" toward the European Union newcomers and their supposed right to enjoy the freedom and prosperity that a unified continent under liberal democracy would provide to them. Germany would invest more than half of the West's total in eastern European countries.[142] As a result, by the beginning of the world crash in 2007, much of central and eastern Europe became part of the German supply chain, giving Germany an inbuilt competitiveness advantage relative to other Eurozone economies.[143] It also aligned to a large extent the economic interests of the eastern European countries with those of Germany and thus increased German power within the union.[144]

But German economic take off from the second half of 2000s had also much to do with the already mentioned reforms undertaken by the Schröder government between 2002 and 2005 that concerned the German workers themselves, and that led to an internal devaluation once the single currency had been established. Shortly after Chancellor Schröder took office in October 1998, in June 1999, Germany was described by *The Economist* as "the sick man of Europe." Economic growth was lower than in the rest of the newly created Eurozone, unemployment remained high, German exports had declined, and the continued costs of unification remained a burden.[145]

The Schröder government, of Social Democrats in coalition with the Greens, had to undertake structural reforms that would have delighted the liberals and the conservatives in order to align Germany with the needs of a global competitive economy (not surprisingly Schröder's initiatives in economic policy would split the German left and, at the end of the day, would serve the chancellery to the Christian Democrats in 2005 under the figure of Angela Merkel).

The most significant set of measures introduced by that government was a package of reforms announced in March 2003 labeled as the "Agenda 2010" that cut unemployment and health care benefits and reduced state pensions.[146] The reforms also made it easier for very small companies to fire employees and eliminated social security contributions on earnings of less than 400 euros a month, which helped reduce unit-labor costs and thus encouraged the creation of part-time jobs. This wage restraint, together with the elimination of the social security contributions on low-paid jobs, instigated the drop of unit labor costs and opened up a competitiveness gap between Germany and other Eurozone countries. In this way, Germany consolidated itself as a manufacturing and exporting colossus that flooded with its goods not only Europe but also the rest of the industrialized world and the emergent economies such as China, Russia, or Brazil. Since the wage restraints among German workers made the domestic demand low within a framework in which German exports gained new records every year, a huge German trade surplus was created that needed to be invested somewhere.

The boom in German exports was accompanied by a credit boom that German banks channeled toward southern European countries in part to allow their population to buy the goods that German companies produced. Huge surpluses were also invested, among other things (such as the mortgage-backed securities in the United States that were in the origins of the world crises) in buying sovereign bonds of the alluded southern European countries such as Greece, Italy, or Spain.

Unsurprisingly, when the crises of the Eurozone exploded, the German authorities, backed by both the German finance system and German industry, strongly opposed any measure taken by the European authorities and the global financial governance leading to debt-relief in such countries or even to a sizing in the bonds markets able to restrain the cost of the debt that may deprive German debt holders of the enormous benefits that they expected.

However, as the crisis evolved, it was clear even for German agents that it was better to renounce some of those benefits (in fact threatened by a total default of the countries besieged by the debt) and focus themselves on a strategy of displaying a direct political influence grounded on Germany's privileged economic position. As the biggest creditor country in a crisis of a currency made up of sovereign states, Germany could impose conditions on debtor countries in exchange for an agreement to stand behind their debt and thereby reduce the interest rates that they paid. German economic power ambitioned, thus, to entrench its control over great parts of Europe by holding other countries' sovereign debt and making them accomplish the political agenda decided in Frankfurt and Berlin.

XXVI

"Schäuble's plan" said the former Greek minister of finance Yanis Varoufakis shortly after stepping down as a protest against the third bailout for the country asked for by Tsipra's government in July 2015 "is to impose the *troika* everywhere: in Madrid, in Rome and, especially, in Paris."[147]

Wolfgang Schäuble, German minister of finance during the Eurozone crisis, adopted a hard line toward southern European countries in handling their sovereign debt. He refused any debt relief and urged the political establishment of such countries to adopt austerity measures in order to grant the bailout loans. The decisions concerning the bailout programs were taken by what was known as the Troika (the European Commission, the European Central Bank, and the International Monetary Fund), but Varoufakis suggested, first, that behind such decisions lay the German political control exercised as the biggest debt holder and, second, that the final German aim of the crisis in relation to debt was to seize political control of France. In that vein, economics would make gain for Germany what it didn't reach by military means in two world wars: a stable dominion over France.

The Eurozone crises, nevertheless, did not produce this outcome. Even its macroeconomic factors in the 2010s such as its debt-to-GDP ratio, its public deficit, or its economic growth were not much more favorable than those of Italy or Spain; its sovereign debt bond yields did not critically fall into the clutches of unsustainability. If there had been any attempt by the German authorities to adopt toward France measures with a strong political impact such as the ones decided in the cases of Greece or Spain, the strategy did not succeed. France came through the crisis being still a big power of Europe, a power that faced up to political turbulences and that needed a range of reforms but still a power after all.

As we have seen, the European Union was fractious, due its members' weaknesses. If one of them, as might have happened with Germany, had reached an overwhelming superiority upon the others, the organization would not have survived, at least in the fashion designed through the constituent treaties. The scenario of total German hegemony looked more plausible with the withdrawal of the United Kingdom, but it did not rush into a continental transformation since France's power remained relevant and Varoufakis's soothsaying was not accomplished.

If we compare the European process with other experiences on regional integration, we will find that the cornerstone of European evolution lay in the lack of hegemonic power. Integration did not reach European levels in North America or in Asia given the influence of the giants such as the United States or the People's Republic of China, respectively. Even in South America, the only place in which continental relations between the countries have gone far, although not as far as in Europe (with organizations such as the American States Organization with its system of human rights protection exercised through the Inter-American Court, the Andean Community, or the Southern Common Market), Brazil represents approximately one third of the whole Latin America population and 39 percent of the whole of Latin America's GDP, being still the world's ninth largest economy, in spite of the economic and political crisis registered by the second half of the 2010s.

In a context marked by the interaction between a huge nation and smaller ones the latter have few incentives to go beyond in the struggle for a closer union fearing to be absorbed by the larger one. At the same time, the big one, if it is powerful enough, does not need a common framework designed under egalitarian parameters among the different nations to sell its goods or to display both its political and cultural influence. In fact, that is what happened in the whole of America (both North and South) with the United States.

But in Europe the landscape after the Eurozone crisis was that Germany became a hegemonic power that found itself within a continental integration built under other premises. After Brexit, France appeared as the only counterbalance. But at some point it was doubtful if such an equilibrium would be maintained for long. French far-right pressure, Emmanuel Macron's incapacity in his presidential terms to face up to the economic challenges, and social unrest (aside from the social fragmentation provided by an unsuccessful cultural integration and the Islamic radical terrorist threat within the most Islamized society in a European Union Member)[148] undermined French political stability (indeed the French traditional party system completely vanished by the beginning of the 2020s). The crisis caused by the COVID-19 pandemic only made things worse and, together with Spain and Italy, sent France to the wagon of the states most dependent on European solidarity.

France's fall could well have been added to the fall of the western European states. Spain, Britain, France, the three of them once empires, were crossed by divisive forces able to jeopardize their territorial integrity and their social peace. Two of them, France and the United Kingdom, were the empires against which Germany fought since the first unification of the latter in the nineteenth century. The Federal Republic had some conditions to emerge as Europe's empress exercising economic colonization of those around her and, furthermore, with a whole institutional and bureaucratic apparatus, the rest of the European Union, at her service.

But the German institutions of the twenty-first century had never been interested in transforming the indirect domination that they had developed upon their neighbors into direct domination backed by the use of physical force. That renunciation, somehow grounded in the traumas inherited from the memories of the Third Reich and its total defeat in World War II, was fatal for the Germany of the 2020s once political developments in eastern Europe began to be expressed in a military contest and it became clear that disorders caused by Russian imperialist ambitions would cut Germany's access to crucial sources of energy. In the Federal Republic, thus, the same vulnerabilities that beset the European Union as a whole are certainly condensed on a smaller scale: the reliance on an outside power for external security (that of the United States which in turn was sustained through its own and independent sources of energy) and the need to legitimate themselves through the idea that the notion of nation-state is archaic made both Germany and the European Union extremely open to disturbance from geopolitical change.[149]

Meanwhile, the Europe that emerged from the 2012 sovereign debt crises was chaotic (in the same fashion that was the management of the political consequences of the 2020 COVID-19 challenge), which included the raising of populism and, in the case of the United Kingdom and Spain, the threat of territorial disintegration.

We have seen to which extent the creation and the evolution of the European integration of the first decades was associated with the decline of the western European empires. We have also remarked to which extent the crises involving some of such western European former empires were guided by the fantasy that somehow problems may be solved through a kind of imperial revival such as happened with the United Kingdom in the Brexit era, or as happened with Spain in harshly repressing the democratic claims for Catalan secession.

The paradox, though, was that the one that was going to approximate an imperial dimension, Germany, was the one that did not formally demand any empire or, rather, that even rejected to be moved by imperial ambitions given a past from which such a power sought to be rehabilitated. The Federal Republic was likely to opt, instead behaving as every power has behaved in the past, to exercise its domination in a different, "post-national," way. But the political and economic turbulences that surrounded the world in the 2020s did not leave room to believe that such a "post-national" way of leading a continental union and, through it, to become a superpower within the global arena, was possible at all.

XXVII

German European hegemony in the twenty-first century appeared within a context in which territorial occupations such as the ones that the Nazi regime fostered were considered obsolete. The euro crises of the 2010s showed that capitalist occupation, probably in a definitive way, replaced territorial imperialism.[150] Through both a permanent trade surplus and debt holdings (in a series of bail outs defining conditions able to deprive other member states' budgetary and legislative autonomy), Germany transformed the European periphery into its economic colony.

Such a movement also entailed profound consequences from the democratic perspective; the priority conferred to the repayment of the loans and the monetary stability induced both the German and the European Union institutions to be relatively indifferent toward the authoritarian turn that some other member states suffered as a consequence of the succession of economic crises.

In spite of several warnings at the European Union level regarding the activation of article 7 of the Treaty on European Union against some member states in order to avoid serious breaches to the foundational values of the union (such as democracy, human rights, or the rule of law), the truth was that no robust response was given to the rise of illiberal authoritarianism in places such as Hungary or Poland,[151] not to mention the silence around the Spanish repression against the democratic and pacific Catalan secession attempt. In this fashion it might be remembered that most of the German European MPs belonging to the conservative, the liberal, or even the socialist groups voted for lifting the immunity as European MP of the former Catalan president, Carles Puigdemont, in spite of the fact that a German court itself, the Schleswig-Holstein High Court, had previously refused his extradition.[152] The human rights violations against several Catalan separatists appreciated by several United Nations bodies[153] did not instigate, either, any movement from German political authorities to claim against the Spanish abuses or to display some degree of influence within the European Union bodies to isolate Spain in its siege to some of the European Union values declared in article 2 of the Treaty on European Union. Thus avoiding the Spanish economic implosion that the loss of the 20 percent of its GDP would imply following Catalonia's independence, and the possible chain reaction of insolvencies that would affect European banks holders of the Spanish debt, was a more compelling interest than preserving the human rights of the Catalan citizenry and its representatives.

The German Federal Constitutional Court, in a different vein, was very concerned in protecting the German democracy from decisions adopted at the European Union level (such as the purchasing of member states' sovereign debt by the European Central Bank), which supposedly lacked democratic accountability. But the German court's struggle to preserve the democratic values within the German constitutional system had been dispatched at the cost of attending to the collapse of the same values across some of the European neighbors and associates.

Economic asymmetry within the European Union led, given the requirements of the financial markets, to democratic asymmetry as well. But capitalist occupation and tolerance toward the democratic default of other European Union members had its risks if there was someone bigger in the geopolitical arena able to jeopardize Germany's preeminent regional position.

Germany had economically colonized the European periphery, but it could be transformed at its turn as an object of capitalist occupation by another superpower. Such was the horizon envisaged through the European Union–China Comprehensive Agreement on Investment, whose negotiations concluded in December 2020. Relying on the Chinese capital supply was the main evidence that showed the eagerness of the European (and German) elites to make the logic of economic profit prevail upon the logic of democracy and human rights. A Chinese capitalist would not witness any kind of disturbance by the European democratic standards infringed while waiting for the investment rate returns, but, what was perhaps worse for the European Union's proclaimed values, the German investor would not express any concern either for, let's say, the genocide perpetrated against the Uyghurs or the crippling of political rights in Hong Kong or Tibet while receiving the benefits of the capital transferred to extract lithium in Lake Zhabuye.

Chinese authoritarianism was in that fashion ready to be integrated to the German and European dynamics entrenching the democratic crush already experienced both by the European periphery and the European Union institutions. At least in terms of political organization, Chinese capitalist occupation over Europe would represent also an imperial occupation by forcing regime changes. The capitalist occupation that the unified Germany exercised from the euro crises with mastery would eventually swallow Germany and the rest of Europe by a country that ironically the European powers had partially dominated and dismembered in the past.

The German lack of political influence, together with the progressive economic dependence and technological backwardness, shackled the competitiveness of the European Union as a bloc in the struggle for global hegemony. Focusing on mercantilist economic policies and strengthening manufacturing export power was not enough to avoid a scenario in which the big superpowers, embodied in the United States or in the People's Republic of China, were in the position to dictate anything to Germany (and hence to the whole European Union) by threatening to reduce imports.[154]

Similar dependence links under which the German economy had subjected itself regarding Russia in energy matters had been developed regarding China in manufacturing, raw material extractions, and capital resulting from that process an extreme economic and political vulnerability.

XXVIII

In assessing Angela Merkel's sixteen years as chancellor, Wolfgang Münchau highlighted, among the different elements lacking in Merkel's rule, her inability to transform the fabulous gains obtained as a consequence of the euro crises into successful technological progress.[155] According to Münchau, losing positions as an innovative power resulting from poor investment lay behind the German decline that Merkel's successors had to deal with.

The German economic and political establishment entered into panic when they realized, for instance, that they might not be in a couple of years competitive in one of the economic sectors that was chiefly responsible for German postwar growth (and that still was the jewel of the German exports) namely, the automobile industry.

With the abandonment of the combustion engine given the pressure of the climate change phenomenon, the transition to the fully electric car represented the obsolescence affecting all the products linked to the fossil power regarding to which the German industry had attained high specialization levels (no combustion engine means no pistons, no carburetor, or no spark plug). To make things worse, the German automobile conglomerates showed some shortcomings in attaining the technological levels concerning the development of the electric cars' hardware and their software equipment able to compete with American industry or the Asian companies of Korea, Japan, or China, including the technology required to produce cars driven by artificial intelligence. China, on the other hand, dominated the market for several raw materials on which electric cars rely. China was about to ban by 2023 the export of rare-earth magnets, which were critical for wind turbines and electric engines. China was also the world's largest product of lithium, an essential ingredient for car batteries, with a market share of 80 percent to 90 percent. The market share for rare-earth magnets were in the same category.[156]

The self-imposed restrictions, given the environmental preservation imperatives, on nuclear power or derived from the de-carbonization targets, together with the endemic lack of raw materials under German soil, particularly minerals related to the fabrication of technological devices, were factors also burdening German industrial capacity. While such dependence was shown toward Germany's European partners, as happened regarding an eventual dependence on French nuclear power, the weakness of the German economy was theoretically not so worrying as long as the European integration was preserved and strengthened.

But the 2022 energy crises in reality contributed to make more acute the rivalries between supposed partners. Thus, for instance, Macron's government did its best to veto any initiative to establish a partnership between Germany and southern European countries such as Spain or Italy in transferring oil and gas through pipelines from northern Africa to central Europe. The French instances sought in that way to ensure that those member states of southern and central Europe would not place themselves in the position to do without France in obtaining the sources of energy that they needed to maintain their levels of industrial development.[157]

Competition among allies tied through the framework of a higher political organization might work and help to advance the whole body as long as a minimum of federal trust is contemplated (as the models of competitive federalism might suggest).[158] But in a context in which, given a scarcity and a very hostile external atmosphere, such a minimum of federal trust is in different forms abandoned in order to satisfy national interests (as Germany did in managing the debt in the Eurozone from the 2008 crises and France did regarding energy resources in 2022), the system might be compromised to the extent of posing an existential threat to its continuity.

XXIX

From the beginning of the twenty-first century, European economic, industrial, and technological capacities suffered a considerable setback in contrast to China and other Asian competitors, a change of scene that was even more astonishing when remembering that Europe had been the cradle of the industrial revolution and the modern economy.

China's economic growth between 2000 and 2007, reaching an annual rate of 14 percent at its peak, had been partially responsible for the shock that reverberated in the Western economies from 2008. The assemblage of tech and electronic products, as well as production in the retailing sector, was massively transferred to China and eastern Asia, causing unemployment in America and Europe. China's industrial output forced a growth on energy demands that pushed up oil and gas prices. On the other hand, the large trade deficits that the West maintained with China were transformed by the latter into an enormous storage of Western debt (mainly American, to the point of becoming the Unites States' largest state creditor). The macro-economic strategic preponderance gained by the Asian superpower through those means was fabulous.[159]

By 2022 more than the 80 percent of the semiconductors output was settled in Asia (mainly in Taiwan, South Korea, and China). In that time no firm fabricated chips with more precision than Taiwan Semiconductor Manufacturing Company, better known as TSMC. Chips from Taiwan provided 37 percent of the world's computing each year. Two Korean companies produced

44 percent of the world's memory chips. Even the United States, where the basic science applied to semiconductors manufacturing had been developed, lagged behind in the technological race.

Semiconductor supply chains were bewilderingly complex but, with one remarkable exception mentioned below, Europe played a tiny role in producing such products crucial for economic development: a typical chip might be designed with blueprints from a Japanese-owned company, by a team of engineers in California and Israel, using design software from the United States. When a design was completed, it was sent to a facility in Taiwan, which bought ultra-pure silicon wafers and specialized gases from Japan. The design was carved into silicon using some of the world's most precise machinery, which could etch, deposit, and measure layers of materials a few atoms thick. These tools were produced primarily by five companies, one Dutch (ASML, the exception to which we referred before) one Japanese, and three Californian. Then the chip was packaged and tested, often in Southeast Asia, before being sent to China for assembly into a phone or a computer.[160] While China's authorities main economic and technological struggle relied on controlling the future of the chip industry (which meant controlling the future of computing and the power of artificial intelligence), Europe remained completely backward in those fields. Europe, in short, entered into a technological glaciation.[161]

However, as suggested by the beginning of 2020s, there were exceptions to such a dark horizon for the Europeans. Despite the mentioned energy deficiencies and the incomplete replacement of both nuclear and fossil sources by renewable energy, some companies had been able to maintain a high market share given their specialization in high-tech detailed components.

The most prominent example of the latter was represented by the Dutch ASML Holding, which was specialized in the development and manufacture of photolithography systems, being by 2022 the largest supplier of photolithography systems, primarily for the semiconductor industry. ASML Holding crucially manufactured machines for the production of integrated circuits. Some German companies were competitive in producing specific technological devices (such as Mann+Hummel producing air filtering devices), but none of them could attain the level of technological competitiveness of ASML, not to mention the level of the Asian (and some Northern American and Israeli counterparts).

China's industry was in the position to create by itself such photolithography systems to be applied to its own supply chain of integrated circuits. While the movement toward the full availability of capacities in the photolithography field was not completed, China opted to trade with companies like ASML that had developed such a technology. In the ASML photolithography systems' case it was nonetheless appreciated to what extent the West was able to block its liberal doctrine about globalization when it benefited a political rival. When an agreement between the ASML Holding and China was on the brink of being broken (to wit, an agreement between the European Union regarding one of its scarcely technological competitive advantages and an emergent China), the Biden administration sought to veto ASML from selling to its potential customer those machines crucial to advanced microprocessors.[162] Again, European political insignificance and lack of perspectives were likely to jeopardize both technological and economical preeminent positions.

The transition in the United States from the Trump administration (which had blocked any comprehensive trade agreement with the European Union and had forced the latter to embrace China's trade and investment appeal) to the Biden administration led to a complete disorientation both among German officials and the European Union institutions. When asked if Germany and Europe would stand on the side of the United States given the Biden administration's struggle to forge a closer alliance with Europe against China, the German defense minister Annegret Kramp-Karrenbauer, in Merkel's last government, replied that "Germany would take a position of equal distance between China and the United States,"[163] a statement that, given the above-mentioned EU-China trade and investment treaty (which was supposed to replace another Germany-China investment treaty already in force from 2005) and the German dependence on China for telecommunication systems, manufacturing trade, capital,and raw materials for producing technological devices, was likely to tip the scales of the German-EU foreign priorities clearly in favor of China.

The Biden visit to his European Allies in June 2021 clearly expressing American concerns on China's rising power and the demand of support to contain such a threat was reluctantly adopted by the European Union actors and particularly by Germany, which had not stopped the process of the EU-China bilateral investment agreement's ratification (let alone the vigorous working of the already existing bilateral investment treaties between China and other EU member states as that mentioned between Germany and China).

While before Russia's "special military operation" against Ukraine, there were already different approaches toward Kremlin's regime among the European Union members, such incompatible visions were hardly appreciated regarding China. European critical voices against the latter were almost absent within governments and political establishments in spite of the totalitarian character of Xi Jinping's rule and the serious violations of human rights and the genocidal practices against ethnic minorities that it caused. Even in the midst of the Russian military campaigns in Ukraine, the configuration of a Sino-Russian alliance, the United States pressure toward the European governments and China's reiterated menaces of invasion against Taiwan, the European political and economic agents did not cease their trade and diplomatic exchanges with Beijing. The formal freezing of the ratification of the comprehensive investment treaty did not conceal that relations of all kinds between China and Europe continued at full capacity, as for instance, Olaf Scholz's visit to Xi Jinping with a delegation of German business representatives in November 2022 demonstrated.[164]

Contrary to what happened in the relationship between China and the European Union, no comprehensive trade and investment agreement was concluded between the European Union and the United States. The involvement of the Obama administration in that aim was not regained by the Biden administration once Trump lost the reelection in the fall of 2020. Instead, the Biden presidency followed his predecessor in confronting China, a movement that was not accompanied by the European Union partners.

Regarding China, thus, there was appreciated a fracture between the more hostile strategy displayed by the United States, the post-Brexit United Kingdom, and other members of the Anglosphere, such as Australia, and the more submissive approach shown by the European Union governments and particularly by the German one, apparently more concerned in building a kind of Eurasian commercial relationship than in opening a front of conflict in the Pacific.

European decline in all terms before China and America, with Germany relinquishing to any political ambition in the global arena, made the historian Nils Gilman ironically suggest that the only role left for Europe would be to host meetings between the Chinese and the American delegations at grand old palazzos after their wrangling.[165]

Through investment commitments and debt repayment obligations, in sum, nations such as China that once felt under Western influence (or that were directly colonized by it through territorial acquisition) were going to inflict to the former rulers of the world the same constraints that they had suffered in the hands of the old colonial European powers. European economic integration, and its ability to negotiate trade and investment agreements with China, or with any other new geopolitical giant, as a single bloc, was an alternative to prevent the extinction of the nostalgic empires, but the result that the European intra-relations between Germany and the periphery had already anticipated, was that by surviving in the midst of economic and technological dependences the European political system was willing to jettison the values (democracy, human rights, rule of law, etc.) and even to question some of its Western alliances that were supposed to represent the ethos of the European integration process.

XXX

The lack of national ambition, the lack of project, the lack of will to power, led Germany to economic stagnation and to geopolitical irrelevance.

The self-inflicted wound caused by renouncing nuclear power and, at the same time, surrendering to the arms of the Russian dependence on sources of energy proved disastrous for the German economy and its political position within the European Union and the world. The trade surpluses on which the German Federal Republic had built its economic supremacy in the postwar period, and thereafter allowed the unified country to colonize both eastern and southern Europe through its privileged lender and investor condition, evaporated by July 2022. For the very first time in decades, Germany's trade balance sunk into deficit.

Inflation (whose annual rate was over 10 percent by November 2022) and the lack of provision of raw materials severely hit German manufacturing competitiveness and put the German economy on the edge of recession. The only solution relied on cajoling the European Central Bank to respond to the German needs in monetary policy but that represented a direct confrontation with the interests of other members of the Eurozone. The struggle against inflation required the European Central Bank to stop the purchasing of peripheral countries' debt, and that was indeed what the Bundesbank urged the European Central Bank to do by summer 2022, but German demands went even beyond this: German authorities pushed to veto Christine Lagarde's initiative to sell stronger Eurozone sovereigns in order to buy Spanish, Italian, Greek, or Portuguese debt.[166]

However, and differently as happened in 2008, the divergence of needs between the Eurozone core and its periphery was not decided in favoring the core. It happened that the supposedly more vulnerable and indebted economies, given their lower exposure to geopolitical and energetic dependences toward Russia, did better by the end of 2022 through the European Central Bank rise in interest rates.

While Spain, for instance, in 2022 almost recorded a 4 percent of GDP annual growth rate, Germany only reached an anemic 1.3 percent (and Italy doubled such rate: 2.6 percent). Though reviewing long term indicators, such as the ten-year borrowing costs did not allow to foresee particular investor trust in southern European macroeconomic positive evolution vis-à-vis the German one (the Italian sovereign ten-year bond yield [3.8 percent] still doubled the German one [1.88 percent] by December 2022), the point was that the European Central Bank monetary policy adopted to fight inflation did not momentarily endanger the Eurozone peripheral economies (but it did not solve German economic problems either). Somehow, southern European economies and other Eurozone peripheral ones were likely to be detached from German difficulties perhaps to the degree of reversing the German economic colonization displayed in the previous decade. By the beginning of 2023, Germany seemed in the transition to lose even its hegemonic character in the economic field within Europe.

In spite of those profound political and economic turbulences by summer 2023, social discontent had not gone beyond disapproval in the opinion polling in relation to Scholz's social-democratic, green and liberal coalition. Differently as other European jurisdictions, far-right nationalistic tendencies have not invaded German representative institutions. That political spectrum is still disorganized and, again, the extremist *Alternative für Deutschland*'s rise is still modest (and particularly focused on eastern Germany) compared to other ultra conservative political forces in other western European countries such as France, not to mention Italy. It is true that on December 7, 2022, twenty-five members of a suspected far-right terrorist group were arrested for allegedly planning a coup d'état. The group, called Patriotic Union, was a part of the German far-right extremist *Reichsbürger* movement. But that attempt, spectacular as it was, was not likely to be representative of a generalized social uproar able to cause a disruption in Germany's constitutional democracy.

The failures of German nationalistic groups did not however conceal that Germany's geopolitical weight was seriously damaged in the months that followed Ukraine's invasion by Russia. Such a movement revealed the profound German weakness in military and geo-strategic terms and the complete dependence on the system provided by NATO. Putin's 2022 strike showed that economic predominance without hard power, which Germany had developed since the end of World War II, might mean a lack of power altogether. That impotence might eventually lead to a radical change in the German political landscape.

The irony of destiny is traceable by observing that, at the end of the day, the western European power that is more exposed to a multiple risk on all sorts of fronts (economic, social and political) even to a scenario of total failure able to drag the whole European project into the abyss, would be that power which had expressly refused, at least until these lines are written, to be nostalgic at the eventual resurrection of a nation.

NOTES

1. This statement on Germany comes from the historian Dr. Carles Sirera Miralles. I am in debt to him for allowing me to include the observation in my essay.

2. Christian Joerges, "Europe a *Großraum*? Shifting Legal Conceptualizations of the Integration Project," in *Darker Legacies of Law in Europe: The Shadow of National Socialism and Fascism over Europe and Its Legal Traditions*, eds. Christian Joerges and Navraj Singh Ghaleigh (Oxford and Portland, OR: Hart Publishing, 2003), 167–68.

3. See Richard Blanke, *Orphans of Versailles: The Germans in Western Poland, 1918–1939* (Lexington, KY: University Press of Kentucky, 1993), 32.

4. See Mark Mazower, *Hitler's Empire: Nazi Rule in Occupied Europe* (London and New York: Penguin, 2008), 41.

5. See Kristina Spohr, *Post Wall, Post Square: Rebuilding the World after 1989* (London: William Collins, 2019), 307.

6. Mazower, *Hitler's Empire*, 2.

7. See, for instance, John Darwin, *After Tamerlane: The Global History of Europe* (London: Allen Lane, 2007), 417–18; Hans Kundnani, *The Paradox of German Power* (Oxford/New York: Oxford University Press, 2015), 13–15; and Uta G. Poiger, "Imperialism and Empire in Twentieth Century Germany," *History and Memory* 17, no.1–2 (Spring-Summer 2005): 117–43.

8. Niall Ferguson, *Empire: How Britain Made the Modern World* (London: Penguin Books, 2004), 234.

9. Niall Ferguson, *Civilization: The West and the Rest* (London: Penguin, 2012), 176.

10. Mazower, *Hitler's Empire*, xxxiv–xxxv.

11. Matthias Häussler, *The Herero Genocide: War, Emotion, and Extreme Violence in Colonial Namibia* (New York and Oxford: Berghahn, 2021).

12. Ferguson, *Civilization*, 189–90.

13. See Woodruff D. Smith, "Friedrich Ratzel and the Origins of *Lebensraum*," *German Studies Review* 3, no.1 (February 1980): 51–68.

14. Mazower, *Hitler's Empire*, xxxix.

15. See Gordon A. Craig, *Germany, 1866–1945* (Oxford: Oxford University Press, 1980), 175; Gerald Reitlinger, *The House Built on Sand: The Conflicts of German Policy in Russia, 1939–1945* (New York: Viking Press, 1960), 176.

16. Ian Kershaw, *Hitler: 1936–1945: Nemesis* (London: Allen Lane/Penguin Books, 2001), 415.

17. Mazower, *Hitler's Empire*, 59.

18. On that point see Adam Tooze, *The Wages of Destruction: The Making and Breaking of the Nazi Economy* (New York: Penguin, 2006), 387.

19. Dieter Gosewinkel, "Europe antilibérale ou anti-Europe? Les conceptions européennes de l'extrême droite française entre 1940 et 1990," *Politique européenne* 62, no. 4 (2018): 161.

20. Keith Lowe, *Savage Continent: Europe in the Aftermath o fWorld War II* (London: Penguin, 2013; first edition 2012), 230–48; Mazower, *Dark Continent*, 216–21.

21. See Tooze, *The Wages of Destruction*, 672.

22. Giles McDonogh, *After the Reich: The Brutal History of the Allied Occupation* (New York: Basic Books, 2009), 1.

23. See Alfred-Maurice De Zayas, *A Terrible Revenge: The Ethnic Cleansing of the East European Germans* (New York: Palgrave Macmillan, 2006), 156.

24. See Wilfried Röhrich, "Die 'Stunde Null'" In *Deutschland nach 1945: Ein Lesebuch zur deutschen Geschichte von 1945 bis zur Gegenwart*, eds. Eckart Conze and Gabriele Metzler, (München: Verlag C.H.Beck, 1997), 30.

25. Tooze, *The Wages of Destruction*, 672.

26. Lowe, *Savage Continent*, XIII.

27. Michael R. Marrus, *Unwanted: European Refugees in the Twentieth Century* (Oxford and New York: Oxford University Press, 1985), 324.

28. Tooze, *The Wages of Destruction*, 672.

29. Control Council Law No. 46 of February 25, 1947 (Abolition of Prussia). The preamble of the Control Council Law states, "The Prussian State which from early days has been a bearer of militarism and reaction in Germany has de facto ceased to exist," see Ernst R. Huber, *Quellen zum Staatsrecht der Neuzeit (Deutsche Verfassungsdokumente der Gegenwart 1919–1951)*. Volume 2 (Tübingen: Matthiesen 1951), 648.

30. On that plan, see Winston Churchill, *The Second World War, Vol. 6: Triumph and Tragedy* (London: Educational Book Company, 1954), 138–39.

31. Andrew Moravcsik, *The Choice for Europe Social Purpose and State Power from Messina to Maastricht* (London: UCL press, 1998), 96.

32. See Hans Kundnani, *The Paradox of German Power* (Oxford and New York: Oxford University Press, 2015), 24.

33. See Peter Schöttler, "Three Kinds of Collaboration," in *Anti-liberal Europe: A Neglected Story of Europeanization*, ed. Dieter Gosewinkel (New York and Oxford: Berghahn, 2015), 141.

34. Joseph Weiler, "Integration through fear," *Blog of the European Journal of International Law*. April 13, 2012. Available at https://www.ejiltalk.org/integration-through-fear/.

35. See Bruno Maçães, "La Realidad de Eurasia," *Política Exterior* 204. November 1, 2021. Available at https://www.politicaexterior.com/articulo/la-realidad-de-eurasia/.

36. Hanns W. Maull, "Germany and Japan: The New Civilian Powers," *Foreign Affairs* 69, no. 5. (1990–1991). Available at https://www.foreignaffairs.com/articles/asia/1990-12-01/germany-and-japan-new-civilian-powers.

37. See, for instance, Kohl's speech at the European Parliament of November 22, 1989. Available at https://my-european-history.ep.eu/myhouse/story/921. "*Deutschlandpolitik* and *Europapolitik* are two sides of the same coin," stated the German chancellor in that address.

38. See Spohr, *Post Wall, Post Square*, 177.

39. Stanley Hoffmann, "Obstinate or Obsolete? The Fate of the Nation-State and the Case of Western Europe," *Daedalus* 95, no. 3 (Summer 1966): 862–915, 894; Dietrich Thränhardt, *Geschichte der Bundesrepublik Deutschland* (Frankfurt am Main: Suhrkamp, 1996), 80.

40. Hèctor López Bofill, *Law, Violence and Constituent Power. The Law, Politics and History of Constitution Making* (London and New York: Routledge, 2021), 134–69.

41. Michael A. Wilkinson, "The Reconstruction of Postwar Europe: Lineages of Authoritarian Liberalism," *LSE Law, Society and Economy Working Papers* 05/2016. May 2016. Available at https://eprints.lse.ac.uk/66570/1/__lse.ac.uk_storage_LIBRARY_Secondary_libfile_shared_repository_Content_LSE%20Working%20Paper_The%20Reconstitution%20of%20Postwar%20Europe_Wilkinson_The_Reconstitution_of_Postwar_Europe_Author.pdf, 11.

42. Fritz W. Scharpf, "The Asymmetry of European Integration or Why Europe Can't Have a Social Market Economy," *Socio-Economic Review* 8, no. 2 (April 2010): 211–50.

43. Michael A. Wilkinson, *Authoritarian Liberalism and the Transformation of Modern Europe* (Oxford: Oxford University Press, 2021), 74.

44. Karl Loewenstein, "Militant Democracy and Fundamental Rights, I," *American Political Science Review* 31, no. 3 (June 1937): 417–32.

45. Wilkinson, "The Reconstruction of Postwar Europe," 37.

46. Moravcsik, *The Choice for Europe*, 91–92.

47. Mark E. Spicka, *Selling the Economic Miracle. Economic Reconstruction and Politics in West Germany, 1949–1957* (New York and Oxford: Berghahn Books, 2007), 2–3).

48. See Christoph Möllers, "We Are (Afraid of) the People: Constituent Power in German Constitutionalism," in *The Paradox of Constitutionalism, Constituent Power and Constitutional Form*, eds. Martin Loughlin and Neil Walker (Oxford: Oxford University Press, 2007).

49. See Chris Thornhill, *A Sociology of Constitutions: Constitutions and State Legitimacy in Historical-Sociological Perspective* (Cambridge: Cambridge University Press, 2011), 335.

50. See Michaela Hailbronner, *Tradition and Transformations: The Rise of German Constitutionalism* (Oxford: Oxford University Press, 2015).

51. See Wilkinson, *Authoritarian Liberalism*, 74.

52. Heinrich A. Winkler, *Germany: The Long Road West: 1933–1990* (Oxford: Oxford University Press, 2007), 112.

53. Tony Judt, *Postwar: A History of Europe since 1945* (London: Penguin, 2005), 53.

54. Tooze, *The Wages of Destruction*, 100.

55. See Walter Scheidel, *The Great Leveler: Violence and the History of Inequality from the Stone Age to Twenty-First Century* (Princeton, NJ, and Oxford: Princeton University Press, 2017), 152.

56. Tooze, *The Wages of Destruction*, 673.

57. See Judt, *Postwar*, 57.

58. Ulrich Herbert, *Hitler's Foreign Workers: Enforced Foreign Labor in Germany under the Third Reich* (Cambridge: Cambridge University Press, 1997), 143–50.

59. Judt, *Postwar*, 51.

60. Mazower, *Hitler's Empire*, 571.

61. Perry Anderson, *The New Old World* (London and New York: Verso, 2009), 12.
62. Mazower, *Hitler's Empire*, 6.
63. Schöttler, "Three Kinds of Collaboration," 141.
64. Tooze, *The Wages of Destruction*, 252 and 721 (n. 29).
65. Judt, *Postwar*, 58.
66. Hermann Lübbe, "Der Nationalsozialismus im politischen Bewußtsein der Gegenwart," in *Deutschlands Weg in die Diktatur*, Martin Broszat, et al., eds (Berlin: Siedler, 2005).
67. See "Bertelsmann Offers Regret for Its Nazi-Era Conduct," *The New York Times*, October 8, 2002. Available at https://www.nytimes.com/2002/10/08/world/bertelsmann-offers-regret-for-its-nazi-era-conduct.html. Besides the independent commissions of historians promoted by private bodies or academic institutions the German federal government also supported the creation of such commissions to examine the role of public bodies during the National Socialist era, as was represented, for instance, by the establishment of an independent commission in 2005 within the framework of the German Federal Ministry for Foreign Affairs to analyze the involvement of the diplomatic agents during the Third Reich and to assess how much continuity or otherwise existed with the pre-1945 Foreign Service. See "Independent Commission of Historians," *Federal Foreign Office*. Available at https://www.auswaertiges-amt.de/en/aamt/geschichte/historikerkommission-node (visited October 19, 2022).
68. Mazower, *Hitler's Empire*, 234.
69. See Norbert Frei, *Vergangenheitspolitik: Die Anfänge der Bundesrepublik und die NS-Vergangenheit* (München, CH Beck, 1996); and Michael Stolleis, "Prologue: Reluctance to Glance in the Mirror: The Changing Face of German Jurisprudence after 1933 and Post-1945," in *Darker Legacies of Law in Europe: The Shadow of National Socialism and Fascism over Europe and Its Legal Traditions*, eds. Christian Joerges and Navraj Singh Ghaleigh (Oxford and Portland, OR: Hart Publishing, 2003), 3.
70. See Vladimir M. Zubok, *A Failed Empire: The Soviet Union in the Cold War from Stalin to Gorbachev* (Chapel Hill, NC: The University of North Carolina Press, 2007), 81.
71. David J. Gerber, "Constitutionalizing the Economy: German Neoliberalism, Competition Law and the 'New' Europe," *American Journal of Comparative Law* 42, no. 25 (January 1994): 25–84
72. James C. Van Hook, "Translating Economics into Politics in Cold War Germany," *German Politics & Society* 25, no. 2 (Summer 2007): 104–16, 104–5.
73. Perry Anderson, "Ever Closer Union?," *London Review of Books* 43, no. 7 (January 2021). Available at https://www.lrb.co.uk/the-paper/v43/n01/perry-anderson/ever-closer-union.
74. Mauve Carbonell, *Des hommes à l'origine de l'Europe: Biographies des membres de la Haute Autorité de la CECA* (Aix-en-Provence, Publications de l'Université de Provence, 2008).

75. Vera Fritz, *Juges et avocats généraux de la Cour de Justice de l'Union Européenne (1952–1972): Une approche biographique de l'histoire d'une révolution juridique* (Frankfurt am Main: Vittorio Klostermann, 2018).

76. Mazower, *Hitler's Empire*, 571.

77. Gosewinkel, "Europe antilibérale ou anti-Europe?, 152–79, 156.

78. Mark Mazower, *Governing the World: The History of an Idea* (London: Allen Lane, 2012), 411.

79. Anderson, "Ever Closer Union?"

80. Fritz, *Juges et avocats généraux de la Cour de Justice de l'Union Européenne*, 287–99.

81. Thomas Horsley, "Reflections on the Role of the Court of Justice as the 'Motor' of European Integration: Legal Limits to Judicial Lawmaking," *Common Market Law Review* 50, no. 4 (2013): 931–64, 934–35.

82. European Court of Justice Judgment C-26/62 *Van Gend and Loos* of February 5, 1963. See a brilliant account on the significance of the *Van Gend and Loos* case for the European integration process in Luuk van Middelaar, *The Passage to Europe: How a Continent Became a Union* (New Haven, CT, and London: Yale University Press, 2014), 49–53.

83. European Court of Justice Judgment C-6/64 *Costa v. ENEL* of July 15, 1964.

84. Morten Rasmussen, "The Origins of a Legal Revolution—The Early History of the European Court of Justice," *Journal of European Integration History* 14, no. 2 (2008): 77–98, 94.

85. Antonin Cohen, "Constitutionalism without Constitution: Transnational Elites between Mobilization and Legal Expertise in the Making of a Constitution for Europe (1940s–1960s)," *Law and Social Inquiry* 32, no. 1 (Winter 2007): 109–36, 127–28.

86. See Antoine Vauchez, "The Transnational Politics of Judicialization: *Van Gend en Loos* and the Making of EU Polity," *European Law Journal* 16, no. 1 (January 2010): 1–28, 2.

87. Cohen, "Constitutionalism without Constitution," 112.

88. Antoine Vauchez, "Statesmen of Independence: The International Fabric of Europe's Way of Political Legitimacy," *Contemporary European History* 27, no. 2 (April 2018): 183–201.

89. The so called „Berlin Agreement" of 1951 on the German currency areas [*Abkommen über den handel zwischen den Währungsgebieten der Deutschen Mark (DM-West) und den Währungsgebieten der Deutschen Mark der Deutschen Notebank (DM-Ost)*] by which the respective jurisdictions existed side by side through the political conflict on Berlin. On the Western side a trusteeship was set up for inter-zonal trade. Initially this was an agency of the German "*Industrie-und Handelstag*," an institution of self-government of the West German economy, later an institution which was de facto bound to the Federal Ministry for Economic Affairs, though it did not share the character of government authority.

90. Dietmar Petzina, "The Economic Dimension of the East-West Conflict and the Role of Germany," *Contemporary European History* 3, no. 2 (July 1994): 203–15, 206.

91. See Ethan B. Kapstein, *The Insecure Alliance: Energy, Crises and Western Politics since 1944* (New York: Oxford University Press, 1990), 137.

92. Helen Thompson, *Disorder: Hard Times in 21st Century* (Oxford: Oxford University Press, 2002), 51.

93. Judt, *Postwar*, 497–498.

94. Zubok, *A Failed Empire*, 212 and 217.

95. Petzina, "The Economic Dimension of the East-West Conflict and the Role of Germany," 209.

96. Zubok, *A Failed Empire*, 230.

97. Judt, *Postwar*, 470.

98. Lawrence J. Brainard, "Overview of East's Europe's Debt: The Evolution of Creditworthiness in the 1980s," *Business Economics* 25, no .4 (October 1990): 10–16, 10.

99. See Spohr, *Post Wall, Post Square*, 113.

100. André Steiner, *The Plans That Failed: An Economic History of the GDR* (New York: Berghahn, 2010), 172.

101. Maximilian Graf, "Before Strauss: The East German Struggle to Avoid Bankruptcy during the Debt Crises Revisited," *The International History Review* 42, no. 4 (2020): 737–54, 737.

102. So Stephan Kieninger, "Freer Movement in Return for Cash: Franz Josef Strauss, Alexander Schlack-Golodkowski, and the Milliardenkredit for the GDR, 1983–1984," in *New Perspectives on the End of the Cold War: Unexpected Transformations?*, eds. Bernhard Blumenau; Jussi M. Hanhimäki, and Barbara Zanchetta (London: Routledge, 2018), 117.

103. Graf, "Before Strauss," 750.

104. See Thompson, *Disorder*, 58.

105. See Spohr, *Post Wall, Post Square*, 171–78.

106. Fritz Bartel, *The Triumph of Broken Promises: The End of the Cold War and the Rise of Neoliberalism* (Cambridge, MA, and London: Harvard University Press, 2022), 321–30.

107. Judt, *Postwar*, 642.

108. Thomas Piketty, *Capital in the Twenty-First Century* (Cambridge: Belknap Press of Harvard University Press, 2004), 186. See also David Stark and László Bruszt, *Postsocialist Pathways: Transforming Politics and Property in East Central Europe* (Cambridge: Cambridge University Press, 1998).

109. Stephen Kotkin, *Armageddon Averted: The Soviet Collapse 1970–2000* (Oxford and New York: Oxford University Press, 2001), 138.

110. Aurélie Bros, Tatiana Mitrova, and Kirsten Westphal, "German-Russian Gas Relations: A Special Relationship in Troubled Waters," *Stiftung Wissenschaft und Politik Research Paper* 13, December 2017. Available at https://www.swp-berlin.org/publications/products/research_papers/2017RP13_wep_EtAl.pdf.

111. Roland Götz, "Germany and Russia—Strategic Partners?," *Geopolitical Affairs* 4 (2007). Available at https://www.swp-berlin.org/publications/products/fachpublikationen/Strategic_Partners_ks.pdf.

112. Judt, *Postwar*, 642.

113. Spohr, *Post Wall, Post Square*, 307.

114. Judt, *Postwar*, 501–3.

115. Hanns Jürgen Küsters, *Der Integrationsfriede: Viermächteverhandlungen über die Friedensregelung mit Deutschland, 1945–1990* (München: Oldenbourg, 2000).

116. See Mattias Kumm, "Constituent Power: Boundaries and Identity: On the Justificatory Depth of Constitutionalism—A Rejoinder to Neil Walker," *International Journal of Constitutional Law*, 14, no. 4 (October 2016): 914–24, 923.

117. Spohr, *Post Wall, Post Square*, 307.

118. Thompson, *Disorder*, 94.

119. Judt, *Postwar*, 643.

120. See *BverfG* 2 *BvF* 2/98 of November 11, 1999.

121. Judt, *Postwar*, 643.

122. Agnia Grigas, *The New Geopolitics of Natural Gas* (Cambridge, MA: Harvard University Press, 2017), 137–73.

123. See "German Lawmakers Warn Gerhard Schröder over Russian Projects," *Deutsche Welle*, September 6, 2020. Available at https://www.dw.com/en/gerhard-schr%C3%B6der-russia-germany/a-54829142.

124. See Thompson, *Disorder*, 32.

125. See Alexey Anishchuk, "Germany's Scholz Seeks 'Prudent' Sanctions against Russia," Bloomberg, January 23, 2022. Available at https://www.bloomberg.com/news/articles/2022-01-23/germany-s-scholz-seeks-prudent-sanctions-against-russia-s-z.

126. See Thompson, *Disorder*, 10.

127. Wolfgang Münchau, "Networks of Resistance," *Euro Intelligence*, May 1, 2022. Available at https://www.eurointelligence.com/column/networks-of-resistance, 99.

128. *Lisbon* Judgment *BVerfG* 2 *BvE* 2/08 of June 30, 2009. On this ruling see, for instance, Daniel Halberstam and Christoph Möllers, "The German Constitutional Court Says 'Ja zu Deutschland!,'" *German Law Journal* 10, no. 8 (August 2009): 1241–57; Frank Schorkopf, "The European Union as an Association of Sovereign States: Karlsruhe's Ruling on the Treaty of Lisbon," *German Law Journal* 10, no. 8 (August 2009): 1219–40; and Christian Tomuschat, "The Ruling of the German Constitutional Court on the Treaty of Lisbon," *German Law Journal* 10, no. 8 (August 2009): 1259–62.

129. See the German Federal Constitutional Court ruling on the OMT Program *European Central Bank OMT-Programs* Judgment *BVerfG* 2 *BvR* 2728, 2729, 2730, 2731/13, 2 *BvE* 13/13 of 21 June 2016.

130. See Adam Tooze, *Crashed. How a Decade of Financial Crises Changed the World* (New York: Viking, 2018), 378; Carlo Bastasin, *Saving Europe: Anatomy of a Dream* (Washington, DC: Brookings Institution Press, 2015), 223.

131. See Wolfgang Münchau, "Overrated—Now Fading," *Euro Intelligence*, June 26, 2021. Available at https://www.eurointelligence.com/column/merkel.

132. Judgment *BVerfG* 2 *BvR* 859, 1651, 2006/15, 2 *BvR* 980/16 of 5 May 2020.

133. See France C. Mayer, "To Boldly Go Where No Court Has Gone Before: The German Federal Constitutional Court's Ultra Vires Decision of May 5, 2020,"

German Law Journal 21, no. 5 (July 2020): 1116–27, 1117. On the Judgment *BVerfG* 2 *BvR* 859, 1651, 2006/15, 2 *BvR* 980/16 of May 5, 2020, see also Jürgen Basedow, Jan Dietze, Stefan Griller, Manuel Kellerbauer, Marcus Klamert, Luigi Malferrari, Tibor Scharf, Dominik Schnichels, Daniel Thym, and Jonathan Tomkin, "European Integration: Quo Vadis? A Critical Commentary on the PSPP Judgment of the German Federal Constitutional Court of May 5, 2020," *International Journal of Constitutional Law* 19, no. 1 (January 2021), 188–207.

134. European Court of Justice Judgment C-493/17 *Weiss and Others* of December 11, 2018.

135. In January 2012, the Czech Constitutional Court declared ultra vires the ruling of the European Court of Justice in Landtová case (European Court of Justice Judgement C-399/09 Landtová of June 22, 2011), which prohibited the discrimination between Czech and Slovak citizens in accessing to pension benefits, claiming that this ruling "failed to respect the European history" and specifically the events leading to the dissolution of Czechoslovakia (Pl. ÚS 5/12 Judgement of January 31, 2012, Slovak Pension XVII). In 2016 the reformed Constitutional Court of Hungary, according to the 2011 Hungarian Fundamental Law, also issued a ruling concerning the relocation mechanism across the European Union for asylum seekers who had entered the Schengen area in the course of the 2015 refugee crisis in which the court provided an interpretation of the constitutional identity in matters related to the participation of Hungary in the European Union as a limit of the Hungarian authorities' obligations vis-à-vis the EU institutions. See Hungarian Constitutional Court Decision 22/2016 of November 30 (XII.5.) AB.

136. Order *BVerfG* 2 *BvR* 2728/13 of February 7, 2014. See on this point Federico Fabbrini and András Sajó, "The Dangers of Constitutional Identity," *European Law Journal* 25, no. 4 (July 2019): 457–73, 459.

137. Wolfgang Münchau, "When Did We Lose the Fight," *Euro Intelligence*, January 23, 2022. Available at https://www.eurointelligence.com/column/when-did-we-lose-the-fight.

138. See "Primacy of EU Law: EU Commission Sends Formal Notice to Germany for Breaching Fundamental EU Law Principles," *Insight EU Monitoring*, June 10, 2021. Available at https://portal.ieu-monitoring.com/editorial/primacy-of-eu-law-eu-commission-sends-formal-notice-to-germany-for-breaching-fundamental-eu-law-principles.

139. Order *BVerfG* 2 *BvR* 1651/15 and 2 *BvR* 2006/15 of April 29, 2021.

140. See "EU Commission Closes Infringement Procedure against Germany on Primacy of EU Law and Authority of the EU Court of Justice," *Insight EU Monitoring*, December 2, 2021. Available at https://portal.ieu-monitoring.com/editorial/eu-commission-closes-infringement-procedure-after-germany-recognising-the-primacy-of-eu-law-and-authority-of-the-eu-court-of-justice.

141. Kundnani, *The Paradox of German Power*, 74.

142. Mazower, *Dark Continent*, 389.

143. See "Europe's Future in an Age of Austerity," *Centre for European Reform Conference Report*, November 9–10, 2012. Available at https://www.cer.eu/sites/default/files/ditchley_event_rpt14dec12.pdf.

144. Kundnani, *The Paradox of German Power*, 74.

145. Kershaw, *Roller-Coaster*, 472.

146. Adam Tooze, *Crashed: How a Decade of Financial Crises Changed the World* (New York: Viking, 2018), 94–95.

147. See "El tercer rescate de Grecia está diseñado para fracasar," interview with Yanis Varoufakis, *El País*, August 2, 2015. Available at https://elpais.com/internacional/2015/08/01/actualidad/1438462320_301878.html.

148. By 2012 the Muslim community share of the French population was already around 10 percent according to the data provided by Niall Ferguson in Ferguson, *Civilization*, 290.

149. See Thompson, *Disorder*, 6.

150. Wilkinson, "Authoritarian Liberalism as Authoritarian Constitutionalism," 335.

151. See Gráinne De Búrca, "Poland's and Hungary's EU Membership: On Not Confronting Authoritarian Governments," *International Journal of Constitutional Law* 20, no. 1 (January 2022): 13–34.

152. Schleswig-Holstein High Court, Aus(A) 18/18 (20/18) (July 12, 2018).

153. See for instance the Opinion 6/2019 (Spain) adopted by the Working Group on Arbitrary Detention at its 84th session A/HRC/WGAD/2019/6 or the decision of the United Nations Human Rights Committee regarding the Communication No.3297/2019, CCPR/C/135/D/3297/2019 adopted on July 12 2022.

154. I'm in debt to Sebastien Cochard for this observation on both the United States' and China's ability to blackmail Germany (and indirectly the European Union) by imposing a reduction on German imports.

155. Münchau, "Overrated—Now Fading."

156. Wolfgang Münchau, "The Case for Strategic Autonomy," *Euro Intelligence*, April 13, 2023. Available at https://www.eurointelligence.com/page-5.

157. See "Macron Reiterates Opposition to Building New Iberia Gas Pipeline," *Le Monde*, 6 October 2022. Available at https://www.lemonde.fr/en/europe/article/2022/10/06/macron-reiterates-opposition-to-building-new-iberia-gas-pipeline_5999403_143.html.

158. The classical contribution to the theory of competitive federalism is provided by Charles M. Tiebout, "A Pure Theory of Local Expenditures," *The Journal of Political Economy* 64, no. 5 (October, 1956): 416–24.

159. See Thompson, *Disorder*, 126–29.

160. See Chris Miller, *Chip War: The Fight for the World's Most Critical Technology* (London, New York, Sydney, Toronto, New Delhi: Simon & Schuster, 2022), XX–XXV.

161. Afiq Fitri, "The US Wants to Cut Off East Asian Chip Exports to China: Some Asian Countries Are Set to Reap the Benefits," *Techmonitor*, November 14, 2022. Available at https://techmonitor.ai/technology/emerging-technology/us-east-asian-semiconductor-exports-china-asian-countries-benefit.

162. See Stu Woo and Yang Jie, "China Wants a Chip Machine from the Dutch: The U.S. Said No," *Wall Street Journal*, July 17, 2021. Available at https://www.wsj.com/articles/china-wants-a-chip-machine-from-the-dutch-the-u-s-said-no-11626514513.

163. See “This Is a Huge Break with the Past,” interview with Annegret Kramp-Karrenbauer. *Internationale Politik Quarterly*, April 28, 2021. Available at https://ip-quarterly.com/en/huge-break-past.

164. See Shannon Tiezzi, “China Celebrates German Chancellor’s Trip,” The Diplomat, November 5, 2022. Available at https://thediplomat.com/2022/11/china-celebrates-german-chancellors-trip/.

165. Gilman, Nils (@nils_gilman) “The Role of Europe Will Be to Host Meetings between the Chinese and the Americans at Grand Old Palazzos,” April 28, 2021, 16.39. Tweet.

166. See Neil Unmack, “Lagarde Will Struggle to Do a Mario Draghi,” Reuters, June 21, 2022. Available at https://www.reuters.com/breakingviews/lagarde-will-struggle-do-mario-draghi-2022-06-21/.

Conclusion

National Horizons or the War and the Peoples

I

During recent decades we have witnessed former colonies strike back toward their western European metropolises in the form of massive migration, security threats, and, overall, the challenge that emerging economies have posed to European competitiveness and European social welfare.

However, maybe the first example of the revenge against Europe undertaken by former colonies is provided by those coming from the American states. After the Northern-American colonies' independence in 1776 and the creation of the Federation of the United States, the population of a territory once dominated by Europeans was able to accumulate such an enormous amount of wealth and military power that would propel them to global hegemony after rescuing some of their former European imperial masters in both World War I and World War II.

Somehow, by the end of 1945, western Europe had become no less than a colony of the United States and the creation of the European Communities, beginning with the foundation of the European Coal and Steel Community, may be interpreted as a reaction orchestrated by some European nation-states to face up to that situation. Surprisingly, the postwar United States, to which the founders of the European project were economically and military dependent altogether, consented to an initiative that may enshrine the seed of an economic and political competitor.

There was nonetheless a clear explanation for the United States authorities' attitude toward the western European movements: the existence of the Soviet Union and the beginning of the Cold War. The alternative of not backing European economic development through integration would have probably seen the fall of the whole continent into the hands of Communism. The political divisions experienced within some European nation-states given the shadow of the Eastern bloc and the role of the European Communities in pacifying them, as remarkably happened in France or in Italy, illustrate such a dynamic.

The fear of a Communist movement seizing power somewhere in western Europe whether by democratic means or by direct action (as happened in Czechoslovakia in 1948) pushed Conservative, Democratic-Christian, and Social-Christian political groups to create supranational structures to protect liberal democracies grounded in property rights and free market economies. The European Communities were a step forward in that direction but also the Council of Europe, the conclusion of the European Convention on Human Rights, and the foundation of European Court of Human Rights, which were even sponsored by the United Kingdom (in a time in which the United Kingdom had little interest, or none at all, in strengthening ties with the continent regarding other issues). The Council of Europe provided a framework of safeguards allowing liberal democracies in western Europe to contain any radical measure adopted by an eventual left-oriented government ruling in any other contracting party of that organization. Postwar European supranational structures were, in short, the product of a conservative approach.

Things were likely to change from 1989 onward with the spectacular disintegration of the Communist bloc in Eastern Europe. While a superpower, the Soviet Union was a collapsing power that had been defeated in World War II; Germany was, via national unification, emerging again. But the reluctance toward revolutionary movements that had been hovering in western Europe since the end of the war was still vivid once the Berlin Wall fell.

Thus, in the beginning of such a process, the former victors of the war, including the Soviet Union on the verge of its extinction, tolerated German's resurrection as long as it was constrained through the structure of the European Union that was going to be formed through the 1992 Maastricht Treaty. So the German chancellor, Helmut Kohl, among the other arguments that he held in order to achieve his political goals as we saw, convinced the former Allies to push forward with German unification by promising them that a united Germany would only be developed within the framework of a closer supranational European integration. According to Kohl's approach, which would be the prevalent German narrative in the following years, nobody had to be afraid of the revival of German national identity since this time German identity would be intertwined with the invocation of a common European identity (expressed, for instance, with the introduction of the so-called Europa Article in article 23 of the German Basic Law at the domestic law level, or with the creation of European citizenship in the 1992 Treaty on European Union at the supranational law level).[1]

The European Union forged in 1992 somehow co-opted the logic of the West German state's postwar trajectory (that is a trajectory of an occupied country). The union, as the Federal Republic, renounced to pretensions as a military power and followed the limited ambitions of its predecessors, the European Communities, in entrenching a project built around peace, economic prosperity, and social welfare. European identity would be developed within a space committed to democracy, the rule of law, human rights, and, not to mention, the free market economy with some social constraints. But in the supranational European bodies, the obsession of stability and tranquility that had marked the original design in the 1950s would be maintained; at the end of the day, Europe (beginning with the member state that spearheaded it, Germany) was cramped by its adherence to dogmas forged after 1945 and hobbled by its chronic lack of independent political and military power.[2]

Helmut Kohl, nevertheless, died in 2017 and so is fading the generation that lived the last throes of the war and Germany's partition (including also the ones that Kohl vested as their heirs, such as Angela Merkel whose retirement took place in 2021). Soon there will not be anyone in the leading edge belonging to those that rendered the promise of the German contention within a framework of continental union. Soon, indeed, there will not be anyone engulfed by the post-1945 dogmas and fears that were reproduced by 1989 and that might explain the relatively pacific means by which the collapse of the European Communist world was managed.

II

In the first stage the former Allies, beginning with the United States, had not to be very concerned about Germany's progress; unification required the Germans to deal with enormous economic and social complexities and sacrifices that slowed Germany's capacity both to consolidate its power within the European Union and to compete in the global sphere. The costs of German reunification saddled the country for more than a decade with stagnation, high unemployment, and mounting public debt, to the extent that by the beginning of the twenty-first century Germany (together with France, it should be added) repeatedly breached the stability pact criteria agreed to in order to underpin monetary union.[3]

It would not be until the middle of the 2000s, when the drastic economic reforms undertaken by the Schröder government at the beginning of the decade began to show their effects, that the unified Germany took the road of becoming an economic hegemon. But not only this, taking advantage of several circumstances such as the crisis of the sovereign debt that devastated southern Europe, the French decline, the rise of populisms in Italy and eastern

Europe, and, above all, Brexit, Germany found itself in the position of reinforcing its leadership in the European Union to the extent that the European Union legal, political, and economic framework would be ready to serve Germany's *national* interests.

By 2022, nevertheless, Germany had squandered all such advantages. By not having any clear national ambition nor any European project German authorities relinquished to lead anything and dragged both the country and the European Union to economic decline, technological backwardness, energy dependence, and not to mention, political irrelevance.

The conflict between Russia and Ukraine unchained in February 2022. The collapse of Germany's energy sources, given the dependence on Russian gas, the decision to close the nuclear power plants, and, from September 2022, even the sabotage against the Nord Stream pipelines accelerated German economic unsustainability. The seeds of Germany's sudden downturn, however, were already planted before Putin's regime sent its tanks to Kiev and might be summarized in one idea: Germany's lack of a collective project.

Even at the peak of its predominance when southern and eastern European countries were up to their necks in debts, most of which were in German hands, Berlin renounced to transform this economic subjugation into some expression of more defined direct political domination. And what was worse for German interests, the benefits obtained in the privileged position as manufacturing and financial supplier were not reinvested in promoting a real technological leap forward. Perhaps because military ambitions of physical coercion toward other peoples are the main bait to explore new technologies (and that was a path that German authorities were not willing to take), they had no incentives to delve into new sources of progress.

Territorial expansion, or even cultural expansion, eastern from the Oder-Neisse line to those parts of Europe that before 1939 were the German Empire had always been completely out of the political agenda. Only a bunch of far-right nostalgic elements dared to think about the imperialist aspirations of redrawing boundaries closer to what the *Kaiserreich* was. While Russia was challenging Europe and the West with a large-scale invasion, Germany reasserted itself in abstaining from repeating the courses of action that marked its past (at least for the moment, despite the warnings issued by the far-right gangs placed in the political fringes).

III

It might be thought that the election of Ursula Von der Leyen to the presidency of the European Union Commission in July 2019 expressed German ambitions to rule over the European Union without intermediaries (in the fashion that might be interpreted that the Juncker Commission operated). But Von der Leyen's mandate was just as sullen and uncharismatic as that of most of her predecessors basically because trying to define a political line emancipated from the member states, Von der Leyen's commission did not take any clear direction in one sense or in another.

It was likely that even in the case of the last Merkel government, encouraging Von der Leyen's commission to develop a more ambitious European common and independent policy[4] the commission's performance went at the end of the day no further than introducing one patch after another, seeking to avoid deeper divisions among the partners and deeper political, financial, or ecological catastrophes—not to mention the hesitance and the lack of determination when responding to the threats posed by authoritarian and militarily endowed neighbors such as Russia, Turkey, or, to a lesser extent, Morocco.

In sum, although the German Federal Republic materially became a nation-state with the whole carcass of the European Union at his disposal, its institutional apparatus (maybe with the exception represented by the constitutional court) did not exercise an explicit dispatch of national domination upon its weaker European partners. German authorities gave up on making visible any association between the union and a German national political hegemony. We might envisage such hesitations in translating economic power into explicit cultural and political power (in national power) by observing, for instance, the feeble defense of the German language vis-à-vis the overwhelming predominance of the English as European lingua franca (in spite of the fact that after the withdrawal of the United Kingdom from the European Union, English remains an official language only in the Republic of Ireland and Malta). The linguistic claudication appears as a sign of such a German refusal to endanger the union's multinational façade.

Germany did not take over the union, but the union did not develop, either, an autonomous policy able to trump over its member states at any field. The European Union institutions were even impotent to assert the primacy of its law upon its more disobedient members, were constantly tarnished by corruption scandals (as the one that besieged some members of the European Parliament, including one of its vice presidents, Eva Kailí, in relation to the bribes of Qatar to improve the image of this country in Europe in the midst of the 2022 World Cup celebration in Qatar), and they could not avoid the lack of performance of the Next Generation funds that did not cover the needs arising from the energy crisis and climate change.

The decline of the European Union as a political body was also translated to the external dimension and the hesitance of their authorities in building an independent project from the global superpowers and, particularly, from both China and the United States. In the new global disorder caused by China's continuous rising as a key center of economic and geopolitical power,[5] it was likely that European elites and the European institutional performance sought to secure autonomy from the United States, even by suggesting, as Macron did on several occasions, to resuscitate a European military organization[6] and weave a closer economic alliance with China. At the end of the day, however, and particularly when the European security pillars staggered with the Russian general attack against Ukraine, both the European governments and the representatives within the supranational level embraced again the United States leadership, and they took refuge in the American military and monetary supremacy as well as they accepted the Biden administration's *diktat* on avoiding strengthening economic ties with China.

IV

Aside from the path finally taken by Germany and the conjugation of its national interests within the European Union, it is interesting to follow the attitudes in the United States every time that an emancipated European Union under German political and economic predominance has been envisaged.

Bullying toward the European Union coming from the United States began much before President Trump's bravado when in July 2018 he stated that "the European Union is a foe." Already the prospects of war against Saddam Hussein's Iraq in the beginning of the 2000s became more intense when the Iraqi regime started selling oil in euros instead of doing it in dollars under the United Nations oil-for-food program. With this gesture, the euro was enshrined as a serious competitor to the dollar as a global currency and made the United States authorities under the George W. Bush administration fear about a global flight from the petrodollar to the euro that would have had a severe inflationary impact on the United States' economy.

Unsurprisingly, when the American government, backed by the British, decided to go ahead with the invasion of Iraq in the first months of 2003, the two pillars of the recently created Eurozone, France and Germany, under President Chirac and Chancellor Schröder respectively, strongly opposed the war. The Bush administration responded through its defense secretary, Donald Rumsfeld, by stirring anti-European feeling in the United States and denouncing France and Germany as representatives of "Old Europe."

Without the threat of Communism, any step forward to European economic and political unity leading to an entrenchment of the European Union as an independent and a strong actor in the world was seen from the other side of the Atlantic with reluctance. A strategy, particularly adopted by the American neo-conservative governments from George W. Bush to Trump, would be focused in fostering European divisions. The invasion of Iraq in 2003, confronting France, Germany, Belgium, and Luxembourg with the United

Kingdom, the Netherlands, Italy, Spain, Portugal, Denmark, and the eastern European states that were going to accede to the European Union in months, represented a high point of this maneuver.

But, in addition to those intra-European disputes fostered by American geopolitical interests, the European energy and monetary fragility did not take long to be revealed after Iraq's occupation. Though the 2007–2008 crash originated in the United States, its wave would be more devastating in Europe precisely because of the European banking sector's dependence on Eurodollar loans earned by Middle Eastern oil producers.[7]

Northern European banks, including the German ones, were involved in the massive growing of the Eurodollars lending markets transferring large volumes of money to corporations and governments in the southern Eurozone and Ireland. This lending, financed by short-term dollar funding from money markets, including repurchase agreements (repo) and Eurodollar markets, left those banks with large liabilities in a foreign currency and a mismatch between their longer-dated financed international assets and their short-term dollar borrowing.

When the Eurodollar credit markets on which the European banks relied stopped functioning and the cost of borrowing for all banks in inter-bank markets spiked, the American Federal Reserve moved to provide dollar swaps to the European Central Bank to pass on to European banks engaged in the Eurodollar credit market. Such initiatives did not prevent the Eurozone crisis, which between 2009 and 2013 still had to experience its worst shocks, but contained the disaster in North America and, overall, entrenched the dollar as a globally preeminent currency, confirmed the role of the Federal Reserve as a lender of last resort to the Eurodollar markets and, in short, reasserted the United States financial power vis-à-vis any challenge that the euro and the unified European monetary policy may pose.[8]

V

In its own way, the post-Brexit United Kingdom governments followed the lead of the European Union in terms of disorientation. The vote to withdraw from the supranational organization was a consequence of both a financial crisis and constitutional crises, which only worsened once the divorce was achieved. By 2022, inflation, jeopardized supply chains, lack of labor force, and disastrous decisions on fiscal policy led to an economic cataclysm.

On the other hand, the fact that a British democracy had decided to retire the consent of belonging to the European Union demonstrated that, according to the same democratic logic, the Scottish and the Irish republicans may retire their consent of belonging to the United Kingdom. By 2023, however, the Scottish SNP government did not obtain the referendum on independence that its prime minister had been asking for, nor was the Northern Irish shared government even capable of adapting itself to the leadership of Michelle O'Neill's Sinn Féin, which had won the May 2022 elections.

The "special relationship" between the United Kingdom and the United States was likely to mirror the geopolitical destabilization that the separation between the United Kingdom and the European Union might bring. Indeed, the Brexit phenomenon, in which America took advantage of that "special relationship" with its former motherland to coach the British decision of breaking up with Britain's former partners, might be interpreted as another divisive momentum encouraged from Washington to cajole any European pretension to jump into the premier of the superpowers.

However, during the administration of the vote and the negotiation of the rupture, President Trump did not hesitate in letting the British prime minister of that time, Theresa May, down every time she had to face up with an insurmountable opposition both within her own Conservative Party and within the British Parliament. Once the British definitive status in its relationship with Europe entered into force, under Biden's administration in the United States, it was not still clear that the Americans would be sympathetic with the British position by concluding the trade and investment agreement that had never been concluded between the United States and the European Union. Would America participate in the resurrection of an Anglo-Saxon empire able to confront other global superpowers for which the Brexiters had dreamed? Biden's need to regain the Europeans meant that the British-American "special relationship" was likely to be displaced in order to satisfy the European Union partners (and to prevent the latter from falling into the arms of the Chinese). In the meantime, the British status regarding the European Union culminated, with American indifference, by accepting the erection of a customs border in the Sea of Ireland, which meant the establishment of *a border in the middle of a sovereign state,* something that to some extent left clear that the United Kingdom had lost its grip on the international sphere. After all, dividing a country had been the punishment reserved to Germany once it had dragged the whole continent into the catastrophe. In the round triggered by Brexit the European Union returned the humiliation to the British, though in a more postmodern fashion.

The United Kingdom was not likely to be considered at any rate an economic competitor of the United States since America held a goods and services trade surplus of almost $20 billion. But something different might have happened with the remaining countries of the European Union, spearheaded by Germany, with which the United States goods trade deficit increased almost by 20 percent every year. The COVID-19 crisis, first, and later the economic debacle caused by the war in Ukraine, inflation, and the lack of competitiveness of German industry changed, however, such a relationship.

VI

Disregarding the details of the macroeconomic triangle formed by the United Kingdom, the United States, and the European Union, the point here is that every time there emerges a new power, there will be always someone interested in destroying it.

European integration was a project devoted to creating power with pieces that represented the most recent manifestations of the colonial empires. As we have seen in the previous pages, if the European nation-states joined in a common enterprise, it was because they had no other alternative if they wished to survive in the context of the postwar and the Cold War. As was written by Jean Monnet in his *Memoirs*, Europeans had to choose "either unity or decline" though it would have been more precise to observe that the union would make the decline smoother.[9]

Integration entrenched democracy within western European nation-states in a context in which their empires were disintegrating. But, contrary to what is commonly explained, such a process relating the building of a supranational structure and democratic stabilization was not deprived for many years of political turmoil, violent clashes and even the possibility of authoritarian reversals, as the constitutional transformations experienced in France by the Algerian decolonization war revealed. Still, the abuses perpetrated by the nation-states in their agonic attempts to retain their possessions occurred under the indifference, when not the complicity and the acquiescence, of the European partners. Some of those reminiscences on the European solidarity in avoiding the empires' dissolution would also surround the European authorities' mood when in more recent times the danger to the nation-states' territorial integrity would be translated to the European mainland of those entities.

To some extent, liberal and democratic revolutions in western Europe, from the British Glorious Revolution onward, and their consolidation were possible through the benefits provided by colonial exploitation. Overseas imperialism was the other side of domestic liberal progress in the eighteenth and nineteenth centuries up to the first half of the twentieth century, at least for the United Kingdom or France. As we have highlighted, the European Communities provided a protective mesh to minimize the costs that the anti-colonialist movements in Asia or in Africa caused to their respective metropolis.

The European supranational experiment created an alternative market to that focused on the exchanges between the metropole and its dependencies safeguarded by a supranational legal order which, in fact, designed a bulwark against the global liberalization system and allowed the maintenance of an acceptable standard of living for popular strata within each of the European nation-states. The economic growth of the so-called European golden age in the 1950s and the 1960s (that is, by the first years of the communities) made it possible to swallow the bitter pill of renouncing external sources of domination without tearing European societies apart and, in this way, helped to confine domestic political radicals to the fringes.

The 1970s crises flared up such a social understanding in places like Italy or the German Federal Republic, but it also convinced some of the dismembering empires that until that moment had remained outside the integration project (both democratic as the United Kingdom or until then authoritarian, such as Portugal or Spain) to join the enterprise. Getting back on the growth path from the 1980s, apart from definitively burying the Communist counter-model by the end of that decade, would enable the western European nation-states to participate in the ongoing process of economic globalization from a more solid position, though the political detachment regarding their former dominions had already been almost complete and even some of such former European colonies began to transform themselves into relevant economic powers.

VII

Such a new global balance that continued to favor the European experiment was more or less fruitful well into the first decade of the twenty-first century, a time when the optimistic discussions on federalization, relocation of powers, and institutional reengagements prospered within the European political agenda and reached their high point by the drafting of the Treaty Establishing a Constitution of Europe by which, though the reform outlined therein was indeed less profound than it appeared, was permitted at least briefly to envisage a Europe less supervised by the nationalistic aspirations of its members.

Until then the European project had demonstrated that it was possible to strengthen the power of the nation-states that integrate it by consolidating at the same time a supranational power. But the illusion burst into pieces with the 2008 crash, which revealed that strengthening a particular European nation-state was only possible at the expenses of *other* European members.

The 2012 sovereign debt crisis showed this tension in all its intensity and reaffirmed through economic means the German political predominance as a national power upon some European southern and eastern states. That power that had avoided facing the extinction of a colonial empire (because it had already lost it by the aftermath of World War I and because World War II had finished with the attempt to impose the European internal project of colonization that the Third Reich conceived) emerged from the 2012 sovereign debt crisis as the pole around which all the European legal, economic, and political structure spun.

But by the beginning of the 2020s, the Federal Republic of Germany was no longer a benchmark for much. At that time the European Union had lost any sense of a future blueprint as a supranational organization; in spite of masquerade conferences as the one organized by the French presidency of the European Council in 2022 nobody talked about federalization nor closing ties among the European peoples or even seriously developing new policies in the fiscal, social, or military fields. But the German crisis reaffirmed that no nation would take the lead either. The European space, thus, got into the third decade of the twenty-first century in an impasse in which both the national and the supranational perspectives completely lacked horizons and hopes beyond the attempt of desperately maintaining the European population's standards of living. Such a claim was nonetheless in the economic and geopolitical situation of that moment difficult if not impossible to achieve.

VIII

The memories of the past—the remnants of the Nazi times, the war, the Holocaust—have probably refrained Germany from clearly adjusting its economic and political influence within the European Union to the level of power (or superpower) that it deserved. But the German defense of an incomprehensible and vaporous post-national *Weltanschauung* provided nothing but the perfect conditions to be smashed by other superpowers, these being the United States, China, Russia, or whomever. Such superpowers, on the other hand, played the card in different degrees of fostering intra-European national disputes in order to debilitate still more the German predominance.

Russian authorities had been truly champions at such a game; from the close ties that were developed with Germany under Schröder's governments (which included relevant economic trumps in the energetic field) to causing all sort of confusions and distrusts among the European partners on occasion of the Russian seizing of Ukrainian territories, the backing of Lukashenko's Belarusian's regime, or, generally, of the aggressive Russian policy toward the former members of the Soviet sphere of influence.

If the German Federal Republic had relinquished any strong nationalistic discourse, Vladimir Putin's regime had not: it took advantage of that contrast long before the 2022 war in Ukraine and also during the conflict. The union reprimand on Russia had adopted more or less severe measures, but the fact was that, by the beginning of the 2020s, the central and eastern Europe dependence on Russian energy was overwhelming. That political stress had not prevented, at least until the Russo-Ukraine war, the Russian-European understanding in consolidating a system of offshore natural gas pipelines running under the Baltic Sea from Russia to Germany. Additional gas pipelines beyond those crossing Ukraine were supposedly devoted to ensure the Russian gas supply to Europe, and it might have continued like this if the will to power in the Kremlin had not entered into an excessive phase.

Despite the immense contradiction that represented alluding to gas supply in the times of climate change and the necessity to reduce the dependence on fossil fuel energy sources, the issue was that an energy-deficient Europe still crucially relied on Russian gas. During the 2010s, the Russian government played with that circumstance as a geopolitical deterrence card in order to minimize any European response to Russian behavior in those places—Armenia, Azerbaijan, Belarus, Georgia, Moldova, or Ukraine—that the Russian regime considered its area of influence since they once belonged to the extinguished Soviet Union. Any attempt from Germany or the European Union to punish Russia for the military aggression in those areas, for the abuses of the Russian regime concerning human rights, or for fostering waves of massive migration toward the European Union borders (as happened in autumn 2021 in the border between Belarus and Poland) was always far from being effective.

As we have seen, the West German relationship with the East on energy matters already began in the heart of the Cold War and associated the West German private and public actors mainly with the authorities of a single sovereign power: the Soviet Union. But the disruption already was appreciated when the actors involved in the business of providing gas and oil to central and western Europe multiplied and some of them, becoming sovereign powers by themselves, even acceded to economic and military organizations such as the European Union or NATO. On their way to Germany, energy resources had to cross the Baltic States, Belarus, Ukraine, or Moldova in a manner that any dispute that a Russian government might hold against such states would automatically have an impact on German energy policy and, generally, on the energy policy of an economically integrated Europe.

Instead of hurting the Russian economy by not consuming Russian extracted energy within Europe, Russia was the one that was able to make both the European economy and welfare extremely vulnerable by cutting the gas supply to the West. Until 2022 the Russian regime was not strong enough to challenge Europe with an open conflict but it had a wider range of resources to cause European instability and Putin's regime used such strategies on some occasions (by sending immigrants to the union during the Syrian crisis in 2015, for instance, or by consenting Afghanistan's fall into the hands of the Taliban in 2021, or simply by supporting populist movements across Europe) in order to lead the European order to chaos.

IX

The European ambition to be an island of stability in a confusing world became an illusion and a weakness that the Russian rulers had always been eager to exploit.[10] And so they did until Vladimir Putin changed the approach and decided to double down by triggering a total war in the heart of Europe.

While Russian authorities displayed, regarding the European Union, a strategy that might be described under the motto "since you cannot become stronger you must make the stronger weaker,"[11] China had for a long time opted to become straightforwardly the strongest. Chinese authorities had not even to delve into the disputes among the European Union members; some of them are quite dependent on China's financial and industrial supplies and some (such as Greece, Hungary, Malta, Italy, or Spain) are *fully* dependent on Chinese productive, investment, and technological capacities.

As we mentioned, the path to the conclusion of a comprehensive agreement on investment between China, the European Union, and its twenty-seven members went forward in spite of the serious flaws that China exhibited regarding the human rights file (which, theoretically, represents the core value that defines the European Union project). Only direct intervention from U.S. president Biden, in the midst of China's threat to take over Taiwan, was able to dissuade his European allies from strengthening ties with China through the investment treaty. But even the momentary stoppage of such a ratification process did not conceal that most of the European Union member states maintained bilateral investment treaties with China, beginning with Germany. It did not either conceal that every time that some European partner dares to open a diplomatic crisis with Beijing, as Lithuania did by reasserting its support for Taiwan in 2022, European Union authorities offered, at best, a lukewarm support to the European dissident and, at worst, an ominous silence.[12]

While with regard to Russia there had been differences among the member states even in the midst of a war of aggression on European soil, with China what prevailed instead was rather the unanimity, with the exceptions mentioned, in not complaining too loudly against Beijing about its policies of threat and oppression in relation to Taiwan, Hong Kong, Tibet, or East Turkestan.

During the 2010s there had been a strong European component to the Chinese project of the Eurasian channel of economic exchange known as the Belt and Road. To carry its exports to Europe, China sought new train links and ports. It also encouraged European states to join a new Asian Infrastructure Investment Bank, launched in 2013 to fund Belt and Road infrastructure projects. Italy joined the Belt and Road in March 2019, and, though the German and French governments criticized the Italian decision, they had already decided to advance in a deeper commercial relationship with China regarding to which the conclusion of the European Union investment treaty with Beijing represented the chief evidence. Though Germany was not a formal member of the Belt and Road project, in practice it was very much part of China's Eurasian trade routes; the German city of Duisburg became the rail and river hub for Chinese exports coming to Europe, and the port of Mukran was the end point of a new railway route running from central China. By the middle of the 2010s China became Germany's single largest overall trading partner. When the firm Huawei faced President Trump's attempts to ban that company's leading role in establishing 5G networks, Deutsche Telekom increased its collaboration with Huawei, disregarding American reproaches.[13] In short, European dependence on Chinese investment and trade opened the prospect of tensions between the European Union members and the United States and as such was able to destabilize the geopolitical balance of power.

X

The reaction to overcoming the 2020 COVID-19 crisis introduced some novelties maybe pressed by the urgency to avoid the dismantlement of the European project given the immediate danger of social and economic collapse of the southern European countries. The northern and "frugal" countries (spearheaded by a Germany more deferential toward the south than it had been in 2010) agreed for the very first time to create a supranational structure of debt issuance in a way that wealthy countries would cover a substantial part of the expenses of the most hit European Union members.

The funds created to rebuild economies devastated by the virus, particularly the 390 billion euros provided in grants, revealed a sort of a transnational political logic encouraged by the need to preserve the single market and the European corporations value chains (menaced by the ambition of extra-European capitals from the United States, China, or the Arabic monarchies to capture European assets). The decision to fund European fiscal stimulus to confront a recession was, certainly, a big innovation. It made credible the idea that in serious socioeconomic situations the European Union would not leave some of its members behind.[14] However, such a proposal designing a system by which the European Commission would be vested with the power to borrow money in the European Union's name was not accompanied by a redefinition of taxes to serve the European Union debt. The formal proposal that followed the announcement of the Recovery Fund outlined a European Union corporation tax tied to access to the single market and a European Union tax on technological giants. But the actual agreement on the Recovery Fund contained no reference to supranational tax on corporations nor to commitment devoted to harmonize national corporation tax rates. In that package the European Union acquired the authority to tax nonrecyclable plastic waste, and committed itself to future discussion on carbon and digital taxes.[15] The final outcome in the end was that, beyond marginal figures, the supranational organization failed again in displaying a structure able to directly tax citizens to support the European debt.

In addition to the recurrent problem of reaching agreements on a common fiscal policy, the execution of the Recovery Funds had to tackle with the domestic guardians of the nation-state interests, particularly with the German ones led by the German Constitutional Court, which were permanently supervising the attempt to shape a European common space of welfare and prosperity through the capacity of the Commission to borrow money. Sometimes those agents within the "frugal" economies caused delays in the implementation of the measures or even jeopardized them. They did it so, for instance, in assessing the measures adopted in the 2012 crisis (such as the sovereign debt purchasing in the secondary markets by the European Central Bank) in a fashion to justify an eventual blocking of transfers regarding to the funds provided in 2020. The amounts finally agreed to in July of that year were, at the behest of the Netherlands, Sweden, Denmark, and Austria, the result of accepting rebates to the original grant package, of more than one hundred billion euros. The rebates obtained by the mentioned states were accompanied by threats of opting-out in a way that sometimes resembled the maneuvers shown by the United Kingdom in the 1980s under the leadership of Margaret Thatcher when demanding a reduction of the European Communities' budget.

The fact that the United Kingdom finally left the European organization after such a sequence of disagreements did not permit the prediction of any movement favorable to the cohesion of the European economies if the "frugal" countries considered that the commitments on the debt regarding the recovery funds would not satisfy their expectations and that their development was burdened as a consequence of financing southern countries' decisions on expenditure.

As with many other debates, the objections regarding the contribution of northern European economies to support the modernization of the southern and eastern European ones were silenced by the Russian military pressure from 2022. But the economic slump caused by a high-scaled armed conflict made the struggle of hoarding resources by nation-states and the abandonment of solidarity mechanisms more likely. An inflation around the 10 percent rate in countries such as the Netherlands, Sweden, Austria, or Germany posed enormous difficulties to the implementation of the redistributive measures adopted in the stage defined during the health crisis. If the "frugal" countries had problems in keeping their economies and the well-being of their population afloat, still less would they be concerned about supporting the development of other countries.

XI

Divisions spread among European nation-states and also within the nation-states. If the European Union was not capable of ensuring the integral territory and political stability of a nation-state, they would consequently have fewer incentives to be committed to the European project. Anyone interested in undermining the union would strike against the weak link, that is, the unconfident, nationally disperse, and economically meager nation-states. The fear of opening territorial fault lines within the common European space instigated the supranational organization to defend without qualms the unity of the members that compounded it.

By providing assistance to the European old empires through human rights violations, however, the union was also risking descending into hell. In such a circumstance, unknowing the values that supposedly inspired the foundation of the continental integration, the agreement on Europe would be transformed into the antagonist of the pacific, human rights friendly, and democratic model about which generations of Europeans have dreamt from the first postwar years until now. Leaving the nation-states to their fate would be bad, but supporting such nation-states eager to commit abuses to save their national integrity would be worse. So was the tragic runaround still persisting in the present.

From the 1970s the European Union institutions, beginning with the Court of Justice of the European Communities (today the Court of Justice of the European Union; CJEU) provided an increasing legal definition of fundamental rights able to trump certain conceptions of civil liberties outlined by the supreme legal interpreters within the nation-states. Despite the different positions sometimes held by the European legal system vis-à-vis the national courts and the fact that some of those resolutions represent the canon of the European legal developments both institutional levels (European versus national) indeed never came to blows. The point was that, at the end of the day, there was not a very profound disagreement, and existential question, separating the conceptions of human rights, rule of law, and democracy between domestic and supranational courts.

But the legal and political conflict between European institutions and the member states escalated not only regarding the allocation of resources in a context of economic crisis (as might be considered that it happened in the clash between the CJEU and the German Federal Constitutional Court) but also in the case of the deviation of some member state from the standards on human rights protection and the democratic European consensus in order to protect their respective national interests, a path that was taken not only by Poland, Hungary, or Romania but also by Spain, though in the latter circumstance, which was more serious, the outright conflict between that member state and the European Union did not explode since the European institutions, aware of the danger that the fragmentation of Spain might pose to the core of the European integration project, turned a blind eye toward the human rights violations perpetrated by Spanish authorities against Catalan pro-independence politicians and activists.

At any rate, European national courts tested a way to dodge the member states' obligations toward the European Union through the doctrine of respect for the national identity that in fact was already coined in the European Constituent Treaties (article 4.2, Treaty on European Union [TEU]). While more or less abstractly announced and developed such doctrine from the times of the failed Treaty Establishing a Constitution for Europe (as, for instance, the Spanish Constitutional Court[16] or the French Constitutional Council[17] did) and the conclusion of the Lisbon Treaty (with the more elaborated jurisprudence on the issue developed by the German Federal Constitutional Court)[18] several constitutional jurisdictions applied in the 2010s and the 2020s the national identity clause to set aside the application of EU law in specific cases, beginning with the German Federal Constitutional Court in order to contain the European Central Bank quantitative easing programs or several courts in Eastern Europe (such as the Czech, the Polish, or the Hungarian ones) in order to reassert their path to their conversion, particularly both in the Hungarian and Polish cases, into illiberal democracies.

XII

In October 2021 the Polish Constitutional Court outrightly overruled the European Law primacy doctrine arguing that in the adoption of measures devoted to ensure Polish judicial independence, the European Union authorities have acted beyond the scope of the competences conferred upon them by the Republic of Poland in the Treaties.[19]

The Polish Constitutional Court, thus, reasserted the supremacy of the Polish Constitution upon the European treaties and declared its ability to nullify the European Union rules that violate the core of the Polish

Constitutional system. Though such a decision generated a scandal across the European institutions, the truth was that the power to review the European Law provisions represented the logical consequence of the German Federal Constitutional Court jurisprudence outlined in the *Lisbon* case and reiterated in the *Monetary Transactions programs* cases that we mentioned in the previous chapters.[20] On those occasions, however, the European actors reacted in a more moderated form than when sovereigntist reassertions came from the eastern European constitutional courts.

Maybe the German Constitutional Court pronouncements were not as extreme as the ones dictated by some eastern European constitutional courts such as the Polish one but indeed years of anti-European legal rhetoric in Germany created a fertile ground for secessionist juridical decisions in Poland, Hungary, Spain, Italy, or elsewhere.[21] Different to experiences in France, the Netherlands, or Ireland in which the contestation to the European Union legal order had been expressed through rejecting constitutive treaties in referenda, the German path to questioning integration (given the fact that the Weimar collapse advised not to include national popular referenda within the constitutional system designed by the 1949 Basic Law) was led by the German Federal Constitutional Court.[22] That was a strategy that other European courts imitated.

Until the Brexit experience it was believed that if a member state was not committed to applying European Union law, they would have to leave the union (as certainly the United Kingdom did without having previously raised any existential challenge able to clash with the European Union normative architecture). But the attitude revealed from different national instances supported by the national identity idea refers to a subtler maneuver than that expressed by a secessionist procedure, namely, a *way to remain in the European Union without respecting the European Union law*, particularly the most basic ones related to the defense of democracy, the rule of law, or human rights. In other words, the "constitutional identity" device allows member states to enjoy from the benefits (such as the recovery funds in case of crisis) without paying the cost of meeting some basic obligations.

The only way to stop such a trend would probably be that the European Union institutions applied more firmly the procedure to suspend a member state from their voting rights in the European Union institutions in case of breaching the basic values entailed in article 2 TEU (a procedure provided by article 7 TEU). But, at the moment, the European Union institutions have been reluctant to begin an open fight against one or more of its members by pressing the "nuclear button" that article 7 TEU represents to defend the supposed European Union values. The European institutions have not even gone all the way in the application of article 7 TEU in the case of a clear authoritarian drift as the one experienced in Hungary and, consequently, they are not likely to take this option in other pressing circumstances, being still less imaginable that they would have the courage to challenge large states such as Spain or Italy for not respecting human rights or democratic principles.

Taking again the background of the United States political developments, it might not be superfluous to remember that also in that scenario when the federation sought to impose the federal law upon issues regarding to which some states authorities thought that they had exclusive powers to regulate (such as the slavery) a civil war was needed to clarify who held the legal supremacy. The discussions that nowadays confront the European courts against the national constitutional courts have some analogies with those that concerned the federation and the American states before the Civil War, such as the scope of application of the Federal Bill of Rights. Only after the Civil War, and with the Southern States occupied, it began to be accepted that the civil liberties recognized at the federal level had to be imposed upon the states' authorities.[23]

XIII

The global and authoritarian superpowers would be eager to see the collapse of both European democratic values and some of the western European nation-states, even if their leaders declare explicitly, as Putin did in the Spring 2019, that they are not interested in the wreck of any of the European members (in an evidence that sometimes the statements provided by some sly politicians have to be interpreted with the exact opposite of their literal meaning).

But also *some* European member states, particularly if they would follow a strategy grounded on maximizing their national interests, would be pleased to see an erosion of democracy within their European rivals. In fact, this is what already happened regarding the German authorities' attitude toward the authoritarian turn affecting some eastern European members: they did nothing beyond some rhetorical laments.

Some agents within the European Union's political system soon realized that the old principle according to which the thriving of the union was equivalent to the thriving of its nation-states had been transformed into the opposite principle, namely, that the maximization of the nation-state's interest is only possible through the waning of the surrounding nation-states. Such was the logic that led the old European empires to fight amongst themselves during the struggle for imperial dominion in World War I, and it was able to pose a decisive threat in the aim of retaining some influence vis-à-vis the other superpowers in the globalized world.

The European Union was, in sum, the last expression of the former decadent empires whose only chance to survive as nations required being attached to a framework of power created in common. But in the geopolitical circumstances of the 2010s and 2020s, some national rulers as well as growing citizenry majorities punished by the decline in their standards of living as a consequence of integration and monetary union believed that the only way to maintain the nation-states would require the destruction of the European Union values proclaimed in article 2 of the Treaty on European Union: human rights, democracy, and the single market.

We have seen several examples of that: for Spain the only way to crush the Catalan democratic separatism relied on crushing democracy and human rights in Catalonia; in Italy the only way to contain the immigration from northern Africa and from the Middle East (or, basically, the only way to use the immigration to create a second-class category of citizens deprived of human rights) relied on the sacrifice of the values of the Union, human dignity among them; and, finally, in Great Britain, the only way envisaged by the British nationalists to resuscitate the old empire relied on the straightforward separation from the union and the disintegration of the single market.

Notice that the crises indicated on relating the fate of the European Union with the fate of the nation-states affect the *existing* nation-states, but not the concept of nation-states *per se*, nor the idea of the European nation-states either. Certainly, the secessionist challenges in Spain or in the United Kingdom did not question the reality of the nation-state but confirmed its triumph in a form of smaller and more homogeneous national communities transformed in sovereign entities. The eventual dissolution of Spain or that of the United Kingdom, revealing the emergence of a multiplicity of new nation-states, would rather show the definitive crises of the old empires of western Europe,[24] precisely the ones that, according to the thesis in these pages, joined the European process with the aim of stopping the disintegration that had commenced overseas.

XIV

The creation of the European Communities and the further constitutional developments concerning such particular legal order nourished by the transfers of sovereignty consented by the nation-states reflected, after all, the same operation that has characterized any constituent movement: the entrenchment of a given allocation of powers through its translation into law.[25] It is in that way that might be more clearly appreciated the preeminence of the "rule of law" as the systemic source of legitimacy in the European integration process from its outset, since it did not question the structure of power displayed within each of the members (at the same time that it strengthened the bonds between the elites of the different states by given them a common framework to provide economic growth and stability).[26]

The "rule of law" would be in this fashion a tantamount of a safeguard devoted to protect the diverse national orders within a common framework occupied by the elites of those orders. As soon as the European institutions pretended to hold a more invasive notion of the "rule of law," colored by a substantial view of that principle attached to fundamental rights, problems emerged.

Indeed, fundamental rights as well as democracy had been for a long time absent from the European foundations, and even when they were recognized from the 1970s, they would play a secondary role partially because their expansion to a European level would undermine the existing distribution of power within the states. Democracy was mainly exercised within the framework of the nation-states because it was not possible to be fully translated to something that *was not a nation*. Democracy was, at the same time, a barrier to integration and a safeguard to preserve the member states. When for instance, the German Constitutional Court stated that some European institution, such as the European Central Bank, had acted outside the scope of its competences the court was in reality considering that something had been decided without the consent of the German people. According to the German Court, thus, there were basic decisions on power (called the "sovereignty of the German people") that could not be transferred to any supranational instance.

If, in our perspective, European integration embodied from its origins the aim *of preserving the existing situations of political, economic, and social domination within each state*, there would not be a transfer of democracy to a superior level able to threaten such allocation of wealth and power decided within the nation-state. That explained also why when such reallocation was intended through the creation of the single currency and the consolidation of the single market the nationalistic backlash under a supposed democratic expression was not long in coming.

The integration, the transfer of powers mainly in the economic field and even some checks to the development of those mainly economic competences, were tolerated as long as they did not endanger the basic power structures of the nation-states. The emergence of a supranational power was established in the heart of the Cold War through weak democratic foundations given the desperate circumstances that characterized the European elites that sought legitimacy through economic growth after the devastation of the war, the rise of Communism in eastern Europe, and the loss of the empires. Once that legitimacy grounded on prosperity vanished (which beyond the slump in the 1970s was after 2008 most poignantly revealed) and the principles that had been invoked to restrain the supranational performance such as "the rule of law" or " protection of human rights" might be applied *against* the nation-states the incentives at the domestic level to continue in the union became lower and lower. At any point the same question that arose in Britain in the 2010s would emerge in some other part of the continent: why continue being together?

War in Ukraine and the threat that Russia posed somehow concealed momentarily such a question, but the mere defense before the possibility of an aggression was not a project of future and, still less, a project of a future in common.

XV

The political crisis of the European Union would be, thus, the last evidence of the collapse of the empires that had composed it. If France, the United Kingdom, or Spain were the "Masters" of the treaties, exercising their prerogatives for the sake of their national benefits, the doubts on their continuity as "Masters" forced to rethink both the sense and the objectives of the common organization that they shared. The latter leads to another significant point: the existential crisis of the European Union is related to the lack of common objectives among its members, but that happens mainly because the European nation-states, at least the most powerful of them, *also lack a national project for themselves*.

While small non-state nations such as Catalonia and Scotland have at least a clear collective endeavor, to become sovereign states, Germany, for instance, was during the 2010s on the verge of consolidating not only its economic but also its political hegemony without knowing for what it was going to use its power and its enormous influence both in Europe and in the world. A nation that only hopes to remain in the same stage of tranquility as long as possible may easily follow the path of the decay as, indeed, happened in the German case. The lack of collective ambitions threw a nation into a secondary role at the mercy of others' decisions, essentially at the mercy of those, like Putin's Russia, that reshaped their political ambitions by regaining clear territorial expansive goals. While the German authorities after 1990 wanted nothing to do with recovering the territories they had lost in their defeat in 1945, Putin's regime placed at the center of its political agenda restoring direct rule or at least influence over some of those territories that had fallen out from under Russian control by the time of the Soviet Union's dissolution.

Germany's resignation on avoiding its transformation as a superpower after its success on taming the European economic crises of the 2010s also made Germany's export strength dependent on the vicissitudes of the trade war between China and the United States. While the United Kingdom sought to cut its ties with the European Union given an excess of imperial nostalgia (and with their pro-Brexit political elites believing that they would be able to reconstruct their empire by resurrecting the links with the Commonwealth of Nations and the former British Dominions), Germany got into a political depression given their elite's reluctance to be involved in an explicit imperial logic.

Something even more disturbing may be suggested about France, which case was not only a matter of not having collective ambitions to reproduce imperial grandeur (and to cope with the fact of being humiliated every time in which a French president invokes an imperial rhetoric and he is accompanied by a bewildering lack of means that makes the loss of French influence in the world more evident) but a matter of passing the years with the only hope of avoiding economic and social default and complete political irrelevance. Different phenomena, among which the marginalization and alienation of various strata of the population (and in particular the descendants of immigrants from the former French colonies) appeared as the most serious, reaffirming the difficulties to preserve the cultural and social cohesion required to ensure the French national continuity within the European borders. The reemergence of the cultural and linguistic claims by the minority nations, including the Corsican claim for statehood, supposed an additional line of pressure able to stress France's national system.

Common ideals of other western European minor powers were not less disappointing. In Italy it was likely to be settled by criminalizing immigration or, one might say, by creating an unfair society to provide welfare for the Italians at the expense of the newcomers in order to conceal the economic bombs that in the form of public debt or toxic banking systems might explode at any time.

The situation was even worse in Spain in which the defense of the national unity regarding the Catalan secessionism by the Spanish central authorities was placed above human rights and the democratic principle while the European Union institutions, for instance, left millions of citizens without representation in the European Parliament, as happened between May and December 2019 when the parliament's presidency refused to recognize the condition as parliamentarians of some Catalan leaders that had been elected that year because, since they were in prison or in exile, they could not fulfill the requirements established by the Spanish electoral regulations. The question of the representation of Catalan pro-independence politicians in the European Parliament (together with the attempts of the Spanish judicial authorities to remove the immunity from those who had managed to access the status of MEPs) would open a long sequence of cases before the Court of Justice of the European Union that would last through the decade of the 2020s.

At any rate, as we explained, the European integration project was conceived to strengthen the nation-states, but also was designed to consolidate a community of values grounded in democracy, the rule of law, and human rights in order to avoid any other disgrace similar to the confrontations experienced in the two world wars of the twentieth century. However, when the economic crisis from 2008 began to put pressure on the system, the political consequences of such disruption developed in the second half of the 2010s made clear that the movements toward the protection of the nation-state would even trump the common values of democracy, rule of law, and human rights and that with the horse of the nationalistic option bolting again on the European field every actor, both the nation-states and the union, would face the risk of losing it all.

The contradiction between asserting the values of democracy and fundamental rights while at the same time showing a contempt for them in practice (at least in three precise practices that might be grouped in the disdain against national minorities, in the agreements with non-democratic global powers or in the hostility against some fluxes of extra-European immigration) had another delegitimizing effect in defining the European Union position in the world.

At least, one possibility of renewed imperial aspirations might have centered on the universal character of human rights (in a similar fashion as the first conquistadores in America sought legitimacy in their actions through giving the peoples that they were discovering the opportunity to know the truth of the Christian message). Europe might have in this way wrapped any expansionist enterprise through the messianic excuse of bringing universal liberties to everyone (now including with special emphasis relatively new Western moralities regarding gender equality or protection for LGTBI groups) but such a political reassertion grounded on the defense of liberty or democracy was hardly credible to address while at home, both at the nation-state and at the European Union levels, such principles were tarnished with hurtful deficits.

XVI

The fate of the European Union, as was inferred from the political debates in Italy or in the United Kingdom regarding immigration, opened another question of global transcendence.

The integration process had promoted an economic development that entrenched a progressive inequality between the Europeans and the rest of the world including some of the societies in Africa, Asia, and America that once belonged to some of the European empires. The European Union had thus allowed the Europeans to maintain and to increase their wealth even though they had witnessed the evaporation of their empires.

But the nationalistic turn experienced within some European member states fostered inequalities among the European societies themselves and debilitated all the European states before any assault, pacific or not, organized from an extra-European power aimed at extracting European wealth to cover the social needs of their own societies.

One of the main theses of these writings has been that both, the European State-Nations and the European Union as an organization, relinquished to extend their political power to non-European territories as had been constant in the "Age of the Empire."[27] But, in the lack of possibilities to maintain predation outside the European continent the European system of powers was likely to opt to display their predatory appetites *inward* under the form that I have qualified as "internal colonization."

"Internal colonization" means besieging minority nations dissidence within the nation-states borders, subjecting non-European immigration almost to conditions of serfdom, and promoting the concentration of wealth—if not directly kleptocratic policies—in the hands of few oligarchs of every nation-state as a result of the combination between neo-liberal economic policy and authoritarian regression.

The design of the single currency to consolidate the single market was an artifact to neutralize the popular demands of generalized welfare fostered by democratic policies that had produced debt and inflation. But the decision to impose the monetary union "whatever it takes," as Mario Draghi stated, caused the precariousness and the alienation of large sectors of the population and, at the end of the day, the corrosion of the channels through which such discontentment might be democratically expressed.

The European Communities were born to ensure welfare for their populations after the European empires but the disputes among the European states in their fight to guarantee the welfare only of some of their inhabitants at the expenses of other Europeans and migrant workers prepared the ground for the definitive dismemberment of the union in the hands of renewed global empires.

XVII

Western European powers might have renounced imperialism, but (leaving aside the fact that some of the European Union members have not renounced imperial visions *within their borders*) some of the eastern European neighbors have not taken the same restrained path.

As eloquently demonstrated Vladimir Putin's regime by encircling Ukraine with the most impressive troop movement in Europe since the end of Cold War (and finally by invading Ukraine in February 2022), not everybody was willing to abandon their nationalistic dreams, even at the risk of pushing the world toward the abyss of a nuclear conflict.

The Russian president perceived the weakness of the European rulers entangled in their disputes and desperately concerned in ensuring social comfort. Under such circumstances Putin launched his gamble in order to restore some of the Russian grandeur that had vanished by end of the Soviet Union.

Against the expectative of the European nations, nevertheless, being calm, having social peace,and maintaining a thriving economy cannot last in the struggle for power that characterizes geopolitical challenges. The German federal government spearheaded by Olaf Scholz found itself cutting channels of economic exchange with Russia, or at least it simulated to renounce to those sources of energy regarding to which German capital had made great investments.

By the beginning of the conflict in Ukraine, and in unprecedented decision that represented a radical turning point in German policy toward Russia, the German government decided to send weapons and ammunition to Ukraine and fostered a rearmament program by increasing defense spending above 2 percent of the German GDP and setting up a 100 billion euros *Bundeswehr* fund.[28] With such movements Scholz reasserted Germany's alignment with the Western Allies though the countries' core interests, including the purpose to entrench Germany's position as an economic hegemon, were endangered.

As most of the European countries, whether in the European Union or not, as was the case of Switzerland, the German Federal Republic understood that Putin's aggression over Ukraine represented an existential threat not only for the supranational organization but also for the survival of the nation-states that integrated it. That was also understood, at least during the first week of the Ukrainian war, by those governments of such states which, though belonging to the union, remained neutral in military terms and had not joined the North Atlantic Treaty Organization (NATO) during the Cold War; that was expressed by the attitude of the Swedish and the Finnish governments both pondering and imminent application to the mentioned defense structure once Putin's regime also included them as potential victims of its attacks.

Prosperity and wealth derived from economic growth meant nothing for the European nations if their territories were menaced by a foreign full-scale invasion. The latter observation perceives that the evolution of human interactions, even in one of the most prosperous and technologically developed areas in the world as Europe, is still fully dependent on the territorial factor and its physical control by an authority basically grounded on coercion. We have seen along these pages to which extent other possibilities outlined to define political subjects beyond the force of the arms, such as the developments around the idea on the right of peoples' self-determination and its legal translation, tend to collapse before raw violence.

XVIII

War in Ukraine was only one episode of a long story of failures in trying to underpin the states' political authority on the democratic variable that the peoples' free decision might represent.

It was the Russian military support and not the referendum held in 2014 in Crimea that ensured the annexation of that territory from Ukraine to the Russian Federation. Likewise, in 2022 the Russian military intervention and a high intensity conflict were preferred over negotiation and the respect toward the democratic will of the people in the Donbass in order to overcome the political differences existing in that area. The intention to promote constitutional arrangements in Ukraine by recognizing some self-government structure in certain areas of the Donetsk and Luhansk regions (as was stipulated in the 2015 Minsk Agreement)[29] was never implemented. Instead, the conflict in eastern Ukraine persisted in a more or less dormant manner until it was reignited with the Russian recognition of the Donetsk and Luhansk republics at the start of the open war between Russia and Ukraine. Again, tanks and artillery trumped upon peoples' freedom to decide on their political status since tanks and artillery, at the end of the day, defined *the framework* in which any democratic decision might be adopted.

As we saw, the redrawing of the border by invoking the right to self-determination also emerged in that area once dominated by the Tsarist Empire during World War I. It is likely to accompany any recognition of sovereign entities in the twenty first-century Ukraine only *after* the avatar of arms decides the dispute in one sense or another. Somehow that was what the Russian government tried to do when the Ukrainian army threatened to regain some territories in an offensive in fall 2022: fostering referenda in those provinces in dispute to be annexed to Russia in order to confer legitimacy to a previous invasion. First comes the carnage and then the vote in the midst of the ruins.

XIX

War and violence would decide, as well the future of the European Union and that of the nation-states that compose it. In the similar way by which the European Communities were founded (and the former enemies of World

War II were forced to reach an agreement) before the shadow of the Soviet Union, Russian's challenge in 2022, and the horizon of global confrontation was likely to avoid, at least temporarily, the fragmentation trends that have been crossing the Union since the 2008 economic crisis and that had Brexit as their peak.

All such a range of controversies appeared minute in comparison with the total annihilation that may come about as the result of a military clash. Suddenly, the union's most wayward members such as Poland or Hungary closed lines with the other partners in deciding severe sanctions against Putin's regime despite the fact that Orbán had become one of the most condescending figures toward the Russian president and that part of the Hungarian imperial dreams were inspired by expanding Budapest's influence upon the Magyar minority within Ukraine. Orbán's equilibrium between aligning with the European Union while at the same time maintaining terms with Putin gave outstanding results for the Hungarian prime minister: the April 2022 legislative elections were a sweeping victory for his party, the Hungarian Civic Alliance, though the entire opposition, including the far right Jobbik party, had run together against Orbán.

But neither the Hungarian government's ambiguities in foreign policy nor Polish or Romanian incompliances with the rule of law mattered much when the Russian columns advanced toward the Ukrainian cities in a scenario that some eastern European governments read as the prelude of an advance toward their own capitals.

Poland began feverishly helping its Ukrainian neighbor. Historic resentments concerning the former Polish dominion upon some parts of Ukraine, which had caused several massacres between Poles and Ukrainians by the border displacements resulting from World War II,[30] were conveniently forgotten in the same fashion that happened with more recent grievances that confronted Polish authorities with the European Union institutions. War in Ukraine rapidly erased the suggestion made by Polish authorities only a couple of weeks before Russian armored unities struggled to encircle Kiev according to which Poland would respond with withdrawal from the European Union, in response to the decision on blocking the funds for the post-COVID era given the Polish encroachments against European Law.

All those quarrels seemed to belong to another past political life compared with the Ukrainian emergency. The reluctance which Poland and other eastern European States showed in hosting the refugees that came from Syria in 2015 after Russian aircrafts dropped bombs on the cities of that Middle East country turned into enthusiasm in welcoming the hundreds of thousands of Ukrainian citizens that were fleeing from the war and the occupation.

However, promises of direct military aid to Zelensky's government made by Poland, Bulgaria, Romania, or Slovakia soon faded away when the NATO

Allies realized that the involvement of the mentioned countries in order to stop the Russian invasion on Ukraine might lead to a total war with a certain risk of triggering nuclear exchanges. The latter was admitted by the NATO secretary general, Jens Stoltenberg, in the press conference following a meeting of NATO foreign ministers on March 4, 2022, when he announced that the military organization had refused the reiterated Ukrainian demands of establishing a no-fly zone over the country in order to avoid Russian bombing on the Ukrainian besieged cities and other strategic facilities.[31] Though pledging "the courage of the Ukrainian people and their armed forces," the truth was that the NATO members did their best to avoid a direct clash between one of its members' units and the Russian ones in Ukrainian space.

Also the measures adopted in the first week of the conflict with the intention to undermine Russian's economy were contained, or even not implemented at all, as long as the conflict advanced. The Russian gas supply to western Europe continued to flow and Germany rejected the proposed European embargo on Russian oil imports by arguing, as Chancellor Scholz did, that the pressure on Moscow had to be "sustainable" in order not to impose "a too heavy burden on Germans."[32] In the decisive moment, Europe, and particularly Germany, could not afford a disconnection of Russian energy supply overnight. Consequently, payments were still transferred to Russia in order to cover such imports and Western purchases were still financing Putin's regime military struggle.

In spite of the extreme difficulties that the Russian army had to entrench its control upon the Ukrainian territories that it occupied (disregarding the truly military aims that the Russian operation had which no one was likely to know with exactitude) the scarce European capacity to suffer, even at the economic level, was conveniently exploited in Moscow. The High Representative of the Union for Foreign Affairs and Security Policy, Josep Borrell, admitted more than one month after the war started that in that time the European Union spent thirty-five billion euros on Russian energy while only one billion euros were transferred to Ukraine as humanitarian aid.[33] By April 2022 the European Union's consumption of Russian raw material was still scandalous despite the supposed sanctions that were awkwardly implemented to the extent, for instance, that Ukrainian's President Zelensky refused to meet with the German president Frank-Walter Steinmeier arguing that Germany was still purchasing Russian gas through the Nord Stream pipelines and that the former German Social Democratic chancellor, Gerhard Schröder, was still holding a management position in Gazprom.[34] The European economic detachment from Russia was an arduous task to achieve precisely because the ties established since the times of the Soviet Union had been strong.

Globalization was likely to evaporate territoriality and territorial disputes, but the Russo-Ukrainian conflict made it clear not only that economic exchanges relied on a previous territorial design but also that economic sanctions were hardly ineffective in retaliation against an invasion. The intertwined character of the economic relations that the globalization provided meant that economic consequences would affect both the one that was sought to be punished and also the ones that dictated the sanctions. The damage against the target might be huge, and in fact Russian actors, included private Russian fortunes settled in the West, suffered some of the biggest limitations ever, but the shock wave toward those that approved the measures were also harsh unless, as Germany tried to do during the first weeks of the confrontation, they were breached by the back door.

XX

The war between Russia and Ukraine called for the reconfiguration of the world order that had emerged from World War II. It probably did it because the end of the Cold War and the disintegration of the Soviet Union occurred in a relatively smooth way. With the perspective of the years, it is hard to believe the predisposition that, for instance, led Russian's new authorities to allow the maintenance of the Crimea Peninsula within Ukrainian borders or the Ukrainian acquiescence in transferring to Russia the remains of the Soviet nuclear arsenal that might have fallen into Ukrainian's hands with the country's independence.

Russia went through the decade following the Soviet Union's collapse besieged by economic and political default. It saw also how the Western organizations such as the European Union or NATO laid the ground for their expansion by absorbing eastern European members that once belonged to the Soviet influence area or even had been a Soviet Republic themselves. But Russia also retained some trumps that allowed it to preserve a relevant geopolitical status: its territory contained enormous energy reserves of gas and oil (regarding to which Europe became more and more dependent), and it had a powerful army vested with nuclear weapons and a privileged position at the global diplomatic level.

One evidence of the latter point was represented by Russia's recognition as the Soviet Union's successor in several international fora, including the permanent member condition of the United Nations' Security Council and the correspondent holding of the veto power in that body, which was devised as the inheritance of the Soviet Union's victory in World War II. Even with the Russian crises in the 1990s, that political entity still was remembered and respected as the crucial actor that defined the global power relations, playing an important role in the process of economic liberalization that followed the abandonment of the Socialist credo. In that regard Russia was admitted to the

World Trade Organization, the International Monetary Fund, and to the wide range of international structures that defined the global capitalist architecture.

Ukraine's invasion was a shock to all that system. Russia's veto power in the United Nations' Security Council blocked any backlash against a military performance that was clearly in contravention of the core principles of the organization coined in the charter. It was true that after the Cold War Russia had already offered examples of an aggression against a sovereign state with the intention to preserve its circle of domination, which was already shown in the war between Russian and Georgia in 2008. But such a conflict did not have the length, the destructiveness, and the capacity to threaten the world's economy and the balance of power as the war in Ukraine did regarding to which, despite the overwhelming majority of opposition in the United States General Assembly against the Russian aggression, such an organization remained impotent to restore peace.

Economic sanctions against Putin's regime were adopted by more than forty states and several organizations. However, they had to be compatible with avoiding a total economic crash resulting from damage to the global free market economy. That explained partially the difficulty of their implementation. Russian's marginalization of the international economic system (beginning with the possibility of being expelled from the World Trade Organization) would anticipate the path toward the scenario that had already been experienced in the Cold War according to which economic systems were organized separately in a way that they were more dependent on political power.

Breaking economic ties with Europe pushed Russia to strengthen its relationship with China, fostering the creation of a Eurasian bloc able to compete, and eventually to prevail, upon Western liberal democracies. As we saw, Germany, the first European Union power, already had designed a project to be aligned in such a bloc by cultivating all sorts of economic agreements with both Russia and China. But what was outside the mind of the German planners, and that the Ukrainian war's cruelty revealed, was the impossibility to maintain liberal democratic structures dependent on geopolitical giants that are not democratic.

XXI

Another organization stressed, if not ruined, as a consequence of an open full-scale military conflict in the heart of Europe was, of course, the Council of Europe and the system of human rights protection designed by the European Convention of Human Rights and the jurisprudence of the European Court of Human Rights. The inefficiency of that device was already envisaged with the alluded war in Georgia in 2008, which in fact confronted two member states of the Convention (Russia and Georgia); but the consequence regarding human rights in only twelve days of military operations with around two hundred causalities was hardly comparable with the conflict in Ukraine producing more than such number of victims *per day*, the complete annihilation of entire cities, the displacement of millions of people, and the damage of industrial facilities and sources of energy and commodities with direct impact upon the most dynamic economic areas of the planet.

The 2022 war was not even comparable either with former experiences of massive human rights violations in the context of high intensity clashes developed in European territory during the 1960s or the 1970s in places such as Cyprus, Northern Ireland, or the military coup d'états launched in Greece or in Turkey (in some of those episodes the state responsible for human rights violations was at least suspended or expelled from the convention). The situation in Ukraine was even worse than in the mentioned scenarios essentially because, with exception of the former Yugoslavia, which did not belong to the convention, Putin's aggression represented the first war of extermination in Europe since 1945 precisely encompassing the degree of destruction and war crimes able to transform the structures, such as the Council of Europe and the European Convention of Human Rights, that emerged from that time in order to prevent the reproduction of another havoc of that dimension.

Not surprisingly, on March 10, 2022, the Russian government announced that the Russian Federation would withdraw from both the Council of Europe and the European Convention of Human Rights with the aim of not assuming any responsibility for the deeds perpetrated in Ukraine.

A new war in Europe demonstrated that neither the global economy structures nor the law, and particularly human rights law, were sufficient to chain the will to power. Putin's regime maybe was not in the position to translate its thirst of domination into political and military world hegemony, but it showed that it is enough with the performance of a national structure grounded on relatively strong structures of coercion to corrode, at least momentarily, the basic pillars of a given economic and legal order. Some of those principles in organizing societies by the beginning of the twenty-first centuries that might have been taken for granted (from those mentioned human rights to the free movement of capital) might be wiped out by any flaw in the security system. The sequence that had been implicit during decades suddenly became explicit: first comes the defense of a given political order by violence and then comes the legitimacy of that order through the welfare provided by economic growth and the safeguards of liberty's spheres designed by normative mechanisms.

XXII

The European challenge, in sum, relies on the ability of Europe's political structures to maintain the sources of social stability (welfare, democracy, political freedom). This book has described the main threats focusing on the internal divisions that cross the continent, which are somehow rooted in the developments of the nation-states experienced after World War II.

Some of those weaknesses came from the incompatibility of building a supranational political entity while at the same time struggling for the consolidation of national interests still attached to exercising the monopoly of violence upon a given territory and a given population. No wonder that such a monopoly of the physical force still defines, according to the German Federal Constitutional Court, the core of a state's constitutional identity not able to be transferred to the European Union without a major constitutional transformation.[35] Even the frame of the European liberal democracies of the twenty-first century relies on the coercive devices conceived in the times of imperialist expansion. The first thing that war in Ukraine demonstrated was, as suggested, that territory still mattered. After all, in Europe, at least in eastern Europe, people were still willing to die for a piece of land.

Disintegrating forces began to operate with predictably irreversible effects by the 2008 economic crisis, which began to severely hit the European project with the Greek debacle and the subsequent 2012 sovereign bond crises. The economic crush fostered nationalistic demands and oppositions (beginning by those expressed in the German discourse that masqueraded in economic terms what was a political project of domination). The second half of the 2010s saw Brexit, Catalan secessionist aspirations, the growth of anti-immigration discourse, and the authoritarian turn and defiant attitude against the European rule of law mainly manifested by the Polish and Hungarian governments but also expressed by the growth of the far-right and populist movements everywhere in Europe, acceding to government in Italy in fall 2022 under Giorgia Meloni.

Nevertheless, by the beginning of the 2020s, the external threats proved to be still more dangerous for the European supranational experiment than its internal wrangling. Though some European powers, again spearheaded by Germany, sought to ensure their economic welfare and their stability by forging alliances and promoting economic exchanges with authoritarian Eurasian regimes (mainly with the People's Republic of China and the Russian Federation), Russian hubris by causing a catastrophe in Ukraine changed all the geopolitical parameters.

XXIII

At the end of the twentieth century, Alberto Alesina, Enrico Spolaore, and Romain Wacziarg wrote a very celebrated article in which the authors argued that trade openness led to political "disintegration,"[36] but, in fact, the history of the European Union showed that in the world's most trade-opened area internal borders have been preserved with stability for decades.

Brexit would represent, of course, the only clear exception. But the relationship between the United Kingdom and the European integration presented some relevant differences in regard to what the European Union represented to the other members. The United Kingdom was the only one (maybe together with Sweden) that joined the European Union under almost entirely voluntary parameters. The others sought to accede to the European promise after a military defeat in World War II, after the internal devastation as a consequence of the Third Reich expansion in that war, after the mentioned colonial disasters, because of the need to overcome an authoritarian regime from the right (Spain, Portugal, and Greece) or from the left while preventing potential invasions triggered by a powerful neighbor (as happened regarding most eastern European countries). If the British government's attitudes were the closest to be not forced regarding the belonging to the European Union, they were also the closest to be free to withdraw. Moreover, the "political disintegration" caused by economic freedom in the case of Great Britain (that may suit with Alesina, Spolaore, and Wacziarg's idea) was rather represented by the major trade openness of that area with the global system defined by special and direct links with big economic areas, the architecture formed by the World Trade Organization, the International Monetary Fund, and the World Bank, and the United Kingdom's privileged free trade position regarding its former dominions and colonies. In short, Brexit as a "political disintegration" derived from economic openness toward the European Union was associated with the trade ties displayed within a wider sphere.

When Alesina and his colleagues developed their hypothesis pointing out the process of the Soviet Union dismemberment and the changes in the eastern European Communist satellites, they rather described the political fragmentation *in the transit* between Socialist and authoritarian regimes to liberalism and democracy. The political disintegration was not, thus, a consequence of a consolidated free trade system but as the *expectation toward* the liberalization and the integration of the markets. And such disintegration spun around claims on territorial sovereignty usually expressed in the most brutal terms (as in the former Yugoslavia).

The point here is that the frame of the economic integration that indeed provides political stability requires *the previous territorial definition* through unities emerged from ominous conflicts that retain a wide margin of political decision (as the European Union member states). The conflict between Russia and Ukraine precisely exploded before the Ukrainian expectation to join a closer space of economic integration represented by the European Union against the will of the agent, Russia, that represented the previous regional hegemon.

Ukrainian's struggle to find political stability provided by an economically integrated space, the European Union, was not liberated from the "political disintegration" and the bloodbath that tends to accompany the determination of the political unities that are called to participate in another economic integration process. The "political disintegration" would not, in conclusion, derive from the economic integration but rather from a *change* concerning the areas of geopolitical influence.

XXIV

One of the main theses of this book was that the European integration that began with the European Communities represented the last struggle to save for the European Nations the remnants of the benefits obtained with imperialism. The antecedent of the globalization developed by western European empires until World War I was not a true globalization grounded on free trade and economic competition but the creation of areas of commercial exchange that directly derived from European military occupation, colonization, and exploitation. Europeans invented liberalism and the free-market economy and were prone to defend their principles *as long as they benefited from them through the resorts of domination that they had displayed overseas*.

When the colonial building began to crack, the European position toward free trade began to totter. In fact, we have seen to what extent the emergence of the European Communities sought to shield the declining western European metropolis from the world capitalist system designed in Bretton Woods. The European Communities, first, and the European Union, after, had been always *an exception* within the GATT system (and the subsequent World Trade Organization system) and that explained why the hardliner ordo-liberals indeed abhorred the European integration project.

But the tiny European nations, suddenly almost confined to their European territories, after the loss of both their colonies and the direct apparatus of coercion upon their former dominions could only economically thrive by exploiting such exceptionalism within a free trade biased version, a movement that always required the consent of the United States.

On the other hand, during the decades following decolonization, the former metropoles got rid of the burden of the costs associated to direct ruling and enforcement, but they still retained a privileged position in the process of extraction of raw materials and the commercialization thereof, let alone the circumstance that the cultural influence of the former empire was still very present in the new independent entities. Mineral and oil companies operating in the former colonies were still mostly based in London, New York, Paris, or Brussels, trade and migration was mainly directed toward the metropolitan areas, and the majority of the local elites that constituted the political and economic cadres of the emerging sovereign state had been educated in one of the languages of their former masters.

While during the Golden Age of European colonialism capital-exporting nations were devoted to conquering other countries (or to make sure that they would control the economic policy of quasi-colonies in places like China, Egypt, Tunisia, or Venezuela, which had no choice but to protect the property rights of foreigners), the global economic law emerged after the decolonization processes appeared as a subtler structure of imperialist dominance. The pillars of the global economic order, such as the International Monetary Fund, the World Bank, and the World Trade Organization, together with hundreds of bilateral and multilateral trade and investment treaties, maintained the economic preeminence of the West's industrialized powers (which at their turn had grounded their growth on the benefits obtained through colonialist expansion) within the myriad of the formally sovereign nations that resulted once the Europeans withdrew from Asia or Africa.[37] Resource empires disappeared as major actors, but the opportunity for neo-imperial transfers of wealth hardly disappeared, they were transmuted not into some enduring post-imperial commonwealth but into capital assets.[38] The crisis of the Communist bloc in the 1990s opened the horizon of the world's unification under the coordinates of property rights and free circulation of capitals, goods, and people in a process of political liberalization that looked unstoppable.

But at some point, tables began to turn in favor of the peoples that had been colonized. When globalization began to be taken seriously by the non-European nations that had entrenched themselves in their independence, only a couple of years after the extinction of the Soviet Union, Europe was absorbed by a spiral of uncertainties. Economic globalization, on the other hand, was not accompanied in many places by political liberalization, and it was precisely in some of those autocracies, as remarkably in China (in which the path to democracy had been crushed in Tiananmen a few months before the fall of the Berlin Wall) where the economic and technological progress was most impressive.

Such nations that once had been under the yoke of an empire, thus, began to purchase assets of their former masters. Examples of such penetration of the emergent economies in the Western and industrialized economies already flourished by the beginning of the twenty-first century. In 2006, for instance, the Indian company Mittal Steel acquired Luxembourg's most important industrial concern, Arcelor, giving birth to the largest steel conglomerate in the world.[39]

The Qatar sovereign wealth fund had been for decades holding shares in the world's most important stock markets, largest automotive companies, and most prominent financial institutions. Struggling to surmount its energy deficit that was damaging its economy as a consequence of the war in Ukraine, the German Federal Republic agreed by November 2022 to a fifteen-year liquid gas supply deal with Qatar by which the Gulf state would provide to that federation two million tons of liquid gas.[40] Once again it was found that the German authorities were more interested in solving their energy emergency than demanding respect for human rights or maintaining their commitments in the matter of decarbonizing the economy. Qatar, on the other hand, even became one of the top countries in terms of individual property ownership in the United Kingdom, its former metropole. Something similar regarding investments in shares of European technological, financial or energetic companies, as well as investments in real state located in western Europe might be said about the Arab Emirates, Bahrain, or Oman, not to mention the case of Saudi Arabia though the latter, leaving apart the British influence in encouraging the revolt against the Ottoman Empire during World War I, was never formally a western European power's colony or protectorate.

The 2008 crash, which in Europe reached its peak in the sovereign debt crisis by 2012, urged the European system to perform within *a real liberal frame* without the support of an empire. We have here analyzed some of the shocking consequences resulting from such a change in some member states: the authoritarian turn, the rise of the far-right (and the rise, to a lesser extent, of the far-left which in some occasions joined forces with the conservatives in order to fight such a real globalization), the anti-immigration discourses, the nationalistic reassertion, and secessionism both within the member states and from the European Union.

When it was realized that globalization could promote a political and an economic leadership different from that of the West, the demands of protectionism in those former colonial powers increased. The ideal of a completely liberalized and economically integrated world was not going to happen under the aegis of the West, so globalization began to be perceived, even by those nations that had promoted it, with reluctance. In addition to that, and regardless of how cautiously Western liberal capitalist democracies began to view the workings of a runaway free market, the more intense political conflicts unfolded by the beginning of the 2020s favored a bloc dynamic, which still placed the globalization process in a more delicate situation.

XXV

China was no longer the corroded empire occupied in huge parts of its territory by direct European jurisdictions as happened until the beginning of the twentieth century. Already by 1999 the Chinese regime had swallowed the two last remnants of European colonialism: Macao from Portugal (1999) and, one of the most valued financial and trade world's centers, Hong Kong from the United Kingdom (1997).

By the beginning of the twenty-first century, China has been transformed into an economic, political, and military superpower defining the global framework in which the movement of goods and capitals is developed. The above-mentioned investments from India or from some Arabic monarchies in the Persian Gulf on western European assets dwarf in comparison to those supplied by Chinese capital including public debt bonds to the extent that before 2008, the crisis that some analysts envisaged was not that of the sub-primes but that of a sovereign debt crisis in the West (in Europe and in the United States) due to a massive Chinese bond sell-off. By the beginning of the 2020s, Chinese ascendancy, beginning with its leading world position in scientific development, not only threatened the European world but even five hundred years of Western predominance including those contributions to Western hegemony provided by the United States.[41]

China had been during the first decades of the twenty-first century dictating the rules of the economic game to the extent that Europeans had no other option but to abide, as we saw in mentioning the trade and investment agreements that some member states maintain with the Peoples Republic, let alone the comprehensive agreement on that matter that was on the verge to be ratified by the European Union's authorities and its twenty-seven member states if the United States had not pressured to block it.

In the midst of the conflict between Russia and Ukraine to which it may be added the increasing of tension in eastern Asia regarding Chinese plans to seize Taiwan and the consequent formation of a Sino-Russian/ Euro-Asiatic Axis against the West, it is disturbing to think about the European possibilities to display a strategy of reindustrialization, technological development, and energetic independence able to entrench the European position in the world.

The two world wars of the twentieth century represented the climax of a cycle in which the European world imperial powers, after they had occupied and subjected thousands of peoples all over the rest of the continents, decided to descend into hell by attacking each other and setting in motion the same genocidal impulses that they had previously tested in some other parts of the globe. The lack of ambition, leadership, or project exhibited by the European Union members, and most notoriously by Germany, have dragged the European sphere to a situation resembling that in which World War II concluded: a continent that instead of being the area of the metropoles' coexistence is called to be the battleground of confrontation among other global powers. The difference, however, was that during the Cold War a direct clash between the two superpowers within a European scenario was avoided. Instead, the war in Ukraine outlined a darker fate for the former cradle of Western imperialism in which a "European scramble" perpetrated by more vigorous and self-asserting powers is not unthinkable even when some of such powers at first sight do not exhibit an economic, technological, or demographic weight comparable to that of some European states.

After all, exhibiting a stronger aspiration of collective hegemony than that which has been envisaged within the European societies is not very difficult. European national pluralism and a desperate sense of maintaining at any cost the standards of living able to tame European societies have reduced the ability of that region's organizations to compete globally.

One might conclude that the history of western European imperialism ends with the European Union position by the third decade of the twenty-first century. Witnessing the abrupt European decline, even the extinction of the supranational integration saga, one is lead to the conclusion that what is ahead will be written, for good or for ill, by non-European empires.

NOTES

1. Joseph H. H. Weiler, *The Constitution of Europe: "Do the New Clothes Have an Emperor?" and Other Essays on European Integration* (Cambridge: Cambridge University Press), 324–57.

2. See Kristina Spohr, *Post Wall, Post Square: Rebuilding the World after 1989* (London: William Collins, 2019), 8.

3. Perry Anderson, *The New Old World* (London and New York: Verso, 2009), 50–52.

4. For instance, when Merkel answered to the German Constitutional Court ruling of May 5, 2020, regarding the European Central Bank quantitative easy program by stating that "the nation-state on its own has no future" and that "Germany only shall thrive if Europe thrives." See Harold James, "Why Angela Merkel Is Coming to the Rescue in Europe," in *Financial Review*, June 3, 2020. Available at https://www.afr.com/world/europe/why-angela-merkel-is-coming-to-the-rescue-in-europe-20200602-p54yu3.

5. See, Scott Lavery and Davide Schmid, "European Integration and the New Global Disorder," *Journal of Common Market Studies* 59, no. 5 (February 2021): 1322–38.

6.See, for instance, Daniel Keohane, "Macron's European Defense Doctrine," *Strategic Europe*, Carnegie Europe, September 28, 2017. Available at https://carnegieeurope.eu/strategiceurope/73246.

7. Carlo Eduardo Altamura, *European Banks and the Rise of International Finance: The Post-Bretton Woods Era* (London: Routledge, 2017), 88–136.

8. Helen Thompson, *Disorder: Hard Time in 21st Century* (Oxford: Oxford University Press, 2002), 129–54.

9. Jean Monnet, *Memoirs* (London: Collins, 1978), 75.

10. See Bruno Maçães, "Is Vladimir Putin Preparing for War?," *The New Statesman*. November 24, 2021. Available at https://www.newstatesman.com/world/asia/2021/11/is-vladimir-putin-preparing-for-war.

11. Timothy Snyder, *The Road to Unfreedom* (London: Penguin Random House, 2018), 249.

12. See "China Downgrades Diplomatic Ties with Lithuania over Taiwan Row," BBC News, November 22, 2021. Available at https://www.bbc.com/news/world-asia-china-59370521.

13. See Thompson, *Disorder*, 164–66.

14. Pilar Más Rodríguez, "The EU Budget: The New MFF and the Recovery Instrument: Next Generation EU," *The Euro in 2021*, IEAF/ Fundación ICO, 2021, 169–95. Available at https://www.ieaf.es/images/Publicaciones-FEF/Anuarioeuro2021/10_The_EU_budget.pdf.

15. Thompson, *Disorder*, 200.

16. Spanish Constitutional Court Declaration 1/2004, of December 13, 2004.

17. French Constitutional Council Decision no. 2004–505 DC, of November 19, 2004.

18. *Lisbon* Judgment BVerfG 2 BvE 2/08 of June 30, 2009.

19. Polish Constitutional Court Judgement K-3/21 of October 7, 2021.

20. See *Lisbon* Judgment BVerfG 2 BvE 2/08 of June 30, 2009, and, on the German Federal Constitutional Court ruling on the OMT Program European Central Bank, see the *OMT-Programs* Judgment BVerfG 2 BvR 2728, 2729, 2730, 2731/13, 2 BvE 13/13 of June 21, 2016, and the Judgment BVerfG 2 BvR 859, 1651, 2006/15, 2 BvR 980/16 of May 5, 2020, all of them commented above.

21. See Wolfgang Münchau, "Ultra Vires," *Euro Intelligence*, October 10, 2021. Available at https://www.eurointelligence.com/column/ultra-vires.

22. Thompson, *Disorder*, 228.

23. See, for instance, the so-called interposition doctrine elaborated by J. C. Calhoun, who was the U.S. vice president between 1824 and 1828. According to the mentioned doctrine the States act "in their separate and sovereign capacity" and that "the Constitution of the United States is in fact a compact, to which each State is a party, in the character already described; and that the several States or parties, have a right to judge of its infractions, and in cases of a deliberate, palpable, and dangerous exercise of power not delegated, they have the right, in the last resort, to use the language of the *Virginia resolutions*, 'to interpose for arresting the progress of the evil, and for maintaining within their respective limits, the authorities, rights and liberties appertaining to them,'" see Calhoun *Fort Hill Address* speech July 26, 1831 available at https://akhilamar.com/wp-content/uploads/2021/03/Furman-Calhouns-Fort-Hill-Address-1831.pdf.

24. Istvan Hont, "The Permanent Crises of a Divided Mankind: 'Contemporary Crises of the Nation State' in Historical Perspective," *Political Studies* 42, no. 1 (August 1994) 166–231, 177.

25. See López Bofill, *Law, Violence and Constituent Power*, 41–89.

26. See Antoni Abat Ninet and Acar Kutay, "Europe's Lack of Solidarity in its Response to the Humanitarian Crisis: Jeopardizing the European Union's Constitutional Imaginary," *Revista Catalana de Dret Públic* 61 (December 2020): 99–111, 103.

27. Eric Hobsbawm, *The Age of Empire, 1875–1914* (London: Weidenfeld & Nicolson, 2010).

28. See Die Hundert-Milliarden-Überraschung," *Süddeutsche Zeitung*, February 28, 2022. Available at https://www.sueddeutsche.de/politik/ukraine-russland-bundeswehr-scholz-1.5538616?reduced=true.

29. The 2015 Minsk Agreement, available at https://www.ft.com/content/21b8f98e-b2a5-11e4-b234-00144feab7de.

30. Keith Lowe, *Savage Continent: Europe in the Aftermath of World War II* (London: Penguin, 2013; first edition 2012), 212–29.

31. NATO Secretary General Press Conference at Foreign Ministers Meeting held on March 4, 2022. Available at https://www.nato.int/cps/en/natohq/opinions_192739.htm?selectedLocale=en.

32. See Hans von der Burchard and Merlin Sugue, "Germany's Scholz Rejects Calls to Ban Russian Oil and gas," Politico, March 7, 2022. Available at https://www.politico.eu/article/germany-rejects-calls-for-banning-russian-oil-and-gas/.

33. See "EU Has Spent €35bn on Russian Energy since the War Began and Just €1bn on Aid to Ukraine," Euronews, April 6, 2022. Available at https://www.euronews.com/my-europe/2022/04/06/eu-has-spent-35bn-on-russian-energy-and-just-1bn-on-aid-borrell.

34. See "Pressure Mounts on Berlin as Kyiv Snubs German President," *France24*, April 12, 2022. Available at https://www.france24.com/en/live-news/20220412-pressure-mounts-on-berlin-as-kyiv-snubs-german-president.

35. *Lisbon* Judgment BVerfG 2 *BvE* 2/08 of June 30, 2009 (para 249).

36. Alberto Alesina, Enrico Spolaore, and Romain Wacziarg, "Economic Integration and Political Disintegration," *American Economic Review* 90, no. 5 (December 2000): 1276–96.

37. Branko Milanovic, *Capitalism Alone: The Future of the System That Rules the World* (Cambridge, MA; London: The Belknap Press of Harvard University Press, 2019), 147–48. On the relationship between the global economic law designed from the Bretton Woods Agreements and the previous colonial law, see Karen J. Alter, "From Colonial to Multilateral International Law: A Global Capitalism and Law Investigation," *International Journal of Constitutional Law* 19, no. 3 (July 2021): 798–864.

38. See Charles S. Maier, *The Project-State and Its Rivals. A New History of the Twentieth and Twenty-First Centuries* (Cambridge, MA: Harvard University Press, 2023), 16.

39. See Giuliano Garavini, *After Empires: European Integration, Decolonization, and the Challenge from Global South, 1957–1986* (New York: Oxford University Press, 2012), 1.

40. See Patrick Wintour, "Germany Agrees 15-Year Liquid Gas Supply Deal with Qatar," The Guardian, November 29, 2022. Available at https://www.theguardian.com/world/2022/nov/29/germany-agrees-15-year-liquid-gas-supply-deal-with-qatar.

41. See Niall Ferguson, *Civilization: The West and the Rest* (London: Penguin, 2012), XV.

Bibliography

Abat Ninet, Antoni, and James A. Gardner. "Distinctive Identity Claims in Federal Systems: Judicial Policing of Subnational Variance." *International Journal of Constitutional Law* 14, no. 2 (April 2016): 378–410.

Abat Ninet, Antoni, and Acar Kutay. "Europe's Lack of Solidarity in its Response to the Humanitarian Crisis: Jeopardizing the European Union's Constitutional Imaginary." *Revista Catalana de Dret Públic* 61 (December 2020): 99–111.

Ackerman, Bruce. *Revolutionary Constitutions: Charismatic Leadership and the Rule of Law*. Cambridge, MA, and London: The Belknap Press of Harvard University Press, 2019.

Aja, Eliseo. *El Estado Autonómico: Federalismo y hechos diferenciales*. Madrid: Alianza, 1999.

Alber, Elizabeth "Qualified Autonomy versus Secessionist Discourses in Europe: The Case of South Tyrol." In *States Falling Apart? Secessionist and Autonomy Movements in Europe*. Edited by Eva Maria Belser, Alexandra Fang-Bär, Nina Massüger, and Rekha Oleschak Pillai, 267–296. Bern: Stämpfli Verlag, 2015.

Albert, Richard. "Constitutional Amendment and Dismemberment." *The Yale Journal of International Law* 43, no. 1 (Winter 2018): 1–84.

Alberto Alesina, Enrico Spolaore, and Romain Wacziarg. "Economic Integration and Political Disintegration." *American Economic Review* 90, no. 5 (December 2000): 1276–96.

Albertus, Michael, and Victor Menaldo. *Authoritarianism and the Elite Origins of Democracy*. Cambridge: Cambridge University Press, 2018.

Altamura, Carlo Edoardo. *European Banks and the Rise of International Finance: The Post-Bretton Woods Era*. London: Routledge, 2017.

Alter, Karen J. "From Colonial to Multilateral International Law: A Global Capitalism and Law Investigation." *International Journal of Constitutional Law* 19, no. 3 (July 2021): 798–864.

Álvarez Chillida, Gonzalo, and Rosa M. Pardo Sanz. "La independencia de Guinea Ecuatorial: El hundimiento de un proyecto neocolonial (Septiembre de 1968 a Mayo de 1969)." *Hispania* 82, no. 270 (January–April 2022): 201–32.

Anderson, Perry, *The New Old World*. London and New York: Verso, 2009.

Anderson, Perry. "Ever Closer Union?" *London Review of Books* 43, no. 7 (January 2021). Available at https://www.lrb.co.uk/the-paper/v43/n01/perry-anderson/ever-closer-union.

Anghie, Antony. *Imperialism, Sovereignty and the Making of International Law*. Cambridge: Cambridge University Press, 2004.

Arendt, Hannah. *The Origins of Totalitarianism*. San Diego, New York, and London: Harvest/HBJ Book, 1973 (first edition 1951).

Arneil, Barbara. *Domestic Colonies: The Turn Inward to Colony*. Oxford: Oxford University Press, 2018.

Balibar, Etienne. "The Rise and Fall of the European Union: Temporalities and Teleologies." *Constellations* 21, no. 2 (August 2014): 202–12.

Bardèche, Maurice. "Une nouvelle carte du monde." *Défense de l'Occident* 34 (June–July 1956): 3–10.

Bartel, Fritz. *The Triumph of Broken Promises: The End of the Cold War and the Rise of Neoliberalism*. Cambridge, MA, and London: Harvard University Press, 2022.

Basedow, Jürgen, Jan Dietze, Stefan Griller, Manuel Kellerbauer, Marcus Klamert, Luigi Malferrari, Tibor Scharf, Dominik Schnichels, Daniel Thym, and Jonathan Tomkin. "European Integration: Quo Vadis? A Critical Commentary on the PSPP Judgment of the German Federal Constitutional Court of May 5, 2020." *International Journal of Constitutional Law* 19, no. 1 (January 2021): 188–207.

Bassetto, Marco. "Fiscal Policy and Price Stability: The Case of Italy, 1992–98." *Chicago Fed Letter* 233 (December 2006). Available at https://www.chicagofed.org/publications/chicago-fed-letter/2006/december-233.

Bastasin, Carlo. *Saving Europe: Anatomy of a Dream*. Washington, DC: Brookings Institution Press, 2015.

Bayly, Christopher, and Tim Harper. *Forgotten Wars: Freedom and Revolution in Southeast Asia*. Cambridge, MA: Belknap Press, 2006.

Bickerton, Christopher J. *European Integration from Nation-States to Member States*. Oxford: Oxford University Press, 2012.

Blanke, Richard. *Orphans of Versailles: The Germans in Western Poland, 1918–1939*. Lexington, KY: University Press of Kentucky, 1993.

Bossacoma, Pau. *Morality and Legality of Secession: A Theory of National Self-Determination.* Cham: Palgrave Macmillan, 2020.

Bossacoma, Pau. *Secessió i integració a la Unió Europea*. Barcelona: Institut d'Estudis d'Autogovern, 2017.

Brainard, Lawrence J. "Overview of East's Europe's Debt: The Evolution of Creditworthiness in the 1980s." *Business Economics* 25, no. 4 (October 1990): 10–16.

Breda, Vito. *Constitutional Law and Regionalism: A Comparative Analysis of Regionalist Negotiations*. Cheltenham and Northampton: Edward Publishing, 2018.

Bros, Aurélie, Tatiana Mitrova, and Kirsten Westphal. "German-Russian Gas Relations. A Special Relationship in Troubled Waters." *Stiftung Wissenschaft und Politik Research Paper* 13 (December 2017). Available at https://www.swp-berlin.org/publications/products/research_papers/2017RP13_wep_EtAl.pdf.

Brown, Megan. "Drawing Algeria into Europe: Shifting French Policy and the Treaty of Rome (1951–1964)." *Modern & Contemporary France* 25, no. 2 (March 2017): 191–208.

Brown, Megan. *The Seventh Member State: Algeria, France and the European Community*. Cambridge and London: Harvard University Press, 2022.

Buettner, Elizabeth. *Europe after Empire: Decolonization, Society, and Culture*. Cambridge: Cambridge University Press, 2016.

Bull, Martin J. "In the Eye of the Storm: The Italian Economy and the Eurozone Crisis." *South European Society and Politics* 23, no. 1 (January 2018): 3–28.

Bull, Martin J., and Pasquino, G. "Introduction: Italian Politics in an Era of Recession: The End of Bipolarism." In *Italy Transformed: Politics, Society and Institutions at the End of the Great Recession*. Edited by Martin J. Bull and Gianfranco Pasquino, 1–11. London and New York: Routledge, 2020.

Cain, Peter. "Was It Worth Having? The British Empire 1850–1950." *Revista de Historia Económica/Journal of Iberian and Latin American History* 16, no. 1 (March 1998) 351–76.

Carbonell, Mauve. *Des hommes à l'origine de l'Europe: Biographies des membres de la Haute Autorité de la CECA*. Aix-en-Provence, Publications de l'Université de Provence, 2008.

Carli, Guido. *Cinquant'anni di vita italiana*. Bari: Editori Laterza, 1993.

Casals, Xavier. *La Transición Española: El voto ignorado de las armas*. Barcelona: Pasado y Presente, 2016.

Cassese, Antonio. *Self-determination of Peoples: A Legal Reappraisal*. Cambridge: Cambridge University Press, 1995.

Cassuto, Aldo, and Muriel Grindrod. "The Regional Experiment in Italy." *The World Today* 26, no. 7 (July 1970): 305–12.

Cavatorta, Francesco. "The Role of the Northern League in Transforming the Italian Political System: From Economic Federalism to Ethnic Politics and Back." *Contemporary Politics* 7, no. 1 (2001): 27–40.

Chakrabarty, Dipesh. *Provincializing Europe: Postcolonial Thought and Historical Difference*. Princeton, NJ: Princeton University Press, 2007.

Chaloult, Beatriz, and Yves Chaloult. "The Internal Colonialism Concept: Methodological Considerations." *Social and Economic Studies* 28, no. 4 (December 1979): 85–99.

Churchill, Winston. *The Second World War: Vol.6: Triumph and Tragedy*. London: Educational Book Company, 1954.

Claude, Inis Lothair. *National Minorities: An International Problem*. Cambridge: Harvard University Press, 1955.

Clayton, Anthony. *The Wars of French Decolonization*. Abingdon and New York: Routledge, 2013.

Cohen, Antonin. "Constitutionalism without Constitution: Transnational Elites between Mobilization and Legal Expertise in the Making of a Constitution for Europe (1940s–1960s)." *Law and Social Inquiry* 32, no. 1 (Winter 2007): 109–36.

Colitti, Marcello. *Energia e sviluppo in Italia: La vicenda di Enrico Mattei*. Bari: De Donato, 1979.

Craig, Gordon A. *Germany, 1866–1945*. Oxford: Oxford University Press, 1980.

Crawford, James. "Self-Determination of Peoples: A Legal Reappraisal: By Antonio Cassese." *American Journal of International Law* 90, no. 2 (April, 1996): 331–33.

Curli, Barbara. "Italy, Euratom and Early Research on Controlled Thermonuclear Fusion (1957–1962)." In *Nuclear Italy: An International History of Italian Nuclear Policies during the Cold War*. Edited by Elisabetta Bini and Igor Londero, 57–76. Trieste: Edizioni Università di Trieste, 2017.

D'Alimonte, Roberto. "How Populists Won in Italy?" *Journal of Democracy* 30, no. 1 (January 2019): 114–27.

Darwin, John. *After Tamerlane: The Global History of Europe*. London: Allen Lane, 2007.

Davis, Muriam Halleh. "Restaging *Mise en Valeur*: 'Postwar Imperialism' and the Plan Constatine." *Review of Middle East Studies* 44, no2 (Winter 2010): 176–86.

De Búrca, Gráinne. "Poland's and Hungary's EU Membership: On Not Confronting Authoritarian Governments." *International Journal of Constitutional Law* 20, no. 1 (January 2022): 13–34.

De Figueiredo António. "The Empire Is Dead, Long Live the EU." In *The Last Empire. Thirty Years of Portuguese Decolonization*. Edited by Stewart Lloyd-Jones and António Costa Pinto, 127–44. Bristol and Portland, OR: Intellect, 2003.

De la Cuadra, Bonifacio, and Soledad Gallego-Díaz. *Crónica Secreta de la Constitución*. Madrid: Tecnos, 1989.

De Madariaga Álvarez-Prida, María Rosa. *Marruecos, ese gran desconocido: Breve historia del protectorado español*. Madrid: Alianza, 2013.

De Zayas, Alfred-Maurice. *A Terrible Revenge: The Ethnic Cleansing of the East European Germans*. New York: Palgrave Macmillan, 2006.

Delgado, Mariano. "Kolonialismusbegründung und Kolonialismuskritik: Der Januskopf Europas gegenüber der außereuropäischen Welt." In *Herausforderung Europa: Wege zu einer europäischen Identität*. Edited by Delgado, Mariano and Lutz-Bachmann, Matthias, 153–70. Munich: Beck, 1995.

Delledone, Giacomo. "La resistenza in Assemblea Constituente e nel testo costituzionale italiano del 1948," *Historia Constitucional* 10 (August 2009): 217–41. Available at http://www.historiaconstitucional.com/index.php/historiaconstitucional/issue/view/12.

Doyle, Michael, W. *Empires*. Ithaca, NY: Cornell University Press, 1986.

Elgey, Georgette. *Histoire de la IVe République: La République des Tourmentes (1954–1959) Tome 3. La fin*. Paris: Fayard, 2008.

Elliott, John H. *Scots and Catalans: Union and Disunion*. New Haven, CT, London: Yale University Press, 2018.

Ellison, James. "The European Rescue of Britain." In *Alan S. Milward and a Century of European Change*. Edited by Fernando Guirao, Frances M. B. Lynch, and Sigfrido M. Ramírez Pérez, 444–58. New York and London: Routledge, 2012.

Evans, Malcolm. "The Italian Constitutional Court." *International and Comparative Law Quarterly* 17, no. 3 (July 1968): 602–33.

Fabbrini, Federico. *Brexit and the Future of the European Union: The Case for Constitutional Reforms*. Oxford: Oxford University Press, 2020.

Fabbrini, Federico, and András Sajó. "The Dangers of Constitutional Identity." *European Law Journal* 25, no 4 (July 2019): 457–73.

Fennell, Rosemary. *The Common Agricultural Policy: Continuity and Change.* Oxford: Oxford University Press, 1997.

Ferguson, Niall. *Empire: How Britain Made the Modern World.* London: Penguin Books, 2004.

Ferguson, Niall. *Civilization: The West and the Rest.* London: Penguin Books, 2012.

Ferguson, Niall. *The Ascent of Money: A Financial History of the World.* London: Penguin Books, 2019.

Ferraz, Ricardo. "The Financial Costs of the Portuguese Colonial War, 1961–1974: Analysis and Applied Study," *Revista de Historia Económica/Journal of Iberian and Latin American History*, October 20, 2021. Available at https://cambridge.org/core/journals/revista-de-historia-economica-journal-of-iberian-and-latin-american-economic-history/article/abs/financial-costs-of-the-portuguese-colonial-war-19611974-analysis-and-applied-study/31B3C7ADFAAB352A4D4EBAF0BFB7E3CA.

Finkelstein, Monte S. *Separatism, the Allies and the Mafia: The Struggle for Sicilian Independence, 1943–1948.* Bethlehem, PA: Lehigh University Press, 1999.

Fradera, Josep Maria. *Colonias para después de un imperio.* Barcelona: Edicions Bellaterra, 2005.

Frei, Norbert. *Vergangenheitspolitik: Die Anfänge der Bundesrepublik und die NS-Vergangenheit.* München: CH Beck, 1996.

Fritz, Vera. *Juges et avocats généraux de la Cour de Justice de l'Union Européenne (1952–1972). Une approche biographique de l'histoire d'une révolution juridique.* Frankfurt am Main: Vittorio Klostermann, 2018.

Garavini, Giuliano. *After Empires: European Integration, Decolonization, and the Challenge from Global South, 1957–1986.* New York: Oxford University Press, 2012.

Garry, John, Brendan O'Leary, and John Coakley. "How Northern Ireland Voted in the EU Referendum—and What It Means for Border Talks." *Queen's Policy Engagement*, 28 April 2017. Available at http://qpol.qub.ac.uk/border-talks-brexit/.

Gerber, David J. "Constitutionalizing the Economy: German Neoliberalism, Competition Law and the 'New' Europe." *American Journal of Comparative Law* 42, no. 1 (Winter 1994): 25–84.

Gildea, Robert. *France since 1945.* Oxford: Oxford University Press, 2002.

Giles, Frank. *The Locust Years: The Story of the Fourth Republic, 1946–1958.* London: Secker & Warburg, 1991.

Gillingham, John. *European Integration 1950–2003: Superstate or New Market Economy?* Cambridge: Cambridge University Press, 2003.

Gilman, Nils. *Mandarins of the Future: Modernization Theory in Cold War America.* Baltimore, MD: Johns Hopkins University Press, 2007.

Gilman, Nils. "Modernization Theory Never Dies." *History of Political Economy* 50, no. 1 (December 2018): 133–51.

Ginsborg, Paul. *A History of Contemporary Italy: Society and Politics, 1943–1988.* London: Penguin Books, 1990.

Ginsborg, Paul. *Italy and Its Discontents: Family, Civil Society, State. 1980–2001*. London: Allen Lane/The Penguin Press, 2001.

Girardet, Raoul. *La crise militaire française 1945–1962: Aspects sociologiques et idéologiques*. Paris: Colin, 1964.

Gordon, Bertram M. *Collaborationism in France during the Second World War*. Ithaca, NY: Cornell University Press, 1980.

Gordon Levin, Norman. *Woodrow Wilson and World Politics: America's Response to War and Revolution*. New York: Oxford University Press, 1968.

Gosewinkel, Dieter. "Introduction. Anti-liberal Europe—A Neglected Source of Europeanism." In *Anti-liberal Europe: A Neglected Story of Europeanization*. Edited by Dieter Gosewinkel, 3–32. New York and Oxford: Berghahn, 2015.

Gosewinkel, Dieter. "Europe antilibérale ou anti-Europe? Les conceptions européennes de l'extrême droite française entre 1940 et 1990." *Politique européenne* 62, no. 4 (2018): 152–79.

Götz, Roland. "Germany and Russia—Strategic Partners?" *Geopolitical Affairs* 4, 2007. Available at https://www.swp-berlin.org/publications/products/fachpublikationen/Strategic_Partners_ks.pdf.

Gourinchas, Pierre-Olivier, Philippe Martin, and Todd Messer. "The Economics of Sovereign Debt, Bailouts and the Eurozone Crisis." *CEPR Discussion Papers*, 14891, June 2020. Available at https://papers.ssrn.com/sol3/papers.cfm?abstract_id=3628214#.

Gowa, Joanne. *Allies, Adversaries and International Trade*. Princeton, NJ: Princeton University Press, 1994.

Graf, Maximilian. "Before Strauss: The East German Struggle to Avoid Bankruptcy during the Debt Crises Revisited." *The International History Review* 42, no. 4 (2020): 737–54.

Grieco, Joseph M. *Cooperation among Nations: Europe, America and Non-Tariff Barriers to Trade*. Ithaca, NY: Cornell University Press, 1990.

Grigas, Agnia. *The New Geopolitics of Natural Gas*. Cambridge, MA: Harvard University Press, 2017.

Guirao, Fernando. "Reflexiones desde la historia." In*¿Una Unión Europea en crisis? Reflexiones para un debate urgente*. Edited by Fernando Guirao and Josep Pich, 27–48. Madrid: Catarata, 2019.

Guirao, Fernando. *The European Rescue of the Franco Regime, 1950–1975*. Oxford: Oxford University Press, 2021.

Häberle, Peter. *Gibt es eine europäische Öffentlichkeit? Vortrag gehalten vor der Juristischen Gesellschaft zu Berlin am 15 Dezember 1999*. Berlin and New York: Walter de Gruyter, 2000.

Habermas, Jürgen. *The Divided West*. Cambridge: Polity, 2006.

Hahn, Erich C. J. "The Occupying Powers and the Constitutional Reconstruction of Germany (1945–1949)." In *Cornerstone of Democracy: The West German Grundgesetz 1949–1989*. Edited by Erich C. J. Hahn, Detlef Junker, et al., 7–35. Washington DC: German Historical Institute, 1995.

Hailbronner, Michaela. *Tradition and Transformations: The Rise of German Constitutionalism*. Oxford: Oxford University Press, 2015.

Halberstam, Daniel, and Christoph Möllers. "The German Constitutional Court Says '*Ja zu Deutschland*!' *German Law Journal* 10, no. 8 (August 2009): 1241–57.
Hametz, Maura Elise *Making Trieste Italian, 1918–1954*. Woodbridge/Rochester: The Boydell Press, 2005.
Hansen, Peo, and Stefan Jonsson. *Eurafrica: The Untold History of European Integration and Colonialism*. London: Bloombsbury, 2014.
Hansen, Peo, and Stefan Jonsson. "Building Eurafrica: Reviving Colonialism through European Integration, 1920–1960." In *Echoes of Empire: Memory, Identity, and Colonial Legacies*. Edited by Kalypso Nicolaidis, Berny Sèbe, and Gabrielle Maas, 209–26. New York: IB Tauris, 2015.
Harari, Yuval Noah. *21 Lessons for the 21st Century*. London: Jonathan Cape, 2018.
Hartley, Stephen. *The Irish Question as a Problem in British Foreign Policy, 1914–1918*. New York: Palgrave Macmillan, 1987.
Harvey, Colin "The Irish Border." In *The Law and Politics of Brexit: Volume II: The Withdrawal Agreement*. Edited by Federico Fabbrini, 148–68. Oxford: Oxford University Press, 2020.
Harvey, David. *The New Imperialism*. Oxford: Oxford University Press, 2003.
Häussler, Matthias. *The Herero Genocide: War, Emotion, and Extreme Violence in Colonial Namibia.* New York and Oxford: Berghahn, 2021.
Hechter, Michael. *Internal Colonialism: The Celtic Fringe in British National Development*. New Brunswick, NJ, and London: Transaction Publishers, 1999.
Henningsen, David M. "The Origins of Italian Sovereign Debt Crisis." *Claremont McKenna College Senior Theses*, Paper 379, May 2012. Available at http://scholarship.claremont.edu/cmc_theses/379, p. 9.
Herbert, Ulrich. *Hitler's Foreign Workers: Enforced Foreign Labor in Germany under the Third Reich*. Cambridge: Cambridge University Press, 1997.
Hermida del Llano, Cristina. "Reflexiones sobre el Tratado por el que se instituye una Constitución para Europa." *Anuario de Filosofía del Derecho* 21 (2004) 287–312.
Hickson, Kevin. *The IMF Crisis of 1976 and British Politics*. London: I.B. Tauris, 2005.
Hobsbawm, Eric. *The Age of Empire, 1875–1914*. London: Weidenfeld & Nicolson, 2010. (first edition 1987).
Hobsbawm, Eric. *The Age of Extremes. A History of the World, 1914–1991*. New York: Vintage Books, 1994.
Hoffmann, Stanley. "Obstinate or Obsolete? The Fate of the Nation-State and the Case of Western Europe." *Daedalus* 95, no. 3 (Summer 1966): 862–915.
Hont, Istvan. "The Permanent Crises of a Divided Mankind: 'Contemporary Crises of the Nation State' in Historical Perspective." *Political Studies* 42, no. 1 (August 1994): 166–231.
Horsley, Thomas. "Reflections on the Role of the Court of Justice as the 'Motor' of European Integration: Legal Limits to Judicial Lawmaking." *Common Market Law Review* 50, no. 4 (2013): 931–64.
Huber, Ernst R. *Quellen zum Staatsrecht der Neuzeit. (Deutsche Verfassungsdokumente der Gegenwart 1919–1951)*. Volume 2, Tübingen: Matthiesen, 1951.

Jackson, Ashley. "Empire and Beyond: The Pursuit of Overseas National Interests in the Late Twentieth Century." *English Historical Review* 122, no. 499 (December 2007): 1350–66.

James, Harold. "Why Angela Merkel Is Coming to the Rescue in Europe." *Financial Review*, June 3, 2020. Available at https://www.afr.com/world/europe/why-angela-merkel-is-coming-to-the-rescue-in-europe-20200602-p54yu3.

Joerges, Christian. "Europe a Grossraum? Shifting Legal Conceptualizations of the Integration Project." In *Darker Legacies of Law in Europe: The Shadow of National Socialism and Fascism over Europe and Its Legal Traditions*. Edited by Christian Joerges and Navraj Singh Ghaleigh, 167–92. Oxford and Portland, OR: Hart Publishing, 2003.

Judt, Tony. *Postwar. A History of Europe since 1945*. London: Penguin Books, 2005.

Kaiser, Wolfram, Brigitte Leucht, and Morten Rasmussen. "Origins of a European Polity. A New Research Agenda for the European Union History." In *The History of the European Union: Origins of a Trans- and Supranational Polity 1950–72*. Edited by Wolfram Kaiser, Brigitte Leucht, and Morten Rasmussen, 1–11. London and New York: Routledge, 2009.

Kapstein, Ethan B. *The Insecure Alliance: Energy, Crises and Western Politics since 1944*. New York: Oxford University Press, 1990.

Keohane, Daniel. "Macron's European Defense Doctrine." *Judy Dempsey's Strategic Europe*, Carnegie Europe, September 28, 2017. Available at https://carnegieeurope.eu/strategiceurope/73246.

Kershaw, Ian. *Hitler. 1936–1945: Nemesis*. London: Allen Lane/Penguin Books, 2001.

Kershaw, Ian. "War and Political Violence in Twentieth-Century Europe." *Contemporary European History* 14, no. 1 (February 2005): 107–23.

Kershaw, Ian. *Roller-Coaster. Europe 1950–2017*. London: Allen Lane/Penguin Books, 2018.

Kieninger, Stephan. "Freer Movement in Return for Cash. Franz Josef Strauss, Alexander Schalck-Golodkowski, and the Milliardenkredite for the GDR, 1983–1984." In *New Perspectives on the End of the Cold War: Unexpected Transformations?* Edited by Bernhard Blumenau, Jussi M. Hanhimäki, and Barbara Zanchetta, 117–37. London: Routledge, 2018.

Klose, Fabian. "Europe as a Colonial Project: A Critique of Its Anti-liberalism." In *Anti-Liberal Europe: A Neglected Story of Europeanization*. Edited by Dieter Gosewinkel, 47–71. New York and Oxford: Berghahn, 2015.

Koskenniemi, Martti. "International Law as Political Theology: How to Read *Nomos der Erde*?" *Constellations* 11, no. 4 (December 2004): 492–511.

Kotkin, Stephen. *Armageddon Averted: The Soviet Collapse 1970–2000*. Oxford and New York: Oxford University Press, 2001.

Kumar, Krishan. "Nation States as Empires, Empires as Nation States: Two Principles, One Practice?" *Theory and Society* 39, no. 2 (March 2010): 119–43.

Kumm, Mattias "Constituent Power: Boundaries and Identity: On the Justificatory Depth of Constitutionalism—A Rejoinder to Neil Walker." *International Journal of Constitutional Law* 14, no. 4 (October 2016): 914–24.

Kundnani, Hans. *The Paradox of German Power*. Oxford and New York: Oxford University Press, 2015.

Küsters, Hanns Jürgen. "West Germany's Foreign Policy in Western Europe, 1949–1957: The Art of the Possible." In *Western Europe and Germany: The Beginnings of European Integration, 1945–1960*. Edited by Clemens Wurm, 55–85. Oxford and Washington: Berg, 1995.

Küsters, Hanns Jürgen. *Der Integrationsfriede: Viermächteverhandlungen über die Friedensregelung mit Deutschland, 1945–1990*. München: Oldenbourg, 2000.

Lafont, Robert. *Per una teoria de la nació: El cas de França*. Barcelona: Edicions 62, 1969. (Catalan translation by Miquel Martí i Pol [first edition 1968]).

Lansing, Robert. *The Peace Negotiations—A Personal Narrative*. New York and Boston, MA: Houghton Mifflin Company, 1921.

Laqueur, Walter. *Europe in Our Time: A History 1945–1992*. London: Penguin, 1992.

Lavery, Scott, and Davide Schmid. "European Integration and the New Global Disorder." *Journal of Common Market Studies* 59, no. 5 (September 2021): 1322–38.

Lenin, Vladimir Ilyich Ulyanov. "The Right of Nations to Self-Determination." In *Lenin's Collected Works: Vol 20: December 1913–August 1914*. Moscow: Progress Publishers, 1972. (Translation by Bernard Isaacs and Joe Fineberg [first published 1914]).

Lennkh-Yunus, Alvise. "Italy: Bond-Buying Shift from ECB to private Sector Requires Policy Flexibility, Political Stability." *Scope Ratings*, June 15, 2022. Available at https://www.scoperatings.com/ratings-and-research/research/EN/171430.

Lieshout; Robert H., Mathieu L.L. Segers, and Johanna Maria van der Vleuten. "De Gaulle, Moravcsik and the Choice for Europe: Soft Sources, Weak Evidence." *Journal of Cold War Studies* 6, no. 4 (November 2004): 89–139.

Loewenstein, Karl. "Militant Democracy and Fundamental Rights, I," *American Political Science Review* 31, no. 3 (June 1937): 417–32.

López Bofill, Hèctor. "The Limits of Constitutionalism: Politics, Economics, and Secessionism in Catalonia (2006–2013)." In *Constitutionalism and the Politics of Accommodation in Multinational Democracies*. Edited by Jaime Lluch, 70–85. Houndmills: Palgrave Macmillan, 2014.

López Bofill, Hèctor. "Hubris, Constitutionalism, and 'the Indissoluble Unity of the Spanish Nation': The Repression of Catalan Secessionist Referenda in Spanish Constitutional Law." *International Journal of Constitutional Law* 17, no. 3 (July 2019): 943–69.

López Bofill, Hèctor. "Catalonia: The Right to Self-Determination and the Consent of the Governed." In *Constitutional Law and the Politics of Secession*. Edited by Antoni Abat Ninet. London and New York: Routledge, 2023.

Lowe, Keith. *Savage Continen:. Europe in the Aftermath of World War II*. London: Penguin Books, 2013 (first edition 2012).

Lübbe, Hermann. "Der Nationalsozialismus im politischen Bewußtsein der Gegenwart." In *Deutschlands Weg in die Diktatur: Internationale Konferenz zur nationalsozialistichen Machtübernahme im Reichstaggebäude zu Berlin*. Edited by Martin Broszat, Ulrich Dügger, et al., 329–49. Berlin: Siedler, 1983.

Lynch, Frances M. B. "Resolving the Paradox of the Monnet Plan: National and International Planning in French Reconstruction." *Economic History Review* 37, no. 2 (May 1984): 229–43.

Maçães, Bruno. "La Realidad de Eurasia." *Política Exterior* 204. November 1, 2021. Available at https://www.politicaexterior.com/articulo/la-realidad-de-eurasia/.

Maçães, Bruno. "Is Vladimir Putin Preparing for War?" *The New Statesman*. November 24, 2021. Available at https://www.newstatesman.com/world/asia/2021/11/is-vladimir-putin-preparing-for-war.

Maier, Charles S. *The Project-State and Its Rivals. A New History of the Twentieth and Twenty-First Centuries*. Cambridge, MA: Harvard University Press, 2023.

Majone, Giandomenico. "The Politics of Regulation and European Regulatory Institutions." In *Governing Europe*. Edited by Jack Hayward and Anand Menon, 298–312. Oxford: Oxford University Press, 2003.

Majone, Giandomenico. *Dilemmas of European Integration: The Ambiguities and Pitfalls of Integration by Stealth*. Oxford: Oxford University Press, 2005.

Manela, Erez. *The Wilsonian Moment: Self-Determination and the International Origins of Anticolonial Nationalism*. Oxford and New York: Oxford University Press, 2007.

Marrus, Michael R. *Unwanted: European Refugees in the Twentieth Century*. Oxford and New York: Oxford University Press, 1985.

Martinico, Giuseppe. "Between Mimetism and Parasitism: Italian Populism in a Comparative Perspective." *European Public Law* 26, no. 4 (2020) 921–40.

Más Rodríguez, Pilar. "The EU Budget. The new MFF and the Recovery Instrument: Next Generation EU." *The Euro in 2021*, IEAF/ Fundación ICO, 2021, 169–95. Available at https://www.ieaf.es/images/Publicaciones-FEF/Anuarioeuro2021/10_The_EU_budget.pdf.

Maull, Hanns W. "Germany and Japan: The New Civilian Powers." *Foreign Affairs* 69, 5 (1990–1991): Available at https://www.foreignaffairs.com/articles/asia/1990-12-01/germany-and-japan-new-civilian-powers.

Mayer, France C. "To Boldly Go Where No Court Has Gone Before: The German Federal Constitutional Court's Ultra Vires Decision of May 5, 2020," *German Law Journal* 21, no. 5 (July 2020): 1116–27.

Mazower, Mark. *Dark Continent: Europe's Twentieth Century*. New York: Vintage Books, 2000 (first edition 1998).

Mazower, Mark. *Hitler's Empire: Nazi Rule in Occupied Europe*. London and New York: Penguin, 2008.

Mazower, Mark. *Governing the World: The History of an Idea*. London: Allen Lane, 2012.

McDonogh, Giles. *After the Reich: The Brutal History of the Allied Occupation*. New York: Basic Books, 2009 (first edition 2007).

McDonagh, Luke. "Losing Ireland, Losing the Empire: Dominion Status and the Irish Constitutions of 1922 and 1937." *International Journal of Constitutional Law* 17, no. 4 (October 2019): 1192–1212.

McEwen, Nicola, and Mary C. Murphy. "Brexit and the Union: Territorial Voice, Exit and Re-Entry Strategies in Scotland and Northern Ireland." *International Political Science Review*, March 12, 2021. Available at https://journals.sagepub.com/doi/full/10.1177/0192512121990543.

McKittrick, David. *Making Sense of the Troubles: The Story of the Conflict in Northern Ireland*. New York: New Amsterdam Books, 2002.

McQueen, Norrie. "Portugal: Decolonization without Agency." In *The Oxford Handbook of the Ends of Empire*. Edited by Martin Thomas and Andrew S. Thompson, 162–78. Oxford: Oxford University Press, 2018.

Meehan, Elizabeth. "Britain's Irish Question: Britain's European Question? British-Irish Relations in the Context of European Union and the Belfast Agreement." *Review of International Studies* 26, no. 1 (January 2000): 83–97.

Michel, Marc. *Décolonisation et émergence du Tiers monde*. Paris: Hachette, 1993.

Milanovic, Branko. *Capitalism Alone: The Future of the System That Rules the World*. Cambridge, MA, and London: The Belknap Press of Harvard University Press, 2019.

Milanovic, Branko. "What If Putin's True Goals Are Different? The Trade-Off between Sovereignty and Income." *Global Equality and More*, June 2, 2022. Available at https://branko2f7.substack.com/p/what-if-putin-true-goals-are-different?r=16uxt&s=w&utm_campaign=post&utm_medium=web.

Miller, Chris. *Chip War: The Fight for the World's Most Critical Technology*. London, New York, Sydney, Toronto, New Delhi: Simon & Schuster, 2022.

Milward, Alan S. *The Reconstruction of Western Europe, 1945–1951*. London: Methuen, 1984.

Milward, Alan S. *The European Rescue of the Nation-State*. London and New York: Routledge, 2000 (first edition 1992).

Milward, Alan S. *The United Kingdom and the European Community: Vol I: The Rise and Fall of a National Strategy, 1945–1963*. London: Whitehall History Publishing in association with Frank Cass, 2002.

Molinero, Carme, and Pere Ysàs. *El règim franquista: Feixisme, modernització i consens*. Vic: Eumo, 1997.

Möllers, Cristoph. "We Are (Afraid of) the People: Constituent Power in German Constitutionalism." In *The Paradox of Constitutionalism, Constituent Power and Constitutional Form*. Edited by Martin Loughlin and Neil Walker, 87–106. Oxford: Oxford University Press, 2007.

Monnet, Jean. *Memoirs*. London: Collins, 1978.

Montanelli, Indro, and Mario Cervi. *Storia d'Italia: Volume IX (1943–1948)*. Milano: Rizzoli Editore, 2006.

Moran, Matthew. "Terrorism and the Banlieues: The Charlie Hebdo Attacks in Context." *Modern & Contemporary France*, 25, no. 3 (April 2017): 315–32.

Moravcsik, Andrew. *The Choice for Europe: Social Purpose and State Power from Messina to Maastricht.* London: UCL Press, 1998.

Morone, Antonio Maria. *L'ultima colonia: Come l'Italia è tornata in Africa 1950–1960*. Bari: Laterza, 2011.

Moyn, Samuel. *The Last Utopia: Human Rights in History*. Cambridge, MA, and London: The Belknap Press of Harvard University Press, 2010.

Müller-Armack, Alfred. *Auf dem Weg nach Europa*. Stuttgart: C. E. Poeschel, 1971.

Münchau, Wolfgang. "Overrated—Now Fading." *Euro Intelligence*, June 26, 2021. Available at https://www.eurointelligence.com/column/merkel.

Münchau, Wolfgang. "Ultra Vires." *Euro Intelligence*, October 10, 2021. Available at https://www.eurointelligence.com/column/ultra-vires.

Münchau, Wolfgang "Unicorn in the Room." *Euro Intelligence*, December 12, 2021. Available at https://www.eurointelligence.com/column/unicorns-everywhere.

Münchau, Wolfgang. "When Did We Lose the Fight." *Euro Intelligence*, January 23, 2022. Available at https://www.eurointelligence.com/column/when-did-we-lose -the-fight.

Münchau, Wolfgang. "Networks of Resistance." *Euro Intelligence*, May 1, 2022. Available at https://www.eurointelligence.com/column/networks-of -resistance, 99.

Münchau, Wolfgang. "The Case for Strategic Autonomy," *Euro Intelligence*, April 13, 2023. Available at https://www.eurointelligence.com/page-5.

Muñoz, Jordi, and Raül Tormos. "Identitat o càlculs instrumentals? Anàlisi dels factors explicatius de suport a la independència." *Papers de Treball Centre d'Estudis d'Opinió*, April 2012. Available at https://ceo.gencat.cat/web/.content/30_estudis /03_publicacions/Papers_treball/2012_04_04_papers_treball_identitat2.pdf.

Nietzsche, Friedrich. *The Will to Power: An Attempted Revaluation of All Values*. New York: Barnes & Noble, 2013. (Translation Anthony M. Ludovici [first edition 1901]).

Novak, Bogdan C. *Trieste, 1941–1954: The Ethnic, Political and Ideological Struggle*. Chicago, IL: University of Chicago Press, 1970.

O'Brien, Patrick K. "The Costs and Benefits of British Imperialism: 1846–1914." *Past and Present* 120, no. 1 (August 1988): 163–200.

Ortega y Gasset, José. *España Invertebrada: Bosquejo de algunos Pensamientos Históricos*. Madrid: Alianza, 1988 (first edition 1922).

Pahlavi, Pierre Cyril. *La Guerre Révolutionnaire de l'Armée Française en Algérie 1954–1961: Entre esprit de conquête et conquête des esprits*. Paris: Harmattan, 2004.

Pasquino, Gianfranco. "Italy's Transition to Democracy: 1943–1948." In *Transitions from Authoritarian Rule: Southern Europe*. Edited by Guillermo O'Donnell, Philippe Schmitter, and Laurence Whitehead, 45–70. Baltimore, MD: Johns Hopkins University Press, 1986.

Pavone, Claudio. *Una Guerra civile: Saggio storico sulla moralità nella Resistenza*. Turin: Universali Bollati Boringhieri, 2006.

Petzina, Dietmar. "The Economic Dimension of the East-West Conflict and the Role of Germany." *Contemporary European History* 3, no. 2 (July 2008): 203–15.

Piketty, Thomas. *Les hauts revenus en France au XXe siècle: Inégalités et redistributions 1901–1998*. Paris: Grasset, 2001.

Piketty, Thomas. *Capital in the Twenty-First Century*. Cambridge, MA: The Belknap Press of Harvard University Press, 2004.

Pinto, António Costa, and Severiano Nuno Teixeira. "From Africa to Europe: Portugal and Europe Integration." In *Southern Europe and the Making of the European Union, 1945–1980's*. Edited by António Costa Pinto and Nuno Severiano Teixeira, 3–40. Boulder, CO, and New York: Social Science Monographs and Columbia University Press, 2002.

Piris, Jean-Claude. "La Unión Europea, Cataluña y Escocia (cuestiones jurídicas sobre recientes tendencias secesionistas en los Estados Miembros)." *Teoría y realidad Constitucional* 37 (2016) 101–34.

Poiger, Uta G. "Imperialism and Empire in Twentieth Century Germany." *History and Memory* 17, no. 1–2 (Spring-Summer 2005): 117–43.

Pujol, Jordi. *Memòries (1930–1980)*. Barcelona: Proa, 2007.

Ranieri, Ruggero. "Unlocking Integration: Political and Economic Factors behind the Schuman Plan and the European Coal and Steel Community in the Work of Alan Milward." In *Alan S. Milward and a Century of European Change*. Edited by Fernando Guirao, Frances M. B. Lynch, and Sigfrido M. Ramírez Pérez, 299–306. New York and London: Routledge, 2012.

Rasmussen, Morten. "The Origins of a Legal Revolution—The Early History of the European Court of Justice." *Journal of European Integration History* 14, no. 2 (2008): 77–98.

Reitlinger, Gerald. *The House Built on Sand: The Conflicts of German Policy in Russia, 1939–1945*. New York: Viking Press, 1960.

Ripka, Hubert. *Munich: Before and After: A Fully Documental Czechoslovak Account of the Crises of September 1938 and March 1939*. London: Victor Gollancz, 1939.

Röhrich, Wilfried. "Die 'Stunde Null.'" In *Deutschland nach 1945: Ein Lesebuch zur deutschen Geschichte von 1945 bis zur Gegenwart*. Edited by Eckart Conze and Gabriele Metzler, 30–32. München: Verlag C.H. Beck, 1997.

Sacchi, Stefano. "Conditionality by Other Means: EU Involvement in Italy's Structural Reforms in the Sovereign Debt Crises." *Comparative European Politics* 13, no. 1 (January 2015): 77–92.

Salzano, Giovanni, Demetrios Pogkas, and Ben Sills. "Why Italy's Debts Are Europe's Big Problem." February 3, 2019. Available at https://www.bloomberg.com/graphics/2019-italian-banks/.

Sartre, Jean-Paul. *Life/Situations: Essays Written and Spoken*. New York: Pantheon Books, 1977.

Scharpf, Fritz W. "The Asymmetry of European Integration or Why Europe Can't Have a Social Market Economy," *Socio-Economic Review* 8, no. 2 (April 2010): 211–50.

Scheidel, Walter. *The Great Leveler: Violence and the History of Inequality from the Stone Age to Twenty-First Century*. Princeton, NJ, and Oxford: Princeton University Press, 2017.

Schmitt, Carl. *Theorie des Partisanen: Zwischenbemerkung zum Begriff des Politischen*. Berlin: Duncker & Humblot, 2002 (first edition 1963).

Schmitt, Carl. *Nomos der Erde: Im Volkerrecht Des Jus Publicum Europaeum*. Berlin: Duncker & Humblot, 2012 (first edition 1950).

Schorkopf, Frank. “The European Union as an Association of Sovereign States: Karlsruhe’s Ruling on the Treaty of Lisbon.” *German Law Journal* 10, no. 8 (August 2009): 1219–1240.

Schöttler, Peter. “Three Kinds of Collaboration.” In *Anti-liberal Europe: A Neglected Story of Europeanization*. Edited by Dieter Gosewinkel, 128–56. New York and Oxford: Berghahn, 2015.

Schwarzenberger, Georg. *Power Politics*. London: London Institute of World Affairs/ Stevens & Sons, 1951.

Segers, Mathieu. *The Netherlands and European Integration, 1950 to Present*. Amsterdam: Amsterdam University Press, 2020.

Shipway, Martin. *Decolonization and Its Impact: A Comparative Approach to the End of the Colonial Empires*. Oxford: Blackwell, 2008.

Simon Tarrés, Antoni. *La unitat d’Espanya com a valor polític: Una arqueologia intel·lectual*. Catarroja, Palma and Barcelona: Editorial Afers, 2022.

Sirera Miralles, Carles. “Neglecting the 19th Century: Democracy, the Consensus Trap and Modernization Theory in Spain.” *History of the Human Sciences* 28, no. 3 (April 2015): 51–67.

Skoutaris, Nikos “What’s in an Irish Border? *Brexit*, the Backstop(s) and the Constitutional Integrity of the UK.” *DCU/Brexit Institute. Working Paper* 2, February 24, 2020. Available at https://papers.ssrn.com/sol3/papers.cfm?abstract_id=3543514.

Slobodian, Quinn. *Globalists: The End of the Empire and the Birth of Neoliberalism*. Cambridge, MA: Harvard University Press, 2018.

Smith, Woodruff D. “Friedrich Ratzel and the Origins of Lebensraum.” *German Studies Review* 3, no. 1 (February 1980): 51–68.

Snyder, Timothy. *On Tyranny: Twenty Lessons from the Twentieth Century*. London: The Bodley Head, 2017.

Snyder, Timothy. *The Road to Unfreedom*. London: Penguin Random House, 2018.

Spevack, Edmund. *Allied Control and German Freedom. American Political and Ideological Influences on the Framing of the West German Basic Law*. Münster, Hamburg, Berlin, and London: Lit Verlag, 2001.

Spicka, Mark E. *Selling the Economic Miracle: Economic Reconstruction and Politics in West Germany, 1949–1957*. New York and Oxford: Berghahn Books, 2007.

Spohr, Kristina. *Post Wall, Post Square: Rebuilding the World after 1989*. London: William Collins, 2019.

Springhall, John. *Decolonization since 1945: The Collapse of European Overseas Empire*. Basingstoke/New York: Palgrave, 2001.

Stark, David, and Bruszt, Liszld. *Postsocialist Pathways: Transforming Politics and Property in East Central Europe*. Cambridge: Cambridge University Press, 1998.

Stephens, Philip, “The Meaning of Rishi Sunak’s Northern Ireland Deal.” *Encompass*, March 2023. Available at https://encompass-europe.com/comment/the-meaning-of-rishi-sunaks-northern-ireland-deal.

Steiner, André. *The Plans that Failed. An Economic History of the GDR*. New York: Berghahn, 2010.

Stettinius, Edward R. *Roosevelt and the Russians—The Yalta Conference*. Garden City: Doubleday & Company, 1949.
Stoessinger, John G. *The Might of Nations: World Politics in Our Time*. New York: Random House, 1962.
Stolleis, Michael. "Prologue: Reluctance to Glance in the Mirror: The Changing Face of German Jurisprudence after 1933 and Post-1945." In *Darker Legacies of Law in Europe: The Shadow of National Socialism and Fascism over Europe and its Legal Traditions*. Edited by Christian Joerges and Navraj Singh Ghaleigh, 1–18. Oxford and Portland, OR: Hart Publishing, 2003.
Sutton, Michael. *France and the Construction of Europe, 1944–2007: The Geopolitical Imperative*. New York and Oxford: Berghahn Books, 2007.
Tertrais, Hugues. *Le piaster et le fusil: Le coût de la guerre d'Indochine 1945–1954*. Vincennes: Institute de la gestion publique et du développement économique, 2002.
Tesauro, Alfonso, and Ginevra Capocelli. "The Fundamentals of the New Italian Constitution." *Canadian Journal of Economics and Political Science* 20, no. 1 (February 1954): 44–58.
Thatcher, Margaret. *The Downing Street Years*. London: HarperCollins, 1993.
Thompson, Helen. *Disorder: Hard Times in 21st Century*. Oxford: Oxford University Press, 2022.
Thornhill, Chris. *A Sociology of Constitutions: Constitutions and State Legitimacy in Historical-Sociological Perspective*. Cambridge: Cambridge University Press, 2011.
Thränhardt, Dietrich. *Geschichte der Bundesrepublik Deutschland*. Frankfurt am Main: Suhrkamp, 1996.
Tiebout, Charles M. "A Pure Theory of Local Expenditures." *The Journal of Political Economy* 64, no. 5 (October, 1956), 416–24.
Tomuschat, Christian. "The Ruling of the German Constitutional Court on the Treaty of Lisbon." *German Law Journal* 10, no. 8 (August 2009): 1259–62.
Tooze, Adam. *The Wages of Destruction: The Making and Breaking of the Nazi Economy*. New York: Penguin Books, 2006.
Tooze, Adam. *The Deluge: The Great War, America and the Remaking of the Global Order, 1916–1931*. New York: Penguin, 2014.
Tooze, Adam. *Crashed: How a Decade of Financial Crises Changed the World*. New York: Viking, 2018.
Top, Sibel. "Explosive Case: Cautious Ruling: The CJUE Prudently Favors Cooperation in the Puig Case." *EJIL: Talk! Blog of the European Journal of International Law*, February 20, 2023. Available at https://www.ejiltalk.org/explosive-case-cautious-ruling-the-cjeu-prudently-favours-cooperation-in-the-puig-case/.
Torres Delgado, Gemma. *La virilitat d'Espanya a l'Àfrica: Nació i masculinitat al colonialisme al Marroc (1880–1927)*. Catarroja: Editorial Afers, 2020.
Townsend, Mary Evelyn, and Cyrus H. Peake. *European Colonial Expansion since 1871*. Chicago, IL: Lippincott, 1941.

Tully, James. "Modern Constitutional Democracy and Imperialism." *Osgoode Hall Law Journal* 46, no. 3 (December 2008): 461–93.

Urwin, Derek W. *The Community of Europe: A History of European Integration since 1945*. London and New York: Longman (first edition 1991), 1993.

Van Hook, James C. "Translating Economics into Politics in Cold War Germany." *German Politics & Society* 25, no. 2 (Summer 2007): 104–16.

Van Middelaar, Luuk. *The Passage to Europe: How a Continent Became a Union*. New Haven, CT, and London: Yale University Press, 2014.

Van Wegenberg, Astrid. "'Europe' on Display: A Postcolonial Reading of the House of European History." *Politique Européenne* 66, no. 4 (2019): 44–71.

Vauchez, Antoine. "The Transnational Politics of Judicialization. » *Van Gend en Loos* and the Making of EU Polity." *European Law Journal* 16, no. 1 (January 2010): 1–28.

Vauchez, Antoine. "Statesmen of Independence: The International Fabric of Europe's Way of Political Legitimacy." *Contemporary European History* 27, no. 2 (May 2018): 183–201.

Vilar, Juan B. "Franquismo y descolonización española en África." *Historia Contemporánea* 30 (2005): 129–58.

Violini, Lorenza. *Una forma di stato a regionalismo differenziato? Percorsi e argomenti per l'attuazione dell'Art. 116, III comma, Cost*. Torino: G Giappichelli Editore, 2021.

Watkins, Susan Cotts. *From Provinces into Nations: Demographic Integration in Western Europe 1870–1960*. Princeton, NJ: Princeton University Press, 1991.

Weiler, Joseph H. H. *The Constitution of Europe: 'Do the New Clothes Have an Emperor?' and Other Essays on European Integration*. Cambridge: Cambridge University Press, 1999.

Weiler, Joseph H. H. "The Political and Legal Culture of European Integration: An Exploratory Essay." *International Journal of Constitutional Law* 9, no. 3–4 (October 2011): 678–94.

Weiler, Joseph H. H. "Integration through Fear." *Blog of the European Journal of International Law*, April 13, 2012. Available at https://www.ejiltalk.org/integration-through-fear/.

Weiler, Joseph H. H. "Brexit, the Irish Protocol and the 'Versailles Effect.'" *Blog of the International Journal of Constitutional Law*, September 7, 2021. Available at http://www.iconnectblog.com/brexit-the-irish-protocol-and-the-versailles-effect/.

White, Nicholas J. "Reconstructing Europe through Rejuvenating Empire: The British, French, and Dutch Experiences Compared." In *Post-War Reconstruction in Europe: International Perspectives, 1945–1949*. Edited by Mark Mazower, Jessica Reinisch, and David Feldman, 211–36. Oxford: Oxford University Press, 2011.

Wiley, James. *The Banana Empires, Trade Wars, and Globalization*. Lincoln, NE: University of Nebraska Press, 2008.

Wilkinson, Michael A. "Authoritarian Liberalism in the European Constitutional Imagination: Second Time as a Farce?" *European Law Journal* 21, no. 3 (May 2015): 313–39.

Wilkinson, Michael A. "The Reconstruction of Postwar Europe: Lineages of Authoritarian Liberalism." *LSE Law, Society and Economy Working Papers* 05 (2016). Available at https://eprints.lse.ac.uk/66570/1/__lse.ac.uk_storage_LIBRARY_Secondary_libfile_shared_repository_Content_LSE%20Working%20Paper_The%20Reconstitution%20of%20Postwar%20Europe_Wilkinson_The_Reconstitution_of_Postwar_Europe_Author.pdf.

Wilkinson, Michael A. "Authoritarian Liberalism as Authoritarian Constitutionalism." In *Authoritarian Constitutionalism*. Edited by Helena Alviar García and Günter Frankenberg, 317–37. Cheltenham: Edward Elgar Publishing, 2019.

Wilkinson, Michael A. *Authoritarian Liberalism and the Transformation of Modern Europe*. Oxford: Oxford University Press, 2021.

Winkler, Heinrich A. *Germany: The Long Road West: 1933–1990*. Oxford: Oxford University Press, 2007. (Translation Alexander Sager [first edition 2000]).

Winock, Michel. *L'agonie de la IVe République*. Paris: Gallimard, 2006.

Zaslavsky, Victor. *Lo Stalinismo e la Sinistra Italiana: Dal mito dell'Urss alla fine del communismo 1945–1991*. Milano: Mondadori, 2004.

Ziblatt, Daniel. *Structuring the State: The Formation of Italy and Germany and the Puzzle of Federalism*. Princeton and Oxford: Princeton University Press, 2006.

Zubok, Vladislav M. *A Failed Empire: The Soviet Union in the Cold War from Stalin to Gorbachev*. Chapel Hill, NC: The University of North Carolina Press, 2007.

Index

About the Author

Hèctor López Bofill is an associate professor of constitutional law at Pompeu Fabra University in Barcelona. He is a prolific author, having written ten books and over thirty articles in the field of constitutional theory, constitutional law history, fundamental rights, federalism, secessionism, and judicial review of legislation. His most recent publication, "Law, Violence, and Constituent Power" (2021), focuses on constitution-making processes and has garnered praise from notable law scholars, historians, and political philosophers such as Peter Häberle, Walter Scheidel, and Giorgio Agamben. Over the course of more than a decade, López Bofill has dedicated his research to studying the origins and legal foundations of the European Union. This book represents the culmination of his extensive research in this area.

www.ingramcontent.com/pod-product-compliance
Ingram Content Group UK Ltd.
Pitfield, Milton Keynes, MK11 3LW, UK
UKHW041449071026
15587UKWH00010B/698

9 781666 920963